Systemic Racism

Systemic Racism
A THEORY OF OPPRESSION

Joe R. Feagin

Routledge
Taylor & Francis Group
New York   London

Published in 2006 by
Routledge
Taylor & Francis Group
270 Madison Avenue
New York, NY 10016

Published in Great Britain by
Routledge
Taylor & Francis Group
2 Park Square
Milton Park, Abingdon
Oxon OX14 4RN

Printed in the United States of America on acid-free paper
10 9 8 7 6 5 4 3 2 1

International Standard Book Number-10: 0-415-95278-6 (Softcover) 0-415-95277-8 (Hardcover)
International Standard Book Number-13: 978-0-415-95278-1 (Softcover) 978-0-415-95277-4 (Hardcover)
Library of Congress Card Number 2005022345

Library of Congress Cataloging-in-Publication Data

Feagin, Joe R.
   Systemic racism : a theory of oppression / Joe R. Feagin.
        p. cm.
   Includes bibliographical references.
   ISBN 0-415-95277-8 (hb) -- ISBN 0-415-95278-6 (pb)
   1. United States--Race relations. 2. Racism--United States--History. 3. Oppression (Psychology)
I. Title.

E184.A1F385 2005
305.896'073--dc22   2005022345

informa
Taylor & Francis Group
is the Academic Division of Informa plc.

Visit the Taylor & Francis Web site at
http://www.taylorandfrancis.com

and the Routledge Web site at
http://www.routledge-ny.com

To my many and diverse students,
from whom I have learned much
over more than four decades

CONTENTS

PREFACE

Let me begin with a question to the reader: Do you know who Ann Dandridge, William Costin, West Ford, and John Custis were? Very few Americans can answer this question in the affirmative. Yet these Americans should be well known, for they were all close relatives of George and Martha Washington. Two were part of the first "First Family." Ann Dandridge, Martha Washington's half-sister, was born to an enslaved black woman (her name unrecorded) who was likely co-erced into sexual relations by Martha's powerful slaveholding father, John Dandridge. Martha later enslaved Ann Dandridge for some years as a servant at this country's most famous slave plantation, Mt. Vernon in Virginia. In addition, around 1780, Martha's son from her first mar-riage, Jacky Custis, likely raped his aunt Ann Dandridge, who thus had a son named William (later, William Costin). William, Martha's grandson, was also enslaved. Significantly, Martha's black half-sister and grandson were freed only after George Washington died.[1]

In addition, Martha's first father-in-law, the wealthy Virginian John Custis, had raped a woman he called "his Negro Wench Young Alice," who thus had a black son named John (nicknamed "black Jack") whom he enslaved. Yet another enslaved black child, West Ford, also came into Washington's extended family as a result of sexual coercion. The child's mother was Venus, an enslaved servant of Washington's brother John's wife, and his father was one of the Washington men, most likely John Washington or Bushrod Washington (John's son).[2]

Fundamental lessons about our society are suggested by even this brief history of a few powerful white men and the enslaved black girls and women whom they coerced into sexual relations. Wealthy and in-fluential white men periodically engaged in sexual violence against and degradation of black girls and women, whom they clearly regarded as less than human. They engaged in this predatory behavior in spite of their professions of religious virtue and personal integrity. For the most

ix

part, these men also enslaved the biracial children resulting from their predatory actions. One important lesson here is how commonplace and well-institutionalized these rapacious practices were. Over more than two centuries of slavery, hundreds of thousands of white men raped and attacked black girls and women.

Generally, the dominant social and political institutions, and the leaders therein, typically supported or ignored this sexual predation. White rapists did not fear condemnation from their peers or relatives, nor even from their religious leaders, who for the most part winked at or sometimes participated in this depredation. These white men generally had no fear of punishment under the law. Indeed, some of them or their white relatives had written the U.S. Constitution, with its numerous provisions protecting slavery, and they and their ilk continued thereafter for several decades to make laws and render court decisions buttressing the slavery system. In addition, prominent white men and their white contemporaries rarely commented on this widespread rapacious behavior in their writings and public commentaries, but instead mostly kept it concealed. As far as I can discover, at no point in their writings did the wealthy and powerful founders, George Washington and Thomas Jefferson, acknowledge the black Americans who were their close kin. One other lesson is also quite clear from these historical data: This society was, in the founding era as today, a white social space within which black Americans and other Americans of color typically were trapped and thus had to submit to whatever exploitative and oppressive actions privileged whites might wish to impose on them.

There are deep lessons here for our era as well. Why have so very few Americans ever heard or considered seriously these accounts of racialized sexual attacks and rape involving whites from various backgrounds during the founding generations? These stories of the first First Family almost never appear in history textbooks. White history-telling has generally cut off many significant connections between the present and the past, except for certain sugar-coated stories of "founding fathers." Few U.S. children are taught much about the two-centuries-plus slavery era or about the eight or so decades of legal segregation that followed slavery, a segregation era that ended only in 1968. For the most part, these historical realities have remained hidden from public view, and today very few non-black Americans are aware of them or of their profound significance for this society.

Indeed, in my experience, many whites will deny the evidence even as it is presented to them, in part because they have never heard it before. Truths are difficult to face when they are as bloody as this country's deepest racial truths. Yet, one can better understand the rage and resistance of black Americans and other Americans of color in the past and present if one understands that many critical events of racial violence and other oppression are part of a huge white coverup of this country's extremely racist history.

As these accounts of the First Family suggest, African Americans were the first non-European group to become so central and internal to the white-controlled economy and society, and especially central to white families and to the white sense of self. In this book, I focus mainly on what early became the archetypal oppression generated by European Americans for non-European groups: The nearly 400-year-old oppression of African Americans. For centuries now, African Americans have been central to the important events and developing institutions that so well imbed color-coded oppression. As essayist James Baldwin once put it, the "black man has functioned in the white man's world as a fixed star...and as he moves out of his place, heaven and earth are shaken to the foundations."[3] White oppression of African Americans is archetypal because it is the original model on which whites' treatment of other non-European groups entering later into the sphere of white domination has largely been patterned.

This archetypal oppression of black Americans is responsible for a substantial portion of the initial white wealth on which the American economy and government were built. For more than two centuries, enslaved African Americans labored arduously (usually on land stolen from Native Americans) to develop agricultural and other economic prosperity for millions of white Americans in many walks of life. For many white families, this early prosperity led to some assets being passed down over later generations of whites to the present day. This wealth generation could be seen in many areas. For example, the trade in enslaved Africans and African Americans was a central reason why New York City early became one of the world's major cities. World-famous Wall Street was early on a center for slave buying and selling. In addition, enslaved workers built many of the country's first great houses and mansions, including such famous homes of presidents as Thomas Jefferson's Monticello and George Washington's Mount Vernon. Enslaved African Americans also built major educational facilities, such as buildings at early colleges and universities like William and Mary and the University of Virginia. Enslaved workers also constructed the great buildings that have become the most important political symbols of the United States—the White House and the Capitol in Washington, D.C. Ironically, these enslaved black workers put a bold Statue of Freedom on the top of that Capitol dome.[4]

The white founders' vision of a "nation of equals," stated eloquently by Virginia slaveholders like Thomas Jefferson, was fatally flawed at its beginning by whites' oppression of black Americans in the bloody and profitable arrangements of slavery. The country has never recovered from being founded in this extensive white-on-black oppression. As I will show in this book, substantial aspects of this racial oppression persist to the present day in a contemporary guise—in the form Supreme Court Justice William O. Douglas once called "slavery unwilling to die."[5] Similarly reflecting on contemporary racism, influential historian Edmund Morgan has asked the rhetorical question, Is the United States "still colonial Virginia writ large?"[6] The answer is, in numerous significant ways, "yes."

This truth about systemic racism in this society is not easy to communicate to many Americans, especially to most white Americans. One of the great nineteenth-century English philosophers of liberty and opponents of African slavery, John Stuart Mill, once put it this way:

> The real advantage which truth has, consists in this, that when an opinion is true, it may be extinguished once, twice, or many times, but in the course of ages there will generally be found persons to rediscover it, until some one of its reappearances falls on a time when from favourable circumstances it escapes persecution until it has made such head as to withstand all subsequent attempts to suppress it.[7]

In this book I undertake a major effort in what might be termed "leukology"; that is, a focused study of the reproduction of white power and privilege in this society over several centuries. I search out numerous truths about white-on-black oppression as it has persisted, in shifting forms, over a very long period. Here I build on analysis in a previous Routledge book, *Racist America*, and lay out a developed conceptual framework accenting systemic racism as a better way of understanding centuries of racial oppression. As I will demonstrate, systemic racism encompasses a broad range of racialized dimensions of this society: the racist framing, racist ideology, stereotyped attitudes, racist emotions, discriminatory habits and actions, and extensive racist institutions developed over centuries by whites.

Herein I make use of two general metaphors in describing the white-on-black oppression that has persisted from the seventeenth century to the present day. I use a type of body metaphor in the term "systemic racism," which I consider the best overview term for this centuries-old oppression. In addition, to convey how important this oppression is, I also make use of a building metaphor in describing this white-on-black oppression as foundational for society. The reader should also note that, in order to avoid cumbersome phrasing in some historical discussions, I utilize "racial oppression" and "systemic racism" as shorthand terms for the European American oppression of African Americans since the 1600s—even though in the earliest period the African American targets of color-coded oppression were viewed by their oppressors as primarily different in terms of skin color and culture, and not yet fully in terms of "race" as biologically conceived (a view that emerges in full in the mid-1700s).

As I will show, this white-generated and white-maintained oppression is far more than a matter of individual bigotry, for it has been from the beginning a material, social, and ideological reality. For a long period now, white oppression of Americans of color has been systemic—that is, it has been manifested in all major societal institutions. This oppression has long been a dialectical reality; while it has been an intense system of oppression, it has also constantly encountered resistance.

Indeed, an additional sign of the centrality of black Americans in this country's history can be seen in the impact that centuries of black resistance to oppression have had on society. For centuries, black Americans have fought against their oppression, as individuals and in groups. They have engaged in slave revolts, in fleeing slavery to Canada, in legal challenges in court, in civil rights organizations and movements, and in urban riots and revolts. Indeed, over the long course of this history, black Americans have probably been the most consistent and insistent carriers of the much-heralded values of expanded liberty, equality, and social justice for this society. Not long before he died, the great black abolitionist and social analyst, Frederick Douglass, underscored in a major speech the importance of these values: "The spirit of justice, liberty, and fair play is abroad in the land. It is in the air. It animates men of all stations....States may lag, parties may hesitate, leaders may halt, but to this complexion it must come at last."[8]

Today, fortunately, these values are still very much in the air, but local, state, and federal governments in this country still lag greatly, and political parties still hesitate, in eradicating racial discrimination and other forms of racial oppression. Research study after research study demonstrates that African Americans, as well as other Americans of color, still must struggle against placement by whites at the bottom of this country's racial hierarchy. For example, a recent survey of 202 black Bostonians found that 80 percent viewed racial discrimination in Boston as a significant problem. More specifically, 85 percent of the respondents felt that African Americans lose out on good housing because of fear of how they will be received in certain Boston communities. Substantial percentages reported facing discrimination from the police or in workplaces, and nearly half felt they were unwelcome in shopping areas or restaurants in the metropolitan area.[9]

Another recent study in Milwaukee had black and white male applicants, all with good self-presentations, apply for 350 less-skilled jobs in the city. While 34 percent of the white job applicants were called back, only 14 percent of equally qualified black applicants were called back. Even the subgroup of white applicants who indicated they had been in prison for cocaine possession were more likely to be called back than the black applicants with no criminal record. Evidently, employers drew on stereotypes of black men in screening them out of their hiring pools.[10] Similarly, researchers at the Massachusetts Institute of Technology recently sent applications to ads by Chicago and Boston employers. Using made-up names that sound (especially to whites) like typical white or black names, they found that applicants with white-sounding names were 50 percent more likely to be contacted by employers than those with black-sounding names. Improving the reported qualifications of the applicant was far more likely to get whites a callback than blacks. Being black with eight years of job experience was necessary to get the same treatment as a white applicant with no experience.[11] Significantly, a research study in Florida examined the school records for 55,000 students from families with at least two children in a major school district's schools and found that black students with distinctive black-sounding names (like LaQuisha) averaged lower scores on reading and math tests, and got fewer recommendations for gifted classes, than brothers or sisters without such names. The researcher suggested that black children with exotic-to-whites names get less attention and help from teachers who likely assume from their names that they will not do well.[12]

Racial discrimination is found in many other areas for African Americans and other Americans of color. Thus, a 2005 report by the New Jersey Citizen Action (NJCA) cited data indicating for New Jersey, and nationally, a pattern of black and Latino car buyers being quoted substantially higher finance rates (with a greater undisclosed markup) than comparable white car buyers. Financing markup charges for black buyers have averaged as much as 60–70 percent higher than for white buyers.[13] In addition, black patients being treated for physical or mental illness are, depending on the illness, less likely or far less likely than white patients to get standard and adequate care.[14] To take one final example of recent research, which demonstrates the long-term impact of racial discrimination, an analysis of U.S. family wealth found that the median net worth of black families was just $5,988, which compared to a median net worth for white families of $88,651.[15] The median wealth of black families is substantially less than one tenth of the median wealth of white families and has declined relative to that of whites over the last decade. This is even more striking, given the reality that the average black American likely has ancestors going back more generations in this country's history than the average white American. As I will show in later chapters, this huge wealth gap is substantially the result of the processes of individual, family, and institutional reproduction of unjust enrichment for white Americans and unjust impoverishment for black Americans over centuries of systemic racism.

In August 2005, as I was writing this preface, one of the greatest hurricanes ever to hit the United States (Katrina) slammed into the Gulf Coast and brought much death and destruction to areas in southern Louisiana, Mississippi, and Alabama, including the city of New Orleans. For four days, the world watched as the virtually all white federal officials moved very slowly to assist those stranded and dying in flooded houses and overcrowded shelters in New Orleans and other southern coastal areas. For a time, media commentators and others raised the reasonable question of whether the fact that a majority of those hit hardest by severe flooding in New Orleans were low-income black residents had affected the slowness of the federal government response. Those seen in the mass media suffering terribly in streets and shelters were mainly black and poor, including a large number of black families with children. Many black women, men, and children died in the combined natural and man-made disaster.

Some underlying reasons contributing to the human disaster were clear. Many black residents were very poor. More than one third of New Orleans' black residents did not own a car, yet the mandatory evacuation orders for the city did not provide the necessary public transportation out for those too poor to own or rent a car. Many of the city's black residents were forced by their low-wage jobs to live in cheap housing in low-lying areas likely to flood, while whites disproportionately lived in more affluent, higher-up areas less likely to suffer major flooding. Like many black Americans in the South, many black residents in these hurricane-hit areas have endured much unjust poverty and inequality now for many generations. Over the generations relatively little of the government aid provided for the mobility of whites, such as the provision of substantial homestead land, has been provided to facilitate blacks' economic mobility. Indeed, even today the states of Louisiana and Mississippi are near the bottom of the list in state spending per capita for such critical government programs as public education and public health.[16]

Why are there today so many poor black Americans in these Deep South areas? There is a clear historical reason that was never noted in the *public* discussions of the 2005 hurricane disaster. In the first decades of the nineteenth century, major U.S. slaveholders and politicians, including the famous slaveholding military leader (later president) Andrew Jackson, led a drive to kill off or drive out the Native Americans who inhabited the lands (now Alabama and Mississippi) desired by whites already in the Deep South areas or seeking to move there. One goal was to open up much new land for slave plantations, which were soon created in that area and in Louisiana. African Americans were brought in by force, often through the thriving New Orleans slave markets. Because of this dramatic increase in slave plantations, the ancestors of many African Americans who now live in the region were forced to move there in chains. Thus, New Orleans became a major center of the slavery-centered economy of the region.

After slavery, the near-slavery of legal segregation kept many of the slaves' descendants in the Deep South, usually as poor sharecroppers and tenant farmers working on white-owned farms or as low-wage laborers in white homes or businesses in southern towns and cities. After desegregation came slowly and partially in the 1960s and 1970s, many children and grandchildren of those severely impoverished by Jim Crow segregation continued to reside in southern towns and in cities such as New Orleans. The great and disproportionately black suffering of men, women, and children after 2005's Hurricane Katrina was, simply put, substantially the result of slavery still unwilling to die. Scenes of black mothers and fathers in these Deep South areas being unable to feed, clothe, and protect their children were in some respects reminiscent of the eras of slavery and Jim Crow when black mothers and fathers were often powerless to care for their children properly. The large-scale suffering and death in the Deep South revealed once again that a majority of whites have long been unwilling to give up any significant share of the unjust enrichment that they have collectively gained over centuries of systemic racism and to do something substantial about the unjust impoverishment faced by enslaved African Americans and passed along to their descendants over several centuries to the present day.

Today, very few white political, economic, religious, or educational leaders are speaking out about, and working diligently to reduce, the devastating consequences of centuries of white-on-black oppression. Indeed, from the 1970s to the present day, most of the country's white leadership has supported a slowing of progress toward, or an actual backtracking on, the task of remaking this country into a true democracy where there really is "liberty and justice for all." Today, we are once again in a deep struggle for the soul of this country, for, in spite of the widespread profession of certain religious commitments, a great many white Americans still put much effort into maintaining the well-entrenched system of racial oppression.

Still, we must not lose hope, for the long history of resistance to racial oppression by African Americans and other Americans of color, working with their white allies, suggests that major changes can be made in this system of racism. This will be true in the future only if concerned Americans of all backgrounds organize on a large scale for their, and their society's, liberation from racial oppression. Human beings can bring significant change in racial oppression, but that task is long and arduous. A young black friend of mine, Mattie Rush, when she was just nine years old, wrote the following statement to her mother, titled as "My Word to the World":

> I give you my word that I will stop all racism. I don't care how long it takes, I will stop all racism. It could take 100, 1,000, 100,000, 1,000,000 [years]. I will reach that goal. I could die but I still would reach my goal. I would die and my spirit would go into the right person, and if they didn't reach it before they died, then their spirit would go into someone else. They would go on and on and on until my goal was reached. But I can't reach my goal without everyone's cooperation. I need your help to reach that goal. All you need to remember is that no matter if you're black or white, Asian or American, boy or girl, you are just as special as anyone else in the world. I will stop all racism.[17]

ACKNOWLEDGMENTS

I am indebted to numerous scholars for their helpful comments and critical suggestions on various incarnations of this book's arguments. I am especially indebted to Hernán Vera, Bernice McNair Barnett, Roy Brooks, Gideon Sjoberg, Melvin Sikes, Sharon Rush, and Tony Orum, who over many years have helped me hone my ideas and improve my field research projects on racial matters. I would also like to thank the following colleagues for their critical comments on sections of this manuscript and on related research work: José Cobas, Karen Glover, Chris Chambers, Glenn Bracey II, Jennifer Mueller, Connie Shehan, Nijole Benokraitis, Felix Berardo, Donny Barnett, Crystal Copeland, and Mary Ann Davis. I especially would like to thank my current and former graduate students, Ruth Thompson-Miller, Ana S. Liberato, Kristen Lavelle, and Leslie Houts, for critical comments and for permission to use interview data in this book that they collected in the field.

1

SYSTEMIC RACISM

INTRODUCTION

Some time after English writer Henry Fairlie immigrated to the United States in the 1960s, he visited Thomas Jefferson's Monticello plantation in Virginia and took the standard tour. When the white guide asked for questions, Fairlie asked, "Where did he keep his slaves?" Fairlie reports that the other white tourists looked at him in disturbed silence, while the guide "swallowed hard" and said firmly that the slave quarters were "not included in the official tour."[1] Today, racial segregation in various areas and institutions, and the well-entrenched, systemic racism such segregation reveals, are still not in the "official tour" of this society.

In the late 1700s, Thomas Jefferson and the other white founders of the new United States advocated strongly an "all men are created equal" perspective. Yet their broadly stated phrasing of equality was hypocritical, for they intentionally and openly excluded African Americans, indigenous peoples, and women from the scope of this ideal. The new nation of the United States was explicitly designed to create wealth, privileges, and status for European Americans, people who had long stolen by various means, including much violence, the lands of indigenous peoples and the labor of Africans.

From the first decades of colonial America, European Americans have made oppression of non-Europeans basic to the new society. For the first 90 percent of this country's history (about 350 years) slavery or legal segregation was generally in place. Only for the last 10 percent or so of our entire history have we been free of slavery and legal segregation. Thus, racial oppression makes the United States very distinctive, for it is the only major Western country that was explicitly founded on racial oppression. Today, as in the past, this oppression is not a minor addition to U.S. society's structure, but rather is systemic across all major institutions. Oppression of non-European groups is part of the deep social structure. Beginning with the genocidal killing off of Native Americans and the theft of their lands, and the extensive enslavement of Africans as laborers on those stolen lands, European colonists and their descendants created a new society by means of active predation, exploitation, and oppression.

In this book, I develop a theory of systemic racism to interpret the racialized character, structure, and development of this society. Generally, I ask, What are the distinctive social worlds that have been created by racial oppression over several centuries? And what has this foundation of racial oppression meant for the people of the United States?

A CRITICAL EXAMPLE: RACISM AS FOUNDATIONAL AND SYSTEMIC

Beginning in the seventeenth century, the Europeans and European Americans who controlled the development of the country that later became the United States positioned the oppression of Africans and African Americans at the center of the new society. Over the long history of the country, this oppression has included the exploitative and other oppressive practices of whites, the unjustly gained socioeconomic resources and assets of whites, and the long-term maintenance of major socioeconomic inequalities across what came to be defined as a rigid color line. Today, as in the past, systemic racism encompasses a broad range of white-racist dimensions: the racist ideology, attitudes, emotions, habits, actions, and institutions of whites in this society. Thus, systemic racism is far more than a matter of racial prejudice and individual bigotry. It is a material, social, and ideological reality that is well-imbedded in major U.S. institutions.

Historically, and in the present, the routine operation of the economy has greatly favored many millions of white Americans. Before the late 1960s, the many wealth-generating resources provided by state and federal governments to U.S. citizens were overwhelmingly or exclusively for whites. Indeed, prior to the end of slavery in 1865, African Americans were not regarded by most whites, including the Supreme Court, as citizens, and thus very few had any access to wealth-generating resources such as the public lands provided by state and federal governments to many white citizens.

After the Civil War, African Americans freed from slavery were for the most part barred from new government-provided resources, such as good land for homesteading, by the rapidly expanding and violent Klan-type organizations and by whites implementing racial segregation. Strikingly, in the peak decades of the official segregation era, in the late nineteenth and early twentieth centuries, the U.S. government provided huge amounts of wealth-generating resources to many white families and businesses. The federal government distributed hundreds of millions of acres of land, billions of dollars in mineral and oil rights, major airline routes, major radio and television frequencies, and many other government-controlled resources almost exclusively to white Americans, while black and other non-European Americans were mostly excluded by racial violence or the racial apartheid system of the era.

Let us briefly consider systemic racism as it operated in just one historical period of the U.S. economy. Under the federal Homestead Act—passed in the 1860s and in effect until the 1930s—the U.S. government provided about 246 million acres of land (much of it taken from Native Americans by force or chicanery) at low or no cost for about 1.5 million farm homesteads. Because of the extensive racial exclusion and violence directed at African Americans, including those recently freed from slavery, those who gained access to these wealth-generating resources were almost entirely white. The homesteads of about 160–320 acres provided land resources on which many white families, including new European immigrant families, built up substantial wealth in the initial generation and subsequent generations. These white-controlled programs of land provision have had major long-term consequences. Drawing on demographic projections, one researcher's careful data analysis suggests that perhaps 46 million white Americans are the current descendants of the fortunate homestead families and are substantial inheritors and beneficiaries of this wealth-generating government program.[2] In addition, many millions more of white Americans are the current descendants of those whites who received millions of acres of public lands allocated by the government or private companies for farms before the 1860s.

Even though they may not now be aware of it, many white families today are comfortable or affluent because of these past and vast federal giveaways. The enhanced incomes and wealth garnered by white Americans in one generation have generally been transmitted by them to later generations. This type of inheritance has enabled later generations of whites to provide much better educational, housing, and other socioeconomic opportunities for their children than the later generations of black Americans whose ancestors did not receive access to such wealth-generating resources because of massive racial discrimination and segregation. The other side of this centuries-long unjust enrichment for white Americans is the centuries-long unjust impoverishment for African Americans; this unjust impoverishment has often, with the help of continuing white discrimination, been passed along from one generation of African Americans to the next.

MAINSTREAM APPROACHES TO "RACE"

One remarkable thing about this intergenerational transmission of unjust enrichment and unjust impoverishment over centuries is that virtually no mainstream scholars and other mainstream analysts of "race" in the United States have given serious attention to its reality and operation. The unjust, deeply institutionalized, ongoing intergenerational reproduction of whites' wealth, power, and privilege is never the center of in-depth mainstream analyses and is rarely seriously discussed. Today, mainstream analysts of the racial-ethnic history and contemporary reality of this society usually adopt some variation of an "understanding race and ethnicity" approach that ignores or downplays the centrality and injustice of white wealth, power, and privilege and instead accents the buzzing complexity of U.S. racial-ethnic groups and their socioeconomic demographics, geography, recent history, attitudes, or patterns of sociocultural adaptation and assimilation.[3] This is generally true for most scholars assessing immigration patterns, for they analyze the adaptation and assimilation of various racial-ethnic immigrant groups with no sustained discussion of the implications for these groups' socioeconomic situations of whites' unjustly gained, centuries-old dominant racial status, power, and privilege in the host society.[4]

Most mainstream analysts approach the histories and experiences of each U.S. racial-ethnic group as more or less distinctive and/or as taking place within a U.S. society whose major institutions are now reasonably democratic and generally open to all groups in terms of socioeconomic opportunities—and thus no longer (if ever) systemically racist. This mainstream approach tends to view persisting racial-ethnic tensions and conflicts today as being matters of prejudice and stereotyping or of individual and small-group discrimination mainly directed against

Americans of color. Racial-ethnic inequality is periodically discussed, but it is typically presented as something that is not fundamental, but rather an unfortunate socioeconomic condition tacked onto an otherwise healthy society.[5]

In most mainstream analyses of "race and ethnic relations," whites as a group often seem to be just one of many contending racial-ethnic groups. Whites are typically included in demographic comparisons of racial-ethnic groups' socioeconomic status and are often noted as the more advantaged group, especially in comparisons with black Americans and Latinos, yet rarely are whites seen as currently the central propagators and agents in a persisting *system* of racial discrimination and other racial oppression. Data on group differences in regard to such variables as income, occupation, health, and residence are frequently presented, but these differences are rarely if ever conceptualized in terms of a deeplying system of racial oppression.[6]

Even many social analysts who recognize the still difficult conditions faced by certain racial groups, such as contemporary discrimination against African Americans, do not assess how deep, foundational, and systemic this racial oppression has been historically and remains today.[7] While there may be some discussion of subordinate groups and allusions to institutional discrimination, these ideas are typically not built into a thoroughgoing perspective on racism in U.S. society. Many mainstream analysts give significant attention to divisions and conflicts among racial-ethnic groups, but their acceptance of the existing society as more or less sound in its sociopolitical foundation leads to well-intentioned analyses of these divisions that accent the need for a societal "vision" that will promote the "values of racial and intergroup harmony."[8] Yet such a perspective does not take into account the well-institutionalized power and wealth hierarchy favoring whites, nor the centuries-old social reproduction processes of unjust enrichment and impoverishment that lie just beneath the surface of the recognized disharmonies.

Interestingly, when racial discrimination issues are raised by some mainstream scholarly or media analysts, they are often discussed in ways that remove the dominant white agents of discrimination largely from view. Thus, these discussions of discrimination are put into the passive tense in order to remove white agents from the center of attention; or they are couched in an abstract language, so that it is some vaguely specified "institution" that may occasionally discriminate against black Americans or other Americans of color.[9]

RACIAL FORMATION THEORY

Currently, a major alternative framework to this traditional race and ethnic relations approach is the racial formation theory pioneered by the creative sociological theorists Michael Omi and Howard Winant. This perspective has advanced our thinking about racial and ethnic matters because it accents the important ideological and political processes that have imbedded racial-category thinking in U.S. laws and other institutions. This framework accents ideas and ideology, that is, "how concepts of race are created and changed, how they become the focus of political conflict, and how they come to permeate U.S. society."[10]

From this perspective, the concept "racial formation" refers to historical and governmental processes by which various racial categories have been socially created and destroyed.[11] The category of "race" symbolizes social conflicts by referring to human physical characteristics, yet it is not fixed, but rather variable over time. Omi and Winant recognize the importance of racial inequality, and for them a "racial project" is one where racial symbols are often linked to an unequal distribution of resources. Governments appear as the most important institutions in the racialization process because their actors have imbedded the "race" category into many public policies and laws.[12] This is a major contribution of racial formation theory, for much mainstream analysis gives little or no sustained attention to the role of government in creating racial-ethnic groups.

SYSTEMIC RACISM: AN ALTERNATIVE AND DEEPER APPROACH

Unlike the systemic racism perspective that I use in this book, however, the racial formation perspective does not view U.S. racial formations as being first and fundamentally about long-term relationships of racialized groups with substantially different material and political-economic interests—group interests that stem from greatly different historical experiences with economic exploitation and related oppression. The accent in racial formation theory on the racial categorization process is very important, but mainly in the context of these historical relationships of material oppression. In the U.S. case, these racial-group interests have generally arisen out of large-scale racial oppression over a long period. In racial formation theory there is not enough consideration of the grounding of U.S. society today, as in the past, in the provision of large-scale wealth-generating resources for white Americans; nor is significant attention given there to the intergenerational transmission of these critical material and related social assets. Racial formation theory assesses well and insightfully the critical importance of racial ideology, but not so much the historical foundation and systemic character of contemporary racial oppression. Also accented in this approach is how other racial formations have developed alongside antiblack racism.[13] Like other scholars operating from this perspective, Omi and Winant view the past of North American slavery and legal segregation as not weighing "like a nightmare on the brain of the living," but rather as lingering on "like a hangover" that is gradually going away.[14]

Thus, missing in both the mainstream race-ethnic relations approach and much of the racial formation approach is a full recognition of the big picture—the reality of this whole society being founded on, and firmly grounded in, oppression targeting African Americans (and other Americans of color) now for several centuries. Given that deep underlying reality of this society, all racial-ethnic relationships and events, past and present, must be placed within that racial oppression context in order to be well understood.

White-on-black oppression is systemic and has persisted over several centuries without the broad and foundational racial transformations that many social analysts suggest should have happened. While some significant changes have certainly taken place, systemic racism today retains numerous basic features that perpetuate the racial views, proclivities, actions, and intentions of many earlier white generations, including white founders like Thomas Jefferson. Because of its power and centrality in this still racially hierarchical society, white-on-black oppression has shaped considerably all other types of racial oppression that whites later developed within this still white-controlled society. To make sense out of the experiences of all non-European Americans, we must constantly accent the role of whites, especially elite whites, as the originators, enforcers, and remodelers of systemic racism in the United States. In addition, white-on-black oppression is an independent social reality that cannot be reduced to other social realities such as class stratification, though all major forms of oppression do interact and intersect with it historically. Indeed, white-on-black oppression today remains a major nightmare weighing on the brains and lives of Americans of all backgrounds.

In thinking about what a better theory of racial oppression might look like, I here suggest three features: (1) it should indicate clearly the major features—both the structures and the counterforces—of the social phenomenon being studied; (2) it should show the relationships between the important structures and forces; and (3) it should assist in understanding both the patterns of social change and the lack of social change. There are a number of key questions about racial oppression in the long history of this country that such a theoretical approach should help answer: What role has racial oppression played in making the United States a wealthy and powerful nation with great international influence and impact? Why has "race" remained so central to this society's development and reality for such a long period? Why have periods of significant change, such as the ending of slavery after the Civil War or the ending of legal segregation in the 1960s, been followed by major periods of reaction in which racial oppression has been reinvigorated and reinforced?

An approach accenting systemic racism differs significantly from the conventional race-and-ethnic relations framework. The word "systemic" comes from two Greek words meaning to place or stand together. I use it here in the sense of an organized societal whole with many interconnected elements.[15] In later chapters, drawing on the commentaries of many black and white Americans in major historical eras, I explore how U.S. institutions have been thoroughly pervaded by enduring racial stereotypes, ideas, images, emotions, proclivities, and practices. This system of white-on-black oppression was not an accident of history but was created intentionally by powerful white Americans. Whites labored hard to bring it forth in the seventeenth and eighteenth centuries and have labored to perpetuate this system of oppression ever since. While significant changes have occurred in systemic racism over time, critical and fundamental elements have been reproduced over this period, and U.S. institutions today reflect and imbed the white-over-black hierarchy initially created in the seventeenth century. Today, as in the past, this oppression is not just a surface-level feature of U.S. society, but rather pervades and interconnects major social groups, networks, and institutions across the society.

I will show in chapter 2, using important accounts of long-term enslavement by African Americans, that the traditional race-and-ethnic relations perspective is too underdeveloped for an adequate understanding of the white-on-black oppression that undergirded and riddled the early American colonies and, later, the nation called the United States. Consider that the word "oppression" comes from a Latin word meaning "to crush," and thus white-on-black oppression literally means keeping black people down—that is, crushing them physically and in many other ways. Examining the lived experiences of African Americans who endured slavery and subsequent racial oppression, I will show that they constantly contended with exploitation and coercion, including physical and psychological violence, at the hands of white oppressors acting as individuals and in groups. These black Americans describe their oppression as crushing physically and psychologically, yet they also recount much personal and collective resistance to it. To understand profoundly and well the nearly four hundred years of white-on-black oppression and other white oppression in North America, one should study closely the experiences, views, understandings, and interests of those oppressed, as well as the experiences, views, understandings, and interests of their oppressors.

In this analysis, I show that the black accounts of everyday, micro-level experiences with white oppressors reveal a macroworld of institutionalized oppression that, in its numerous and bloody manifestations, constantly crashes in on and warps the everyday microworlds of African Americans, to the present day. I also use white voices and accounts to show how many whites assess these same oppressive realities. They reveal the limited extent to which whites have been able to grasp the impact of racial oppression on its targets, yet have been able to rationalize the structures and processes of oppression. My sociological approach understands individual lives, including personal troubles and recurring barriers, as not only personal but also social and societal. Personal troubles are almost always set in the context of the family, economic, political, educational, and religious institutions of society. The many accounts presented in subsequent chapters document well these social interconnections, and they show as well the omnipresent reality of human agency in whites' oppressing blacks and in blacks' resisting that oppression.

THE SOCIAL GENERATION OF RACIAL OPPRESSION

If we are to comprehend the enduring and systemic character of racial oppression in this country, we must look carefully at the material reality and social history of the colonial society created by the European invaders of North America. North American colonialization was part of a process of European imperialism, and from the start, the society that became the United States was founded on the idea of "a dominion, state or sovereignty that would expand in population and territory and increase in strength and power."[16]

From the beginning, European and European American dominion and expansion took the form of oppression, genocide, and slavery. The central reality of the new country was economic exploitation of Native Americans, African Americans, and (later) other Americans of color in order to generate prosperity, wealth, and status for generations of European Americans. The centuries-long theft of Native American lands and of African American labor by European Americans constituted the economic foundation of the new nation, and the unjust enrichment stemming from that theft generated not only income, assets, and wealth for the white families directly involved, but soon an extensive capitalistic economy benefiting most whites. This economy was substantially centered in the slavery system and its associated farms and commercial enterprises and later evolved into closely related forms of racial exploitation such as legal and de facto segregation. Over the centuries, this color-coded economic exploitation has greatly facilitated the economic mobility and substantially enhanced the assets and socioeconomic status of white Americans.

The Predatory Ethic, Ethnocentrism, and Xenophobia

The early European colonists came to North America mainly from northern European areas, often from what is now Great Britain. While they differed significantly in their attitudes toward such matters as religion and politics, most held firmly to a distinctive predatory ethic. This predatory ethic encompassed the view that the land and labor of non-European peoples were fully available for European colonists to steal and to exploit economically. European colonists and slavers used extensive violence as the means to secure Indian land and African labor and, thus, to develop what they frequently called their advanced "civilization."

The majority of colonial immigrants came dreaming of owning their own farms, a dynamic that created a chronic shortage of white labor. Many seized land and drove away or killed the indigenous inhabitants. They built their new society with strategies of overt savagery and genocide directed at Native American peoples and a strategy of enslavement for Native American peoples (for a short time) and for African peoples (for long centuries). In the process, the colonists developed the age-old rationalization that they were taking "vacant land."[17] Yet, when they invaded, North America already had an estimated population of ten million people divided into hundreds of different Native American societies. Soon, however, much of the indigenous population nearest European settlements was dead or dying because of violent attacks from the European invaders or from the diseases and environmental destruction that the latter brought to North America.

Today, the early Puritans, perhaps the most celebrated of the early colonists, are portrayed as coming to North America looking for religious liberty and to "tame the wilderness." In reality, they were intolerant of others' religious views and saw themselves as a "chosen" people—with the right to kill and displace indigenous populations whom they demonized as uncivilized, savage, and non-Christian.[18] Referring to Native Americans, the Puritan minister and influential pamphleteer Cotton

Mather argued that the New England "woods were almost cleared of those pernicious creatures, to make room for a better growth."[19] Other groups of immigrants from England and nearby European areas, as well as their descendants, also exuded such a predatory ethic. They, too, usually drove away or exterminated most indigenous peoples in the process of stealing their lands. Moreover, many colonists came under the auspices of capitalistic corporations such as the London Company, which accented the freedom of immigrants to build personal assets and company wealth by using violent and genocidal tactics against the many indigenous inhabitants and their societies.

Coupled with this "your land and labor are mine" ethic were two associated perspectives: An ethnocentrism asserting European superiority in culture (especially religion) and society, and a xenophobia showing hostility to indigenous peoples and holding that they were not really human. European colonists generally held to a view of their cultural (later racial) superiority, a superiority that in their view gave them the right to prey on and dominate other peoples.[20] In addition, European colonists typically viewed indigenous peoples as dangerous and uncivilized "savages" to be overcome, not as fully human beings. Native Americans were said by Cotton Mather to be "wild beasts" who should be hunted down, or they were "agents of the Devil."[21] Africans and other people of color were also viewed as non-people who could be killed off or made the subordinated property of whites.

Predatory oppression has been central to the society now known as the United States since the seventeenth century. U.S. origins lie in the violent shedding of the blood of millions of indigenous peoples of America and Africa. One can make full sense out of nearly four hundred years of colonial and U.S. history only by understanding the reality and consequences of this violent and predatory history of North America.

Archetypal Racial Oppression: African Americans

Systemic racism exists because of critical decisions made by important European American decision makers at key points in North American history. For centuries, the European American elite has actively shaped major social, economic, and political institutions to support and maintain its oppression of Americans of color.

Thus, we see the centrality of white-on-black oppression for the elite minds at the Constitutional Convention that brought forth the new nation called the United States in the late eighteenth century. In 1787, fifty-five white men met in Philadelphia to create a U.S. Constitution. All were of European origin, and about 40 percent had been or were slaveowners. Many others were operating as merchants, lawyers, or bankers profiting from an economy centered around servicing slave plantations and selling slaves or slave-produced products. In their new Constitution, these elite white men dealt *at length* with the domination and exploitation of only one non-European group in colonial America— people of African descent. Concerned with the large population of en- slaved African Americans that they had built up for their profit, these white men placed numerous provisions protecting slavery in their new document, including articles counting those enslaved as three fifths of a person, preventing the international slave trade from being abolished before 1808, and requiring the return of fugitive slaves.[22]

The centrality of white-on-black oppression has been clear in many political debates and government actions ever since. For example, in the important 1830s congressional debates over whether antislavery peti- tions should be received and read by Congress, Representative Henry Wise of Virginia summed up what the majority of contemporary white leaders thought about their new nation:

> Sir, slavery is interwoven with our very political existence, is guar- anteed by our Constitution, and its consequences must be borne by our northern brethren as resulting from our system of govern- ment, and they cannot attack the system of slavery without attack- ing the institutions of our country, our safety, and our welfare.[23]

By "our very political existence," Wise meant that of white Americans. The centrality of white-on-black oppression for white economic and po- litical existence can also be seen in the fact that many founders, includ- ing leading northerners such as John Hancock and Benjamin Franklin, were slaveholders, and that between 1790 and 1869, ten men who served as U.S. president had at some point enslaved black Americans.

One might ask, What about the case of Native Americans that we just noted? Various Native American societies were indeed the first groups to be exploited economically, often in genocidal extreme, by the early European colonists. These colonists stole land and even some labor from Native Americans. Attempts were made by some white colonists to enslave Native Americans in the early decades, but this effort proved to be insufficient to produce the amount of labor they felt to be necessary for their prosperity. For a number of reasons, including their destruction by genocidal white actions and their ability to flee beyond white control, Native Americans never became a labor force well integrated into, and thus internal to, the everyday operation of the white-dominated economy and society. Indeed, by the time of the 1787 Constitutional Convention, Native Americans were barely mentioned in the founding document.

African American labor was a central consideration at that Convention, having become so central to the new country created by European colonists that the African American presence was early on commonplace in most colonies. From at least the late seventeenth century onward, that African American presence frequently obsessed or preoccupied white minds and generated special laws, especially in regard to matters of racial interaction. Enslaved black laborers soon became essential to the general prosperity of the white-dominated society as a (if not *the*) major labor source for the generation of economic assets for many yeoman farmers as well as elite farmers, plantation owners, and urban entrepreneurs. This slavery-centered economy and society involved not only economically successful slaveholders but other capitalists such as merchants, bankers, and shippers, as well as a very large number of ordinary whites in the South and the North who worked in occupations linked to a substantial degree to the growing slavery system. The latter whites included

> ...the fisherman whose low-grade, "refuse fish" was dried and sold as slave meal in the Indies; the New York farmer who found his market for surpluses in the Southern plantations; the forester whose timber was used by shipyard workers rapidly turning out slave ships; the clerk in the New York City export house checking bales of tobacco awaiting shipment to London; the master cooper in the Boston rum distillery; the young Virginia overseer building up his "stake" to try and start his own plantation; the immigrant German farmer renting a team of five slaves to get his farm started; and on and on.[24]

Indeed, in one way or another, the majority of whites benefited from the slavery-centered economic complex, which encompassed the slave trade, trade with and support of slave plantations, the international trade in slave-produced products, and the panoply of slavery-support occupations and businesses.

Moreover, from the seventeenth century forward, many colonial and U.S. laws and customs have been developed by whites in response to black resistance to enslavement and other oppression. Over the centuries, the recurring white responses, legal and extralegal, to the many types of black resistance—slave runaways, rebellions, abolitionism, and recent civil rights movements—are additional evidence of the centrality of white-on-black oppression in the development of systemic racism in North America.

The case of black Americans is also prototypical because the standard examples for such racial categories as "inferior race" or "non-whites" that have been deeply imbedded in a great many white minds, indeed since at least the eighteenth century, have involved black Americans. Cognitive science has discovered that many categorizations that people make are in terms of prototypes; that is, in terms of one primary example for a major category.[25] By the mid- to late-1700s, the emerging racial ideology accenting a hierarchy of "races" in what would soon be the United States was crafted substantially in connection with rationalizing the enslavement and other oppression of African Americans. At an early point in the new nation's history, moreover, the typical white mind made the centrality of black labor for the white-controlled society clear in phrases like "working like a nigger" (by 1800) and "wage slave" (by the 1850s).

Indeed, white Americans of all classes often seemed obsessed with black Americans, a point that the great abolitionist Frederick Douglass once made eloquently in a nineteenth-century speech:

> Go where you will, you will meet with him [the black American]. He is alike present in the study of the learned and thoughtful, and in the play house of the gay and thoughtless. We see him pictured at our street corners, and hear him in the songs of our market places. The low and the vulgar curse him, the snob and the flunky affect to despise him, the mean and the cowardly assault him, because they know…that they can abuse him with impunity.…To the statesman and philosopher he is an object of intense curiosity.…Of the books, pamphlets, and speeches concerning him, there is literally, no end. He is the one inexhaustible topic of conversation at our firesides and in our public halls.[26]

Over the centuries many whites have been obsessed with black Americans, their families, or their communities. This remains true today. To take a recent example, Charles Gallagher has reviewed various surveys and shown that a majority of whites greatly exaggerate the size of the U.S. black population, at 30 percent or more—two and a half times the actual black population size of about 12 percent. A significant number of whites insist that black Americans are at least 40 percent of the population. Black Americans are the only group of color whose size looms so large in the typical white racial imagination. Indeed, some research shows that whites discuss their own numerical position in the society principally in relationship to their image of the number of black Americans, and much less often in regard to other Americans of color.[27]

Consider too that, in its use for human groups, the word "white" was originally defined by the English colonists mainly in contrast with "black." According to Winthrop Jordan, the European American colonists developed the relatively new and distinctive term "white" for themselves in the last half of the seventeenth century mainly to contrast themselves to those they had named as "blacks." Prior to that time, European colonists mostly distinguished themselves as "Christians" in counterpoint to "Negroes" and "Indians." About 1680, they began contrasting themselves as "whites" with "Negroes," and soon with "blacks" (or "Africans").[28] This English language development is an indicator of the thorough and methodical institutionalization of African American oppression by that early point in time, as well as of its emerging rationalization. "White" defined who the European Americans were, and who they were not. Whiteness was indeed a major and terrible invention, one that solidified white thinking into an extensive and racialized either/or framework and that came to symbolize for whites the "ownership of the earth" and "civilization."[29]

African Americans have been rather distinctive among the non-European groups encountered and exploited by whites, for they have generally become the "othered" group against which most whites in this society have long defined themselves. Even today, if asked about a general category like "non-white person" or "person of color," a majority of whites will likely think in terms of a black person, probably most often an image of a black man or woman in working-class dress. In such cases, a social stereotype often stands in for the category "non-white person" as a whole.

Another reason for the centrality of black Americans in this white-dominated society, as well as in the white mind, is the fact that whites played a very important role historically in the creation of the diverse ancestries of many millions of black Americans. Recall from the preface that under the gendered racial oppression that was slavery and legal segregation, very large numbers of black women were raped, at will and generally with impunity, by white men in the elite and in the working and middle classes. As we will see in later chapters, the children resulting from these rapes during the long slavery era were typically labeled as "black" and usually enslaved. This coercive pattern continued in many areas during the legal segregation period following slavery. The physical makeup of African Americans as a group has been fundamentally shaped by the widespread sexual violence perpetrated by white men historically. Perhaps the white focus on and obsession with black Americans historically, and the frequently extreme character of white rationalizations of antiblack oppression, are linked to the fact that white Americans as a group have for centuries oppressed a group of people who are often, in reality, their *unacknowledged kin*.

Significantly, by the mid-nineteenth century, many thousands of whites were moving ever more aggressively westward across North America, thereby bringing more people of color into the white-controlled economically and politically exploitative framework. Beginning in the 1840s, the deep structure of racialized oppression set in place by European colonists and their descendants to exploit and oppress African Americans was gradually extended to other people of color. Next in chronological order, in the 1840s and 1850s, whites brought the lands and labor of Mexicans and the labor of Chinese immigrants—as well as the lands of more Native American societies long beyond white intrusion—into the expanding framework of exploitative racism that had been so profitable for whites in the early centuries of North American development.

MAJOR DIMENSIONS OF RACIAL OPPRESSION

From a systemic racism perspective, U.S. society is an organized racist whole with complex, interconnected, and interdependent social networks, organizations, and institutions that routinely imbed racial oppression. This system has changed somewhat over time in response to pressures within the societal environment. We can view it at particular points in time, that is, synchronically, or we can view it as it changes over several points in time, that is, diachronically. Significantly, most *basic* elements and institutions of racial oppression in U.S. society have endured over time, even as some significant changes have taken place.

Economic Domination and Its Many Costs

In Figure 1, I trace out key features of systemic racism in this country to show just how this racism works. However, we should keep in mind that the various features of systemic racism are often in effect at the same place and time, and all are *integrally connected* to one another. None stands alone, and each is but an aspect of a much larger whole.

What are the motor forces that drive systemic racism? Why does one form of systemic racism, white-on-black oppression, have such centrality and staying power over the course of this society's long history? One major answer to these questions lies in the long-term dependence of white Americans on African American labor. As I have noted, systemic racism began historically with extensive economic domination and vigorous economic exploitation, that is, with the violent theft of other peoples' land and other peoples' labor. Less than a decade after they arrived, in 1637, New England colonists asserted their control over indigenous peoples by massacring the inhabitants of a Pequot village

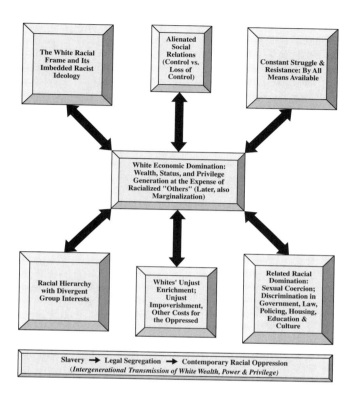

Figure 1 Dimensions of Systemic Racism

and sending the survivors into slavery. Unable to secure enough labor from Europe or from such attacks on Indian societies, European colonists soon turned mainly to enslaved African labor. The brutality of the European violence used in enslaving Africans is recounted by an African who was forced to labor in North America:

> I was soon put down under the decks, and there I received such a salutation in my nostrils as I had never experienced in my life: so that with the loathsomeness of the stench, and crying together, I became so sick and low that I was not able to eat….On my refusing to eat, one of them held me fast by the hands, and laid me across, I think the windlass, and tied my feet, while the other flogged me severely.[30]

Not surprisingly, such violent treatment led to many deaths of those thus enslaved. From the bloody first decades of European invasion in

North America to the present day, this economic domination has involved the channeling and subordinating of the labor of non-European peoples, usually to maximize the material benefits to European Americans. For centuries now, this domination has encompassed severe and large-scale economic subordination or discrimination in such areas as slave labor, segregated jobs, discriminatory wages, exclusion from other socioeconomic opportunities reserved for whites, and, periodically, marginalization in the economy.

In various ways, economic domination transfers substantial benefits from the labor of one group of people, such as enslaved African Americans, to another group of people, principally white Americans.[31] As I accent in Figure 1, labor and energy exploitation has entailed much unjust enrichment of European Americans and much consequent unjust impoverishment for black Americans and other Americans of color. Unjust enrichment and unjust impoverishment are critical concepts for understanding the past and present reality of this country's constantly exploitative socioeconomic system.

From the seventeenth century to the present day, white elites and rank-and-file whites have aggressively exploited the labor of African Americans (and other workers of color) in order to generate trillions of dollars (measured in today's dollars) in wealth for white Americans. At the time of the American Revolution, one fifth of the population was African American--mostly people who were enslaved--and by the time of the Civil War, millions of enslaved workers had generated substantial material prosperity for many whites in the North and the South. The famous border state slaveholder and U.S. Senator Henry Clay made this clear in his February 1839 speech against abolitionist petitions presented to the U.S. Senate. After estimating that the dollar worth of all "slave property" was then at least $1.2 billion, Clay adds this telling comment:

> This property is diffused throughout all classes and conditions of [white] society....It is the subject of mortgages, deeds of trust, and family settlements. It has been made the basis of numerous debts contracted upon its faith, and is the sole reliance, in many instances, of creditors within and without the slave states, for the payment of debts due to them...there is a visionary dogma, which holds that negro slaves cannot be the subject of property. I shall not dwell long on this speculative abstraction. That is property which the law declares to be property.[32]

Clay, who held many in slavery, was an influential leader of his day, a man whom Abraham Lincoln once said had taught him all he knew about slavery. Stressing heavy white investments in "slave property" was a major argument in the slaveholders' rationalizations of continuing black enslavement. African Americans are here viewed as highly profitable for the U.S. economy. Whites like Clay rationalized their enslavement by placing into the law that they were not full human beings but rather profit-making property.

By 1860, nearly one fifth of all national wealth in the United States was in the value of enslaved African Americans alone, about $3 billion. This was substantially more than the $2.2 billion invested in all manufacturing and railroad enterprises in the country. The income and wealth made off slave-produced products and the slave trade in turn generated large-scale employment for many millions of white workers and white businesspeople in an array of commercial, trade, banking, insurance, and shipping companies, as well as in the local, state, and federal governments. Thus, "no one should have any question where power lay in the antebellum period."[33] Moreover, one scholar has calculated that the value of the slave labor stolen by whites from the 1620s to the 1860s was at least $1 trillion (in current dollars), and perhaps as much as $97 trillion. During the legal segregation era, yet more labor of African Americans was expropriated—an estimated $1.6 trillion just for the years 1929–1969 (in current dollars).[34] If one adds in the value of all the other stolen labor for the years not covered in these estimates, including that still generated today by discrimination in employment, the total cost of antiblack discrimination from the beginning of slavery to the present day is staggering—trillions of dollars. Significant, too, is the fact that large-scale antiblack discrimination in the economy has persisted now into the twenty-first century.

Historically, the enslavement of African Americans encompassed the exploitation of black men's, women's, and children's labor in fields and factories, yet it also involved the exploitation of the procreative (reproductive) labor of those who were enslaved. In the South and the North, the forced breeding of black women and men—and the rape of black women by white slaveholders and their hirelings—accelerated the reproduction of an enslaved people to the economic and sexual advantage of many whites.[35] This unpunished rape of black women continued after slavery during the era of legal segregation, indeed until the 1960s.

This sexual violence by white men during slavery and legal segregation has had major consequences to the present day. For example, Patricia Williams, a distinguished law professor, has recounted the story of Austin Miller, her white great-great-grandfather. Miller, a prominent white lawyer in the South, bought Williams's eleven-year-old black great-great-grandmother during the slavery era. He raped the youngster, who thus became the mother of Williams's great-grandmother Mary. Today, Williams, like many other black Americans, has to cope with the reality of a white slave-holding ancestor who was a child molester and rapist.[36] Indeed, African Americans are the only North American racial group that lost, for centuries, substantial control over their own procreation.

In addition, as I indicate in Figure 1, African Americans, as well as other Americans of color, have paid a heavy price for racial oppression in many other areas of their lives. There are many undeserved costs attached to being the targets of racial oppression, including the dramatic loss of time and energy from having to cope with discrimination, the damage to personal, physical, and psychological health, and the harm to families and communities. These costs can be seen in every era, from slavery to the present day. Thus, a 1990s United Nations report calculated a Human Development Index to assess the quality of life for various groups and countries, an index that included data on education, income, and life expectancy. Among all the countries and groups examined, white Americans ranked *first* in quality of life, while black Americans ranked only *thirty-first* on the list.[37]

Today, the costs of being black in the United States remain very high, costs that signal clearly the long-term impacts of white-on-black oppression. Thus, today the median income of black families is less than 60 percent of that of the white median income, and the median wealth of black families is much less than that of white families. In addition, black Americans on average live about six years less than white Americans. In order to calculate the total cost of antiblack oppression over several centuries, one would need to add to these striking statistics the other personal, family, and community costs over the centuries—the intense pain and suffering, the physical and psychological damage, the rage over injustice, and the huge loss of energy that could have been used for family and community needs. The fact that such comprehensive costs for African Americans have never been discussed seriously by white politicians and other leading government and private officials in public policy discussions of racial matters in the United States is yet another sign of the deep-lying and systemic character of past and contemporary racism. We will return to these issues in later chapters.

Systemic racism, thus, is at bottom a highly unjust system for creating and extending the impoverishment of large groups of people, such as African Americans, to the profit of other large groups of people, principally white Americans.

The Racial Hierarchy: Power Imbalance and Alienated Relationships

Racial domination by whites has been far more than a matter of economic exploitation and the unequal distribution of resources, for it fundamentally involves an extremely asymmetrical relationship of power that enables whites, as individuals and in groups, to take for their own use the land, labor, and lives of non-European peoples. The operation of systemic racism involves the recurring exercise of coercive power by white Americans over black Americans, as well as over other Americans of color. In the process of this oppression, whites attempt to force Americans of color to act as whites would have them act, and thus often to act against their individual and group interests. Thus, whites have created social arrangements where those who are oppressed lose substantial control over their lives and livelihoods. They are generally separated and alienated from their oppressors. They are, to varying degrees, alienated from control over their own bodies as well as from an ability to make decisions about many aspects of their lives. Systemic racism at its core involves separating, distancing, and alienating social relationships.

For several centuries, whites' coercion has kept African Americans from doing much of what they need and desire to do for themselves and their families. Black needs and wants have typically not been given serious consideration by white decision makers in major economic, political, and social institutions, although these needs and desires have often been made clear in black resistance against racial oppression. The imposition of white social and economic power occurs in everyday interactions between individuals and between small groups, but it is always set within the larger system of oppression that constantly asserts whites' group interests over those of African Americans and other Americans of color. White power is always exercised relationally; that is, it is an aspect of a hierarchical relationship that has from the beginning involved a great inequality of socioeconomic resources.

A central aspect of the U.S. racial hierarchy is the reality of divergent racial-group interests. The few scholars who have accented a comprehensive structural approach to racism in the past, such as Bob Blauner and Eduardo Bonilla-Silva, have pointed out that because of this dominant racial hierarchy, white Americans have political-economic interests that are quite different from those of African Americans and other Americans of color.[38] The U.S. racial continuum runs from the privileged white position and status at the top to an oppressed black position and status at the bottom, with different groups of color variously positioned *by whites* between the two ends of this central racial-status continuum. Firmly at the top of the U.S. racial hierarchy are individual whites of all backgrounds and their families. They, as a group, hold the top position in terms of racialized privileges and power. Below whites in this racial hierarchy is the large class of men and women of color and their families. Initially, in the first century of European colonialism, the workers of color included some Native Americans and a great many African Americans, but in the nineteenth century increasing numbers of other workers of color were brought into the racial hierarchy by white employers and expansionists. At points in U.S. history, whites, especially those in the elite, have moved certain groups of color up or down the racial status continuum as they have seen fit. However, no matter what their work efforts, education, or income may be, Americans of color have never been able to attain the *full* array of privileges and power long reserved for whites.

Crosscutting this racial hierarchy are other important stratification systems, including those of gender and class. Women are generally subordinated to men within the racial categories, yet they also occupy societal positions of privilege or subordination depending on their racial-group positioning. There are also class divisions. A white, mostly male elite has the greatest influence and power within white America. Below the elite, and less powerful, is a large category of white workers (called a "labor aristocracy") who not only have benefited from less competition in the many societal areas where black workers and other workers of color have been excluded or marginalized, but also have gained from the socially invented racial privilege that is reserved for white Americans. Historically, white workers often had legally guaranteed "white" jobs. For example, slavery-era laws often required that a white person be hired for every "six Negroes" on plantations and that only whites be trained as skilled workers.[39] Similar exclusive practices were legal during the official segregation era, and many such discriminatory practices have been implemented informally in U.S. workplaces since the end of official segregation in the 1960s.

White workers have generally received what W. E. B. Du Bois called "the public and psychological wage of whiteness." This latter privilege is less tangible but still real, for it involves whites' perceived higher status and a psychological sense of being racially superior. Nothing is more central to U.S. history than the ongoing struggle of working-class and middle-class whites to maintain their unjustly gained material advantages and this psychological wage of whiteness. Indeed, this historical reality is the reason that the United States has much weaker unions and a quite different labor history from numerous European countries: The many better jobs, opportunities, and resources reserved for whites only have constituted a great "social safety-valve," sharply reducing labor struggles with capitalists over the course of this country's long history.[40]

U.S. racism is both complex and highly relational, a true system in which major racial groups and their networks stand in asymmetrical and oppositional relations. The social institutions and processes that reproduce racial inequality imbed a fundamental inegalitarian relationship—on the one hand, the racially oppressed, and on the other, the racial oppressors. For example, at an early point in time, one such inegalitarian relationship counterposed white slaveholders (later, white employers) to enslaved black Americans (later, free blacks). The system of racism aggressively separates and alienates those defined and elevated as the "superior race" from those defined and subordinated as the "inferior race." Generally speaking, those targeted by exploitation and oppression lose substantial control over many important aspects of their lives—over their land or labor, over the products their labor generates, over their relationships to others in their work group and to those in the oppressing group, and ultimately over their ability to develop the full range of their talents and abilities as human beings.

Other Types of Racial Discrimination and Cultural Imperialism

As can be seen in Figure 1, racial oppression has involved discrimination against women, men, and children of color in many institutional arenas besides the economy; these include education, politics, housing, health care, policing, and public accommodations. Generated by or closely associated with economic domination, powerlessness in many institutional areas beyond the economic realm is a key feature of well-developed racial oppression.

Under slavery, African Americans were excluded from schools, public accommodations, and decent housing, and endured much violence by police agencies and by slaveholders. We have already noted the coerced sexual relations imposed on those enslaved. In chapter 2, three enslaved African Americans further describe the extreme oppressiveness of slavery's everyday conditions. Typically, those enslaved arose before dawn and labored until dark, with whips and chains as the means of control. In one account, an enslaved man recounted being moved from Georgia by a white slaveholder:

> Then he chains all the slaves round the necks and fastens the chains to the hosses and makes them walk all the way to Texas. My mother and my sister had to walk....Somewhere on the road it went to snowing, and massa wouldn't let us wrap any-

thing round our feet. We had to sleep on the ground, too, in all that snow.[41]

Black bodies were exploited not just economically, but for an array of other shocking uses that some white minds conjured up. One account provided in the 1850s by William Goodell describes how those enslaved black Americans who were ill and disabled were often bought by white "medical institutions, to be experimented and operated upon, for purposes of 'medical education' and the interest of medical science."[42] These medical institutions advertised in major newspapers for such human guinea pigs.

Later, under the legal segregation that developed after the Civil War, African Americans faced not only large-scale discrimination by whites in the economy—as laborers, sharecroppers, and domestic workers—and in policing, but also exclusion or serious restriction in regard to access to education, housing, political participation, churches, health care, and public accommodations. Policing agencies continued to enforce this legal segregation until the 1960s, only a bit more than a generation back in this country's past.

Today, racial discrimination still confronts African Americans in the areas of education, housing, politics, public accommodations, and policing. Police brutality and other serious harassment remain serious problems across much of the United States, problems rarely experienced by white Americans of any background. A recent ACLU report noted that racial profiling by law enforcement agencies still persists in many states. In Oklahoma, a black father and his young son were victims of discriminatory targeting. A decorated veteran, he and his son were stopped twice by state police officers after crossing into Oklahoma on a highway. When the veteran disputed a white officer's claim that he had not signaled, he and his son were humiliated and put into a very hot patrol car, and their complaints were ignored while their car was searched for drugs that did not exist.[43] Serious hate crimes, often involving personal violence against African Americans, frequently take place in the United States. In a recent government accounting, the largest number of hate crimes reported, including several racialized murders, were those against African Americans.[44]

While most antiblack discrimination is no longer legal, informal discrimination in employment, housing, public accommodations, and other major areas is still widespread and is either perpetrated by or tolerated by most whites. Indeed, white officials at all levels of government, including those in the "justice" system, rarely take aggressive action aimed at significantly reducing racial discrimination in the United States.

Part of the comprehensive system of racism, today as in the past, is an intense cultural imperialism that entails the imposition of many white values and views on those who are oppressed. Whites have imposed the Eurocentric culture they inherited from their ancestors over many generations onto the everyday worlds of this society. They have made a Eurocentric perspective into the national (and, indeed, world) standard for many things cultural and political.[45] Cultural domination by white Americans has long pressured African Americans and other Americans of color to conform to traditional white ways of viewing and doing things—such as conforming to the norms of an old Anglo-Saxon legal system and to the so-called standard (that is, white-middle-class) form of the English language. As numerous critical legal scholars, such as A. Leon Higginbotham and Roy Brooks, have demonstrated, one major area of the cultural embeddedness of racial oppression is the American legal system.[46] The unjust enrichment for the European colonists and their descendants that stemmed from extreme exploitation of Native American lands and African American labor was at an early point protected by the legal system of the North American colonies. This economic domination and the consequent assets and wealth for white Americans were, during both the slavery and legal segregation eras, enshrined in U.S. laws and government policies.

The White Racial Frame

Central to the persistence of systemic racism has been the development of a commonplace white racial frame—that is, an organized set of racialized ideas, stereotypes, emotions, and inclinations to discriminate. This white racial frame generates closely associated, recurring, and habitual discriminatory actions. The frame and associated discriminatory actions are consciously or unconsciously expressed in the routine operation of racist institutions of this society. At an early point in colonial history, the highly structured reality of white-on-black oppression generated the first incarnation of this color-coded framing of society—a composite that has been maintained, albeit with some reworking, to the present day. Antonio Gramsci once noted that

> The personality is strangely composite: it contains…prejudices from all past phases of history at the local level and intuitions of a future philosophy.…The starting point of critical elaboration is the consciousness of what one really is, and is "knowing thyself" as a product of the historical process to date which has deposited in you an infinity of traces, without leaving an inventory.[47]

Not only has racial oppression been foundational to and pervasive within major institutions since before the founding of this nation, but it has historically deposited an "infinity of traces" in the minds and personality structures of European American oppressors of all social backgrounds.

This white framing of society has strongly buttressed anti-Indian genocide, African American slavery, legal segregation, and contemporary incarnations of racial oppression. Today, as in the past, this frame provides an encompassing conceptual and interpretive scheme that shapes and channels assessments of everyday events and encounters with other people.[48] The frame not only explains and interprets the everyday world but also implies or offers actions in line with the frame's explanatory perspective. A strong conceptual frame captures territory in the mind and makes it difficult to get people to think about that captured territory in terms other than those of the accepted frame. If facts do not fit a person's frame, that person typically ignores or rejects the facts, not the frame. In the case of most white Americans, their racial frame includes negative stereotypes, images, and metaphors concerning African Americans and other Americans of color, as well as assertively positive views of whites and white institutions. As in the past, the racialized framing of the societal world today is mostly similar for whites of various backgrounds because they are usually socialized within sociocultural contexts that imbed such framing.

Typically, old racist images, understandings, and related emotions become part of an individual white consciousness at an early age and, indeed, often exist in individual minds at a nonreporting and unconscious level.[49] Thus, researchers have recently found that, when given a test of unconscious stereotyping, nearly 90 percent of whites who have taken the test implicitly associate the faces of black Americans with negative words and traits such as evil character or failure. That is, they have more difficulty linking black faces to pleasant words and positive traits than they do for white faces. Most whites show an antiblack, pro-white bias on psychological tests. In addition, when whites are shown photos of black faces, even for only 30 milliseconds, key areas of their brains that are designed to respond to perceived threats light up automatically. In addition, the more unconscious stereotyping they show on psychological tests, the greater their brains' threat responses when they are shown photos of black Americans.[50]

Over time, by constantly using elements of the white racial frame to interpret society, by integrating new items into the frame, and by applying the learned stereotypes, images, and interpretations in various types of associated discriminatory actions, whites imbed their racialized framing of the world deeply in their minds (brains) and thereby make such framing much harder to counter. Particular cognitive items in a racist frame, such as common stereotypes of black Americans, resist evidence, no matter how substantial, that counters them because of how deeply these cognitions have been implanted in white minds. As a result, most whites do not approach new encounters with black Americans and other people of color with minds that are blank slates open freely to new information and interpretations, but rather with minds framed in terms of the traditional white-racist thinking, interpretations, and inclinations.

Clearly, a white racial frame is more than cognitive, for it also includes racialized emotions that are linked to cognitive stereotypes and visual images. Whites typically combine racial stereotypes (the cognitive aspect), metaphors and concepts (the deeper cognitive aspect), images (the visual aspect), emotions (feelings like fear), and inclinations (to take discriminatory action) within a racist frame that is oriented, in substantial part, to assessing African Americans and other Americans of color in everyday situations, as well as to assessing white Americans and white institutions. While there are clearly variations on the white racial frame across white America, the typical frame doubtless encompasses thousands of these "bits" webbed together. Some are subtly racist cognitions, images, emotions, and inclinations to discriminate, while many others are more blatant and obviously racist. For example, the old white stereotype of the "dangerous black man" typically conjures up in the white mind an array of connected ideas and strong emotions, including the emotionally generated inclination to take precautionary action.[51] As they have for centuries, most whites today likely interpret racial situations and events, and especially interracial encounters, in terms of their white racial framing with its racialized emotions—and usually not in terms of careful reasoning on the basis of aggressively searched-out data.

Recurring discriminatory action and other oppression targeting Americans of color require a breakdown of normal human empathy. Major Western social theorists have mostly missed the central importance of the fact that all human life begins in empathetic networks that are central to human societies. The first network is the dyad of mother and child, a network linked to other relatives. Usually central to these first networks is a basic human empathy, a desire and ability to understand the feelings of others. Thus, as it develops, racial oppression not only severely distorts human relationships but also desensitizes the minds of those involved in oppressing others. Racial oppression requires and stimulates in the oppressors a lack of recognition of the full humanity of the exploited and racialized others. Psychiatrists use the term "alexithymia" to describe individuals who are unable to understand the emotions of, and thus empathize with, other people. Hernán Vera and I have suggested going beyond this individualistic interpretation to a concept of "social alexithymia."[52] Essential to being an oppressor in a racist society is a significantly reduced ability, or an inability, to understand or relate to the emotions, such as recurring pain, of those targeted by oppression. Social alexithymia thus seems essential to the creation and maintenance of a racist society.[53]

The Racist Ideology: Defending Racial Oppression

Critical to the white racial frame is an interrelated set of cognitive notions, understandings, and metaphors that whites have used to rationalize and legitimate systemic racism. Over several centuries now, white Americans have not been content to oppress Americans of color and just admit defiantly that their actions constitute unprincipled group aggrandizement enforced with police and military force. Instead, most whites—including, as we will discuss in chapter 3, early political leaders like Thomas Jefferson, James Madison, and George Washington—have participated in the development of a strong racial ideology, a substantive set of ideas and notions defending white power and privilege as meritorious and natural and accenting the alleged superiority of whites and the inferiority of those who are racially oppressed.

An elite-fostered, color-coded ideology early became central to the new colonial society, one rationalizing the theft of Native American land, the seizure of African American labor, and the passing along of the resulting unjust enrichment to subsequent generations of European Americans. During the slavery era, the mental production of rationalizing antiblack ideas emerged directly from slaveholders as they excused and justified the slavery system for themselves and the society as a whole. Eventually, a well-developed racist ideology permeated the legitimating discourse of the whites who were dominant in major social institutions, including the economy, law, politics, education, and religion.

This color-coded language and discourse did not materialize out of thin air, but rather emerged in the everyday interactions of people in society. Historically and in the present, most people have extended ideas and language taken from their immediate social contexts to their interpretations of the larger society. For example, for centuries, a patriarchal family model has been dominant in Western societies, including the European colonial areas that later became the United States. Historically, well before they engaged in the enslavement of Africans, most Europeans had held strongly to a patriarchal family model that asserted the need for a strict father figure, with the responsibility to protect the family and one to whom wives and children were subordinated and expected to obey. The patriarchal family was part of the experience of life for European colonists and their descendants in North America.[54] The patriarchal family also became one important source of the metaphors used to interpret other important areas of life.

Significantly, patriarchal metaphors have been commonplace in white reasoning about political and racial matters since the days of slavery and the American Revolution. Americans have long spoken of their "forefathers" or "founding fathers," with an understanding that the United States was the "family" of concern. These founders, many of them slaveholders, used the patriarchal symbolism, and they attacked the British king as a "bad father" and abusive parent.[55] Oppressive arrangements in the colonies, such as the enslavement of black Americans, were early characterized in this patriarchal language. A forthright "plantation mentality" on slavery was routinely generated by growing numbers of slaveholders. By the 1660s, the term "patriarchism" was consciously developed by the large plantation owners to characterize their view of society and their prevailing ideology. Slaveholding communities, especially in the South, were usually organized around the idea of supreme male patriarchs—dominant white "fathers" reigning in all things economic, social, and political. Patriarchism explicitly asserted a natural social order with white slaveholders at the top. "The great planters likened themselves to the biblical patriarchs; they were the heads of their families and the governors of society."[56] Their patriarchism encompassed stereotyped notions of white superiority and black (and Indian and female) inferiority and accented stern white control, and extreme and deferential black dependence, within a highly oppressive societal framework.

In addition, historically most white religious groups (mostly Christian) supported slavery and legal segregation, and in their religious teachings long taught white children and adults to accept a racist ideology that portrayed whites as dominant and blacks and other people of color as dependent. For centuries, white religious officials have been leaders in developing the ideology that rationalized slavery and subsequent societal oppression in more or less patriarchal terms.

Consciously or unconsciously, a majority of whites have long extended language and understandings from the patriarchal model and patriarchal family setting to discuss, defend, or prescribe the hierarchy in which whites are generally dominant and people of color are generally subordinated. They have accented and honed the common folk model of a "natural" social order, what has historically been called the "great chain of being." This perspective views men as superior to women, Westerners to non-Westerners, and whites to people of color. This putatively natural social order, in which the strong dominate the weak, is viewed as rightful and moral, and it thereby legitimates existing social inequalities and oppressive social hierarchies.[57]

Today, as in the past, the general perspective that a majority of whites use in interpreting and defending a racially hierarchical world frequently involves, albeit to varying degrees, the folk model of a natural social and racial order. African Americans and other people of color are thus viewed as necessarily dependent beings, even as "children" who should follow the lead of their white "elders." One key aspect of the racist ideology is that adult black Americans are not seen as fully adult beings, a view that is very much a part of historical and contemporary white teachings and rationalizations of racist institutions. African Americans and other Americans of color are expected to defer to whites in regard to the values and operative norms imbedded in the society's major institutions. Indeed, in the contemporary U.S., many African Americans speak of regularly encountering a "plantation mentality" among white Americans. This white-racist mentality can be seen in persisting white images of African Americans as dependent on welfare, as not as work oriented as whites, as less intelligent than whites, and as an intermarriage threat to white families. From this white perspective, indeed, even the phrase "American society" typically means white-controlled social institutions; the phrase "social values" (or "family values") typically means white-determined values; and the word "Americans" typically means "white Americans." Such whitewashed views are inheritances from the antiblack ideology first generated in seventeenth-century North America.

The patriarchal family setting not only has involved the oppression of women and girls, but also has provided, for many whites, a setting where racist prejudices and hostilities may be generated or intensified. Examining the development of systemic racism in recent decades, researchers have discovered that a strict patriarchal family environment can create negative family psychodynamics and have negative consequences for racial attitudes. Children's lessons in unreflective obedience to a strict father can have significant consequences for racial attitudes and relationships in society. In the first major study of racial prejudice and family contexts, conducted in the 1940s, a team of prominent social scientists found that white families with a strong patriarchal character were more likely than less patriarchal families to generate racially prejudiced children:

Prejudiced subjects tend to report a relatively harsh and more threatening type of home discipline which was experienced as arbitrary by the child....Above all, the [white] men among our prejudiced subjects tend to report having a "stern and distant" father who seems to have been domineering within the family. It is this type of father who elicits in his son...the ideal of aggressive and rugged masculinity....[58]

Thus, in strongly patriarchal families, the children, especially the boys, frequently find outlets for suppressed negative feelings toward domineering fathers in very negative attitudes toward subordinated racial outgroups. In strongly patriarchal families many white boys have been likely to accept rather unreflectively the ready-made racist images and stereotypes of socially subordinated groups such as African Americans—personal perspectives that may represent a subconscious transfer of the fathers' harsh attitudes toward them to socially hated and racialized "others" out in the larger society.

Resistance to Systemic Racism

There is a tendency in some sociological theory to see human beings as determined totally by social forces and restrictions, yet people work in many individual and collective ways to try to bring change in the structures and institutions that oppress them. Historically, as I indicate in Figure 1, a very important dimension of systemic racism has been the constant resistance to that racism by African Americans and other Americans of color. For centuries, they have striven as best they can to counter, restructure, and overturn that societal oppression. The omnipresent resistance of oppressed African Americans has shaped the character of the white oppressors' retaliatory actions, and thus the social contours of the larger society itself. The hostile white response, in its turn, has often generated yet more enhanced and reshaped black resistance, a dialectical and difficult process soon to move into a fifth century of struggle in the case of this society. Antiblack oppression, thus, has been constantly shaped and reshaped in an ongoing societal process that has lasted now for centuries. By their resistance, African Americans, as well as other Americans of color, have generated a long struggle for expanded social justice and democracy, a struggle continuing today.

Isaac Newton's third law of motion asserts that in the physical world, "For every action, there is an equal and opposite reaction." There seems to be a similar "law of social motion" in the case of societal oppression, which tends to generate major countering forces. Thus, the protracted struggle by African Americans, now nearly four hundred years old, has involved a major countering force. Oppression in each historical epoch has dialectically triggered distinctive anti-oppression efforts. Overt resistance by African Americans has included nonviolent civil disobedience, such as in the 1950s and 1960s civil rights movements, as well as less frequent armed group resistance, such as in the periodic uprisings of enslaved African Americans in the 1700s and 1800s. During the slavery era, aggressive black resistance took the form of active defense against the violence of individual slaveholders, as well as organized and collective resistance against slaveholders as a group. Some 250 slave revolts and conspiracies to revolt were recorded during the slavery era of this country.[59] For example, in 1831, Nat Turner, an enslaved black man, led a rebellion against slavery in Southampton County, Virginia. Seventy enslaved people rebelled with him, and dozens of whites were killed before white soldiers put down these freedom fighters. They clearly had a sense of what "liberty and justice" really meant, more so than those against whom they revolted. Their rebellion brought great fear of black revolts into white minds, especially in southern areas, and new laws and repressive policing systems were developed by whites in response. This aggressive white response indicates how the action-reaction "law" of social motion works for this society.

Moreover, in the mid-nineteenth century, the actions of hundreds of thousands of formerly enslaved black Americans who served valiantly as Union soldiers and support workers played a critical role in setting the U.S. on the track to becoming a freer and more democratic country (see chapter 2). Similarly, the abolitionist movement in the mid-nineteenth century, composed as it was of both black and white Americans, played a significant role in pushing the enslavement of human beings into the national (white) consciousness as a major moral issue, and thus in providing a moral rationale for the Union side in the Civil War. This abolitionist activism eventually helped secure several critical human rights amendments to the U.S. Constitution just after the Civil War.

Over their centuries-long course of resistance, African Americans have honed a well-developed view of emancipation from oppression and, thus, of the deeper meaning of the age-old ideals of freedom and justice. Indeed, during the Revolutionary era and the first decades of the nineteenth century, free black Americans were the "foremost proponents of freedom and justice in the nation, demanding of the Constitution more than its slave-holding creators dared to dream."[60] During the American Revolution against Great Britain, the commonplace protests against British laws and policies in the cities often involved black patriots, both free and enslaved. These multiracial "mobs" of American patriots were "denounced as a many-headed hydra" by the British authorities.[61]

A little later, after the United States was formed, African American leaders like Absalom Jones and James Forten carried strong petitions to the new U.S. Congress asserting that African Americans were human beings who should have the same "liberties and inalienable rights" that the founding documents decreed to be the birthright of whites.[62] The very people whose racially oppressed condition had been guaranteed by white leaders in several provisions of the founding Constitution were those who most forthrightly asserted the high ideals of equality, liberty, and justice often proclaimed by the same white founders.

The view of the country held by African Americans has long encompassed a more inclusive "family of humanity" understanding that runs counter to the autocratic "white father" view of a rigidly and racially hierarchical society. In their recurring resistance movements, and in their antiracist framing of this society, African Americans have regularly rejected their enforced dependent status and indeed envisioned a world of truly egalitarian social relations. Interestingly, during the 1950s and 1960s and under the influence or pressure of the black civil rights movement, a significant number of white Americans abandoned elements of the old "natural order" language and metaphorical understandings for society in regard to racial issues and understandings. They shifted, at least at the level of public commentary, to a view accenting the more inclusive "family of humanity" in which all people should be treated equally under the law.

THE SOCIAL REPRODUCTION OF RACIAL OPPRESSION OVER CENTURIES

Beneath Figure 1, I have placed a box indicating that the patterns of oppression of African Americans and other Americans of color have continued in an evolved form over the centuries. In the case of African Americans, slavery was replaced in the period from the 1880s to the 1910s by a system of near-slavery usually called legal or official segregation. These rigidly segregated social arrangements lasted in the United States until the late 1960s. In turn, this lengthy era of near-slavery was followed in the late 1960s by the contemporary era of more informal racial discrimination, a racial oppression that is still extensive in U.S. society. The macrosociological box under Figure 1 points to the way in which the American "house" of oppression has been constantly reproduced, though twice remodeled, over a very long period. Systemic racism has seen some important changes, but these changes have done little to alter the deep social structure of an entrenched social hierarchy with its alienated relationships and its well-rationalized inequalities of power and privilege.

The social reproduction of antiblack oppression from the seventeenth century to the present day is a central and abiding theme in the history of this society. Today, most whites prefer to forget the past centuries and to mentally separate that past of antiblack oppression from the present-day racial situation—with many seeking to assert an absence of serious racial problems today and thereby to reduce pressures for major changes. Yet, there are direct connections not only between the racialized institutions of the past and those of the present, but also between the oppressed lives of living African Americans and those who were enslaved not so long ago.[63] Those who are racially oppressed usually see oppression, and periodic changes therein, in quite different ways from the oppressors. Once in place, racial oppression has had a strong social inertia, remaining a fundamental part of society even when modest or significant modifications are made.

The Reality of Social Inertia

Problematic in this slow process of change in societal oppression over time is the difficulty in bringing major alterations to such a well-institutionalized system. In the case of white-on-black oppression, we see in operation what might be termed the "law of social inertia." Isaac Newton's first law of motion, the famous law of inertia, asserts that an object at rest will continue at rest, or an object in motion will continue moving in one direction until an unbalancing counterforce is exerted on it. Applying this to the social realm, one can argue that there is a strong tendency for social oppression's exploitative mechanisms, resource inequalities, basic norms, key images, and buttressing attitudes to stay substantially in place, to remain more or less in force, until a major unbalancing force counters or challenges that oppression. In the case of systemic racism, those with the greater power and privilege, the white oppressors, have worked and strained to keep this system from changing in fundamental and foundational ways over several centuries. From the beginning, whites' maintenance efforts have been both overt and covert, both conscious and unconscious.

When the system of racism does finally change significantly, the law of social inertia typically operates to keep that system more like it was in the past than like the ideal "new" society that many (especially white) analysts like to celebrate. Thus, celebrations of major racial change at the end of the eras of slavery and legal segregation were soon met with sober realizations that less had changed than many had forecast. The major reason for this social inertia is that over the centuries of this country's development, the unbalancing counterforces to the racist system, such as the 1960s civil rights movement, have not been strong enough to dismantle the foundation of that well-entrenched oppressive system.

One striking feature of systemic racism is how long it has now persisted with a very inegalitarian hierarchy in place. The perpetuation of this highly hierarchical system has required a constant reproducing of the major inegalitarian institutions of this society, with their requisite discriminatory arrangements and processes. For white-on-black oppression to persist across many generations since the 1600s, many millions of white individuals and groups have had to participate actively in the ongoing collective and discriminatory reproduction of the family, community, legal, political, economic, educational, and religious institutions that necessarily undergird this oppressive system.

The white elite, as the leading protector of social hierarchy and white privilege, has dealt with the strong pressures coming from the oppressed for change by, at most, making only those changes that will insure social peace and that will not remove whatever is essential to the persistence of the oppressive system. The members of that elite, together with rank-and-file whites, have regularly perpetuated the system of racism by protecting and fortifying existing racist institutions; less often, they have had to change those institutions—sometimes cosmetically, sometimes more substantially—in order to retain the fundamentals of the racial hierarchy and white privilege. The elite has presided over some significant transformations in systemic racism—once in response to the abolitionist movement and the Civil War in the 1860s and again in response to the civil rights movement of the 1960s—yet they have typically acted so as to perpetuate the asymmetrical hierarchy and the sovereignty of white rule and privilege. As Derrick Bell has argued, when the white elite does make changes in the racialized system, it is usually when those societal changes are more or less in line with the interests of whites (or white elites) to do so, including their interests in maintaining societal peace and international political legitimacy.[64]

The Social Reproduction and Transmission of Racial Privilege: Individuals and Families

Because the reproduction of systemic racism over the centuries has been considered more or less normal by most white Americans, and because the ways and mechanisms by which this system of oppression has been reproduced and transmitted over generations have received little attention in social science analyses, let us pause and give specific attention to these critical issues of the social reproduction and social transmission of this hierarchy and inequality.

At the macrolevel, the large-scale racist institutions, such as the racialized economy and governments, have imbedded white-controlled normative structures and social networks and routinely perpetuate—and are routinely perpetuated by the means of—internal racial hierarchies and inequalities. These institutions are constantly created, recreated, and maintained by the processes of institutionalization, such as by legal processes, and by the reproducing and conforming actions at the microlevel by the many individuals in the numerous social networks within these institutions. Which aspects of racial oppression are reproduced, and when and where, varies with the particular institution and with the whites who operate therein, but the accumulating and comprehensive effect of most whites operating in socially reproducing ways within major institutions has been to keep the overall system of racial oppression spanning many generations.

Whether an individual is a member of the oppressor group or a member of an oppressed group, she or he does not exist in isolation from others. Today, as in the past, almost all individuals are firmly imbedded in important small-group contexts that work to socialize and support them. Particularly important are the significant networks of relatives and close friends that surround individuals. For example, within their critical social networks, beginning as young children, whites typically inherit significant socioeconomic resources and learn to operate as part of the racially dominant group in a hierarchical society. In the context of these social networks, whites learn to frame society stereotypically and to take discriminatory action against African Americans and other dark-skinned Americans. In turn, beginning again as young children, the latter typically have inherited modest or no socioeconomic resources and have developed their resources and repertoire of responses to racialized oppression within similarly critical networks of relatives and close friends. Over many generations of North American development, white-on-black oppression has been perpetuated by a social reproduction process that constantly regenerates inegalitarian, segregated, and alienated relationships between the oppressed and the oppressors.

Let me illustrate here with a more detailed discussion of the societal reproduction and transmission of the privileged group—that of white Americans. Consider such matters as white assets, power, and privilege. As a rule, each new generation of whites has inherited an array of resources and privileges that stem ultimately from white control of major societal institutions, but which are transmitted most immediately in the social contexts of family and other intimate networks.

Table 1 Intergenerational Transmission of Resources and Assets: Generations of White Individuals and Families

	Four Generations
Social context	Individual 1→ Individual 2 → Individual 3 → Individual 4
Family circle	Transmission of monetary, cultural/educational, social networking capital
Community circle	Creates/supports segregated family and friendship networks
Institutional circle	Provides supportive economic, political, military, legal, educational, and religious institutions
Societal circle	Envelops and protects major institutions with white-oriented culture

As I indicate in Table 1, for generations a majoriy of whites have inherited some economic resources and/or significant social-capital resources such as access to important social networks (for example, a good job) and access to some cultural capital (for example, a good education). In addition, the inegalitarian character of this routine transmission of economic and social capital is usually so masked in white thinking and societal discussions as to be mostly invisible. The social inheritance mechanisms are disguised to make the intertemporal inheritance of resources, power, and privilege appear to be fair, when in fact the white resources, power, and privilege typically represent the long-term transmission of unjust enrichment across numerous generations of oppressors and oppressed.

Table 1 depicts some major mechanisms in the intergenerational transmission of economic, cultural, and social assets in the everyday operation of this society. A white person in an earlier generation typically passed along some, albeit varying, economic, cultural, or social assets and resources to the next, and this transmission can continue down many generations of whites (in the oldest family trees, perhaps fifteen generations). I suggest four nested social circles that surround individuals as they live out their lives. Typically, an individual, usually situated in the social context of relatives (and close friends), transmits socioeconomic resources and assets to the next generation or two. Each individual is born into a preexisting set of intimate social ties, into a family setting that begins and sustains the often long process of passing along economic, cultural, and social assets, as well as the process of socialization into societal norms, prejudices, values, requirements, and institutions.

Very important in the perpetuation of systemic racism across the generations is the role of social networking, which is an essential type of social capital. For long periods, often centuries, most whites have had access to critical social networks beyond those of their immediate families. These networks of white friends, acquaintances, and neighbors provide access to critical networking resources, such as information about decent-paying jobs, health care, political participation, and educational opportunities.

Let me briefly illustrate these points about cultural and networking capital with reference to four generations of a southern white family whose history I know. Currently, the oldest living generation, now in their sixties, consists of three siblings, all professionals with graduate degrees. The maternal grandfather of this trio, a farmer of modest means who was born in the late nineteenth century, died when his daughter, their mother, was six years old. As a small child, she was farmed out to various relatives across the West. In this difficult process, she gained no significant monetary resources, yet she as a young white woman was able to get a high school degree and to attend a secretarial school at a time when virtually no public high schools or secretarial schools were available to black women in the South. She was thus able to get a job as a secretary before she got married. The paternal grandfather of this trio of professionals was born relatively poor, as a son in a large family whose parents were also small farmers and occasional shopkeepers. His family had migrated from rural Mississippi to rural Texas in a covered wagon when he was a small child. In the early 1900s, he was the first member of his family network to go beyond high school when he spent a year in a business college to learn telegraphy. At that time, there were extremely few such educational programs provided in the South for African Americans. With this education, this cultural capital, he was able to get a job with the U.S. Post Office—again in an era, the early 1900s, when no black southerners were able to get such government jobs because of extensive legal segregation. This employment provided him with a modest but stable income and enabled him and his little family to weather the storms of recession and depression between World War I and World War II. He had a job during the Great Depression of the 1930s, when the country had a 25 percent unemployment rate and more than half of black workers, especially in the South, could not find any work. This job enabled him to build a small house and to assist his son, an only child, to pay the modest tuition fee at a historically white university in the South where he earned the first college degree in this branch of a southern white family.

With this degree, more educational capital, from a public racially segregated university, the son was able to secure a good-paying job in the middle of the Great Depression with a regional oil company. In that period of intensive legal segregation, no white southern employers—indeed, few white employers anywhere—were hiring African Americans with or without college degrees for such jobs. This stable job enabled him, in turn, to send his three children, the professionals mentioned above, to major universities where they all had secured undergraduate and graduate degrees by the early 1970s. All did their undergraduate work in an era when all historically white southern universities were still excluding African American students or, by the late 1960s, admitting very small numbers. These three professionals, in their turn, have been able to assist substantially in providing college educations for their six college-aged children, thereby greatly improving their job opportunities compared to otherwise similar young black Americans who have been much less likely—because of the long history of exclusion and unjust impoverishment—to secure such college educations.

As can be seen in this family's example, a major type of societal resource that facilitated mobility for all these generations was good, nondiscriminatory access to educational and other cultural capital. Each generation was usually able to translate educational capital into decent-paying jobs. In the first three generations, the young white couples were able to earn enough to buy a house in an era when most otherwise similar black couples were able to afford such a house or were excluded by law or informal discrimination from better quality housing if they could.[65]

Like many other whites, those in this particular family can claim that none of their known ancestors directly enslaved African Americans. However, when whites make such dramatic assertions, and many still do, they typically dodge a recognition of the glaring realities of other unjust enrichment for whites over this country's racist history. When whites assert that their families "did not own any slaves" in the past, or "did not segregate any lunch counters," they may or may not be telling the truth, yet at the same time they typically ignore the great importance for their family's social mobility of the asset-generating resources—such as access to farmland or assistance in attending whites-only educational institutions—that they gained from their parents and more distant white ancestors who regularly benefited from the many processes of unjust enrichment central to, and essential to, systemic racism.

If at any point in the reproduction of resources and social privilege across the generations of a family a person had not for some reason been white, the social reproduction process providing these resources and privilege would have substantially ended. Note too that the other side of the social reproduction process that has privileged generations of whites is the one that has more or less guaranteed that generations of

African Americans generally have much less (or no) access to similar asset-generating resources. This ongoing social reproduction process is the principal reason for the many generations now of racial inequality in the United States.

The Social Reproduction and Transmission of Racial Privilege and Inequality: Institutional and Community Aspects

As we can see from this family's example, extensive institutional support over generations is critical to the persistence of racial inequalities in this highly inegalitarian society. As I emphasize in Table 1, the ability or inability of individuals and families to transmit important asset-generating resources from one generation to the next is very dependent on the reproductive support and facilitation of surrounding communities and societal institutions—a point that is essential to an adequate conceptualization of racial oppression and inequality in this society.

Over generations, the perpetuation of systemic racism requires an intertemporal reproducing of major organizational structures and institutions, as well of ideological processes. Reproduced over time are racially structured institutions, such as the economic institutions that exploit workers of color and the legal and political institutions that protect and extend that exploitation. Generation after generation, the major organizational and institutional structures protect the highly racialized processes of enrichment and impoverishment that are central to this society.

The institutional buttressing of the reproduction of racial privilege and racial inequality takes at least two major forms: one of recurring institutional inclusion and the other of recurring institutional exclusion. For example, the ancestors of a majority of whites today benefited significantly not only from the increasing development and provision of supportive institutional facilities in white residential communities such as elementary and secondary schools, government jobs programs, employment agencies, unemployment assistance programs, and sanitary systems in the nineteenth and early twentieth centuries, but also from the substantial exclusion or marginalization of black Americans and their communities in regard to most or all of these institutionalized resources and services. Whites' access to such public (and other private) resources and services has been critical for individual and family mobility now over many generations. Moreover, as a younger white generation has secured racially allocated benefits and prospered from them, that generation has gradually taken control of the racially structured and supportive public and private institutions from its white predecessors. In this manner, white-supportive institutions are socially cloned generation after generation. Because whites have generally remained in control of these critical societal institutions over many generations, they have been the major recipients of an array of resource-providing government and private programs that have historically excluded most, or all, African Americans for centuries.

Because of this social reproduction of white-normed and white-controlled institutions, from the 1600s to the 1960s—about 90 percent of this society's existence—whites were the major or exclusive beneficiaries of almost all major programs of government aid and resource support, such as the homestead (land) acquisitions. Year after year, decade after decade, century after century, major supportive resources and their dispensing institutions were reproduced almost entirely for whites only. For only 10 percent of the society's existence, since the late 1960s, have African Americans and other Americans of color had significant—if still substantially restricted by much racial discrimination—access to many of the major wealth-generating resources provided by an array of local, state, and federal governments in the United States. Moreover, for generations now, literally thousands of local and federal police agencies have protected the governmentally provided resource inequalities from protests and challenges by resisting African Americans and other Americans of color.

Historically and in the present day, whites have also benefited greatly from an array of privately provided services and resources, such as much better access to unions, better-paying union jobs, adequate housing, home buying resources such as mortgages, health care services, and good recreational opportunities. These good quality private services and resources have also been mostly provided by white-controlled and white-cloned private institutions, which have made these services and resources generally unavailable to African Americans for much of their history—or have more recently restricted their availability by means of overt, subtle, and covert discrimination. Over the centuries, systemic racism has reproduced, and been reproduced by, innumerable private workplaces that have excluded black workers and many other workplaces riddled with discrimination and embedding subordination of black labor to white interests. Likewise, systemic racism has reproduced, and been reproduced by, a large array of private real estate and banking organizations operating to exclude or restrict the access of African Americans and other Americans of color to quality housing and to neighborhoods with good services.

In addition, as with public institutions, each younger generation of whites that has benefited in this manner eventually comes into control of the very institutions which have fostered their prosperity. In this manner, discriminatory private institutions have been socially reproduced in recognizable forms over numerous generations. Moreover, each major public and private institution buttresses and reinforces, in cybernetic and interactive fashion, many other public and private institutions in maintaining racial exclusion and other discrimination, as well as in regard to the maintenance of the system of oppression as a whole.

What is the impact today of generations of the reproduction and transmission of racial privilege, resources, and inequality? We can illustrate this by reference to recent measures of family enrichment and impoverishment. Recall from the preface the recent analysis of wealth data that found that the median net worth of black families is currently less than one tenth of the median net worth for white families.[66] This huge wealth gap is the direct result of the processes of individual, family, institutional, and societal reproduction of unjust enrichment and unjust impoverishment. This extraordinary gap shows dramatically how severe white-on-black oppression has been for black families whose ancestry typically goes back some 9–15 generations in this country's history. Over the centuries, far fewer resources and much less wealth for black families as a group have meant much less access to such family attainments as home ownership and college educations for children. As one scholar puts it, "Wealth is critical to a family's class standing, social status, whether they own or rent housing, the kind of community they live in, and the quality of their children's schools."[67]

The usual white interpretation of such great wealth differences by racial groups is that they mainly come from the hard work of whites over generations; yet, blacks have worked at least as hard over those same (or more) generations. What then accounts really for the difference? Today, the major source of startup assets, if there are any, that young families of all racial backgrounds can use to build up their own prosperity and wealth is an inheritance from parents. If headstart assistance is provided for new families, it typically takes the form of parental monetary support for college educations and/or downpayments for houses—parental assistance often not seen as the important family inheritance that it actually is. Sometimes, often later in a family's history, there will be a direct inheritance of money on the death of parents. Generally, whites are much more likely to receive significant parental inheritances, and to receive much more on the average, than otherwise comparable blacks.[68] Once a person or couple has garnered such headstart assets from parents and grandparents, they can use them to build even more assets to pass along to their own children, and so on down many generations. Because of centuries of white-on-black oppression, and its many reproductive mechanisms, white parents and grandparents have been, and still are, far more likely to have significant monetary and other socioeconomic assets to pass along to their children and grandchildren, both during their lives and at their deaths, than are black parents and grandparents. Historically, unjust impoverishment of black Americans parallels directly the unjust enrichment of white Americans. This social reproduction process of enrichment and impoverishment, which substantially accounts for white-black inequality today, is one that most white Americans have great difficulty in seeing and acknowledging.

The Social Reproduction and Transmission of Racial Privilege and Inequality: The White Racial Frame, Social Networks, and the Media

Also important in reproducing systemic racism is the transmission from one generation to the next of the ideological apparatus—the ideology and the concomitant set of attitudes—that legitimates racial oppression. Thus, over long stretches of time, family and friendship networks are important settings for the performance, reproduction, and transmission of whites' racist ideas and understandings, including the overarching and integrating white framing of society discussed previously. A long-term historical creation, this white racial frame is reproduced moment to moment within the dense social networks that contextualize most whites' everyday lives. Maurice Halbwachs suggested that one should not seek where human understandings, images, and stereotypes are "preserved in the brain or in some nook of my mind to which I alone have access." Instead, these understandings and interpretations "are recalled to me externally, and the groups of which I am a part at any time give me the means to reconstruct them, upon condition, to be sure, that I turn toward them and adopt, at least for the moment, their way of thinking." An individual's understandings, images, and knowledge bits hang together because they are "part of a totality of thoughts common to a group."[69] Karl Mannheim also noted that, "Strictly speaking it is incorrect to say that the single individual thinks. Rather it is more correct to insist that he participates in thinking [to] further what other men have thought before him."[70]

Human beings gain most of their color-coded understandings, images, and emotions from observing, imbibing, and testing the comments, reactions, and behavior of parents and other important adults, as well as from peers, the media, and written accounts handed down over generations. They do this learning substantially within important networks of relatives, peers, and friends. Sociocultural inheritances pass from one generation to the next, and adults are major transmitters of collective understandings, interpretations, and memories. In turn, as children become adults, they pass on the collective understandings, images, and emotions to their own children.[71] The collective memory of whites that communicates the white racial frame is instrumental in perpetuating oppression of African Americans and other Americans of color from one generation to the next.

Also important for white perpetuation of, and collaboration in, systemic racism is sustained collective forgetting of society's harsh realities. Perpetuating racial oppression over the long term requires much collective forgetting and much selective remembering, most of which abandons white responsibilities for past oppression or glorifies white achievements, all in line with whites' racial-group interests. The refusal of most white Americans—including many historians—to remember clearly and accept responsibility for a long and bloody past of racial oppression is harmful to them as individuals and to the society as a whole, for no society can forever live a profound social lie. Western psychology has long taught that repressed memories "remain more alive than ever and give rise to severe neuroses. It is better to accept a distressing past than to deny or repress it."[72] This conclusion seems to hold for both individual and collective memories.

Negative stereotypes and images of African Americans and other Americans of color are constantly used, refurbished, played with, amended, and passed along in millions of white kinship and friendship networks, from one community to the next and one generation to the next. Today, as in the past, most whites still view African Americans in terms of at least some of the age-old negative stereotypes—the hoary sincere fictions about black Americans being "unintelligent," "lazy," "immoral," or "criminal." Whites pass along such views even when faced with evidence strongly contradicting them, and many take action on the basis of these unsubstantiated collective notions.[73] In their social networks, whites also pass along an array of sincere fictions about how whites as a group are superior—that is, hardworking, intelligent, and very moral. Most whites initially learn their sense of racial position, of white superiority and outgroup inferiority, as children in critical social networks.

Today, as in the past, the distorted white framing of society is generated and supported by more than childhood socialization. It is supported by a lifetime of moment-to-moment reinforcements within a long series of interactions in recurring and supporting social networks. These family and friendship networks encourage interactions and pressure their members to think and act in line with group stereotyping and allied racial interpretations. Within these networks, frequent repetition of racialized understandings, including conventional negative images and stereotypes of outgroups, and associated emotions and inclinations, keeps them strong and in vital circulation. Accepting these blatant and subtle racial understandings helps whites to fit into their important social networks. While an individual may have a distinctive nuancing of certain understandings of outgroups, even these understandings are likely to be only an elaboration of passed-along group understandings. Today, even though they come from many different areas of the country, have many different occupations, and have been through many different educational systems, the majority of whites report numerous broadly similar images and understandings of African Americans and many other Americans of color. Ongoing interactions in, and the pressures of, these important family and friendship networks just about force individuals to use, reuse, and elaborate bits and pieces of the collective knowledge about outgroups, now over several centuries and across large areas of geographical space.[74]

Another type of intergenerational reproduction and transmission of cultural understandings that sustains systemic racism involves the perpetuation of critical racial images and stereotypes by such cultural institutions as the mass media, which have mostly been controlled generation after generation by whites in power. For example, the image of the white racial self as presented in the mass media has remained essentially positive and unchanged over more than a century. In a pioneering analysis of white self-images in U.S. movies from the earliest days of filmmaking in the early twentieth century to current twenty-first century films, Hernán Vera and Andrew Gordon have shown that heroic, brave, and kind whites routinely prevail in mainstream movie presentations that deal seriously with U.S. racial relations. Noble whites generally dominate these films, and they are usually presented as natural-born leaders who outshine all others—sometimes including a few deviant whites who eventually lose out to the noble white figures and a noble larger society. This positive imagery of the white racial self is as true for the early films that were unremittingly and blatantly racist in their stereotyped images of African Americans, such as *Birth of a Nation*, as for certain recent films, such as *Glory*, that offer much more positive images of African Americans. Sincere fictions about the dominant white self as being heroic, brave, and kind have persisted now for many decades in the mass media, including not only in the movies but also in magazines, in newspapers, on the radio, and on television.

Over the century since the emergence of movies in the early 1900s, white fictions about racialized outgroups such as African Americans have also persisted in the media, even as they have become more positive in certain ways. While there are now many more positive images than in the early 1900s, the white-controlled mass media still routinely circulate negative stereotypes of black men and women. For example, in their news and fictional programs, radio and television networks have long exaggerated the criminality of black men, as compared to the criminality of white men, and they continue to perpetuate negative stereotypes of black women as domineering, oversexed, or on public welfare. The white-controlled mass media accent only a few of the possible positive images of African Americans, such as in their overemphasis on black entertainers and athletes to the neglect of more numerous black managers, lawyers, other professionals and white-collar workers, and blue-collar breadwinners.

The reason for the persistence of these mostly positive racial images of whites, and the varying but still often biased and negative images of racial others, lies in the frame-imbedded rationalizations of systemic racism still present in most whites' minds. Even with the slow but significant changes in racial oppression as this society has moved from slavery, to legal segregation, to contemporary racism, strongly positive sincere fictions of the white self, typically grounded in continuing assumptions of white superiority, have persisted across the society. As Vera and Gordon conclude, "For most Americans, of whatever color, white supremacy is a given, an institutionalized notion, an automatic assumption that requires constant, conscious effort to resist."[75]

The Bottom Line: A Deeply Racist Society

If you break a well-crafted, three-dimensional hologram into smaller parts and shine a laser through one small part, you can project the whole three-dimensional holographic image again just from that part. Like such a hologram, each apparently separate institution of this society—including the economy, politics, education, the family, religion, and the law—on closer examination still reflects in many ways the overarching reality of racial oppression. Thus, each institutional dimension of systemic racism is linked, directly or indirectly, to other major institutional dimensions. While one can separate these institutional aspects of systemic racism for analytical purposes, in the world of the everyday lived reality they are not normally separated but often occur in concert with one another.

From the seventeenth century onward, European colonists and their descendants, who were soon viewed as "whites," intentionally built a new society on a foundation of economic exploitation and oppression. These European Americans began by destroying Indian societies and crafting a slavery-centered society, which grew to great prosperity and success during the eighteenth century. When that oppressive society was later remodeled just after the Civil War, whites made sure that the basic foundation of white-on-black oppression remained intact. As slavery was followed by legal segregation, the racial hierarchy and most of the rest of systemic racism remained substantially in operation. Similarly, as legal segregation was followed by contemporary racism by the late 1960s, again the racial hierarchy and a substantial portion of the rest of systemic racism remained, if often more subtle and covert in its routine operation. In each era, oppressive relationships mark the steps in this racial hierarchy, and these oppressive relationships are reproduced across all major areas of societal life—from one important institution to the next, from one community to the next, and from one generation to the next. Seen comprehensively, this societal reproduction process generates and maintains not only specific institutional, community, and generational aspects of systemic racism, but also the United States as a substantially and foundationally racist society.

Today, we still live in a substantially racist society. Much of the social terrain of this society is significantly racialized. Most major institutional and geographical spaces, acceptable societal norms, acceptable societal roles, privileged language forms, preferred sociopolitical thinking, and favored understandings of history are white-generated, white-shaped, white-imposed, and/or white-authenticated. All people, whether they are defined socially as white or as not white, live largely within a substantially white-determined environment. Those who are not white, whether recent immigrants or long-term residents, are under great pressure, in the language of much social science and policy analysis, "to assimilate" to the white-determined folkways. The word "assimilate," however, does not capture the everyday reality of pressure-cooker-type demands on individuals to conform to that white environment and white folkways. There is often no choice for those who are not white but to more or less accept, mostly emulate, and even parrot the prevailing white folkways, including the white-generated negative images of racial outgroups, usually including one's own group. People of color constantly resist these pressures for conformity, but most have to accept and adapt to some extent just to survive in a white-controlled society.

Consider this societal world today from a typical white person's viewpoint. This person mostly sees this society and its dominant folkways, its dominant customs and way of life, as normal and traditional. Today, most whites enter workplaces, stores, restaurants, and schools and travel the highways viewing the current social norms, roles, and other patterns not as white or white-generated, but just as the normal and correct way of doing things. In addition, much contemporary racism is considered to be normal, including racial discrimination, especially of the covert and subtle type, and the rationalization of this discrimination in terms of the common white frame. This all-encompassing interpretive frame shapes assessments of everyday events and thereby engenders everyday discriminatory action. Prejudiced and discriminatory folkways are often not viewed as racist because they have become the habitual ways of thinking and acting among the majority of whites in society. Indeed, this whitewashed perspective on society goes back centuries and has been adopted by the "best and brightest" of white leaders and intellectuals, from well before Thomas Jefferson and George Washington, to Theodore Roosevelt and Woodrow Wilson, to the majority of white leaders in the present day. A majority of whites have become alexithymic in order to maintain this distinctive orientation to the world. The majority of white Americans have been socialized not to see the racial world as it really is and rarely reflect on that world, even though in recent decades a modest minority of whites have seriously challenged that racialized world on an ongoing basis.

Now consider this same societal world from the viewpoint of a typical black American or other American of color. This person sees much of the society and its prevailing white folkways as imposed and difficult. There is usually some sense of the dominant folkways being white-generated or white-imposed, and of white-imposed discrimination as being very unfair and damaging to individuals and communities. As people of color move through their daily lives, they enter workplaces that are pervaded by white-determined folkways, including norms about wages and working conditions, assigned roles, workplace etiquette, and racial discrimination of a subtle, covert, or blatant type. As they go to shop in many stores and restaurants, they again encounter white-determined and white-maintained folkways. As they travel the highways and as they enter most schools, either as parents or students and at all educational levels, they again encounter a myriad of white folkways to which they must more or less conform. Only at home are they substantially in control of their lives, and even there the white-determined mass media or white ways learned by friends and relatives may intrude to periodically make the home a white-influenced environment as well. For black Americans and other Americans of color, there is no escaping whiteness in this racist society. They often are born and must live and die within the Procrustean bed of white-imposed folkways.

CONCLUSION: CONTINUITIES AND CONNECTIONS

Because of extensive social science research, we know a great deal about the long and sordid histories of slavery and legal segregation. Those histories are still highly relevant to understanding systemic racism today. Rushdy has put it this way:

> Slavery is…the institution we need to explain as a central paradox in the creation of American freedom, the social system that thwarted the ideals of the nation's founding statements.…Two metaphors that resonate effectively in the current dialogue draw on haunted imagery: the American slave past is "that ghost which we have not entirely faced," and the memory of that institution is "a haunted house" we fear to inhabit. These are telling figures. A domestic space haunted by a liminal apparition beyond the grave indicates the ways the past is not dead, but likewise not seen or acknowledged by all.[76]

Today, there is much denial of the bloody ghosts of our haunted past. A chronic problem in both social theory and policy analysis in regard to racial oppression and other forms of social oppression is the failure to link present-day social realities to those of the immediate and distant past. Most analyses of contemporary U.S. society do not make the necessary connections between contemporary social conditions and those of the past.

Powerful U.S. Supreme Court judges have recently ruled that, while there may still be some racial inequality in this society, no analyst can determine who in particular is responsible for that inequality or how to compensate those harmed by institutional discrimination over many years. Thus, in the Supreme Court decision, *City of Richmond v. J. A. Croson Co.*, Justice Sandra Day O'Connor took such a position, noting that there is a "sorry history of both private and public discrimination in this country" and citing the reality of "past societal discrimination."[77] When white judges like O'Connor are forced to consider racial inequality, they often emphasize past realities without connecting them to the present. In the famous *City of Richmond* case, O'Connor naively characterized past societal discrimination as something "amorphous," with no clear link to present-day discrimination against African Americans in business in cities like Richmond. Strikingly, however, at the time of this misinformed Supreme Court decision, there were a great many older African Americans who had suffered much from numerous blatantly racist barriers that kept them from engaging in business in Richmond (and other U.S. cities) just a few decades earlier. Such barriers had kept these Americans from access to necessary resources and thus continued to keep them and their children from doing current business in that area. Indeed, the social science evidence of past and present discrimination against African Americans is very substantial and that research shows that societal discrimination is anything but unstructured and amorphous. Past discrimination can easily be shown to be well-institutionalized and constantly shaping present-day opportunities across the color line.

While one can show some important differences between the "velvet chains" of systemic racism that subordinate African Americans today and the physical chains that subordinated them during slavery or the legal chains that blatantly segregated and subordinated them under legal segregation, to a substantial degree the similarities in the fundamentals of their racialized conditions in all eras—the racialized hierarchy, the alienated group relationships, the sharp group inequalities in assets and incomes, and the persisting unjust enrichment and impoverishment—are at least as striking as the differences.

Examining the most recent shift in U.S. racial patterns, between legal segregation in the 1960s and the modern racism of today, one seems to find that numerous features of systemic racism have changed from earlier days. Tenant farming and rural debt peonage no longer curse most African Americans, and all major institutions are at least officially desegregated. However, in spite of these changes—wrought to a substantial degree by the civil rights organization and movements of African Americans and other Americans of color—there are still fundamental similarities between the systemic racism of the segregation era and that of the contemporary United States. For example, African American children are about as segregated from white children in public schools today as they were in the legally segregated United States of the 1950s. Today, black family income is roughly the same percentage of white family income as it was in the 1960s. While more African Americans are now part of the middle class than in the 1950s, they too face larger-scale discrimination at work, in housing, and in public accommodations. For centuries, no African American has ever held any of the highest elective positions in this country's national government, such as president, vice president, or Speaker of the House—and only a tiny handful have ever served as state governors or in the top ranks of the federal courts. Only three African Americans have ever served in the powerful U.S. Senate over the last twelve decades. Today African Americans are greatly underrepresented in most of the country's state and local legislative bodies. In addition, very large numbers of working-class African Americans are imprisoned, often for relatively minor drug offenses, even as many middle-class white Americans who commit similar or worse offenses manage to stay out of the prison system. In the last few years, local government agencies in some areas of the country have worked diligently to reduce black access to the voting booth, and the history of white-on-black oppression is rarely discussed candidly, or at all, in the mainstream media and school textbooks.

Why are there certain fundamental similarities between white-on-black oppression today and that of the era of Thomas Jefferson, James Madison, and George Washington? The reason is clear, as I have shown in this chapter. The oppressive foundation of the country, laid well during and before the founding era, has never been substantially replaced. Acting in collaborative fashion, whites in various institutional sectors have worked routinely and often aggressively to maintain whites' disproportionate and substantial control over the allocation of the country's major economic resources as well as the country's major political, police, and media resources.

If Jefferson, Madison, or Washington returned to the United States today, they would likely be surprised by the demographic shifts, the urbanization, and the technological changes. Similarly, they would doubtless be surprised that slavery ended with African Americans resident in large numbers in the country and eventually protected by civil rights laws. Yet these founders would have no difficulty in recognizing and supporting the racial hierarchy that still generally positions African Americans at the bottom and whites at the top of this society. And they would likely be pleased that the Constitution, with the undemocratic institutions such as the U.S. Senate and Supreme Court that they and other slaveholders constructed, still governs this putatively democratic country.

Significantly, what changes have come in systemic racism over several centuries have usually been generated by an oppositional dialectic, that is, by individual or group resistance on the part of the oppressed to their racially subordinated conditions. This critical dimension of black resistance will become conspicuous as we move into the interviews in subsequent chapters. Each of the first three circles in Table 1, thus, can also be seen as operating in support of black resistance to oppression in the past and the present. Families, communities, and black institutions such as churches and schools have historically made the difference in enabling African Americans to survive some of the most extreme forms of human oppression ever created. Indeed, these supportive black frameworks have enabled black Americans to survive, even to thrive, and thus make the United States a far better country for all citizens than its white-normed racial structure would otherwise have allowed it to be. To this point in time, however, the racial-oppressor class that includes the white elite and rank-and-file whites has maintained the upper hand and perpetuated an unjustly gained position in a persisting racist system. Whites have greatly limited the potential for the United States to be the fully democratic nation it so often claims to be. It seems to be the time to take the next step, and to follow the honed insights about real racial integration and multiracial democracy that have been offered by so many African Americans and other Americans of color in the past and present.

2

THE WORLD OF SLAVERY: THROUGH THE EYES OF AFRICAN AMERICANS

INTRODUCTION

To understand well the individual and systemic aspects of the racial oppression that developed early in this society, we must probe deeply the actual experiences of real individuals in everyday settings. Their concrete experiences put "flesh" on the conceptual ideas laid out in chapter 1. In the next several chapters, I accent and examine the experiences and standpoints of both the oppressed and their oppressors. I attempt to get as close to everyday experiences and understandings as possible by drawing on accounts or interpretations of what people actually saw and constantly lived. In these chapters we see the worlds of "race" and racism through their eyes.

For African Americans, the centuries-long experience with oppression within the society began in the first moments when twenty Africans were forced ashore at the Jamestown colony in 1619 not long after it was founded in 1607. Bought by white settlers from traders on a Dutch frigate, they were set to work under the dominance of white owners. Over the next two centuries, many thousands more were forced to become

African Americans and thus to do grueling labor to generate sustenance and prosperity for European American colonists. The asymmetrical and hierarchical social relations between those enslaved and their enslavers were central to the well-institutionalized system of racial oppression that persisted over several intervening centuries. Systemic racism begins, thus, not just in the racist minds of Europeans and European Americans, but centrally in their material exploitation of African labor, both productive and reproductive labor.

To understand this system of racial oppression, we should look beneath surface appearances and convenient white rationalizations to the harsh underlying realities that are often ignored or camouflaged by those whites in authority. I begin this examination of the complex reality of racial oppression by examining the experiences of some actual individuals who were enslaved for long periods, until they succeeded in fleeing that enslavement. Typically, this country's history is recounted only from the white point of view. This needs to change. As the old African proverb puts it, "Until lions have their historians, tales of the hunt shall always glorify the hunters." Thus, we need to examine closely the experiences of those actually targeted by systemic racism, who are seldom well represented in the social science and public policy literatures, and not just rely on the account of the oppressors as most historical discussions of racial matters in the United States tend to do.

One does not have to speculate about the experiences of slavery, for we have several poignant and penetrating accounts from those who were enslaved. I focus here on three extensive accounts by African Americans—Frederick Douglass, William Wells Brown, and Harriet Jacobs—who report in detail on their enslavement and on slavery generally, in each case covering experiences during the first decades of the new United States. Once we have examined the enslavement experience from the point of view of those who were long enslaved, we will examine in chapter 3 the perspectives on African Americans and on slavery that were held by three men who were major slaveholders and who were also among the most famous of the country's founders—Thomas Jefferson, James Madison, and George Washington.

Examining these early racialized experiences and understandings of black and white Americans in a comparative and relational framework is in my view essential for developing a grounded theory of systemic racism for the United States. My goal here is to show how attending to the everyday experiences of those who were enslaved and those who were enslavers sharpens our understanding of racial oppression as being as deeply imbedded in this society then as now. By examining these often graphic everyday experiences, we will see not only the dense and painful texture of the lives of the oppressed at the microlevel, but the many ways in which the macrolevel of institutionalized racial oppression crashed into and structured countless aspects of their day-to-day experiences. The micro and the macro are thereby seen to be two dimensions of the same everyday reality.

ACCOUNTS OF THE ENSLAVED: FREDERICK DOUGLASS

In chapter 1, I laid out the array of critical dimensions that have made up white-on-black oppression now for several centuries. We will observe these dimensions documented and analyzed in the accounts of the enslaved African Americans examined in this chapter, as well as in the accounts of leading slaveholders assessed in chapter 3. These experiential accounts give us major insights into what everyday life was like under slavery in the southern and border states, as well as in the numerous northern areas where slavery had persisted into the nineteenth century. During the centuries-long slavery era, racial oppression took the form of widespread white domination of African Americans in major societal arenas, including farming work, urban workplaces, travel, family arrangements, and housing. White slaveholders and their white hirelings routinely enforced the slavery system by means of violence, including that of private and public policing groups such as the infamous slave patrols. Under slavery, most black Americans were coerced to labor to the profit of white slaveholders and their white employees and business associates. Greatly asymmetrical employment relations were imposed on black Americans, and these were linked to an array of economic, social, and political structures essential to the firmly institutionalized slavery system. Those enslaved generally faced poor living conditions, including poor housing, and they faced much racialized control and harassment when they were traveling or in public places. Black enslavement, as I noted in chapter 1, was linked to the vigorous protection of whites' political-economic interests and was firmly rationalized in terms of the white racial framing of the society, with its complex array of racist prejudices, stereotypes, and emotions. Indeed, during this long slavery era, whites developed the extensive racist ideology that persists in significant ways, at the heart of the white racial frame, to the present day.

The early- to mid-nineteenth century autobiographical accounts from two men, Frederick Douglass and William Wells Brown, and from a woman, Harriet Jacobs, who were enslaved, provide us not only a window into their enslavement experiences during the nineteenth century, but also insight into the impact of slavery on the white slaveholders and into the arrangements and apparatus of slavery generally. In some sections of these personal accounts, the authors recount not only their own experiences, but also those of other enslaved African Americans, including those of family and friends.[1]

In this chapter, I examine how those enslaved experienced, felt, and understood the racialized domination and exploitation of the slave masters, and more generally, the reality of slavery as an extremely brutal social system of human oppression. When these African Americans assess the reality of being black in the many institutions controlled by whites, they do not speak just in abstract concepts, but rather voice, in specific and often graphic terms, the oppressiveness of recurring and routinized encounters with whites at various class levels.

The Exploitation and Violence of Enslavement

Repeatedly in the autobiographies of enslaved African Americans, we get detailed accounts of the predatory economic ethic of white slaveholders and the barbaric social system that they created. In his autobiographical account, published in 1845 just a few years after he had fled enslavement, Frederick Douglass reports brutal treatment at the hands of a Mr. Covey, a slave breaker hired by Douglass's slaveowner to destroy resistance in the recalcitrant young black man:

> We were worked in all weathers. It was never too hot or too cold; it could never rain, blow, hail, or snow, too hard for us to work in the field. Work, work, work, was scarcely more the order of the day than of the night. The longest days were too short for him, and the shortest nights too long for him.[2]

At the heart of the slavery system was this superexploitation, of both productive and reproductive labor, for the economic gain of slaveholders and other whites. The discussion of the oppressive work and living conditions—the very long hours in all weather conditions, the lack of wages, the poor clothing (often a dress or one set of pants and a shirt to last a year), and poor food—by those enslaved contrasts sharply with the lack of such candid accounts in the commentaries of prominent slaveholders, such as those examined in chapter 3. Clearly, violence-backed enslavement allowed the extraction of high levels of work effort and extreme amounts of what might be termed "racial surplus value." Douglass continues with much detail about the impact and agony of his enslavement. He notes that he was at first unmanageable,

> But a few months of this discipline tamed me. Mr. Covey succeeded in breaking me. I was broken in body, soul, and spirit.

My natural elasticity was crushed, my intellect languished, the disposition to read departed, the cheerful spark that lingered about my eye died; the dark night of slavery closed in upon me.[3]

Here Douglass notes key elements of the white-controlled, authoritarian system of racial oppression that I listed in chapter 1. In this painful account we glimpse the violence and threat of violence that were central to extreme economic exploitation under slavery in the border state of Maryland, as elsewhere in many areas of the new United States.

The Merriam Webster dictionary defines torture as "the infliction of intense pain...to punish, coerce, or afford sadistic pleasure."[4] The accounts of enslaved black Americans repeatedly show slavery as an institutionalized system of torture—a system designed principally for economic gain yet often undergirded by the socially sanctioned coercive or sadistic inclinations of many whites. The Christian religion of most of these whites did not deter their brutal actions for, as Douglass notes elsewhere in his autobiographical account, this Mr. Covey was a devout member of a Methodist church. Conspicuous too in the Douglass account here is the highly alienating character of slavery, which can be seen in the separation of black workers from the value of their labor and, indeed, the attempted destruction of their spirit and humanity. Also delineated in the Douglass account is the social hierarchy of elite white slaveholders, their white working-class hirelings (the white "labor aristocracy"), and the enslaved black laborers.

Note too an enslaved man's attempted resistance to the well-entrenched system of racial oppression—human resistance that Mr. Covey was explicitly hired to eliminate. From the enslaved person's viewpoint, struggle for physical and psychological survival was routine and essential to survival. In contrast, from the enslaver's point of view, eliminating such resistance by means physical and psychological was essential to maintaining white privilege and autocratic superiority. Both the oppressed and the oppressor were part of a complex societal system of asymmetrical and symbiotic racial relationships that persisted for several centuries and across many geographical areas.

Creating Wealth: Unjust Enrichment for Whites

Labor forced by chains, whips, and dogs created much wealth for white slaveholders and their families, as well as supportive incomes for the large number of whites like Covey who worked for or with the slaveholders. Many sectors of the society were dependent in one way or another on enslaved African American workers. Slave plantations were places where, as Douglass explains, the toil of many "men supports a single family in easy idleness and sin…it is here that we shall find that height of luxury which is the opposite of that depth of poverty and wretchedness [of those enslaved.]"[5] Douglass lists the many luxuries and "immense wealth" of plantations where he did forced labor. Indeed, he is probably the first analyst of U.S. slavery to develop the penetrating sociological ideas of unjust enrichment for whites and unjust impoverishment for blacks that I accented in chapter 1. Douglass adds later that the unjust enrichment of whites amounts to socially sanctioned "robbery," an extreme theft that indeed justifies an enslaved person's rebellion and "helping himself" when possible to the slave master's goods. Unjust robbery of one's labor generates justified and aggressive resistance.

Douglass accents here what is perhaps the most critical point about the development and perpetuation of African American enslavement in U.S. history. It would be difficult to overstate just how important the stolen labor of millions of African Americans was to building up assets and wealth for generations of whites, both those in the elite and those in the middle and working classes. These unjustly gained assets were passed down, for the oldest white families, over a great many subsequent generations. Without such enslaved labor and the prosperity it generated for countless millions of white Americans, the history of the United States would likely have been much different. Indeed, in the eighteenth century, one of the major economic tensions between the white American colonists and their British rulers was generated by increasing American control over the wealth-generating slave trade and related commerce. Even the American Revolution might not have taken place when it did without the huge amount of capital and wealth that the labor of enslaved African Americans brought to the founding generations of white Americans. Directly or indirectly, this slavery-generated wealth was essential to successfully fighting the British for American independence. This is one of the great ironies of American history that is usually missing from accounts of that history in contemporary textbooks.

Breaking up Families: Unjust Impoverishment for African Americans

Violence-backed economic exploitation of African Americans was not the only oppressive feature of the slavery system. Coercive discrimination extended to all other areas of life, including the most intimate and personal of human relationships. Indeed, the arrangements of slavery were very dehumanizing in their impact on enslaved individuals and their families. Earlier forms of slavery, such as those of ancient Greece and Rome, usually allowed the people enslaved to have a greater measure of dignity and stable family life.

At a very young age, Frederick Douglass was separated by his owner from his mother. His grandmother raised him until he was seven, when she too was forced to give him up to be disposed of by his white owner. This routine of family breakup was often an intentional means of repression and control. Describing this experience as extremely brutalizing, Douglass provides insight into the inhumanity and antifamily orientation of most slaveholders:

> The practice of separating children from their mothers, and hiring the latter out at distances too great to admit of their meeting…is a marked feature of the cruelty and barbarity of the slave system. But it is in harmony with the grand aim of slavery…to reduce man to the level with the brute.[6]

Black fathers, mothers, and children could be bought or sold suddenly, and, much like cattle, at the whim of the slaveholder. Frequently, slaveholders ignored or rejected the basic human needs of those they enslaved, such as the need for enduring family relationships. This attempted dehumanization of the oppressed is yet another indication of the alienating character of the slavery system itself. Indeed, enslaved African Americans were legally the property of whites. The legal term for this type of property was "chattel," an English word derived from the same Latin root as "cattle" and "capital."[7] We see in this wording not only how the concept of property evolved but also a suggested link between slavery and early capitalism in North America and elsewhere in the Americas.

Like many of those who were enslaved, Douglass notes in his autobiographical account that he was uncertain about who his father was, although in this case he was likely a white slaveholder. Whites created a system that

> does away with fathers, as it does away with families.…[The slaveholder] often is master and father to the same child. He can be father without being a husband, and may sell his child without incurring reproach…[8]

This separating and alienating character of slavery encompassed those enslaved and their white enslavers, with the latter not only often engaging in the rape of black women, but also inhumanely rejecting and enslaving, even selling, their own children. Recall from the preface that this rape of black women and enslavement of the resulting children reached into the first "First Family," whose black relatives have generally been ignored and concealed in almost all contemporary accounts of the founding era of this society. Dehumanization of all was thoroughgoing and evidently essential to the successful operation of this slavery system, and a convenient forgetting by whites of this history of individual and family dehumanization seems essential to the persistence of systemic racism today.

Certain commonplace words used by many contemporary commentators to describe the family lives of African Americans during the slavery era, as well as in later centuries of oppression, can be somewhat misleading if we accept their traditional dictionary meanings as a guide to the everyday realities of those who were enslaved. Terms like "parent," "child," "mother," and "father" need some qualification or explanation when they are applied to human realities that are dramatically changed under the extreme conditions of enslavement.[9] That is, enslaved "fathers" and "mothers" typically lost much or all control over their children's lives, not to mention over their own family roles. The social realities usually denoted by such English words are often quite different from the actual family conditions faced by enslaved African Americans during their long centuries of brutalization and confinement at the hands of European Americans. A full accounting of the extraordinary impact of slavery on those oppressed and on the whole society would evidently require, indeed, a new English vocabulary of oppression.

Intense Reflectivity and Resistance: The Humanity of Those Enslaved

A common white stereotype, during slavery as now, is that African Americans are generally lacking in intelligence and are unreflective—a view that we will see in the next chapter articulated by slaveholders like Thomas Jefferson, James Madison, and George Washington. Yet nothing could be more inaccurate and unperceptive. Those enslaved often reflected deeply and analytically about their subordinated condition and about how to free themselves. From childhood onward, Douglass reports thinking deeply and intensely about his tortured human condition. Even before he was eight years old, he recounts that he was often asking himself, "Why am I a slave?" and "Why are some people slaves?" He also thought often about the possibilities of flight and freedom, wishing that he was an animal or

> a bird—anything, rather than a slave. I was wretched and gloomy, beyond my ability to describe. I was too thoughtful to be happy. It was this everlasting thinking which distressed and tormented me; and yet there was no getting rid of the subject of my thoughts....

Liberty! The inestimable birthright of every man, had, for me, converted every object into an asserter of this great right.[10]

Systemic racism, including its incarnation in slavery, creates social arrangements where those who are oppressed lose substantial control over, and are thus often alienated from, their own body and their ability to make decisions and take action. Resistance to this loss of control took both mental and interactional forms. Rarely in the writings of the major white founders will one find a greater concern for, and thoughtful stating of, the meaning of liberty and freedom than in the several published accounts of enslaved African Americans. Again, the social reality denoted by the English words "liberty" and "freedom" as used by whites, then or now, is often not quite the same as what is envisioned and treasured by those who have been enslaved. The "everlasting thinking" they did about their possible freedom made their enslavement all the more painful. Such recurring reflection on and planning for freedom are indications of resistance to oppression. It is likely that most of those who were thus severely oppressed worked in significant ways to resist that oppression, even if only in their own minds. However conforming they may have been to the labor and other burdens forced on them, they did not typically become the "happy sambos" of white legend who simply and docilely accepted the oppressive system. Instead, they often resisted as best they could under the extreme circumstances of American enslavement.

Indeed, even in the face of the omnipresent violence of slaveholders and their hirelings, enslaved African Americans often rebelled openly, thereby risking their lives and futures. Plantation houses were burned down, and crops were destroyed. Overseers and slaveowners were attacked, even killed, as black men and women sought to defend or free themselves from bloody oppression. One day, the young Douglass decided he would no longer be savaged by slaveholders and their hirelings without fighting back. He responded heroically to a threatened whipping by successfully defending himself in a long fight with Mr. Covey, a hireling typical of the white working class situated well below the level of the slaveholding elite. After an intense fight—in which Douglass reports that he did not go beyond the point of just defending himself—Covey decided to abandon the fight and, because of the resistance, did not try to whip Douglass thereafter:

> This battle with Mr. Covey was the turning-point in my career as a slave. It rekindled the few expiring embers of freedom, and revived within me a sense of my own manhood. It recalled the departed self-confidence, and inspired me again with a deter-

mination to be free....My long-crushed spirit rose, cowardice departed, bold defiance took its place; and I now resolved that, however long I might remain a slave in form, the day had passed forever when I could be a slave in fact.[11]

Plainly, the enslavement experience was one that necessitated African Americans using their skills, intelligence, patience, and resilience in continuing struggles with whites who regularly treated them as "brutes." We see again just how relational the slavery system was, for it involved many intimate, recurring, and complex interactions between the oppressors and the oppressed. Enslavement pitted body against body and mind against mind, as part of the enduring struggle of those enslaved just to survive. Douglass took a great risk and succeeded in moving from "slave in fact" to only "slave in form." He then adds to this quoted commentary that he let it be known he would never be whipped without retaliation. His confrontation with Covey significantly reduced his alienation in that he gained more control over his life, and this in turn buoyed his "long-crushed spirit" greatly. By his own actions, he had recovered some of his alienated humanity. Elsewhere in his autobiography, Douglass describes how as a young man he also rebelled in less overt and confrontational ways, such as by holding secret schools at which he taught other enslaved men and women how to read and write—a major violation of Maryland state law for which he could have been severely punished.[12] Without a doubt, the full story of the nuanced, complex, and recurring black resistance to slavery and its long-term consequences has yet to be told.

Insights into Oppression: The Complex Knowledge of African Americans

On most pages of the surviving life narratives from enslaved African Americans, one discovers their essential, nuanced, and extensive knowledge about the white practices and institutions of systemic racism. In his autobiographical accounts, Douglass notes that he learned and understood much about the racial ladder that positioned and privileged white workers so that they did not identify with otherwise comparable workers of color. When his owner loaned him out to work in a shipyard, Douglass quickly learned some tough lessons about the animosity and violence that ordinary white workers often directed toward black workers, both those who were legally "free" and those who were enslaved: "They began to ... talk contemptuously and maliciously of 'the niggers'; saying that 'they would take the country,' that 'they ought to be killed.'"[13] He suffered violence at their hands. White workers, and indeed most whites in the North, did not see African Americans as citizens with full civil rights. After he successfully escaped slavery and fled to Massachusetts, Douglass found that in the North ostensibly free African Americans still faced "an inveterate prejudice" against their color and were denied by whites in all classes

> the privileges and courtesies common to others in the use of the most humble means of conveyance…refused admission to respectable hotels—caricatured, scorned, scoffed, mocked, and maltreated with impunity by any one…[who] has a white skin.[14]

Slavery was on the wane in the North by the first decades of the nineteenth century, but still the near-slavery of legal segregation, coupled with much informal segregation, took slavery's place there. Indeed, segregated ("Jim Crow") railroad cars were first used in Massachusetts. In the North and the South, white skin privilege benefited not just slaveholders, but also most other whites no matter what their socioeconomic status might be.

The reflectiveness and critical insights of enslaved men and women about the arrangements and apparatus of slavery frequently reached an extraordinary level, generally much beyond that reached by leading white slaveholders, intellectuals, and political commentators of the period. Thus, Douglass is able to interpret and analyze profoundly not only the oppressed and alienated lives of those who were savagely enslaved, but also the alienating and alienated lives of the white enslavers. At several points in his autobiographical accounts, he dissects in some detail the heavy price paid by white slaveholders under U.S. slavery: "The slaveholder is a subject, but he is the author of his own subjection."[15] The eternal law of justice, in his view, cannot be denied forever.

Delving deeply into how this worked, Douglass gives the example of a white woman who was the wife of a Baltimore relative to whom his slave master had loaned him to work when he was just a child. Economic exploitation took many forms, including being forced to be household servants of whites at such an early age. At first, Douglass notes, the white woman was loving and only regarded him as a child like any other, and not just as her property. Yet she eventually changed dramatically: "It took several years to change this natural sweetness of her temper into fretful bitterness."[16] Her shift to an insensitive, authoritarian slaveholder took place not long after her husband had reprimanded her for teaching the young Douglass how to read. Douglass describes the change in her character thus:

Nature has done almost nothing to prepare men and women to be either slaves or slaveholders. Nothing but rigid training, long persisted in, can perfect the character of the one or the other. One cannot easily forget to love freedom; and it is as hard to cease to respect that natural love in our fellow creatures....How could she, then, treat me as a brute, without a mighty struggle with all the noble powers of her own soul.[17]

Douglass features again his theme of the humanity of those enslaved and in his longer account enumerates the numerous elements of that humanity. With great sociological insight, he suggests a key idea about the routine operation of social oppression: That intensive oppression works to destroy the natural empathy for their fellow creatures that human beings are likely born with. Associated with this declining ability of the oppressor to empathize across the imposed color line is also a declining ability to think clearly about and understand the views and emotions of those who are oppressed. The highly interactive and alienating character of this systemic racism is highlighted as Douglass describes how normal human beings are transformed by "rigid training" over time into the brutalizing oppressors or the brutalized oppressed. Here we observe the socialization process that is a key mechanism reproducing the system of oppression within and across the generations. We observe too the gender hierarchy in which white men of influence use, or even force white women to be enforcers of extreme racial oppression. Of course, in many other settings, white women needed no encouragement from white men to oppress black women, men, or children, for these women typically shared the white racial framing of the world that shaped most antiblack action under slavery, as well as during later eras of systemic racism in the United States.

Indeed, one formerly enslaved blacksmith and abolitionist, James W. C. Pennington, published an 1849 autobiographical account in which he questioned the notion of a meaningful differentiation of slave masters in terms of kindness or Christian religion:

My feelings are always outraged when I hear them speak of "kind masters"—"Christian masters"—"the mildest form of slavery"—"well fed and clothed slaves," as extenuations of slavery; I am satisfied they either mean to pervert the truth, or they do not know what they say. The being of slavery, its soul and body, lives and moves in the chattel principle, the property principle, the bill of sale principle; the cart-whip, starvation, and nakedness, are its inevitable consequences to a greater or less extent, warring with the dispositions of men....The mildest form of slavery, if there be such a form, looking at the chattel principle as the definition of slavery, is comparatively the worst form. For it not only keeps the slave in the most unpleasant apprehension, like a prisoner in chains awaiting his trial; but it actually, in a great majority of cases, where kind masters do exist, trains him under the most favourable circumstances the system admits of, and then plunges him into the worst of which it is capable.

Slavery, whatever its variations, treats human beings like cattle and operates by the whip, chains, and the threat of starvation, A little later Pennington adds this sharp insight about the slave masters themselves:

You cannot constitute slavery without the chattel principle—and with the chattel principle you cannot save it from these results. Talk about the kind and Christian masters. They are not masters of the system. The system is master of them; and the slaves are their vassals.[18]

Systemic racism encompassed and imprisoned not only the enslaved, but also the enslavers, no matter what their individual personalities and propensities might be.

The Greatest American of the Nineteenth Century?

The self-taught, learned, and eloquent Frederick Douglass became one of the principal opponents of racial slavery and racial segregation in his day. A leading abolitionist and advocate for human liberty and freedom, over his long life Douglass gave more than two thousand speeches and wrote literally thousands of editorials, articles, and letters, very often analyzing the many oppressive aspects of systemic racism that he had experienced and observed in the South and in the North. He was one of the greatest orators and intellectuals this country has ever produced.

As an outspoken critic of President Abraham Lincoln's war policies, the learned Douglass played a key role in bringing down the slavery system, including an important role in the critical effort to get many thousands of African Americans, mostly those who had been enslaved, accepted as volunteers in the Union army, soldiers who made the difference in the Union victories in the later years of the South's "War of Rebellion." Significantly, later in life, the ever eloquent Douglass spoke out vigorously against the near slavery of legal segregation for African Americans that had developed to replace slavery, as well as against the gender oppression and sexism faced by women of all backgrounds across the United States.[19] He was, indeed, one of the first outspoken feminists among men in the United States. By any measure, Douglass was one of the greatest leaders and intellectuals to have ever lived in the United States. That Douglass's name is not known to most Americans today, and that there is no major monument to him in Washington, D. C., are telling aspects of the collective forgetting that seems essential to the perpetuation of systemic racism in the United States.

ACCOUNTS OF THE ENSLAVED: WILLIAM WELLS BROWN

Let us now turn to another important abolitionist, William Wells Brown, who was the son of an enslaved black woman raped by a white slave-owner. Brown published his autobiography of enslavement in 1847, an account that is similar in some ways to that of Douglass, but adds significant insights into yet other aspects of the enslavement experience. Brown's account yet again reveals the deep and insightful reflections that those enslaved had about their experience, as well as their strong commitment to the new country's stated ideals of liberty and justice.

Forcing Unpaid Labor: The Violence of Slavery

Like Douglass, William Wells Brown describes slavery as a system of physical and psychological violence, one where infliction of intense pain was routine in whites' attempts to force labor from those they enslaved and dominated. In his case, after several attempts to run away from his slave master, he was caught by slave trackers using dogs. In his accounts, Brown reports numerous beatings and killings of enslaved black men and women by whites during his years of enslavement in the Missouri area: "During a residence of eight years in this city, numerous cases of extreme cruelty came under my own observation."[20]

Brown adds that the cruel actions by whites were so numerous that he does not have the space in his book to record them all. Indeed, in this autobiography, Brown describes how violence relentlessly and routinely undergirded the extensive apparatus of the economic exploitation of African Americans. For example, he explains what happened to an enslaved man known to him, a man called Randall. One day, a white overseer named Grove Cook, who hated Randall's independent spirit, got three white friends to help him. Brown reports that Randall

> was attacked by the overseer and his companions, when he turned upon them, and laid them, one after another, prostrated on the ground. [One man] drew out his pistol, and fired at him, and brought him to the ground by a pistol ball. The others rushed upon him with their clubs, and beat him over the head

and face, until they succeeded in tying him....Cook gave him over one hundred lashes with a heavy cowhide, had him washed with salt and water, and left him tied during the day.[21]

Compounding the physical torture, the men next forced the beaten Randall to work out in the fields with his legs in chains. The recurring coercive violence, and the resistance to it, that were at the heart of U.S. slavery are evident as white hirelings again subordinate the body, and attempt to destroy the spirit, of an enslaved man. We often observe in these surviving enslavement accounts a concern of the authors for the "crushed spirit" of those suffering from violent repression—the fully crushed condition that oppressors everywhere attempt to create in those they oppress, and then often cite as a justification for their conceptual framing of the oppressed as being somehow less than human beings.

Maintaining Family Ties under Extreme Conditions

Enslavement meant a constant battle to maintain what family ties African Americans could. Like Douglass, early in his autobiography, Brown describes the antifamily values of many white slaveholders when it came to enslaved African Americans: "My master sold my mother, and all her children, except myself...to different persons in the city of St. Louis."[22] Those enslaved had to contend regularly not only with their own oppression but also with that of close family members. The conspicuously separating and alienating dimension of the slavery system is evident in the constant attack on and periodic destruction of enslaved black families. Describing one time when he was thinking about the possibility of escaping from a particular riverboat, Brown notes that

> whenever such thoughts would come into my mind, my resolution would soon be shaken by the remembrance that my dear mother was a slave in St. Louis, and I could not bear the idea of leaving her in that condition.[23]

He adds that leaving his mother thus would have been, in his mind, a dereliction of his family duty. Here again is the theme of black resistance in a nuanced account of freedom and family ties. Not only grief and suffering over family separation, but also a strong sense of familial love and obligation fill many pages of the enslavement narratives. Indeed, slaveholders' removal of children and other coerced family separations became part of the collective memory for those enslaved, a reality that had the effect of reinforcing the sense and importance of family among those so regularly abused. Contrary to the expressed ideas of many slaveholders and other white commentators (then and now), family ties, family concerns, and family longings were central to the everyday experiences of most of the African Americans who were chained and tormented by enslavement.

Brown, like Douglass, reports that he constantly thought about and planned for his personal escape from his master's physical and psychological chains. Once, when he was under the control of a white female slaveholder, Brown was vigorously urged by her to take as his wife an enslaved woman. Such white interference in the intimate aspects of the personal lives of enslaved men and women was rather routine and callous. Brown's insistent owner even offered to buy a woman for him to marry, yet he refused the arrangement, not only because it was imposed on him but also because, as he makes clear, he did not want to be tied down when he finally was able to flee from this painful enslavement.[24] Thoughts of resistance and flight likely lay behind many such decisions by black Americans about establishing new interpersonal relationships and family ties.

Extreme cruelty in regard to family matters on the part of slaveholders and slave traders is evident in Brown's accounts. For example, he describes being forced to help a certain Mr. Walker, a white slave trader, march a number of enslaved African Americans twenty miles. When the child of one mother kept crying, Walker asked for the child from the trembling mother:

> He took the child by one arm, as you would a cat by the leg, walked into the house [nearby], and said to the lady: "Madam, I will make you a present of this little nigger; it keeps such a noise that I can't bear it."…The mother…ran up to Mr. Walker, and falling upon her knees, begged him to let her have the child.[25]

Walker ignored her entreaties and had her chained together with the others. Yet again, a white man's vicious and inhumane action treats a black woman as chattel property, as having no family feelings or ties that whites need respect. Here we observe the disregard that whites in the slavery business often had for the families of those they enslaved. (Indeed, we see here the great hypocrisy in much white commentary on the "family values" of African Americans, then and now.) Slavery thoroughly dehumanized the slaveholders and slave traders, as well as those enslaved. Obvious too in this account is the importance of whites other than plantation owners to slavery's persistence over centuries. Both the white slave trader and the (presumably white) woman in the house nearby are heavily implicated in the maintenance and perpetuation of the brutalizing slavery system.

Forcing Deferential Behavior

In numerous sections of his autobiography, William Wells Brown describes the various ways in which large numbers of African Americans were whipped, chained, and penned up. We constantly see the violence underlying the U.S. system of racism. He describes a New Orleans slave pen where planters came to buy and sell the people they enslaved:

> Before the slaves were exhibited for sale, they were dressed and driven out into the yard. Some were set to dancing, some to jumping, some to singing, and some to playing cards. This was done to make them appear cheerful and happy.[26]

This account puts into a new light the "happy slave" stereotype so often articulated by white Americans, including slaveholders, over the last two centuries. Those enslaved were often forced to dance and sing and thus to appear to be the "happy slave," as in the white legend, in order to be saleable to other whites. In this manner, economic exploitation was assisted by emotional domination. This account suggests how mythological the old, and continuing, white images of supposedly "happy slaves" really are, for the truth is generally the opposite of that mythology. Conspicuous, too, is the way in which this deception of whites by other whites had become one more part of the gross immorality at the heart of the everyday operation of the white-controlled slavery apparatus.

Thinking Deeply about Liberty: Mental and Physical Resistance

Like the insightful Frederick Douglass, Brown writes frequently and eloquently about the burden and weight of thinking deeply about human liberty and freedom. Thus, he recounts a situation where his slave master took him near a northern state: "As we traveled towards a land of liberty, my heart would at times leap for joy."[27] Repeatedly in his and other enslavement accounts, we see how central both mental resistance and physical resistance were to the experience of slavery. After Brown and his mother were caught trying to escape from their bondage, Brown worked out a plan to escape yet again. When he met clandestinely with his mother to tell her his plan, she insisted he go: "You have ever said that you would not die a slave; that you would be a freeman. Now try to get your liberty!"[28] Enslaved mothers often had to plan for, and agonize over, the paths to freedom for their children. Watching his mother being taken away by slave traders, Brown unsurprisingly reports experiencing great pain: "The love of liberty that had been burning in my bosom had well-nigh gone out. I felt as though I was ready to die."[29]

The last night that he was enslaved, just before he managed his long trip to Canada, Brown notes how he then reflected deeply on the fact that his mother and siblings would still be left behind in slavery; he accents the great pain that such reflections caused him, pain that he asserts only those who have been through the experience could understand.[30] Later in his autobiography, he writes that "I am satisfied that none but a slave could place such an appreciation upon liberty as I did at that time."[31] Not only is there the torture of slavery for oneself, but there is the excruciating agony that comes from trying to break with slavery when family members are still locked within it. The cruel slavery system frequently forced, for those enslaved, a counterposing of the importance of family ties against the importance of personal human freedom. Thus, such cruel dilemmas were forced on millions of African Americans in the new country that claimed in its public documents to be a land of liberty.

In contradiction to commonplace white assertions, then as now, those enslaved were commonly savvy about the character and meaning of human freedom. Even as they feigned acceptance of the system, they often did not accept it internally in their own minds. At one point, Brown says, with some irony, that he had to escape the "democratic, republican" United States and seek *real* liberty in distant Canada.[32] From his perspective, Canada is the place in North America where the enslaved person can finally become free, for "Wherever the United States Constitution has jurisdiction, and the American flag is seen flying, they point out the slave as a chattel, a thing, a piece of property."[33] Moreover, in an appendix to his autobiography, Brown argues that white slaveholders, no matter how they may appear, are truly enemies of humanity and real civilization. He turns the tables on those whites who have asserted that those enslaved were "uncivilized savages" to underscore the reality of the truly uncivilized whites of his day. After describing the extremely oppressive impact of slavery on black lives, hopes, and families, he sums up this way: "You cannot keep the human mind forever locked up in darkness."[34] He adds, "Not the combined powers of the American Union, not the slaveholders, with all their northern allies, can extinguish that burning desire of freedom in the slave's soul!"[35] The many slaveholders in southern and border states, even though supported by U.S. policing agencies and other government agencies in the South and much of the North, could not prevent large numbers of enslaved African Americans from fleeing enslavement and using other tactics of resistance.

Like Frederick Douglass, once he was finally liberated from his slave master's physical and psychological chains, the courageous Brown devoted himself to the growing abolitionist movement and to lecturing against the inhumanity of U.S. slavery. He even went back into slavery territory and helped many others who were enslaved to flee by means of the "Underground Railroad."[36] This famous means of escape from slavery, contrary to much commentary later on, was substantially black-created and black-maintained. Indeed, constantly in his biographical accounts, Brown shows the importance of black family and other networking ties among African Americans, social networking that was essential to both individual and collective resistance against the group-reinforced oppression of the white slave masters.

ACCOUNTS OF THE ENSLAVED: HARRIET JACOBS

African American women experienced many of the same horrors of slavery as African American men, and they faced the particular burdens of gendered racial oppression targeting them as women. In the slavery system, black women were inherited and owned—in contrast to white women who themselves, though usually dominated and controlled within a patriarchal family system, could inherit and own black women and men (see chapter 3).

In the first published account of enslavement by a black woman—and there are few such accounts—Harriet Jacobs begins her detailed description of enslavement in North Carolina at about the same time as the accounts of Frederick Douglass and William Wells Brown, in her case around the year 1820. In this insightful account, which features a fictionalized character, Linda Brent, as Jacobs herself, the author explains that her slave master was a lecherous and wealthy physician named Dr. Flint (actually Dr. James Norcom), who enslaved at least fifty African Americans. While some scholars have emphasized the point that Jacobs fictionalized names and perhaps some details of her painful experience with enslavement, there is corroborating evidence for her long trial under Norcom, and her account is likely accurate in its essential evaluations and generalizations about enslavement.[37] By hiding key names, Jacobs likely provided some protection for herself and her family. (Here I use Jacobs's own name rather than her pseudonym.)

Coerced Labor and Life: The Commonplace Brutality of Slavery

As in other enslavement narratives, Jacobs describes the extreme brutality and incessant violence that North Carolina slaveholders used to extort labor and compliance from those women, men, and children who were enslaved. Jacobs reports how many slaveholders, including prominent slaveholders, would hide the worst realities of their plantations from a northern or foreign white visitor, and how such a white visitor would often go back home saying that the abolitionists were exaggerating the severity of southern slavery. She harshly criticizes the naïve views of these white visitors:

> What does he know of the half-starved wretches tolling from dawn til dark on the plantations? Of mothers shrieking for their children, torn from their arms by slave traders? of young girls dragged down into moral filth? of pools of blood around the whipping post? of hounds trained to tear human flesh? of men screwed into cotton gins to die? [38]

Speaking from everyday experience, Jacobs is very eloquent here in summarizing the everyday dimensions of enslavement: extreme labor, poor rations, family destruction, child sexual abuse and rape, whipping and other violence, and the intense pursuit of those seeking freedom. Clearly, U.S. slavery was an all-encompassing system. She also comments in her extended remarks on this subject on how the slaveholders intentionally hid these realities from their white visitors. Thus, she underscores an important aspect of U.S. slavery that has gotten relatively little attention in the research literature—the recurring attempts by the white oppressors to hide and disguise its reality from visitors who came from outside the region, in this case mostly to white northerners who seem to have been inclined to accept the deception.

The Centrality of the Racial Hierarchy

Repeatedly, Jacobs offers probing sociological commentaries on the enslavement of black women throughout her autobiographical accounts. She describes and analyzes the experiential reality of the hierarchical, highly patriarchal slavery institution that was ruthlessly overseen and determined by an elite of white male slaveholders—with slaveholding white women, nonslaveholding (working class) white men and women, free blacks, and enslaved blacks as part of a degraded structure of ever decreasing power. For example, at one point Jacobs describes how working-class white men were periodically given the chance by the slaveholding elite to muster and march with muskets, in demonstrations designed to intimidate the local black population. These demonstrations in slavery areas were indicative of the general white fear of open insurrections by enslaved black Americans. Doubtless often lubricated with alcohol, the mustered whites would often take violent action against any blacks they could locate in the surrounding area: "Every where men, women, and children were whipped till the blood stood in puddles at their feet."[39] This arming of the white male population for such demonstrations, as well as for omnipresent slave patrols and slave catching operations, became part of a long history of a strong white male attachment to guns in the southern states. The gun culture so distinctive of the United States today has roots in the violent enforcement of slavery by armed whites over two centuries.

In her nuanced account of slavery, Jacobs, like Frederick Douglass, clearly recognizes the large price paid by ordinary whites for the slavery system. She adds an insightful comment about what W. E. B. Du Bois would later call the "psychological wage of whiteness": That "the power which trampled on the colored people also kept themselves [whites] in poverty, ignorance, and moral degradation."[40] Interestingly, Jefferson Davis, a major slaveholder and later president of the Confederacy, made a somewhat related comment about the privileges of whiteness for all whites just before the Civil War: "One of the reconciling features of the existence [of Negro slavery] is the fact that it raises white men to the same general level, that it dignifies and exalts every white man by the presence of a lower race."[41] This was a common defense of slavery, yet Douglass and Jacobs saw much more deeply into the matter and accented the significant socioeconomic and moral losses that came to the white population of the South—such as the lack of industrial and educational development (for whites and blacks) and the moral depravity of whites that were consequences of the slavery system.

Gendered Racial Oppression: Rape and Other Violence

Jacobs's enslaved life was one of many years in what she terms a "cage of obscene birds." The often violent and threatening slave master, Dr. Flint (Norcom), constantly reminds her of his power to injure her if she does not obey his commands. When she resists his recurring attacks, he reminds her that she is only his "property" and "must be subject to his will in all things."[42] Her slave master regularly used violence in dealing with those whom he had enslaved, no matter their gender or physical condition. For example, when he found out Jacobs was pregnant with another white man's child, he threatened her and then cut her hair off. Nonetheless, she continued to resist him actively and openly. She notes that she "replied to some of his abuse, and he struck me. Some months before, he had pitched me down stairs in a fit of passion; and the injury I received was so serious that I was unable to turn myself in bed for many days."[43] Such vivid images of the treatment of enslaved black women have yet to make their way into the most commonly seen depictions of the pre–Civil War era, such as in the still widely shown racist movie,

Gone with the Wind, and similar media productions produced by whites in more recent decades.

As we have already observed in the accounts of Douglass and Brown, no aspect of the lives of enslaved African Americans, no matter how personal or intimate, was beyond the bounds of extensive slaveholder intrusion. In her detailed accounts, Jacobs provides much evidence of sexual violence directed by white men against enslaved black women, brutal oppression from which there was rarely any lasting escape. She describes many attempts at sexual violence by her slave master (Norcom) when she was just a young teenager. She notes that certain social and ecological circumstances helped in her sometimes successful resistance to the slave master's attacks:

> How often did I rejoice that I lived in a town where all the inhabitants knew each other! If I had been on a remote plantation, or lost among the multitude of a crowded city, I should not be a living woman at this day.[44]

After this foregoing commentary on the racialized geography of slavery, she then adds that

> My master was, to my knowledge, the father of 11 slaves. But did the mothers dare to tell who was the father of their children? Did the other slaves dare to allude to it, except in whispers among themselves? [45]

Jacobs adds that these women dared not make public comments for fear of violent retaliation from their slavemasters.

As I have already suggested, the rape of black women was widespread in many areas of this country during the long slavery era, although most white analysts, then as now, have not been willing to openly grant and assess the significance of this brutal reality. During slavery, many African American women were raped by white slave masters, overseers, sailors, slave traders, and slave catchers. These included, as we have seen, some of the white founders and their close relatives. Under the gendered racial oppression of the day, the children resulting from these sexual attacks were automatically "black" and were normally enslaved, often by their own fathers. It is likely that no other U.S. racial group's physical makeup has been so substantially determined by the sexual depredations of white men, which depredations took place for substantially more than half of this country's total history.

The black female targets of recurring white male violence were usually restricted in acknowledging openly the paternity of children resulting from this rape, though privately they likely discussed the situation and were not fooled by the dominant ideology's attempt to hide this reality. Physical assault was at the heart of much white enslaving practice. Jacobs's account specifically demonstrates the ways in which sexual assault and enforced reproductive labor were gendered; the experiences of black girls and women were thus different in some ways from those of black boys and men. Jacobs notes that when she had a baby girl "my heart was heavier than it had ever been before. Slavery is terrible for men; but it is far more terrible for women."[46] Under slavery, there was not only an exploitation of the labor of production of black men, women, and children, but also an exploitation of the labor of reproduction of black women. We should note too that white slaveholders increased the number of people enslaved not only by raping black women, but also by forcing some black women to "breed" with black men chosen by the slaveholders themselves. Indeed, slave breeding in Virginia was one reason why some powerful and influential Virginia slaveholders had spoken against the overseas slave trade (for example, at the U.S. Constitutional Convention), for they and their colleagues had a surplus of enslaved black people for sale. Clearly, the slavery system was a complicated machine for generating economic wealth and power, which included a well-developed system for the social and sexual control of both black women and black men.

Like most other autobiographical accounts from those enslaved, Jacobs's report accents the strength of love and the value of family relations among those who were enslaved. Resisting the alienation of slavery, as a young woman, she fell in love with a free black man in the local community. When her slave master found out, he was enraged. She pleaded with him, but he refused to let her marry the chosen man. Indeed, he described the particular black man as just a "puppy," and Jacobs replied:

> If he is a puppy, I am a puppy, for we are both of the negro race. It is right and honorable for us to love each other. The man you call a puppy never insulted me, sir; and he would not love me if he not believe me to be a virtuous woman.

She goes on to describe how her slave master attacked her "like a tiger, and gave me a stunning blow." After his violent blow, Dr. Flint (Norcom) again told her that it was in his power to kill her for speaking back, as though she was not already fully aware of that terrifying reality.[47] Clearly, enslaved black Americans, like other human beings, regularly fell in love and sought to marry or sustain such a loving relationship no matter what the contextual difficulties and consequences might be. Such accounts contradict the frequent assertions of whites, including slaveholders like Thomas Jefferson (see chapter 3), that enslaved black Americans had only a physical "desire" for their partners and did not know real love like whites supposedly did.

Seeking solace and freedom from subordination, those enslaved strove to find social support wherever they could, in ways small and large. Thus, like William Wells Brown, Jacobs makes clear in her autobiographical account that the few moments of relaxation among enslaved African Americans were often misread by whites. After describing some blacks who were singing religious songs in a group setting, she comments:

> Precious are such moments to the poor slaves. If you were to hear them at such times, you might think they were happy. But can that hour of singing and shouting sustain them through the dreary week, toiling without wages, under constant dread of the lash?[48]

Long hours of economic exploitation, "toiling without wages," and the constant threat of violence from slaveholders and other whites could not be offset by occasional moments of respite from such recurring harm. These autobiographical reports indicate clearly that enslaved black Americans strove to be full human beings, and in those periods away from whites they could to some degree forget and, perhaps, heal a bit. Significantly, such brief interludes were misinterpreted or disingenuously underscored in the commonplace rationalizations of whites that asserted the local "slaves were happy."

In her recounting, like those of Douglass and Brown, the savvy Jacobs often speaks of personal liberty and freedom, which were indeed constant driving forces for her nearly three decades under slavery. These powerful ideas are central to her enslavement narrative. She often thought of freedom and regularly resisted oppression forced on her. Like Douglass, she taught other enslaved blacks how to read, although the penalty could be great. After several plans to escape from her North Carolina "prison" failed, Jacobs managed to conceal herself in the attic crawlspace of her free grandmother's little house. For seven long years, she lived there, just beyond the touch of her family, and was unable to escape to the North. The winter cold and summer heat caused her much pain, yet she reports this pain of hiding was much less than that of her many years of enslavement.

After escaping to the North, and yet more years of hiding from slave catchers sent by her determined slave master, a white friend finally purchased her freedom. She concludes her account of slavery and liberty thus: "I and my children are now free! We are as free from the power of slaveholders as are the white people of the north."[49] Yet even when freedom came, she had no home of her own, but had to reside with the friend who had helped to liberate her: "The dream of my life is not realized. I do not sit with my children in a home of my own."[50] The economic losses that stemmed from having to work for whites for many of her economically productive years meant that even the free Jacobs had no economic resources of her own to build up a home environment for herself and her children. Lack of access to such resources as home-ownership and housing equities is yet another unjust impoverishment associated with systemic racism for generations of African Americans. Indeed, similar housing discrimination and housing inequality prob-lems have persisted for African Americans over many intervening de-cades , to the present day.

Confronting Racial Oppression in the North and South

Like Douglass and Brown, Jacobs reports that fleeing to the North did not remove her from the devastating and pervasive effects of racial oppression. Some northerners still held African Americans in slavery there, and most non-slaveholding whites were hostile and discrimina-tory toward African Americans, enslaved or free, in the North. True white abolitionists were but a small minority of whites in all regions. In the North, as Jacobs indicates, African Americans faced extensive racial discrimination in most rural and urban areas, including segregation in public places, public transportation, employment, and housing; whites in "the North aped the customs of slavery."[51] African Americans found whites in all areas of the country emulating the discriminatory customs of southern slaveholders. In her nuanced account, Jacobs accurately as-sesses the well-institutionalized character of racism and its impact on all those, black and white, who lived in the relatively new country called the United States.

The North really did not provide a haven where African Americans could live out their lives free from white hostility and discrimination. Writing about these middle decades of the nineteenth century, historian Gary Nash sums up the northern situation this way:

> …hostility against free blacks took the form of bloody attacks on black neighborhoods. Northern whites began demonstrating militantly that they had little commitment to a biracial republic. The republican edifice they were constructing would provide little shelter to those who were black—free or slave.[52]

The foundational reality of systemic racism for African Americans clearly involved a national social grammar, a set of white-generated customs and norms, for everyday oppression of all African Americans wherever they lived and whether or not they were technically free of white enslavement.

ANALYSIS AND CONCLUSION

W. E. B. Du Bois once spoke to whites about the critical contributions of enslaved African Americans to the country that became the United States this way:

> Your country. How came it yours? Before the Pilgrims landed we were here. Here we have brought our three gifts and mingled them with yours: a gift of story and song—soft, stirring melody in an ill-harmonized and unmelodious land; the gift of sweat and brawn to...conquer the soil, and lay the foundations of this vast economic empire two hundred years earlier than your weak hands could have done it; the third, a gift of the spirit.[53]

The past and present prosperity and wealth of the United States, especially that of white Americans, is substantially the result of the enforced labor of millions of African Americans under slavery and under subsequent incarnations of systemic racism. The U.S. might well have not made its way into the "modern world" at the time that it did without all that coerced labor.

The vivid autobiographical accounts by African American men and women of their painful experiences with enslavement as children and adults provide much support for the systemic racism perspective. Viewed from this theoretical perspective, the slavery era was not a brief aberration in an otherwise enlightened and egalitarian history. Instead, the slavery era constituted the founding era during which first the American colonies, and later the United States, were materially and socially constructed. Throughout their consistently perceptive autobiographic accounts, Frederick Douglass, William Wells Brown, and Harriet Jacobs provide masterful social psychological and sociological analyses of the distinctive system of racial oppression that was central to what was then a relatively new United States. These savvy analysts examine systemic racism like social physicians with a scalpel, from different angles and perspectives. Unlike the major white founders of the slavery era discussed in the next chapter—Thomas Jefferson, James Madison, and George Washington—these formerly enslaved African Americans are able to assess the world of slavery deeply and insightfully because they lived it on a quotidian basis. Their detailed and nuanced accounts document and describe how systemic racism was experienced from the point of view of those who were its human targets. They describe the alienating relations of racial oppression forced onto them by whites in the elite and the working class, as well as the relations of resistance African Americans engaged in as they tried to negotiate and survive the many trials of their enslavement. At the heart of the enslavement narratives is this relational interpretation of an alienated life under great life-destroying oppression.

In these accounts, we see that racial oppression involves a set of heavy burdens coercively placed by the dominant group on those subordinated. These burdens are well institutionalized and include economic exploitation, unjust impoverishment, legal enforcement of subordination, family destruction, and a rationalizing racist ideology, as well as a constant and necessary strategizing for survival and resistance. From the black perspective, economic exploitation is central to slavery, as are recurring barbarity and violence in its major forms—physical, sexual, and psychological. The social relations of exploitation are central to this experience and have created much income and wealth, much racial capital, for many generations of whites. That which should most be enslaved black Americans' very own—control over life and work—is that which is most taken away from them by the system of slavery. This is well described in the accounts of Douglass, Brown, and Jacobs. Douglass describes eloquently and in detail how the labor of enslaved people creates wealth for slaveholders' families. He notes the great injustice of this social "robbery" and defends the right of those enslaved to take back what is justly theirs. At the core of the relations of exploitation is unjust enrichment, created by forced production, and a corresponding unjust impoverishment. From the beginning, systemic racism has thus involved a material and social construction of a very oppressive racial reality. It has encompassed the routine exclusion of African Americans from a great many societal opportunities, and thus from the more resource-filled and supportive lives available to the majority of whites over many generations.

These critical issues, not unexpectedly, are entirely missing in the accounts of the slaveholder-founders Jefferson, Madison, and Washington, which we will examine in the next chapter. Not one of the major slaveholders and political leaders of the revolutionary era developed an in-depth analysis of the oppressive slavery system from which they benefited so greatly. While they do note their concern for whites if those enslaved should revolt, they seem relatively oblivious to most of the ways that slavery had a great impact on the lives and hopes of those enslaved and on the country's economy and politics. To be racial oppressors seems to require that white minds be locked in much denial of the harsh everyday realities of systemic racism.

While the economic and political dimensions of racial oppression are central to its origination and reproduction over centuries, racial oppression also affects many other aspects of society. There is thus a significant family impact. Particularly poignant in the enslavement accounts are the many discussions of family disruption and destruction that slaveholders imposed on African Americans. Douglass, Brown, and Jacobs recount how they as children or young adults were torn away from their mothers, and how they suffered greatly over time in trying to maintain their family relationships. The great scale of the white-inflicted family destruction on African Americans is clear in these and other data on the slavery era. One recent study looking at two thirds of a million interstate slave sales before the Civil War estimates that some "twenty-five percent involved the destruction of a first marriage and fifty percent destroyed a nuclear family—many of these separating children under the age of thirteen from their parents. Nearly all of them involved the dissolution of a previously existing community."[54] And many more families were disrupted from intrastate sales.

Significantly, such matters of extreme family destruction are missing in the accounts touching on slavery or African Americans left by slaveholders like Jefferson, Madison, and Washington, as I will show in the next chapter. Also missing is a recognition of the great importance of the family ties and support that were in fact sustained by African Americans under slavery, which social ties are quite evident in accounts of enslaved African Americans. Even under highly disruptive conditions of enslavement, the black extended family was essential to the survival of those enslaved. We see in the autobiographical accounts the great anguish that African Americans faced as they tried to protect those family and friends who were important to them, yet were often unable to do so. Black women and men attempted to protect their children and other relatives from the many ravages of white-generated slavery. Slaveholders often intentionally used threats against black families to try to control black fathers and mothers, brothers and sisters, and uncles and aunts, and thus to keep them from running away. We see this clearly in Brown's painful reflections on leaving his mother to secure his own freedom—a level of agony he says that only those enslaved could understand.

Jacobs, in particular, describes the added layer of oppression faced by black girls and women from the recurring sexual violence at the hands of white men. This is a huge untold story, even today. The data are incontestable, and the evidence can be seen in something as apparently innocuous as nineteenth-century census data—which, for example, shows for 1850 hundreds of thousands of lighter-skinned "mulattos" among African Americans—and in the accounts of enslaved women and men. White slaveholders—including leading slaveholders like Jefferson, John Dandridge (Martha Washington's father), and probably John Washington (George Washington's brother)[55]—sexually coerced and raped myriads of black girls and women over the course of the slavery era. The latter were targets of often horrific sexual violence. In her account, Harriet Jacobs speaks of black women being treated by the slaveholders as sexualized objects to be attacked and passed from one white man to another. Not only were the black women repeatedly and severely affected by such recurring white violence, the black men who were their loved ones also suffered much in watching such white violence, usually without being able to stop it. In addition, black men faced their own gendered racism in the convenient white stereotyping of black men as especially dangerous to white women.[56]

Conspicuous and significant in the writings of Douglass, Brown, and Jacobs are the many and perceptive discussions of reasoning, thinking, and planning, which were part of everyday experience for enslaved black Americans. They frequently thought deeply about the meaning of their enslavement and of the possibilities of flight and liberty. This reflection was not only profound and continuing, but agonizing, as they clearly and poignantly recount. Indeed, the enslaved African Americans who wrote on slavery were generally much more insightful and intelligent about the character and process of that slavery system than the much better "educated" white enslavers who sometimes wrote about that very system. Certainly, those enslaved African Americans had to develop a significant understanding of whites, both slaveholders and nonslaveholders, in order just to survive the brutality of the racial oppression at that time, as indeed their descendants must develop today. Douglass, Brown, and Jacobs carried and articulated the values of human liberty and social justice in profound ways, probably much more so than did any of the famous white founders who time and again spoke of such matters as they revolted against an autocratic British king. Significantly, in 1852, after he had become a major abolitionist leader, Douglass made an eloquent and pointed Fourth of July speech in Rochester, New York:

> What, to the American slave, is your Fourth of July? I answer: A day that reveals to him, more than all other days of the year, the gross injustices and cruelty to which he is the constant victim. To him your celebration is a sham.[57]

Indeed, the real "Fourth of July" came for African Americans much later in U.S. history, on December 18, 1865, when the Thirteenth Amendment to the U.S. Constitution abolishing slavery was finally and belatedly ratified.

Perhaps surprisingly to many white readers, the accounts of those thus oppressed are quite perceptive in regard to matters across the color line. They are able to view enslavement and its consequences as it affected both the enslaved and the enslaver. They see clearly much of the damage done to the white enslavers, more so than the prominent slaveholders we examine in the next chapter. Frederick Douglass and Harriet Jacobs are extraordinarily perceptive in this regard, noting the heavy price paid by the enslavers and their white working-class assistants for their ill-gotten power and privilege. The accounts of Douglass and Jacobs show unmistakably how slavery did have a negative impact on white families—such as in the cases of white wives being forced to counterpose their empathic inclinations toward those enslaved against the coercive demands of their husbands. An adequate theoretical framework for making sense out of systemic racism in this society should note and examine the ramifying impacts of that oppression on all societal arenas and institutions, including the family institutions of both the oppressed and their oppressors.

We see in these autobiographical accounts the central role not only of human reasoning but also, as Douglass accents, of human remembering. Individual and collective memories are central to the reality of racial oppression, both in the past and in the present. For black Americans, collective memories of past experiences move along the generations and assist in honing strategies for resistance to systemic racism. The accurate perpetuation of these strategies has been essential for individual and group survival.

We also observe in these savvy autobiographical accounts references to the importance of parents and others who were enslaved in providing contextual understandings in regard to dealing with enslavement. Human beings can code into their memories events and understandings that they have not personally experienced. When a relative or friend encounters a particular instance of oppression and reports that to another individual, usually that individual records the event in her or his individual memory. Much knowledge about systemic racism, especially for the young, comes from explicit learning about the experiences of older African Americans. This knowledge may be passed along orally or in written form. As one recent analysis of collective memory has put it,

> All such elements of our collective memory...represent tangible records of the past that are external to ourselves. For these external records to pass into an individual's memory, that individual must form a representation of them internally...in his or her own neural networks. This individual can then, through

word and gesture, pass the society's collective memory on to the following generations.[58]

In addition, for white Americans there is also the important reality of much collective forgetting. "Doing racism" requires a certain collective forgetting or misremembering, as we will see frequently in later chapters.

Also significant are the great differences in approaches to resistance to slavery by those who used the whips and chains and those who resisted them. Webbed throughout the enslavement accounts in this chapter, as well as in places in the enslavers' accounts in the next chapter, is the reality of continuing black resistance to slavery. Nothing is more significant in the accounts of enslaved and enslavers than the ongoing interpersonal and intergroup struggle over oppression. The enslaved group seeks to flee or overthrow the system and attain liberty, while the enslaving group seeks to maintain the extreme oppression and legitimate that in white minds. Those who were enslaved frequently sought opportunities to secure their liberty and freedom, and their everyday resistance took many forms. Indeed, Douglass, Brown, and Jacobs were able to write their insightful reports because, after years of attempts, they succeeded in fleeing their brutal enslavement. Such resistance is doubtless greatly liberating, not just for bodies but also for minds. The old African American spirituals captured this deep feeling for liberty at an early point in time. Thus, one enslaved poet once put it this way in one of the greatest of the spirituals: "Free at last, free at last, Thank God Almighty, I'm free at last. The very time I thought I was lost, Thank God Almighty, I'm free at last; My dungeon shook and my chains fell off."

In contrast, as we will see in the next chapter, Thomas Jefferson, James Madison, and George Washington very rarely sense this black desire for, and insightful reflection on, liberty, and they are in fact fearful of black resistance and liberation. Instead, and quite unlike their evaluations of their own individual and organized resistance to the British king's autocratic rule, these "freedom-loving" slaveholder-founders often attribute black resistance to slavery to significant black character flaws and not to blacks' very human love of liberty.

The everyday resistance of enslaved African Americans shaped in major ways the character and contours of this society, North and South, especially where slavery had a major economic presence. As William Link has summarized,

> Black resistance to slavery shaped the way that slaveholders constructed their society, organized their government, and created and maintained their legal system. White southerners' anxieties about an antislavery majority seeking to dominate the national

government and to undermine the institution of slavery...reflected African American discontent. Had slaves been contented, slaveholders would have been less likely to respond violently, to restrict freedom of speech, and to require political conformity.[59]

Broadening this point to include the entire country, one can argue that the rather totalitarian white reactions to black attempts to become free made the country's political and economic system even more autocratic and less democratic than it might otherwise have been. Given the fact that the southern slaveholders had great influence over the federal political system—the executive, legislative, and judicial branches governing the entire United States—until the Civil War, we can see why recurring black resistance to slavery shaped not only the decisions and actions of powerful whites in the major slaveholding states, but also the nationally significant decisions and actions of southern whites in positions of power in the government in Washington, D.C.

3

THE WORLD OF SLAVERY: THROUGH THE EYES OF WHITE AMERICANS

INTRODUCTION

In an early-eighteenth-century letter, one of the largest slaveholders in Virginia, William Byrd II, wrote of himself as a patriarch like those in the Bible:

> Like one of the patriarchs, I have my flocks and my herds, my bond-men and bond-women, and every soart [sic] of trade amongst my own servants, so I live in a kind of independence.... I must take care to keep all my people to their duty, to set all the springs in motion, and to make every one draw his equal share to carry the machine forward.[1]

Byrd demonstrates at this early date a key argument made in chapter 1. Integral to the development and perpetuation of systemic racism in this society has been this development of a white racial frame, which is an organized set of racialized ideas and action inclinations that are expressed in, and constitutive of, the society's racist institutions. In their domination of colonial society, slaveholders like Byrd were dependent on "no one but God," as they put it, and they sought to rule autocratically in the expanding slavery-centered society. Indeed, until the 1770s, the main concern of most planters and other slaveholders was *not* primarily with the grand ideals of "freedom and liberty" for the society they had created, those ideals that were later heralded so strongly for the new United States. Instead, they were principally concerned with creating wealth and power for themselves and their kin at the expense of Native Americans and their lands and African Americans and their labor.

The experience of North American slavery greatly affected the lives and views of white slaveholders, large and small. As a group, they gained much wealth and great privilege at the expense of those they oppressed in the extensive slavery system. Not surprisingly, most white slaveholders spent much time interacting with those African Americans whom they enslaved. What lessons did they take from this recurring experience in house and field? How do their accounts compare with those of the women and men whom they enslaved? What do their accounts tell us about systemic racism in the era of slavery?

To answer these questions, I will now examine the views and accounts of three of the most famous slaveholders of the late eighteenth and early nineteenth centuries—Thomas Jefferson, James Madison, and George Washington. These planter-patriarchs are perhaps the highest ranking icons in U.S. civil religion, and two have large memorials today in Washington, D.C. They were eminent political and economic leaders, and their views and actions on slavery and African Americans had a profound impact on their time and continue to have an impact on our time. Jefferson was probably the leading intellectual of the founding era, Madison was the "father of the U.S. Constitution," and Washington was the preeminent military leader and first president, indeed "the father of his country."

Like other founding "fathers," they welcomed the patriarchal imagery that indicated their great power and privilege. Recall from chapter 1 that by the 1660s the term "patriarchism" was being consciously put forth by planters to characterize their view of society as organized around male patriarchs, who were dominant in all things economic, social, and political. This view explicitly asserted a natural social order with the large slaveholders and associated elites at the top. Jefferson, Madison, and Washington shared a paternalistic, white-supremacist view of society. Because in his era Jefferson was one of the leading advocates of liberty, the most prominent intellectual, and the white analyst who left perhaps the most developed writings on African Americans and slavery, I will give him the most attention here.

In the commentaries of Jefferson, Madison, and Washington on African Americans and slavery, we find relatively little discussion of everyday interactions with African Americans. Instead, we encounter their often stereotyped reflections and prejudicial generalizations about African Americans—and, much less often, their reflections on the impact of slavery on whites or the country as a whole. Even so, we can discern in these commentaries just how essential slavery was to the economy of the new nation in their time.

Recall Figure 1 in chapter 1, which lists critical dimensions of racial oppression. The accounts of enslaved African Americans in chapter 2 touched explicitly on most of these dimensions. In contrast, the accounts of Jefferson, Madison, and Washington do not deal substantially with the multifaceted reality of white domination, with slaveholders' violence, with the profits off slavery as unjust enrichment, with African Americans' poor working and living conditions, with antiblack oppression in settings beyond the economy, or with how government actions constantly undergirded slavery. While they do discuss, sometimes in detail, their views on the possible emancipation and colonization of African Americans overseas, they provide little serious analysis of the institution of slavery as an integral part of society, particularly as it affected their lives and fortunes and those of other slavery-dependent whites. Indeed, we gain a much more insightful analysis of slavery's impact on whites in enslaved blacks' accounts than in those of these white founders. The dimension of systemic racism most demonstrated in their accounts seems to be the white racial frame, which is used to interpret and defend whites' interests.

ACCOUNTS FROM SLAVEHOLDERS: THOMAS JEFFERSON

Thomas Jefferson was the primary author of the Declaration of Independence and other major colonial documents, ambassador to France, and later U.S. president. He was perhaps the leading intellectual of his day. Over his long lifetime, Jefferson had much experience with African Americans, especially the hundreds whom he enslaved on his plantations. Reportedly, his earliest memory was of an enslaved servant carrying him on a pillow.

In discussing life in plantation country, the insightful southern analyst Wilbur Cash has explained the centrality of black Americans in the lives of many white Americans. He explains that this was a society in which the white child of a planter was suckled by a black woman, in which gray old black men were his most loved story-tellers, in which black stalwarts were among the chiefest heroes and mentors of his boyhood, and in which his usual, often practically his only, companions until past the age of puberty were the black boys (and girls) of the plantation—in this society...in which nearly the whole body of whites, young and old, had constantly before their eyes the example, had constantly in their ears the accent, of the Negro, the relationship between the two groups was...nothing less than organic.[2]

While Cash's comment is only from a white viewpoint—a recurring problem in white assessments of "race"—his point about the early and organic relationship of whites and blacks suggests one reason why blacks have a different history and a rather more central position in this society's development than other Americans of color.

Significantly, black servants were with Jefferson for his entire life, from cradle to grave. One enslaved servant, a man named Jupiter, accompanied him on most of his travels until 1800.[3] Enslaved men and women grew his crops, built his plantations, cooked his food, and nursed his children. At his deathbed in 1826, an enslaved servant responded to his last request. Clearly, Jefferson had much contact with African Americans.[4] What views did he develop out of this extensive experience?

Some Myths about Jefferson

Jefferson is such a political icon that much that has been written about him tries to excuse his role in slavery. One contemporary website reports on Jefferson as a great advocate of freedom:

In spite of the fact that he owned slaves himself, as was common with plantation owners of his time, Jefferson spoke out tirelessly throughout his life against the institution of slavery and for the right of black people to be free. Apparently there were many factors, financial, social and political, that prevented him from freeing his own slaves.[5]

Yet, the supposedly liberty-loving Jefferson held in slavery about six hundred black Americans over his lifetime. At no point did he free any significant number of these enslaved men, women, and children. He bought and sold many dozens of them as chattel to create luxury for himself, including when he was president. When he wrote the draft of the Declaration of Independence in 1776, he was a slave master over more than 150 African Americans and resided at slave-built Monticello.[6] He had those whom he enslaved flogged, hired slave catchers to find runaways, and helped to write a slave code for Virginia. Though he periodically indicated discomfort with slavery, he took no significant action to end its importance to his prosperity or to the country's economy. Throughout his adult years, he manumitted only eight or so of the many men, women, and children that he enslaved.

Indeed, when Jefferson had great political power as president, he did little to end the slavery that was central to the new nation's economy. He did oppose the slave trade early on, but as president he abandoned his earlier opposition to the western expansion of slavery and firmly supported its spread into the huge Louisiana Purchase territory.[7]

Wealth and Power Grounded in Slavery

Jefferson knew well black slavery's centrality to society. Not only his wealth but his political power was substantially indebted to the many enslaved African Americans in the South. Once the new nation was created, southern whites got many extra representatives in Congress and extra votes in the electoral college because of the new Constitution's extraordinary three-fifths clause, which counted three-fifths of all enslaved African Americans for the purpose of expanding white political representation in each state.[8] Indeed, Jefferson would not have been elected the third president of the United States without those extra black-based votes in the U.S. electoral college which he secured there against the other candidate, John Adams. The extra white representatives in Congress and the extra votes in the electoral college from the three-fifths clause were likely central in Jefferson's thinking as he gave much support to expanding slavery westward. Every new state in the west with numerous enslaved black workers would mean more national political power for slaveholders like Jefferson.

A Major Intellectual: No Racial Integration Possible

Drawing on his and others' research in agriculture, science, and politics, Jefferson wrote what seems to be the first major book on broad societal issues by a North American scholar, his famous *Notes on the State of Virginia*. Written in the 1780s, *Notes* was a response to European critics of colonial America. One historian has noted that, "The book was very influential from the time of its publication and through a good part of the 19th century."[9]

How did a white man of great intellect and expressed democratic sentiment view the lives, character, and experiences of African Americans? In Query 14 of *Notes*, Jefferson provides the first extended perspective by a white intellectual on enslaved African Americans in the scholarly literature of what would soon be the United States. While his discussion touches on various dimensions of slavery, at no point does he provide an in-depth analysis of that system. Apart from a few fleeting comments, Jefferson seems unconcerned with analyzing the profound impact that slavery had on many institutions of the newly emerging United States.

In Query 14, Jefferson focuses largely on the character and actions of enslaved African Americans and the possibility of their integration into the white population if they were freed. Creation of a racist ideology and the larger white racial frame were essential to perpetuating the system of racial oppression, and in Query 14 much of Jefferson's analysis seeks to rationalize that oppression by denigrating the oppressed. We see that his own character structure was organized in part around a set of racialized habits, emotions, images, and views, the latter including a range of now classical stereotypes of black Americans.

Jefferson begins Query 14 with a discussion of why black Americans could not be freed and integrated into the white-controlled society. After discussing the 1777 Virginia revisal for the overseas colonization of freed African Americans, he raises a rhetorical question: "Why not retain and incorporate the blacks into the state, and thus save the expence of … importation of white settlers…?"[10] In answer, he envisions apocalyptic results from racial integration:

> Deep rooted prejudices entertained by the whites; ten thousand recollections, by the blacks, of the injuries they have sustained; new provocations; the real distinctions which nature has made…will divide us into parties, and produce convulsions which will probably never end but in the extermination of the one or the other race.[11]

Clearly, Jefferson worried much about uprisings by those enslaved, as in this famous comment later in *Notes*:

> Indeed I tremble for my country when I reflect that God is just: that his justice cannot sleep for ever: that considering numbers, nature and natural means only, a revolution of the wheel of fortune, an exchange of situation, is among possible events.…The spirit of the master is abating, that of the slave rising from the dust.…[12]

In these two comments, Jefferson seems fearful of racial conflict and rebellion, a concern that most white founders appear to have had. Jefferson is prescient in recognizing the significance of white prejudices, but his concern for black recollections leading to compulsive retaliation if blacks were freed seems unwarranted, for black Americans rarely responded with retaliatory violence when freed, as we saw in the black narratives. Absent such emancipation, however, African Americans did rebel regularly against their enslavement. Moreover, throughout Jefferson's analysis are racial distinctions that he contends "nature has made." Constantly, he uses the relatively new, white-crafted terminology of "whites" and "blacks," which groups he, like other intellectuals of his day (for example, Immanuel Kant), considered natural "races."

More Rationalization of Slavery: The Superiority of Whiteness

Wearing what he considers to be a scientist's hat, Jefferson argues that the aforementioned arguments against freedom and societal integration for black Americans are buttressed by other "physical and moral" reasons. These include their problematical color, on the origin of which he speculates:

> Whether the black of the negro resides in the reticular membrane between the skin and scarf-skin…whether it proceeds from the colour of the blood, the colour of the bile, or from that of some other secretion, the difference is fixed in nature.…[13]

Jefferson allows his preoccupation with color to carry him into unscientific speculations about skin pigmentation coming from the blood or other secretions. As he views it, this black color is naturally "fixed":

> Is it not the foundation of a greater or less share of beauty in the two races? Are not the fine mixtures of red and white, the expressions of every passion by greater or less suffusions of colour in the one, preferable to that eternal monotony, which reigns in the countenances, that immoveable veil of black which covers all the emotions of the other race?[14]

Important dimensions of the white racial frame are etched here. In these commentaries, we see more than mere cognition, for they reveal emotions and visual images. Beauty and shades of whiteness are associated in his mind. Similarly, another slaveholding founder, Benjamin Franklin, accented that "lovely white" skin color in a comment he made about excluding blacks from the country: "Why increase the sons of Africa, by planting them in America, where we have so fair an opportunity, by excluding all blacks and tawneys, of increasing the lovely white and red?"[15] In both accounts, we encounter sincere fictions of whiteness, in which white physical characteristics are considered far superior to those of "blacks and tawneys." Note, too, that Jefferson's comments suggest whites' fears of what black Americans may be thinking behind the veil of color, a white concern to the present day.

Honing his white-racist framing, Jefferson then adds more negative imagery and stereotyping:

> Add to these, flowing hair, a more elegant symmetry of form, their own judgment in favour of the whites, declared by their preference of them, as uniformly as is the preference of the Oranootan for the black women over those of his own species.[16]

That is, the beauty of whites is demonstrated not only in better hair and body form but also in alleged black preference for whiteness, which preference Jefferson compares to that of the male orangutan for black women—the latter a preposterous notion he likely drew from reports of European travelers in Africa that orangutans mated with African women.[17] This commentary signals the often extreme sexual notions imbedded in much antiblack thought from Jefferson's time to the present.

Jefferson's attempt at rationalizing slavery by reference to black inferiority looms ever larger as he proceeds. He continues in *Notes*, using the new term "race," a word that had only recently emerged in Western thinking in its modern racist meaning:

> Besides those of colour, figure, and hair, there are other physical distinctions proving a difference of race. They have less hair on the face and body. They secrete less by the kidnies [*sic*], and more by the glands of the skin, which gives them a very strong and disagreeable odour.[18]

Pseudoscientific notions, such as that of a natural "bad odor," were apparently common in this era and have remained in much white stereotyping to the present. This language of "a difference of race," asserting a physical hierarchy of "races," was then rather new to North American and European thought.

As part of his white racial frame, Jefferson articulates yet more rationalizations of slavery, for enslaved blacks are "more tolerant of heat, and less so of cold, than the whites."[19] Rationalizing economic exploitation, slaveholders often asserted that without heat-resistant African Americans they would have been unable to develop agricultural operations profitably in the hot, humid, mosquito-filled regions of the southeastern United States. Continuing with his stereotyped notions, Jefferson adds: "They seem to require less sleep. A black, after hard labour through the day, will be induced by the slightest amusements to sit up till midnight."[20] Here he implies the stereotype of African Americans as fun-loving and "happy-go-lucky." The goal again seems to be to justify widespread black enslavement. We also glimpse a fleeting reference to the "hard labour" forced on those enslaved, yet there is no assessment of the importance of this labor to the national economy. Slaveholders' accounts usually avoid a significant analysis of the extreme work and living conditions of those they enslaved, even as they frequently express great concern with black resistance to such enslavement.

Neglecting Wealth Generation

Jefferson's analysis is significant for its major omissions. Thus, the great prosperity and wealth generation for whites that stemmed from massive black labor is nowhere discussed by Jefferson, or by any of his prominent white contemporaries as far as I can determine. Later on, a few slaveholders were occasionally and briefly more candid in their rationalizations. Before the Civil War, the governor of South Carolina defended slavery aggressively:

> In all social systems there must be a class to do the menial duties, to perform the drudgery of life. That is, a class requiring but a low order of intellect and but little skill. Its requisites are vigor, docility, fidelity. Such a class you must have or you would not have that other class which leads progress, civilization, and refinement....Fortunately for the South, she found a race adapted to the purpose of her hand....We use them for our purpose and call them slaves.[21]

Mixing rationalization with candor, he argues that "progress and civilization" (that is, white privilege and power) are impossible without the extensive racial oppression.

Stereotyping Love, Grief, and Reasoning among African Americans

In *Notes*, Jefferson next adds a positive view of black Americans, but quickly takes it back: "They are at least as brave, and more adventuresome. But this may perhaps proceed from a want of forethought."[22] That is, black Americans are as brave as whites, but not as thoughtfully future-oriented, a theme still found today in some white commentaries on African Americans.

Jefferson then turns to more pseudopsychology: "They are more ardent after their female: but love seems with them to be more an eager desire, than a tender delicate mixture of sentiment and sensation." Given the extensive raping of black women by white men during the slavery era, Jefferson's comment on eager sexual desire would seem to be much more applicable to white men (indeed, himself) than to the enslaved black men with whom his mind is preoccupied. Moreover, nothing is clearer in the accounts of those enslaved than that they and their kin had a strong, lasting, and tender familial love.

Further amplifying his racial framing, Jefferson continues with a naïve sociology that indicates how far slaveholders were from understanding black lives: "Their griefs are transient. Those numberless afflictions…are less felt, and sooner forgotten with them."[23] Even though Jefferson sometimes wrote metaphorically, like the patriarch that he was, of his "slave family," he exhibits in these public writings no significant understanding of the everyday black experience and reveals an emotional segregation from the great black suffering that was conspicuous around him. Here we observe again the separating and alienating character of slavery, for whites as well as for blacks. Certainly, as their narratives show, enslaved black Americans were often beaten down, and their griefs over oppression and lack of liberty were anything but transient. They were intense, enduring, and generative of constant resistance.

Next Jefferson offers another enduring stereotype of black Americans that has long been part of the white racial frame. He argues that they are very inferior in key human qualities: "Comparing them by their faculties of memory, reason, and imagination, it appears to me, that in memory they are equal to the whites; in reason much inferior…and that in imagination they are dull, tasteless, and anomalous."[24] Here we see the hoary stereotype of African Americans as less intelligent and creative than whites. There is a striking contrast between Jefferson's racist conclusions and the evidence from the lives of those enslaved. In the narratives of Douglass, Brown, and Jacobs, we see deep reasoning and studied reflections on slavery, as well as the extensive forethought that went into countering, and escaping from, slaveholders. Alienation from those he oppressed, yet lived among, is written all over the pages of Jefferson's *Notes*.

Racial Hierarchy: Is Environment a Factor?

Briefly, Jefferson admits that one should pay attention to the environmental conditions within which African Americans have had to operate, to make substantial allowances "for the difference of condition."[25] Yet, as is his custom, he then tries to refute his counterpoint suggestion: "Yet many have been so situated, that they might have availed themselves of the conversation of their masters.…Some have been liberally educated, and all have lived in countries where the arts and sciences are cultivated to a considerable degree, and have had before their eyes samples of the best works from abroad."[26] He also offers an extensive discussion of how white slaves in Roman times were, in contrast, talented and intelligent.

Accenting the Roman case, Jefferson argues that nature, not environment, accounts for black inferiority. He exudes a plantation mentality that accepts as normal a hierarchy of "masters" and "slaves."

Significantly, Jefferson presents in *Notes* a romanticized image of Indians as brave and noble (albeit lesser) versions of whites: "We shall probably find that they [Indians] are formed in mind as well as in body" much like Europeans.[27] He does not view Indians as a separate race, as he does African Americans. Like George Washington,[28] he envisions in the future a blending of assimilated Indians and whites into one society, which result he could not envision for African Americans. (However, his view of Indians here must be considered in light of his attack on "merciless Indian savages" in his draft of the Declaration of Independence and his genocidal policies when he became president. He would write later that government should pursue Indians "to extermination, or drive them to new seats beyond our reach.")[29]

In *Notes*, Jefferson makes positive comments about the artistic talents and oratorical abilities of Indians and contrasts Indians to black Americans who have never "uttered a thought above the level of plain narration" and have never shown even elementary talents in painting or sculpture.[30] Jefferson proceeds to offer his perspective on music and black Americans, giving praise but again qualifying it: "In music they are more generally gifted than the whites with accurate ears for tune and time....Whether they will be equal to the composition of a more extensive run of melody, or of complicated harmony, is yet to be proved."[31] Though music is the one major area where Jefferson initially ventures to say blacks are more gifted than whites, he hastens to question their ability to handle complicated harmony or composition. Jefferson's negative view of black artistic talents is further underscored in his subsequent contention of an alleged lack of poetry by people of African origin.[32] In his view, African Americans, presumably including the poets of the spirituals, cannot be *real* poets.

Alluding vaguely to interracial mixing, Jefferson then rejects yet again the idea that the environment accounts for a lack of black achievement: "The improvement of the blacks in body and mind, in the first instance of their [physical] mixture with the whites, has been observed by every one, and proves that their inferiority is not the effect merely of their condition of life."[33] Arguing again out of his racist framing, Jefferson views the presence of some "white blood" in "black" veins as improving blacks' intelligence—and says not a word about the rape of black women that created much of that mixture. Then, after another discussion of Roman slaves, whom he argues faced worse conditions than black Americans, Jefferson argues that Roman slaves often became talented artists and scientists. In his view, African Americans—against great evidence at hand—have had it better than Roman slaves, yet have produced no great talent. The reason is that the Romans were "of the race of whites. It is not their condition then, but nature, which has produced the distinction."[34] In this overtly racist analysis, Jefferson nowhere informs the reader about the distinctive character of Roman slavery: For example, Roman slaves often bought their freedom, and those formally manumitted often became Roman citizens.[35] Only infrequently were enslaved black Americans allowed to buy their freedom, and they could not become full citizens anywhere in the United States.

Apparently concerned with his dogmatism, Jefferson belatedly qualifies his comments on black intelligence a little: "Whether further observation will or will not verify the conjecture, that nature has been less bountiful to them in the endowments of the head, I believe that in those of the heart she will be found to have done them justice."[36] While Jefferson does occasionally qualify his views, at no point does he suggest an argument for an alternative conjecture that African Americans might be *superior* to many whites in matters of reason and sociological imagination, a superiority we observe in some of the enslavement accounts of the last chapter. After another digression on ancient slavery, he adds that black Americans often reveal a "rigid integrity, and as many as among their better instructed masters, of benevolence, gratitude, and unshaken fidelity."[37] While positive, this comment is ironic given that enslavement generally forced African Americans to appear grateful or loyal, even servile, in order to protect themselves from some white abuse.

Concluding his white-racist arguments, Jefferson again tries briefly to downplay his dogmatism to some degree: "I advance it therefore as a suspicion only, that the blacks, whether originally a distinct race, or made distinct by time and circumstances, are inferior to the whites in the endowments both of body and mind."[38] Yet, as is his custom, after this passing qualification he reasserts strongly the likelihood of natural racial differences:

> It is not against experience to suppose, that different species of the same genus, or varieties of the same species, may possess different qualifications. Will not a lover of natural history then, one who views the gradations in all the races of animals with the eye of philosophy, excuse an effort to keep those in the department of man as distinct as nature has formed them?[39]

Interracial Sex and Passion

Jefferson then returns to consideration of the emancipation issue that triggered his extended racist discussion in Query 14. Freeing a Roman slave was not a problem because sexual mixing with the master did not involve "staining the blood" of the master, as it does for the case of a freed black American.[40] Again Jefferson accents Roman slaves' whiteness and assimilability if freed, in contrast to presumed unassimilability of enslaved black Americans. This preoccupation with interracial mixture—especially when coupled with Jefferson's assertion that blacks are mainly interested in sexual desire, not real love—is quite ironic given Jefferson's likely relationship with Sally Hemings, a young black teenager whom he enslaved and coerced into his bed a few years after these words were written.

Later, in Query 18, as he does occasionally in his letters, Jefferson briefly offers some insightful concern for slavery's impact on whites. His most critical remarks on slavery appear here:

> The whole commerce between master and slave is a perpetual exercise of the most boisterous passions, the most unremitting despotism on the one part, and degrading submissions on the other. Our children see this, and learn to imitate it; for man is an imitative animal.[41]

He continues in *Notes* with more commentary on the impact of slaveholding on slaveholders' children. While in the first sentence, Jefferson seems to be concerned with both the enslaved and the enslavers, the rest of this paragraph is entirely focused on the impact of slavery on slave masters and their children, not on enslaved adults and their children. This seems to be the closest that Jefferson came to a serious probing of his experiences as a slaveholder, and of the slavery system as a whole.

Later Commentary on African Americans

Over time, Jefferson revealed the depth of his racial framing of society by not altering his negative view of black Americans as racially inferior. Thus, in 1794 he wrote John Taylor about the food needed on his farm to "feed every animal on the farm except my negroes."[42] In 1807, he told a British diplomat that black Americans were "as far inferior to the rest of mankind as the mule is to the horse, as made to carry burthens [*sic*]."[43] Slaveholders often adopted the image of those enslaved as domesticated "animals" created to serve whites, and periodically Jefferson's language is suggestive of this extraordinarily dehumanizing view.

Smarting over criticism of *Notes*, Jefferson occasionally asserted in letters that he did not intend "to enlist myself as the champion of a fixed opinion."[44] In an 1809 letter to Henri Gregoire, who had sent Jefferson his book documenting black talent in the area of literature, Jefferson writes:

> No person living wishes more sincerely than I do, to see a complete refutation of the doubts I have myself entertained and expressed on the grade of understanding allotted to them by nature....My doubts [in *Notes*] were the result of personal observation on the limited sphere of my own state where the opportunities for the development of their genius were not favorable.[45]

This disingenuous comment—his earlier words were much more dogmatic than "doubts" suggests—is quoted by those seeking to portray Jefferson as a man who sometimes considered seriously the possibility of his being wrong about black inferiority. Yet a few months later, Jefferson writes to a friend that the naïve Gregoire's "credulity has made him gather up every story he could find of men of color" and that his book does not amount to much. Jefferson added that Benjamin Banneker, the talented black American who published well-crafted almanacs, had earlier sent Jefferson a long letter which showed Banneker "to have a mind of very common stature indeed."[46]

Moreover, in an important 1814 letter to his young neighbor Edward Coles, the aging Jefferson comments on why enslaved African Americans cannot be freed and integrated into the white population. African Americans are "brought from their infancy without necessity for thought or forecast, are by their habits rendered as incapable as children of taking care of themselves, and are extinguished promptly wherever industry is necessary for raising young."[47] Here, late in life, Jefferson strongly reiterates his explicitly racist notions in *Notes* as to the lack of reflection or forethought among black Americans and his view of their childlike dependency that is implicit in *Notes*. Many slaveholders articulated a patriarchal image of those enslaved as children, and they often commented on their plantations as a large "white and black family."[48] Indeed, George Fitzhugh, a major nineteenth-century apologist for slavery, argued that the slaveholder should be a "parent or guardian" guiding black "children" he had enslaved in his "family circle."[49]

In his letter to Coles, the aging Jefferson also pens a negative assessment of freed blacks: "In the mean time they are pests in society by their idleness, and the depredations to which this leads them."[50] Then he makes a comment indicating yet again his obsession with interracial mixing: "Their amalgamation with the other color produces a degradation to which no lover of his country, no lover of excellence in the human character can innocently consent."[51] For Jefferson, amalgamation of white and black meant great degradation. Not surprisingly, strong white opinions and emotions on this "mixing" matter were evident more than a century before Jefferson wrote this letter. As early as 1662, Jefferson's colony of Virginia had established the first colonial law banning interracial sex.[52]

In his own letter to Jefferson, Coles had called on the aging icon to back the emancipation idea that Jefferson had previously supported, on occasion, in the abstract. Coles said that he was planning to free those he had enslaved and set them up as farmers. Showing his deeper feelings, Jefferson wrote in his letter back to Coles that he was opposed to such manumission. He reasserts his view of black inferiority, writing that "[My views] on the subject of slavery of negroes have long since been in possession of the public, and time has only served to give them stronger root." He then notes that

> the hour of emancipation is advancing, in the march of time. It will come; and whether brought on by the generous energy of our own minds; or by the bloody process of St. Domingo....As to the method by which this difficult work is to be effected...I have seen no proposition so expedient on the whole, as that as emancipation of those born after a given day, and of their education and expatriation after a given age.[53]

Again Jefferson expresses fear over bloody slave uprisings such as those in St. Domingo (today's Haiti), and he is still envisioning the best plan as the expatriation of African Americans overseas.

While Jefferson supports gradual emancipation and export of African Americans, he advises Coles *not* to free his slaves now:

> But in the mean time are you right in abandoning this property, and your country with it? I think not. My opinion has ever been that, until more can be done for them, we should endeavor, with those whom fortune has thrown on our hands, to feed and clothe them well, protect them from all ill usage....I hope then, my dear sir, you will reconcile yourself to your country and its unfortunate condition; that you will not lessen its stock of sound disposition by withdrawing your portion from the mass....[54]

In his phrase, "those whom fortune has thrown on our hands," Jefferson is less than candid in this fatalistic reference, for he knows that white slaveholders like himself had intentionally established slavery as a centerpiece of the country's economy over the previous 150 years. Periodically in *Notes* and in letters, Jefferson advocates shipping freed black Americans outside North America. His long-term advocacy of colonization had helped to stimulate support for the idea among other whites in the country.[55] For Jefferson and many other whites, this colonization idea was substantially motivated by fear of slave insurrections and of sexual relations between whites and blacks.[56] In later years, Jefferson occasionally agonized over the impact of the emancipation: "We have the wolf by the ears and we can neither hold him, nor safely let him go. Justice is in one scale and self-preservation in the other."[57] Similarly, in an 1821 statement he makes this famous comment:

> Nothing is more certainly written in the book of fate than that these people [those enslaved] are to be free. Nor is it less certain that the two races, equally free, cannot live in the same government. Nature, habit, opinion has drawn indelible lines of distinction between them.[58]

Significantly, the first sentence, which sounds antislavery and freedom-loving, is quoted on the wall of the impressive Jefferson Memorial in Washington, D.C., while the rest—indicating his racist views late in life and implying his desire to move those emancipated completely outside the United States—is omitted from that same wall.

Jefferson's Lasting Impact

Because Jefferson seems to have been the major intellectual writer on black Americans in his day, his views have probably had more influence than those of other leading founders. Jefferson's analysis of black inferiority in *Notes* had a major impact on many whites, including key political leaders, of his and later decades.[59] For example, not long after their publication, excerpts were reprinted in key periodicals, such as the *Columbian Magazine* in 1788.[60] In addition, during intense debates on the petitions submitted by enslaved black Americans to the Congress in 1790, southern representatives quoted *Notes* as the authority for their proslavery views.[61] Thus, Finkelman has suggested that *Notes'* arguments about black Americans encompass "very damaging, horrible ideas…used over and over again in the 1840's and 50's by the defenders of slavery to argue in favor of continuing slavery."[62] In the long run, Jefferson's racist views have had a severe and negative impact on U.S. society. Historian John Miller summarizes,

> To a degree which might have astonished Jefferson himself, the dogma of black inferiority proved to be one of the hardy perennials of American anthropological, sociological, and historical scholarship. As late as 1925, the notion of the innate

inferiority of blacks was accepted as axiomatic by most anthropologists and historians.[63]

Today, this idea of innate inferiority is still accepted by a significant number of whites, if often more subtly or covertly articulated than in earlier decades.

ACCOUNTS FROM SLAVEHOLDERS: JAMES MADISON

Other white founders agreed with Jefferson about slavery and black inferiority, although they usually did not comment so publicly on it. Often called, again with the patriarchal metaphor in mind, the "father of the U.S. Constitution," James Madison once said that from a white man's point of view the "case of the black race within our bosom…is the problem most baffling to the policy of our country."[64] He was, like Jefferson, expressly uncomfortable with slavery, yet he owned more than a hundred African Americans over his lifetime and did not free those that he enslaved, even at his death. From childhood, Madison had extensive interactions with enslaved African Americans. They took care of many of his daily needs, and their labor created much of his prosperity and wealth. How then did he view those with whom he had so much contact, and whose work created his luxurious living conditions?

Madison was a very influential participant at the 1787 Constitutional Convention. According to his unique notes on the meeting, the Convention was scissored across a slave/not slave divide among the delegations.[65] At that critical gathering, the learned Madison represented those who felt the enslavement of African Americans was essential to the country's economic prosperity. Slavery was an important issue in the debates, and the new Constitution—under Madison's watchful eye—carefully protected the interests of slaveholders in numerous provisions, including (1) Article 1, Section 2, which counts an enslaved person as only three-fifths of a person; (2) Article 1, Sections 2 and 9, which apportion taxes on the states using the three-fifths formula; (3) Article 1, Section 8, which gives Congress authority to suppress slave and other insurrections; (4) Article 1, Section 9, which prevents the slave trade from being abolished before 1808; (5) Article 1, Sections 9 and 10, which exempt goods made by enslaved workers from export duties; (6) Article 4, Section 2, which requires the return of fugitive slaves; and (7) Article 4, Section 4, which stipulates the federal government must help state governments put down domestic violence, including slave uprisings.[66]

Such constitutional provisions reveal close linkages between the economic exploitation of African Americans and other key institutions such as the legal system and federal and state governments. Madison recognized the inconsistency of the new democracy's Constitution upholding slavery, and thus he argued that it would be wrong to state openly in the Constitution the "idea that there could be property in men."[67] As a result, the words "slave" and "slavery" do not appear in the U.S. Constitution. Instead, euphemistic terminology is used in the numerous provisions legally upholding and protecting the interests of the whites who enslaved black Americans, as well as those who traded with, insured, and financed slaveholders and their plantations.

Enslaved African Americans: Property and Persons

In his defense of the new Constitution in *The Federalist Papers*, Madison coldly describes how the legal framework of the new nation treats enslaved African Americans as both property and persons:

> In being compelled to labor, not for himself, but for a master; in being vendible by one master to another master; and in being subject at all times to be restrained in his liberty and chastised in his body, by the capricious will of another, the slave may appear to be degraded from the human rank, and classed with those irrational animals which fall under the legal denomination of property. In being protected, on the other hand, in his life and in his limbs, against the violence of all others, even the master of his labor and his liberty; and in being punishable himself for all violence committed against others, the slave is no less evidently regarded by the law as a member of the society, not as a part of the irrational creation; as a moral person, not as a mere article of property.[68]

In his racist framing of the society around him, Madison not only recognizes the reality of the rigid master-slave hierarchy of the slavery system, but also assumes the legitimacy of this extreme economic exploitation. He observes the contradiction in some laws in regard to the treatment of those enslaved, yet does not decry the antiliberty aspects of such enslavement. Indeed, he greatly exaggerates the role of law in supposedly providing protection for those enslaved from violence by slave masters and other whites, for violence used with impunity looms large in accounts of those enslaved (see chapter 2). Madison here provides one of the rare analyses of the role of law in protecting slavery in the new nation.

In 1790, when some petitions to end the slave trade early and for black emancipation from slavery were submitted to the new U.S. House of Representatives, Madison led the efforts to pass a resolution buttress-ing the institutionalization of slavery, one stating that Congress had "no authority to interfere" in whites' treatment of enslaved blacks. Madison argued that this resolution made it "unconstitutional" for Congress "to manumit [those enslaved] at any time."[69] Here is an indication of how the new government of a supposed "democracy" operated to buttress long-established racial oppression.

Stereotyping Black Sexuality

Late in his life, in 1823, James Madison replied to a letter from Dr. Jedidiah Morse containing some questions about the U.S. slavery system that were being asked by English abolitionists. Here Madison reveals his own white racial frame with its extremely stereotyped thinking about black Americans. One question to him asked why enslaved African Americans increased rapidly, by 3 percent a year, to which Madison re-plies: "The remarkable increase of slaves, as shewn by the census, results from the comparative defect of moral and prudential restraint on the sexual connexion [sic]."[70] Again we have the stereotypical white think-ing about African Americans as oversexed and defective in morality.

Over the first two centuries, the racialized views of European Americans not only stereotyped the oppressed, including African Americans and Native Americans, but also asserted strongly an array of sincere fictions about white superiority. From the seventeenth century onward, most European Americans appear to have viewed themselves as Christian people of great virtue and civilization, as "virtuous republi-cans," a perspective that provided significant psychological benefits. In the minds of colonial leaders like Jefferson, Madison, and Washington, virtuous white men did not, or should not, have the instinctual qualities of the "creatures of darkness," that is, the black and red Americans they stereotyped in their images of hypersexuality and hedonism. European Americans were positively stereotyped as rational, ascetic, self-govern-ing, and sexually controlled, while African and Native Americans were alleged to be uncivilized, hedonistic, instinctual, and uncontrolled.[71] The accent on white rationality and the fear of instinctual impulses de-veloped as a part of aggressive colonial development. As Ronald Takaki suggests, "As patriot leaders and culture-makers urged white Americans to be self-governing, they cast onto blacks and Indians those qualities they felt republicans should not have," thereby denying these inclina-tions within whites themselves.[72]

White founders like Jefferson, Madison, and Benjamin Franklin viewed their intellectual and political work as pivotal in creating a new white-dominated nation. They were white supremacists and desired eventually "to transform America into a homogenous white society."[73] Their views likely reflected longings for greater personal freedom, happiness, and hedonism than their religious commitments allowed them. Certainly, they did not live up to their professed virtues. Indeed, in his commentary on the black birth rate, Madison does not report the fact that the rate of population increase for whites was about the same as for blacks at that time, nor does he note the significant role of white men in accounting for some increase in the black population stemming from frequent sexual assaults on black women.

Stereotyping Black Character

Asked by the European abolitionists how free blacks' character compared to that of blacks who were enslaved, Madison replies in this frankly stereotyped way:

> Generally idle and depraved; appearing to retain the bad qualities of the slaves, with whom they continue to associate, without acquiring any of the good ones of the whites, from whom [they] continue separated by prejudices against their colour, and other peculiarities.[74]

Using a racist framing like Jefferson, the moralizing Madison responds with common white stereotypes of black idleness and depravity. He too holds to certain sincere fictions about the virtues of whites, although he does not seem to realize that the "prejudices" whites hold contradict his assertion of "good white qualities." Apparently, "prejudices" was a much less negative word in his day. The depth of white commitments to whiteness and its virtues is conspicuous in the letters and other writings of the paramount founders Jefferson, Madison, and Washington. Not only do they benefit economically from slavery in dramatic ways, but they also benefit psychologically from a strong sense of white superiority.

Madison's view of those enslaved as a source of profit is seen in a matter-of-fact answer to another question, this time about the cost of rearing an enslaved black child: "The annual expense of food and raiment in rearing a child may be stated at about 8, 9, or 10 dollars; and the age at which it begins to be gainful to its owner about 9 or 10 years."[75] Note that a black child, a human being, is owned and objectified as an "it." Madison's cold economic calculations have a chilling impact on the contemporary reader.

Black Resistance and Emancipation Schemes

A little later in the letter replying to the English abolitionists, Madison answers a query about whether the increase in free people among blacks increases the "danger of insurrection" with this brief and pointed reply, "Rather increases." He adds that free blacks ally themselves, not with whites, but "More closely with the slaves, and more likely to side with them in a case of insurrection."[76] Here he shares Jefferson's fears of African Americans organizing and protesting their enslavement, fears that are a likely reason for his periodic support of schemes for eventual emancipation. Implicitly, he recognizes the importance of black solidarity across the slavery line and black resistance to enslavement, resistance that forced a constant reinforcement of the system of racism by whites. Madison does not, however, note that free blacks suffered so much discrimination that their main recourse was to network with other black Americans.

Reportedly, Madison rarely spoke in public about his views of African Americans, yet he did publicly support organized efforts to emancipate and expatriate those enslaved. One reason for this was, as he often said, their racial "peculiarities." Near the end of his life, he became president of the American Colonization Society, which sought to move freed African Americans outside the United States. In an 1819 letter to Robert Evans discussing one emancipation plan, Madison suggests that this emancipation should take place only with consent of "the Master & the slave," and then he adds:

> To be consistent with existing and probably unalterable prejudices in the U.S. the freed blacks ought to be permanently removed beyond the region occupied by or allotted to a White population. The objections to a thorough incorporation of the two people are, with most of the Whites insuperable.[77]

Here he asserts, like Jefferson, that the strong prejudices of whites are likely to be "unalterable." In his mind, the reason for white objections lies in black "peculiarities," as he makes clear in the letter:

> If the blacks, strongly marked as they are by Physical & lasting peculiarities, be retained amid the Whites, under the degrading privation of equal rights political or social, they must be always dissatisfied with their condition as a change only from one to another species of oppression.[78]

Madison seems to be suggesting that African Americans are marked by such striking physical peculiarities that it is natural for whites to deprive them of rights, though he also notes the dissatisfaction of African Americans with a continuing privation of rights if they are freed from slavery. In this letter Madison recognizes the imbedded inequality of rights and its corrosive impact over the long term, yet he is most concerned with how such inequality might create problems for the privileged whites. Hierarchy seems in his view to be integral to sustained domination.

In this Evans letter, the moralizing Madison next portrays the character of African Americans as

> always uncontroulled [sic] by some of the most cogent motives to moral and respectable conduct. The character of the free blacks, even where their legal condition is least affected by their colour, seems to put these truths beyond question.[79]

Again we see the white racial frame in operation, as Madison parrots the common stereotype of African Americans as immoral and unrespectable. Like Jefferson, the well-educated Madison reveals a chronic inability to think critically about the racialized system he helps to control.

In another comment in the Evans letter, which is similar to some of Jefferson's suggestions, the more insightful Madison accents problems that white thinking about blacks creates for programs of black emancipation:

> It is material also that the removal of the blacks be to a distance precluding the jealousies & hostilities to be apprehended from a neighboring people stimulated by the contempt known to be entertained for their peculiar features; to say nothing of their vindictive recollections, or the predatory propensities which their State of Society might foster. Nor is it fair, in estimating the danger of Collisions with the Whites, to charge it wholly on the side of the Blacks.[80]

While Madison underscores the supposed problems of blacks' "vindictive recollections" and "predatory propensities" in a future state of substantial emancipation, he also recognizes the problem of persisting white antipathies, albeit stereotyping that is triggered by blacks' "peculiar" features. While he strains to suggest there would be problems on both sides, his language throughout the letter to Evans suggests much more concern with black than white propensities to problematical behavior and with reducing or eliminating the black presence within the new United States.

Recognition of Contradictions: Liberty

Occasionally, as we just noted, Madison put into words a recognition, albeit brief and restrained, that the enslavement of African Americans contradicted the goals of liberty and equality he had long advocated. Significantly, in the mid-1780s he brought an enslaved servant named Billey to Philadelphia for the Continental Congress. He explains in a letter to his father about why he had to sell Billey to a local white buyer:

> On a view of all circumstances I have judged it most prudent not to force Billey back to Va. even if it could be done; and have accordingly taken measures for his final separation from me. I am persuaded his mind is too thoroughly tainted to be a fit companion for fellow slave[s] in Virga [sic]....I do not expect to get near the worth of him; but cannot think of punishing him by transportation merely for coveting that liberty for which we have paid the price of so much blood, and have proclaimed so often to be the right, and worthy the pursuit, of every human being.[81]

Madison combines a concern with Billey tainting the minds of other African Americans in Virginia with a recognition of Billey's reasonable desire for the liberty that Madison himself had long cherished. This paternalistic passage from a "founding father" is perhaps the clearest indication of a certain schizophrenic character to the white-racist mind in this and more recent eras—one that can both hold to the idea of liberty for all and at the same time maintain the firm idea of enslaving men and women to generate white prosperity and wealth for as long as possible. Madison, like Jefferson, lacked the courage to act on his best ideals.

ACCOUNTS FROM SLAVEHOLDERS: GEORGE WASHINGTON

Like Jefferson and Madison, George Washington was made wealthy by the labor of those he enslaved. His much celebrated character incorporated a white-racist orientation to the societal world—stereotypes, emotions, and habitual actions that consistently supported racialized slavery. This orientation remained fairly constant over his lifetime, although it began to change somewhat a few months before his death when he finally decided in his will to free those he enslaved (and then only at his wife's death). By 1783, he held in slavery more than two hundred black Americans, and he continued to hold in slavery such large numbers as president. Indeed, as the first president, he had numerous enslaved workers brought from his Mt. Vernon plantation to serve him and his wife, and he signed the 1793 Fugitive Slave Act, which implemented slaveholders' goals to recover the escaping "property" protected under a new U.S. Constitution. This is the same Constitution that had been prepared by Washington and his fellow founders and that, forthrightly but hypocritically, asserted that it was created to "establish justice,...promote the general welfare, and secure the blessings of liberty" for the American people.

Washington certainly had some awareness of the oppressiveness of African American slavery, for like many white revolutionaries of his day he described the condition of white colonists as one of actual or threatened "slavery" at the hands of the British king. At the beginning of the Revolutionary War for freedom from the British, Washington had made this assessment:

> The crisis is arrived when we must assert our rights, or submit to every imposition, that can be heaped upon us, till custom and use shall make us tame and abject slaves, as the blacks we rule over with such arbitrary sway.[82]

Many of the other white founders, both slaveholders and nonslaveholders, in the emerging United States spoke in such language. (For example, John Adams used the metaphor in his 1765 "A Dissertation on Canon and Feudal Law," where he argued that some English generals treated Americans "More like slaves than like Britons.")[83] The metaphors and images of their own enslavement that were offered by the white founders "reveal how profoundly and disturbingly chattel slavery was embedded in their consciousness."[84] At this early point in time, slavery became an essential metaphor used by whites in conceptualizing certain political inequalities, one used in many revolutionary settings by whites in all regions of the newly emerging nation.

Relying Heavily on Enslaved Servants

Washington left no public writings that provide significant insights into his views about African Americans or slavery. We mainly have the numerous passing comments in his many records, journals, and letters. Reading the records of his several slave plantations, one sees that he viewed black men, women, and children as basically economic units to bring him much profit.[85] These enslaved blacks

> washed his linens, sewed his shirts, polished his boots, saddled his horse, chopped the wood for his fireplaces, powdered his wig, drove his carriage, cooked his meals, served his table, poured his wine, posted his letters, lit the lamps, swept the porch, looked

after the guests, planted the flowers in his gardens, trimmed the hedges, dusted the furniture, cleaned the windows, made the beds, and performed the myriad domestic chores … .[86]

Undoubtedly, Washington had more interaction with African Americans than most whites of his day. Yet he too came away from such interaction with a distinctive alienation, an emotional segregation from their everyday experience of agony, misery, privation, and longing for freedom.

Black Inferiority in Character and Work Ethic

Washington, unlike Jefferson, did not speak or write publicly about the question of black inferiority, but made comments in private, such as in letters, indicating his similarly negative views. Thus, despite the massive amount of labor that black workers did on his plantations—coerced labor he never acknowledges for its wealth generation—Washington confidently observed at one point that, "Blacks were ignorant and shiftless; they were careless, deceitful, and liable to act without any qualms of conscience."[87] (His wife Martha also wrote that blacks were "so bad in thair [sic] nature that they have not the least gratatude [sic] for the kindness that may be shewed to them.")[88] In another context, Washington spoke of an enslaved woman in these terms:

If pretended ailments, without apparent causes, or visible effects, will screen her from work, I shall get no service out of her, for a more lazy, deceitful and impudent huzzy is not to be found in the United States than she is.[89]

Commenting on other black workers, he spoke of "my Negro Carpenters" as an "idle set of Rascals."[90] Washington often spoke of those he enslaved as being untrustworthy: "I know of no black person about the house [who] is to be trusted."[91]

According to one historian, such views were not rare or tailored to just a few individuals: "The thousands of pages of his diaries, correspondence, and agricultural records include a seemingly unending litany of complaints, accusations, sarcastic remarks, and cynical observations with reference to his slave laborers."[92] Two things are clear from Washington's commentaries, as well as from other accounts of life at Mt. Vernon. Washington, like Jefferson and Madison, viewed African Americans as constitutionally ignorant, deceitful, careless, lazy, and without conscience. Clear, too, is that those enslaved did resist their enslavement under Washington, both passively in resisting work and more actively in running away from his oppressive tyranny. In fact, numerous people he enslaved ran away when they had the chance while he was away during the Revolutionary War.

Washington's views on African Americans and on slavery are also signaled in part by his recurring actions in regard to both. As I have noted previously, Washington, like Jefferson, enslaved some of his, and his wife's, relatives in the household at the Mt. Vernon plantation. Recall that those enslaved at Mt. Vernon included Martha's half-sister and her grandson. Her half-sister, Ann Dandridge, was enslaved for many years as Martha's servant at the Mt. Vernon plantation. In addition, Martha's son, John, likely raped Ann Dandridge, who gave Martha a grandson named William Costin.[93] In the case of her first marriage, Martha's father-in-law, John Custis, also had a black son nicknamed Jack. Yet another black child, West Ford, also came into Washington's extended family as a result of rape.[94] As far as I have been able to discover, at no point in his writings or comments to friends did George Washington acknowledge any of the black Virginians who were so close to him in terms of lineage and kinship. In this regard, he was much like Thomas Jefferson.

A Typical Slaveholder

George Washington was known as a profit-oriented slaveholder who was actively involved in most slavery-related institutions of his day. For example, at Williamsburg in 1769, he helped to set up a raffle of the property of a man, Bernard Moore, who owed him money. The raffle was expected to draw gamblers who would spend more money than regular auction buyers. The "property" raffled by Washington included the fifty-five black people enslaved by Moore.[95]

Washington was an authoritarian slaveholder with a view of his plantation as a patriarchal "family." Thus, he was described by one white visitor as speaking harshly to those he supervised: "He spoke differently as if he had been quite another man, or had been in anger."[96] His overseers were allowed to use whips, and he vigorously sought out and punished runaways, as in the case of one man sold to the brutal West Indies' plantations for running away. Such punishment was in effect a death sentence.[97] In the case of another runaway, Oney Judge, Washington had his agent try to kidnap her in New York and return her to his plantation. Even after his agent reported that she fled because of "her thirst for compleat freedom," and that she would come back if Washington promised to free her later on, he refused to compromise and sought to regain her by force.[98] Apparently, Washington could not understand her intense personal desire for freedom, but kept alluding to her in letters as being seduced from his service by devious others.

Washington, like Jefferson and Madison, worked actively to preserve his slavery interests throughout his entire life. Thus, when he became the first president, the capital of the United States was Philadelphia. Southern slaveholders in the new federal government were worried about having the U.S. capital in the free state of Pennsylvania, which had a new law mandating freedom for enslaved individuals resident there for more than six months. President Washington, famous in school textbooks for his supposed integrity and morality, devised a scheme to bypass the Pennsylvania law. He wrote instructions to his secretary to send the enslaved servants periodically back to Virginia so they would not meet the six-month condition: "I wish to have it accomplished under pretext that may deceive both them [the slaves] and the public." Washington suggests for his secretary to send slaves back on an innocent-looking trip to Virginia with his wife Martha and continues: "I request that these sentiments and this advice may be known to none but yourself and Mrs. Washington."[99] Washington intentionally deceived the public as to his motivation in protecting his economic interests in slavery.

The capital of the ostensibly "democratic" United States was soon relocated to Washington, D.C., and away from the major cultural and intellectual centers of Philadelphia and New York. It was moved because powerful slaveholders, including Washington, Jefferson, and Madison, worked behind the scenes to insure that the capital was in a slave-state area where those enslaved by federal government officials would stay enslaved under the law.[100]

Reserving Liberty for Whites

While Washington occasionally spoke of a desire to see the eventual emancipation of those enslaved, mainly in his last years, in everyday practice he viewed enslaved black Americans as undeserving of liberty. He feared that freeing African Americans as a group too soon would mean "much inconvenience & mischief" for whites, though he could see this as something that might be done "by degrees."[101] In 1798, he commented thus in conversation with an English visitor who had smiled as an enslaved man brought them water:

> This may seem like a contradiction, but I think you must perceive that it is neither a crime nor an absurdity. When we profess, as our fundamental principle, that liberty is the inalienable right of every man, we do not include madmen or idiots; liberty in their hands would become a scourge. Till the mind of the slave has been educated to perceive what are the obligations

of a state of freedom, and not confound a man's with a brute's, the gift would insure its abuse.[102]

Like Jefferson's stereotyped comments on the lack of black reflection, this comment about a slave's mind and right to freedom is greatly out of contact with the reality of the black lives that surrounded Washington. One has only to read a few pages of the accounts of Douglass, Brown, or Jacobs to see how much they cherished liberty and how much they understood what a "state of freedom" entailed. Their understandings of, and feelings for, liberty were much deeper than leading white slaveholders were able or willing to comprehend.

EVALUATING THE WHITE FOUNDERS

The public definition of national icons like Jefferson, Madison, and Washington includes an inability of a majority of white Americans to accept a critical evaluation of their racial views and actions. It is often alleged that these famous founders were strongly opposed to slavery and worked much of their lives to seriously question or undermine it. Yet one finds nothing in their writings or actions that provides support for this view of strong opposition to slavery. These powerful slaveholders did periodically express discomfort with slavery in their writings and private comments, and they did occasionally indicate a modest understanding of slavery's negative implications for a society claiming to be oriented to human liberty. On occasion, they said that they supported, to varying degrees, emancipation programs for those enslaved, mainly programs that would export African Americans overseas. Nonetheless, they all lived their entire lives in luxury created off the backs of hundreds of enslaved men, women, and children. Not one of these three major founders liberated a significant number of his enslaved workers and their families during his lifetime, and not one ever called for the full abolition of slavery in their public speeches and commentaries.

Little Critical Discussion

Today, there is little critical discussion in the mass media or school classrooms of these American icons and the systemic racism they created and maintained. There is much that is very important about the country's racial history that is not publicly discussed or presented in the mass media or taught in classrooms. Thus, most Americans have never heard the story of Thomas Jefferson's enslavement of hundreds of people and his white supremacist views rationalizing that enslavement. Even leading historians have difficulty in accepting the full implications of Jefferson's life, views, and actions. Until very recently, most white historical analysts rejected the known story, from the black oral tradition, of Jefferson's sexual coercion of the young black teenager Sally Hemings. Assessing Jefferson's relationship to Hemings, leading historian Winthrop Jordan argued that, if this was true, Hemings was a willing participant. In his view, Jefferson could not have forced himself on Hemings because "he was simply not capable of violating every rule of honor and kindness, to say nothing of his convictions concerning the master-slave relationship."[103] Similarly, in an otherwise critical analysis, historian John Miller argues that Jefferson could not have coerced Hemings: "To give credence to Sally Hemings story is, in effect, to question the authenticity of Jefferson's faith in freedom, in the rights of man, and the innate controlling faculty of reason and the sense of right and wrong."[104] These defensive, rather naïve views of Jefferson's character were made before recent DNA evidence showed the great likelihood of his rape of the young teenager Hemings.

Yet one does not need the DNA evidence to question Jefferson's character, honor, or commitment to human freedom, for he was a life-long slaveholder who held hundreds of human beings in brutal bondage. Any man capable of enslaving other human beings for a lifetime was more than capable of forcing a young teenager whom he owned into a sexual relationship. Many influential white planters, professionals, and politicians in the slave states, as the black enslavement narratives make clear, did the same thing. Indeed, one research study of slave markets in the South found that white slaveholders often sought out and paid very high prices for light-skinned African American women, often called "fancy" or "handsome" girls, to be their sex slaves.[105]

The historian Jordan argues that Jefferson did not free most of those he enslaved in his will because he felt that "his monetary debts constituted a more immediate obligation than manumission. Most Americans would have agreed."[106] Jordan has forgotten that a very large proportion of those "Americans" in Jefferson's Virginia were black Americans who would not have agreed with Jefferson. While Jefferson's white supremacist attitudes have been noted, to varying degrees, by numerous scholars, their significance has often been ignored or rationalized. Thus, Jordan concludes his critical analysis of Jefferson by admitting that Jefferson's view of black Americans was the "most intense, extensive, and extreme formulation of anti-Negro" views put forth by any white person in the three decades after the American Revolution. However, he adds, "Yet Thomas Jefferson left to Americans something else which may now in the long run have been of greater importance—his prejudice for freedom and his larger egalitarian faith."[107] Such assertions come from a narrow white perspective. From the perspective of the overwhelming majority of African Americans, Jefferson's long-term contributions to the freedom tradition are far more than offset by his major contributions to building and rationalizing the bloody totalitarian system of racial oppression and by his unwillingness, when he had the power, to bring an end to that oppression on his own plantation and in the larger society.

In the case of George Washington, a substantial majority of white historians and other analysts have generally portrayed him as a superior leader of great morality in spite of his heavy involvement in slavery. Even critical white analysts, such as Henry Wiencek, portray Washington as a flawed but still great man who was "not a racist."[108] Yet, as we have seen, Washington expressed racist views of African Americans and engaged in much oppressive treatment of those African Americans whom he held as property. Contrary to Wiencek's observation that Washington did not see those enslaved as "inherently inferior," Washington did in fact view African Americans as racially inferior. Wiencek candidly describes Washington's chasing down of runaways, his raffling off of enslaved workers to pay off debts, and his use of whippings and other violence against his enslaved workers. Washington even had the teeth of those enslaved "yanked" from their heads and "fitted into his dentures." After citing this remarkable brutality, however, Wiencek then backs off: "But Washington paid his slaves for the teeth, and the custom of the wealthy buying teeth from the poor was common in Europe."[109] Even Wiencek engages in the deifying panegyric common to less critical analysts:

> Then and now his unique eminence arises from his sterling personal qualities, from the inescapable fact that we Americans owe everything we have to him, and from the eerie sense that, in him, some fragment of divine Providence did indeed touch this ground.[110]

Some analysts insist that we must be careful to evaluate these prominent founders and other slaveholders by the morality and actions of their own time. Yet, if we compare the perspectives and actions of Jefferson, Madison, and Washington with those of numerous other whites in their own time, we see quickly that they come up morally short. There was a significant and vocal minority of whites from the mid-1700s onward who articulated strong views of abolition and equality. These included important European intellectuals who were well-known in the colonies, such as Charles Montesquieu and Adam Smith. Quaker leader, John Woolman, was perhaps the first white American to write empathetically about the conditions of black Americans. In the 1750s, he wrote of the severe impact of slavery on the white mind: "Being concerned with a people so situated that they have no voice to plead their own cause, there's danger of using ourselves to an undisturbed partiality, till, by long custom, the mind becomes reconciled with it, and the judgement itself infected."[111] He saw early on what is still central to racist thought:

> Placing on men the ignominious title, slave, dressing them in uncomely garments, keeping them to servile labour, in which they are often dirty, tends gradually to fix a notion in the mind, that they are a sort of people below us in nature, and leads us to consider them as such in all our conclusions about them.[112]

After noting that whites of the "meanest sort" would never be enslaved, Woolman cited the role of color in whites' enslavement of blacks: "This is owing chiefly to the idea of slavery being connected with the black colour, and liberty with the white: and where false ideas are twisted into our minds, it is with difficulty we get fairly disentangled."[113]

Similarly, the white Quaker David Cooper early wrote of the "power of prejudice over the minds of mankind," noting that

> It is thus we are to account for the fallacious reasonings and absurd sentiments used and entertained concerning negroes, and the lawfulness of keeping them slaves. The low contempt with which they are generally treated by the whites, lead children from the first dawn of reason, to consider people with a black skin, on a footing with domestic animals, form'd to serve and obey.[114]

By the 1770s and 1780s, at the time that Jefferson, Madison, Washington, and other white founders were crafting the Declaration of Independence and the U.S. Constitution, a slowly growing number of white ministers and writers were recognizing and questioning the systemic racism foundational to the new nation. In addition, there were numerous free African Americans, mostly in northern areas, who openly advocated freedom for all African Americans.

Recall, too, the views and actions of a few southern slaveholders, such as the young Edward Coles who wrote Jefferson about freeing his own slaves, but got a negative response. In addition, one powerful Virginia slaveowner, Robert Carter III, freed all five hundred of the African Americans he had enslaved, for he had belatedly come to view slavery as "contrary to the principles of religion and justice."[115] Like other slaveholders such as Thomas Jefferson, Carter was in debt, but did not let that stop him from freeing those many African Americans whom he enslaved. Carter worked out a careful plan for manumission, which he then put into effect. He paid a significant economic price for his actions, but did not become poor. He was strongly criticized and moved from Virginia to Maryland, perhaps to escape some social pressure. Significantly, Carter, like Coles, was well known to Jefferson, Madison, and Washington, so they had a clear *contemporary* example of courageous moral action before them that they never heeded. The modern analysts who claim we must judge Jefferson, Madison, and Washington by the standards of their own time—or who argue that the latter had no practical plan for emancipation before them—simply ignore the clear examples of Robert Carter III and numerous smaller slaveholders.

Indeed, not long before his death, George Washington did write a will in which those he enslaved were to be freed at Martha's (not his own) death. He set aside funds to care for the infirm and insisted on education of the freed youth. These actions indicated a clear moral shift for Washington, and very few southern slaveholders would have approved of his decision.[116] Yet, even then, Washington did not have the courage to emancipate those enslaved while he was still alive, when that action by the leading national icon might have had a very significant impact on the slavery system buttressing U.S. society.

A NOTE ON WHITE WOMEN AND SLAVERY

So far, I have mainly relied on accounts of slavery and slaveholding from three white male slaveholders because they were the most prominent of the founders of the United States, and their views and actions have had a profound impact on most other whites, from their era to the present day. However, I do want to call attention to the views of influential white women in the slavery era, particularly those who were slaveholders. According to available information, the views of these white male slaveholders were largely shared by their wives and other white women in slaveholding areas who left accounts of experiences with slavery. Some white observers in the slaveholding South occasionally suggested that many white women there were "abolitionists in their hearts,"[117] though recent scholars have shown this to have been unlikely.[118] White women in slaveholding families benefited greatly from slavery, even those few who sometimes were critical of it.

One fairly typical diary was written in 1860–1861 by the wealthy Keziah G. H. Brevard, a widow in South Carolina who owned at least three plantations and held more than two hundred African Americans in slavery. Brevard offers little in the way of direct criticism of the slavery system itself, though she writes often of wishing to have "never seen or known of slaves" because of the stress of running her slave plantations.[119] With the southern states seceding and war brewing, she asserts pessimistically that there may be no end to the white South's misery "until a dark age sinks the nation into brutes—I consider the vast body of our slaves little above brutes."[120] She expresses fear of those whom she enslaves, with periodic comments like "we know not what moment we may be hacked to death in the most cruel manner by our slaves."[121] In a number of ways, her views are similar to those of Jefferson, Madison, and Washington. She regards her many black workers as "half barbar-ians" and "barbarous Africans" in a "civilized country." One male ser-vant is described as "very savage like." Enslaved women are said to be females "of the lowest cast" who meddle "with the husbands of others." In her diary, Brevard regularly complains of enslaved servants as being "deceitful and lying" and "impudent" to her (in spite of "all I have done for them"), with no comments on why this might be the case.[122] One father and his four daughters, all of whom she says she has raised, are all very "impudent." She adds that "whipping did very little good and good treatment made them think of themselves better than white people."[123]

Occasionally, Brevard offers some insights into how slavery actually operated, perhaps as only a woman might perceive. At one point in her diary, she adds to her negative statement about black treachery a prob-ing statement that "many white faces" have set a bad example for "our poor negroes." The "sin" is that whites have mixed their blood "with negro blood."[124] She is referring here, rather delicately, to the rape of black women by white men, and perhaps to intercourse between white women and black men in her area. She also shows some awareness that the enslaved workers hide much of their thinking for, as she puts it, "they are far more knowing than many will acknowledge." And late in the diary, she once again expresses a wish to be rid of slaves, yet notes cursorily that she has an obligation to them because they "have worked for us and contributed to our comforts."[125]

One of the most well-connected of the white women who lived on slave plantations before and during the Civil War was the wealthy Mary Chesnut, who left extensive writings recording her experiences before, during, and after the Civil War era. Some of her diary entries offer her assessments of slavery and enslaved African Americans. Chesnut and her husband, South Carolina's Senator James Chesnut, enslaved more than five hundred African Americans on a large plantation. Though the wife of a major politician and Confederate general, Mary Chesnut peri-odically expresses in her writings some significant criticisms of slavery.

In spite of her occasional questioning, Chesnut makes clear that she enjoyed being waited upon by those she enslaved, and she shows little empathy for them. Most of her friends were slaveholders, whom she describes in her writings as "good men and women" or "martyrs" to the southern cause. She portrays the latter as at least as good morally as white northerners, especially the abolitionists whom she despises. At no point does Chesnut criticize the basic racial hierarchy. While she does comment favorably on the loyalty, religion, and family concerns of enslaved blacks, she also asserts strongly racist views. She regards the latter as morally inferior and lacking in intelligence, and refers at one point to their "naked, savage animal nature."[126] Naming them "wooly heads," she characterizes them as "dirty, slatternly, idle, ill smelling by nature."[127] As the Civil War ended in 1865, Chesnut writes in her diary about those that she and others enslaved, "And these negroes—unchanged. The shining black mask they wear does not show a ripple of change—sphinxes."[128] Like some of the male slaveholders previously discussed, she clearly fears what may be going on behind what she regards as a black "mask."

Chesnut's questioning of slavery, doubtless like that of numerous other white women, seems mostly to have been out of fear of black rebellion and because of bitterness about what slavery had done to white "wives, children, and families of the masters, as well as to the masters themselves."[129] In her writings, she discusses with great disapproval the black "mistresses" and "mulatto" children of many white men, including plantation owners she knew. However, she does not empathize with the female targets of this sexual oppression. She views black women as "beastly" and oversexed "animals." She is horrified when a free light-skinned "mulatress" married a free man whom she calls a "horrid negro" because she believes the woman's near-whiteness should have motivated her to reject such blackness.[130]

White women like Chesnut realized the distinctively patriarchal character of slavery, not just for enslaved black Americans but also for white women caught in the racial-gender hierarchy. They were upset at the way in which the patriarchal system held white women under puritanical restrictions. An early feminist, Chesnut described the wives of planters as "slaves" to their husbands. She made use of the metaphor of slavery much like the male founders did when they spoke of their own "slavery" in rationalizing their struggles against the British. Nonetheless, even thoughtful white women like Chesnut rarely in practice broke rank on racial matters with the white men who ran the slavery system.

A NOTE ON THE NORTH AND WEST— IS NOT AMERICA FOR WHITES?

The relations of enslavement for African Americans involved a social grammar, a set of customs and norms, created by white slaveholders and their minions for that everyday oppression. This grammar was honed in the South and in the North in the seventeenth and eighteenth centuries when slavery was widespread in both regions. While enslaved black Americans were not as important to the northern economy as to that of the South, they were numerous enough to have an impact. The families of many leading white northerners—such as those of John Hancock (whose signature looms large on the Declaration of Independence) and of major benefactors of Harvard, Yale, and Brown—were wealthy because of their connections to slavery and the slave trade.[131] Indeed, even as late as the 1860s, New York City stood as the world's leading city because of the slave trade long enshrined there. As one journalist of the time put it, without slavery and the slave trade, "The ships would rot at her docks, grass would grow in Wall Street and Broadway, and the glory of New York, like that of Rome would be numbered with the things of the past."[132]

Movements to emancipate those enslaved were spreading in the North by the late decades of the eighteenth century, and laws were soon passed abolishing slavery, in whole or in part, in most northern areas. Still, the official end to slavery in the North was gradual and did not eliminate the extremely oppressive system of official and informal racial segregation there. Indeed, most whites there viewed black Americans in negative terms and as undesirable residents. In New England, for example, local whites frequently "waged a persistent, if often masked, campaign to remove former slaves and their descendants from their landscape and memory." This white supremacy project involved white New Englanders playing down past slavery in their areas and conceptualizing free blacks as "disorder itself, an innately and permanently inferior element in an otherwise perfectible world."[133]

White New Englanders tried to reduce local black populations by driving them out with settlement laws, taxing them out, working for colonization overseas, and destroying their homes and community institutions. Pamphlets, editorials, and cartoons vigorously stereotyped black Americans and pressed for their removal from the North.[134] New England whites actually invented "Jim Crow" segregation with an extensive array of laws and customs excluding African Americans from public schools, juries, and the voting booth; segregating them in churches and public accommodations; and even unearthing their deceased loved ones for medical use by white doctors.[135] By the time of the Civil War, a majority of whites in most northern areas held to a white-nationalist view. In spite of centuries of residence there, black Americans were seen as dangerous aliens. Across the country, the overwhelming majority of whites held an image of whiteness that was largely generated in counterpoint to the negative imagery of blackness. The new nation was seen by most as ideally a "white republic." As the white-controlled nation spread westward, even Abraham Lincoln and other leading whites unsympathetic to the spread of slavery saw the nation as fundamentally white, and one where black Americans and Native Americans were unwanted. The great nineteenth-century poet of "democracy," Walt Whitman, asked in an 1856 comment in Oregon, "Who believes that the Whites and Blacks can ever amalgamate?" He answered his rhetorical question much as the slaveholding founders like Jefferson did: "Nature has set an impassable seal against it. Besides, is not America for Whites? And is it not better so?"[136]

CONCLUSION

The mainstream social science paradigm on racial matters views anti-black racism as something tacked onto an otherwise healthy society. This perspective typically accents bigots betraying egalitarian institutions and describes an array of intergroup relationships, with whites typically seen as one modestly more powerful group contending with many others. However, the black accounts in chapter 2 and the white accounts here show clearly that the economic and political institutions of the United States have long been basically and systemically racist. Centuries ago, the white elite and their white underlings created and rationalized the extensive system of racial oppression, and whites as a group have remained in control to the present day. This firmly imbedded system of racism has long involved alienating human relationships that are highly exploitative, racially hierarchical, very undemocratic, and rationalized in terms of an old racist ideology.

The accounts of the enslaved and the enslavers are unambiguous in showing the great importance of the centuries-old economic exploitation, which exploitation has created many economic opportunities, resources, and assets for a majority of whites since the long era of slavery ended in 1865. This economic exploitation has also shaped, in very fundamental ways, the development of local and federal governments, as well as the U.S. legal system. The U.S. Constitution was created in part to protect black enslavement and exploitation, and subsequent lawmaking under its aegis—such as the fugitive slave laws and high court decisions like the 1857 *Dred Scott* decision by the Supreme Court asserting that black Americans had no rights that whites needed to respect—substantially reinforced or extended that enslavement and its exploitation. The accounts of Frederick Douglass, William Wells Brown, Harriet Jacobs, and other enslaved Americans reveal how the legal system was almost always on the side of white enslavers, those who worked for the enslavers, and government officials who provided police and judicial enforcement of the enslavement system. As we saw in this chapter, there is little reflective analysis of the relationship of the country's legal system and government to slavery in the accounts of Jefferson, Madison, and Washington, although they sometimes speak about the possibility of government-funded colonization of black Americans overseas.

Indeed, much of their commentary about enslaved African Americans reveals the early and sustained development of a white racial framing of society, a frame strongly asserting white superiority over black inferiority. This frame included a well-buttressed racist ideology that was part of a collective defense of oppression. The racial mentality of whites like Jefferson, Madison, and Washington not only encompassed strong notions of white control and black subordination on plantations and other farms, but also extended the patriarchal plantation as a metaphor for white dominance of society. The white racial framing and related oppressive actions of those in the white elite—originally composed of slaveholders and merchants, but later of industrialists, other entrepreneurs, and major educators—have long been critical to the creation and maintenance of systemic racism. This elite, individually and collectively, has reworked the system of racism somewhat at critical historical junctures, but from the beginning to the present they have been central players in its perpetuation and legitimation.

At the macrolevel, large-scale racist institutions routinely perpetuate racial subordination and inequalities, yet these institutions are created and maintained by actions at the microlevel by particular individuals—with the greatest impact typically coming from powerful whites. Constantly developing a white racial frame, political and economic leaders like Jefferson, Madison, and Washington alleged an array of sincere fictions of the white self, including the supposed superiority of white morality, beauty, reason, work effort, and various other traits. In their framing of society, the white founders and their white subordinates generally regarded African Americans as biologically inferior and incapable of significant grief, sensitivity, or reflection. While the accounts from African Americans indicate the intense pain and grief caused by enslavement, white slaveholders barely allude to these inflicted miseries. Systemic racism breeds a lack of recognition of the humanity of the racialized others. Alexithymic individuals have trouble understanding the emotions of other people and thus have difficulty in empathizing. Essential to being an oppressor is a sharply reduced ability to understand the emotions and pain of those who are targets of oppression. Recall Frederick Douglass's point about the white woman who went from being supportive to being an authoritarian slaveholder. He suggests that "rigid training, long persisted in" is necessary to "perfect the character" of slaveholding whites. Systemic racism seems to require social alexithymia.

Strikingly, given the centrality of slavery to their lives and to the new nation's character, the analyses of Jefferson, Madison, and Washington never offer a significant discussion of the deep institutional realities and impact of slavery. Such unreflectiveness reveals the severity of the impact of systemic racism on the minds of whites. Indeed, many decades later in a 1960s discrimination case, Supreme Court Justice William O. Douglas emphasized that, "The true curse of slavery is not what it did to the black man, but what it has done to the white man."[137]

Webbed throughout the enslavement accounts of chapter 2, as well as in numerous places in the enslavers' accounts, is the matter of ongoing black resistance to oppression. While Jefferson, Madison, and Washington rarely comment on the black desire for liberty and freedom, they are clearly very fearful of black resistance. Their fear of actual and threatened rebellions motivated their occasional support for overseas colonization schemes. Such black resistance constantly signals the dialectical character of racial oppression, in which exploitation and other inhumane action routinely create a studied and recurring determination to resist by whatever means are available.

Unmistakably, the white founders saw the new nation of the United States in white-nationalist terms, and they could not envision a true multiracial democracy. Yet these founders are still regarded as more or less untarnished icons of liberty and justice by the overwhelming majority of white Americans, and perhaps by a majority of all Americans. By covering up the reality of their racist, white supremacist, and anti-democratic impulses and actions, later politicians, executives, journalists, scholars, and media commentators have today allowed these founders to remain influential icons whose lives are not analyzed as intensely as they should be. They and their ideas are still widely and uncritically cited by people working in all types of political movements, even including progressive movements seeking a more democratic and humane United States. Clearly, this use of the founders is highly problematical, as they are far from true icons of freedom and liberty for movements on behalf of Americans of color, the working class, the poor, and women. By claiming these icons, progressive movements not only forget or distort the country's true history, they also overlook the far more important progressive and democratic stands of truly heroic Americans like Frederick Douglass, William Wells Brown, Harriet Jacobs, and John Brown.

4

LEGAL SEGREGATION: THROUGH THE EYES OF AFRICAN AMERICANS

We turn now to the era of formal and legal segregation, which began in the last decades of the nineteenth century and was fully established by the first decade of the twentieth century. After a bloody Civil War and a relatively brief Reconstruction period (circa 1867–1877), during which there was some significant racial integration of southern society, the white elite successfully used violence—especially terrorism by new white supremacist groups like the Ku Klux Klan—to end this era of increasing racial integration. After large-scale terroristic violence by these supremacist groups killed and injured thousands of black southerners and their white allies, Reconstruction governments were severely weakened, and the old slaveholding elite was soon back in control of southern and border states. That extremely racist elite moved to cement into place an extensive system of legal and customary segregation placing black Americans in what was, in effect, a near-slavery system.[1]

Writing in the middle of this legal segregation era, the social historian W. E. B. Du Bois summed up what the white elite in the southern and border states had accomplished. After 250 years of enslaving black Americans, it turned on his emancipation to beat a beaten man, to trade in slaves, and to kill the defenseless; to break the spirit of the black man and humiliate him into hopelessness; to establish a new dictatorship of property in the South through the color line.[2]

After slavery, the whites in control made as few changes as possible in the system of oppression of black Americans, both in the South and in the North. This era of enforced legal segregation lasted, with some variation by area, from about the 1880s to the late 1960s. Systemic racism now took on the form of legally and governmentally sanctioned racial discrimination targeting black Americans in all institutional arenas controlled by whites. The status of being a slave for an individual master was replaced by a condition of all African Americans being, in effect, slaves subordinated to white society collectively. Official segregation, buttressed by much informal segregation as well, was important not only in the eleven states of the former Confederacy, but also in border states and some areas of other northern states. Like slavery, this segregation was implemented under cover of law and was backed by the actions of white officials in local, state, and federal governments.

Once in place, official segregation persisted like a huge ship that is difficult to turn from its destructive path. Over the long era of legally enforced segregation, especially from the early 1900s to the 1960s, there was relatively little racial change in most areas. One of the few whites who has written a critical analysis of his life under segregation, Melton McLaurin has described the relative changelessness in racial oppression in his North Carolina town of Wade: In 1953 that North Carolina town was little different from what it was in 1933, or "except for the presence of automobiles and electricity, from the Wade of 1893."[3]

RACIAL APARTHEID IN THE UNITED STATES

In this era of U.S. apartheid, oppression still took the form of a racial hierarchy with huge differences in power and privileges. African Americans continued to find themselves vigorously subordinated and alienated from substantial control over much of their everyday lives by white-imposed laws that made everyday life very complex and extraordinarily difficult. Moreover, where legal segregation left off, antiblack discrimination of an informal and customary type was frequently strong and blatant. This informal discrimination was commonplace in the South and the North. Thus, when I use the terms "legal segregation" and "official segregation," I often include therein the informal discrimination imposed on black Americans with the collusion or aggressive support of white government authorities.

In the long era of U.S. apartheid, African Americans faced widespread segregation and other discrimination by whites in an array of institutional areas, including employment, housing, education, politics, policing, public accommodations, religion, medical and health care facilities, social services, and recreation. As in the slavery era, the white male elite remained at the helm of society and mandated or supervised the extensive discrimination across the society's many institutions. Discriminatory actions by whites in all classes were generally linked to protection of white political-economic interests and were usually motivated by racist stereotypes and prejudices—understandings and emotions that continued as part of the persisting white racial frame. During legal segregation, the white racial frame was routinely reinforced and remained firmly centered in a thorough racist ideology.

Most black Americans were forced to labor, by law or economic necessity, for white employers at low wages. In most employment areas in all regions, including federal jobs in Washington, D.C., better paying job categories were usually reserved for whites only. In the South and many areas of the North, numerous professional organizations and schools excluded or seriously limited access by African Americans. These included organizations and schools in law, medicine, dentistry, social work, architecture, chemistry, engineering, and publishing. Branches of major private associations, such as the American Medical Association and the American Nurses Association, in the South and other areas were segregated and would not allow black members.[4]

Asymmetrical employment relations continued between white and black Americans and these, in turn, generated, regenerated, and maintained an array of racial inequalities and social structures essential to well-institutionalized segregation. In this era, most African Americans faced much discrimination in many areas, from employment to health services and schools. Thus, public schools were typically run in a racially totalitarian fashion. In the states of Mississippi, Georgia, Louisiana, and South Carolina, any black teacher who joined the National Association for the Advancement of Colored People (NAACP) was prohibited from teaching in public schools. In Florida, a state employee had to take a loyalty oath that included a pledge to support "the race segregation laws of this state." In various southern states, schoolteachers were pressured by white citizens' groups and media campaigns not to teach notions of racial equality and to emphasize white supremacy.[5]

Segregation was rigid and extensive throughout all southern public school districts, where virtually no black children were allowed in schools with whites. Conditions for black children were often extreme, as is indicated in this commentary from a now-elderly black woman interviewed more recently:

> We did not have what white children had. We got the old books and so forth. We had what they discarded at school. We had no transportation. We had to walk many miles. School buses were for those who were way out in the counties and they were bused very far from where they live. They were bused and brought to school early in the morning when there was no one...to watch them....There were two high schools for the black neighborhoods, and we had to walk very far....When a black school got a bus it was always a broken one. The one they did not want in their schools....A high school person could teach black children, but you could not teach white children if you only had a high school diploma.[6]

In addition, most northern school districts used covert or informal means to keep public schools mostly segregated, such as racial gerrymandering of school district lines and discrimination in pupil assignments by school assignment officials.[7] Moreover, housing was rigidly and overtly segregated in the South and the North. Most housing subdivisions in all regions, including those with most of the new housing, had racial covenants prohibiting white owners from selling to non-whites (and often to Jews).[8]

The official segregation era was also marked by the white majority's obsession with "racial purity." In numerous states, the laws defined, and the local and state governments enforced, racial "blood" laws that were much stricter than even the racist laws of Nazi Germany. Numerous U.S. laws stipulated that people with "any ascertainable Negro blood" were to be regarded as and legally segregated as "Negroes."[9] Not surprisingly, white concern over blood purity was a major force lying behind the commonplace laws banning interracial marriages. Into the late 1950s, a majority (29) of the states—including all southern and most southwestern states—had laws prohibiting interracial marriages, most specifically marriages between white and black Americans and between white and Asian Americans. Although there were numerous northern states without laws officially prohibiting intermarriage, there was intense opposition among whites there to white-black marriages, and few couples risked the possible violence that often came down on people in interracial relationships.

The fact that informal and legal racial segregation was common outside the South should not be surprising, for "Jim Crow" segregation of ostensibly free black Americans had first been implemented in the North in the early 1800s to subordinate the growing numbers of black residents there. The Jim Crow system was well in place in the North as a clear model when white southerners aggressively implemented similar practices to subordinate the legally free black southerners in the decades after the Civil War.

ECONOMIC EXPLOITATION: OFFICIAL SEGREGATION

One does not have to speculate about black experiences with systemic racism in the era of legal segregation, for there is a growing number of penetrating accounts from those who were segregated and otherwise racially oppressed. I draw here on interviews done in various settings in regard to life under official segregation from the early 1900s to the 1960s. Most accounts are from rank-and-file citizens, while a few are drawn from black leaders such as W. E. B. Du Bois and Martin Luther King, Jr.

Once I have examined here the experiences with legal segregation from the viewpoint of those who were oppressed, I will examine in the next chapter the views on African Americans and on segregation held by many whites. By again examining the racialized experiences of black and white Americans comparatively, I add interpretive layers to the theory of systemic racism. In reviewing the everyday experiences of black Americans with official segregation, we will see not only the thick texture of their lives at the microlevel, but also the ways in which the macrolevel of institutional oppression constantly intrudes on their daily experience. Note, too, that the accounts from these ever articulate and insightful black women and men offer us not only a window into their segregation experiences, but also insight into the destructive impact of legal segregation on the segregators themselves and on this society generally.

Continuing Economic Exploitation

Central to the era of legal segregation was the continuing exploitation of the labor of black men, women, and children that had long been central to systemic racism in the United States. In many geographical areas, and in all social classes, white Americans still benefited significantly from an economic domination and segregation of African Americans that was in many ways similar to slavery. Whites benefited directly and indirectly from the artificially low wages that black Americans secured under white employers, as well as from blacks' exclusion from other essential economic opportunities, such as access to viable farmland or opportunities for business development. Official segregation in southern and border states and informal segregation in the North meant significantly reduced competition for whites in all social classes, thereby significantly improving their economic options and assets. In addition, much greater economic opportunities and assets meant better access for whites to many housing, educational, and political opportunities or assets.

Recall from chapter 1 that for much of the legal segregation era, the U.S. government provided large amounts of wealth-generating resources more or less exclusively to white Americans. The federal government provided millions of acres of Homestead Act land, billions of dollars in mineral rights, major airline routes, major radio and television frequencies, and many other government-controlled resources to whites, while black Americans were almost entirely excluded by the totalitarian racial system. Today, many white families are affluent or wealthy because of these huge federal giveaways provided to their ancestors in the distant, often forgotten, past. In addition, all whites continued to benefit during this legal segregation era from the "public and psychological wage of whiteness," which gave them a recurring racial preference and dominance over black Americans and other Americans of color in most societal situations and institutions.

Unjust Impoverishment: Tenant Farming and Sharecropping

Officially, the Thirteenth Amendment to the U.S. Constitution had banned both slavery and involuntary servitude. However, in practice, white officials at all levels of government did not interpret this amendment to include the many forms of debt slavery that soon developed across southern and border states. Even an early 1900s white Georgia Baptist Convention statement noted that debt slavery was a serious problem in that area:

> There are more people involved in this diabolical practice than there were slaveholders. There are more Negroes held by these debt-slavers than were actually owned as slaves before the war between the states. The method is the only thing that has changed.[10]

Indeed, for most African Americans, the work-related chains of slavery morphed into the enforced work of legal segregation. In most rural and urban areas, the overwhelming majority worked as farm laborers, sharecroppers, tenant farmers, other small farmers, laborers, or domestic workers and other servants. Most were forced to be highly dependent on exploitative white employers. Writing in 1888 as segregation was becoming legally entrenched, the aging Frederick Douglass noted how slavery had been replaced by exploitation in which a black person was "worse off, in many respects, than when he was a slave....And though he is nominally free he is actually a slave."[11] Legal segregation was in many ways just slavery reincarnated.

Similarly, writing from extensive experience with and sociological research on official segregation, W. E. B. Du Bois reported on the devastating impact of economic exploitation in southern agriculture in the early 1900s:

> The crop-lien system which is depopulating the fields of the South is…also the result of cunningly devised laws as to mortgages, liens, and misdemeanors, which can be made by conscienceless men to entrap and snare the unwary until escape is impossible, further toil a farce, and protest a crime. I have seen, in the Black Belt of Georgia, an ignorant, honest Negro pay for a farm in installments three separate times, and then in the face of law and decency the enterprising [white] American who sold it to him pocketed the money and left the black man landless, to labor on his own land at thirty cents a day. I have seen a black farmer fall in debt to white storekeeper, and that storekeeper go to his farm and strip it of every single marketable article—mules, ploughs, stored crops, tools, furniture, bedding, clocks, looking-glass, all this without a sheriff or officer…and without rendering to a single responsible person any account or reckoning.[12]

The near-slavery of legal segregation meant that whites could usually act thus with impunity, without fear of police intervention. Most blacks were fully alienated from significant control over their economic lives.

The farm situation was often life-threatening for black men during the segregation era. In one Minnesota Public Radio report, an older black man gives an account of going with his father to settle up with a white man after the black tenant family had brought in crops of tobacco, peanuts, and cotton. They followed the usual etiquette and went to the white man's back yard. The son continues, "So we went up to Mr. Thomas' house to the back yard as usual….I had kept a record myself of everything we had got from that man that year and I know we didn't owe him any money."[13] Yet the white man told them that they had no money coming, that they had just broken even. The son then explains that he started to correct the white man about the money that he knew should be coming to his father, but was stopped by his father, who doubtless feared the consequences. In this example, a poor man with a large family is exploited in the extreme by the white farmer, yet cannot dispute such cheating. Note, too, the racial ecology of this segregation era. The respondent and his father must deal with the white man in his back yard, not in his house, and in this account the white man denigrates his father by using just his first name, "John," and not his last name. These are important aspects of the routine degradation ritual that was enforced during legal segregation, just as a similar ritual was enforced under slavery.

We see in such accounts the harsh character of the black experience under official segregation, as well as the existential perspective they honed from that painful experience. Also obvious in farming accounts are the omnipresent racial hierarchy with its extreme differentials of power and the loss (alienation) of control over one's labor imposed on black Americans by the highly racialized economic system. These experiential accounts reveal that whites regularly exploited black farmers and farm workers as they continued to unjustly enrich themselves and to unjustly impoverish those black Americans whom they routinely oppressed.

More Unjust Impoverishment: Domestic Work for Low Wages

Black men, women, and children toiled laboriously in southern agriculture. Often, children in black families were forced to work in the fields, including the very young. In addition, large numbers of black women were pressured by economic necessity to work outside their own homes, mostly doing domestic work for whites. Anthropologist John Gwaltney interviewed numerous women with this experience. One older black woman from Tennessee, at the time of the interview, had worked for sixty-four years "busting the white man's suds and mopping the white man's floors and minding the white man's kids."[14]

In a recent interview, another black woman in her seventies describes helping her mother with domestic work in the 1940s:

> My mother would wash clothes for Mr. Smith, back when I was 16. I would help my mother by using an iron to press the clothes. He always wanted his shirts cleaned and pressed. Back then you did not have bleach. You had to use lye. We used a washing board to scrub the clothes....I remember one day I don't know what happened, but there was one spot on the corner of his collar and he started cussing....He just kept cussing and yelling at my mama. I was so scared for my mama....She just kept saying, "I'm sorry sir, I'm sorry sir, it won't happen again....Yes sir, yes sir, sir I'm sorry. It won't happen again." She was begging and pleading with him.[15]

Black Americans typically experienced the era of official segregation as a type of racial "dictatorship" in which whites, as here, had supreme control. This highly alienated system enforced deferential behavior and generated fear of violence and of losing even this low-wage employment. Here that fear is communicated across two generations. In these experiential accounts, the system of racial oppression is constantly and effectively reproduced, in recurring discrimination from whites and in the requisite defensive reactions of blacks.

While most African Americans lived in the South during the legal segregation era, many did live in the North, largely as the result of the increasing migration out of the racially totalitarian South. Yet the latter also report much everyday discrimination at the hands of whites. For example, in one interview, an older woman comments thus in reply to a question asking if she had faced discrimination: "I was told by my adviser in high school when I wanted to take a secretarial course, 'You cannot take it. Who's going to employ you?...The white businesses are not going to employ you.'"[16] Segregation patterns in the employment sphere often generated discriminatory treatment in the schools, both in the North and the South. Even in the North, black women were often limited to domestic service or restaurant work. A little later in her interview, the previous respondent describes discrimination by a white restaurant owner. She was first screened by that owner to make sure she was a "light-skinned Negro," then given far more work to do than the white waitresses in that workplace. In such situations, black workers had little recourse, for protesting ordinarily meant the loss of a job or worse.

Whether legal or unofficial, racial segregation usually placed black workers in a straightjacket of service and servility in regard to whites. This habitually involved significant contradictions when it came to everyday intimacy. In one interview study, an older black woman recalls such contradictions in the racist etiquette when she was a child. Her mother not only did cooking for whites in the "big house" on the "plantation," but also did breast-feeding for white children:

> Now, a boy used to suck my mother's breast, one tit, and me on the other one. Still, when I'd go to his house, he could go in the front door while I had to go around the back. He was at the table sittin', but they feed me in the kitchen.[17]

She adds that children had to learn the conflicting rituals of segregation as they grew older. There is a recurring pattern here. During the segregation era, black women were often forced by economic necessity to do domestic work for white families. The subordination involved in this work extended even to alienation from one's own body, as in the case of being forced or pressured to breast-feed white infants. In this case, in spite of nursing in proximity to a white boy, the black child was kept by the enforced hierarchy at a distance from white activities. Segregation involved great interpersonal intimacy in some settings (thereby contradicting stereotyped white images of "dirty blacks"), yet it also imposed extreme social distancing in other settings. Note, too, that the language of "plantation" and "the big house," terms left over from slavery, prevailed in many southern and border state areas.

Also important in this account is the reality of white children being raised and cared for by black women, especially in southern areas during the legal segregation era. Indeed, many white children became close to these black women who raised them, a closeness that had to be broken down as those children became adults. The psychological and sociological damage done both to loving black women and loved white children by this typically abrupt severing of intimate human relationships has yet to be fully assessed by social scientists and other researchers concerned with the country's long racial history.

More Impoverishment: Discrimination in the North

In many northern areas, the patterns of blatant discrimination, though enforced informally and often not legally as they were in the South, were widespread from the late nineteenth century to at least the 1960s. African Americans faced significant discrimination in most historically white institutional areas in the North. The great novelist and essayist, James Baldwin, discussed life in the 1960s for a young black person in New York City in this letter to his nephew on the one hundredth anniversary of the Emancipation Proclamation:

> You were born into a society which spelled out with brutal clarity, and in as many ways as possible, that you were a worthless human being....[Y]ou have been told where you could go and what you could do (and how you could do it) and where you could live and whom you could marry.[18]

African Americans who migrated from the South to northern cities faced severe job and housing discrimination. Typically, black men could find little but laborer or service jobs, and many faced serious underemployment or chronic unemployment. Better-paying manufacturing jobs were mostly reserved for whites. Doing research on Philadelphians in the 1890s as segregation became entrenched, Du Bois reported on some of the impact of this employment discrimination:

...in Philadelphia the centre and kernel of the Negro problem so far as the white people are concerned is the narrow opportunities afforded Negroes for earning a decent living. Such discrimination is morally wrong, politically dangerous, industrially wasteful, and socially silly....Industrial freedom of opportunity has by long experience been proven to be generally best for all.[19]

In most areas of the United States until the 1960s, major racial barriers to most types of better-paying employment were officially or unofficially imposed by whites, both employers and rank-and-file workers. Such actions were typically overt and blatant. Such economic discrimination greatly enhanced the opportunities of northern white workers to build up family resources and assets and limited the ability of African Americans to build up similar family resources and assets. The costs of such pervasive discrimination were always more than economic. Commenting on the high rate of stillbirths for black mothers in the early decades of the official segregation era, one black physician concluded:

Why should we be surprised at the great number of still-births among our women?...They do heavy washing, make beds, turn heavy mattresses, and climb the stairs several times during the day, while their more favored white sister is seated in her big armchair, and not allowed to move, even if she wanted to.[20]

In the South and in the North, most whites coming of age in the era between the late 1800s and the late 1960s—including many millions of poor European immigrants—were able to access significantly better opportunities and accumulate greater family resources than most African Americans. For example, European immigrants who came in the late 1800s and early 1900s had far more access to upward mobility resources and channels than did African Americans whose U.S. ancestry went back generations. The immigrants arrived when U.S. capitalism was expanding and job opportunities were relatively abundant, and many had technical skills or a little capital that African Americans were prevented from developing. These white immigrants faced much less employment and housing discrimination than native-born black workers, and thus they could find jobs and housing near immigrant communities in cities, areas where they had the vote and thus access to political resources and power that were also unavailable to most African Americans, in the North or South.[21] Whites from most any background were able to secure the better opportunities and resources, often unfairly and very disproportionately, because omnipresent racial barriers in the South and the

North sharply reduced black workers' and black families' competition with whites for new opportunities in an economically expanding and increasingly affluent United States.

WHITE VIOLENCE AGAINST BLACK WOMEN

Firsthand accounts of the legal segregation era provide much evidence as to how widespread discrimination was in most areas of social life. The various forms of coercive discrimination noted in chapter 1 included much coercion and violence targeting both black women and black men.

Gendered Racism: Rape and Attempted Rape

One of the great ironies in the racist thinking of white Americans, in the past and today, is the constant referencing of black men as major sexual predators and a major threat to white women. Yet, the reality during the slavery and segregation eras was that white men were far more likely to harass and rape black women than the reverse. Indeed, white men usually could do this with impunity. For example, in an interview, one black woman describes extreme harassment from a white man in South Carolina when she was younger. After noting that she did babysitting and cleaning for a white family, she explains what happened after the lady of the house went to take a nap:

> So her husband came in there and he tried…fumbling and pawing all over me. And I told him, I said, "You better get out of here." So he said, "Hush, hush, hush." I said "I'm talking loud because I want your wife to hear."[22]

This woman's experience is suggestive of the fact that many white men, perched atop the racial and gender hierarchies, stereotyped black women as exotic sex objects and as fair game for their sexual advances. Substantial alienation in the form of loss of control over one's body was part of the oppression of slavery and segregation. Note, too, that this woman's experience helped to teach her how to counter attacks from these sexual predators.

Another woman in her eighties, who long worked as a teacher's aide, has tears in her eyes when she describes how as a teenager her family could not protect her:

> I remember one Sunday afternoon…a white man came to our house. I must have been about 15, 16.…This man knocked on the door. My mom was sleeping.…My brother was in the next room sleeping. I answered the door. The man looked like he was

spellbound. It frightened me, so I started backing up, and he started following me. He went straight through my mom's bedroom and my brother's bedroom. I ran,…he was following me. My brother sat up in the bed, to see what was happening.…I can remember…my sister saying, "Oh, no, no, Richard. No, no, no." He was going to hurt him.…I ran up under the house and hid. He walked in the yard looking for me and eventually he went on and got in the car. My dad wanted to know who he was.…I was never able to tell him who he was.…It frightened me. I was young, and it frightened me. I knew that these things happened, and I didn't want that to happen to me.…It was very frightening. My brother wouldn't have been able to do anything about it.[23]

Rape and attempted rape by white men are commonplace in the accounts of black women interviewed about their everyday experiences during legal segregation, especially in southern and border states. In this vivid example from the 1930s, a white man tries to rape a black teenager in her own house with her family looking on. She evaded him, yet her terror and fear were intense then and have stayed with her now years later. Note the similarities here to some enslavement accounts in an earlier chapter. Fathers, mothers, brothers, and other close relatives usually had to stand by helplessly while black girls and women in their families were attacked by white men, typically with no likelihood of punishment. When relatives did try to intervene or protest to the police, they were often attacked and sometimes lynched or otherwise killed. Thus, in 1950 in Kosciusko, Mississippi, three white men, who had been held in jail for a time for raping the stepdaughter of a black man, proceeded to his house where they shot and killed a woman and two children in retaliation for imprisonment.[24]

We should note in several of the previous accounts the central importance and major strengths of the black family in the arduous and ongoing struggle for survival under legal segregation, strengths like those used in the struggle for survival under slavery. Significantly, African American families have often been maligned today as "broken" or "disorganized" by the descendants of those whites who sought to destroy them in earlier eras.

Without a doubt, over the long decades of legal segregation the sexual attacks on black women by many thousands of white men had significant consequences, as we see in one account from a black Georgian who speaks of growing up in the 1940s on land owned by a white family named Smith. He notes that this Smith had been his father, and that when white men like his father "had nothing else to do, they would impregnate black women in his cabins or his fields or his big house....My father was the kind of person who never should have been born!"[25] He then notes that his mother was only thirteen when she was thus raped. Reflection on his mother's rape by his father obviously has had an angering and lasting impact. These accounts of sexual attacks by white men in the segregation era are similar to those recounted by African Americans for the slavery era. As with the white slaveholders, white segregators often gave black families no respect. During this era, many white men still felt they had the license to attack black girls and women. White men of all classes, including members of the elite, could attack black women wherever they wished. These men forced black women to have sex with them, and the women usually had little recourse beyond personal protests. Significantly, white men—hundreds of thousands of them over the long centuries of slavery and legal segregation—have rarely been defined publicly as sexual predators, which in fact they were.[26]

ENFORCING OPPRESSION: MORE VIOLENCE

Killing Black Residents and Burning Their Houses

As was the case during the slavery era, sexual violence was part of a much larger use of violence by whites, and especially white men, to enforce black subordination and segregation. Indeed, white Americans have a very long history of bloodthirsty lynchings of black Americans. From the 1860s to the 1990s, an estimated 6,000 black men and women were lynched by groups of whites, small and large, in many areas of the United States, most often in southern and border state areas. Many of these horrific lynchings were never recorded. Such displays of white violence often involved the ritualized dismemberment of the victim's body and the distribution of its parts to white participants, including women and children. The grotesque and violent rituals generally reflected a strong sense of white supremacy and racial superiority, as well as an intent to keep black Americans fully subordinated to white control.[27]

In most areas, white boys and men could undertake deadly violence against black residents without fear of serious punishment from police authorities. The taunting and terrorizing of blacks were often the "sport" of whites beginning at a rather young age. Another older woman, who was long a health care provider in a rural southeastern area, discusses the constant threat from whites, especially for those black southerners who were prosperous enough to own a nice house:

[Whites] set the house on fire, and they burned him up in the house. When he tried to get out the window, they pushed him back in the house. They're just nasty and mean....Black people weren't supposed to live in no really nice area like that. She [his mother] was living on this lake, and they wanted it. And they probably knew that. She was here in this city, and so they went there, and he was [there], because they left him home by himself. My cousin; he was a young man....And they just burned...the house down and burnt him up in the house. She left that place. She didn't want nothing else to happen....They know who did it, but wasn't nothing they can do about it. All the white people, they stuck together....Back in the forties. Just like Rosewood. They burned him alive.[28]

Note how vivid and detailed these accounts of white terrorism often are in black memories some decades after they happened. In the last sentence, the respondent refers to the Rosewood, Florida, massacre. In January 1923, the relatively prosperous black town of Rosewood was attacked by whites, and at least eight of the 350 residents were killed, with dozens injured. In addition, buildings were burned down.[29] In such cases, black residents fled their homes and communities rather than face more violence, often, as in this case, violence perpetrated with the involvement of white police officers. Whites, usually white men, perpetrated thousands of these racial atrocities during the long era of legal segregation, and few were ever investigated by police agencies. Depending on the situation, the whites involved might include members of the elite, the working class, or both. The white working class often resented black success and engaged in violence to pull successful blacks down to a socioeconomic level below that of local whites.

Another black woman, who moved from the South to the North, gives this account of recurring white attacks and violence while she was growing up under southern apartheid:

We couldn't live in the house. We had to go out and stand in a pond of water up to our waist all night to keep away from the white folks. They would go to our house and bust in....We couldn't come out of the water till the next day. I was scared of everything, scared of everything when I grew up....I prayed to God to let me get my children away from there. The white folks was so mean to us there. If my boy done something they didn't like, they'd kill him and me too.[30]

Emotional scars surface even after long years have intervened. This fearful woman provides detailed and painful memories of extreme experiences with white intrusion and terrorism. Whites could break into black houses without warning and again with impunity. A great and lasting fear was created by this white violence, a fear that few whites, then or now, seem to comprehend. Note, too, her solution for the violence—a move to the North. Millions of African Americans fled the South during the official segregation era, much like some of their ancestors had during slavery. The near-slavery of official segregation—with its common attacks on black individuals, their families, and their homes—led many to seek a (somewhat) better life outside the southern and border states. Indeed, it is only in the last decade or two that significant numbers of black Americans have felt free to return from the North to the South.

Collusion by Southern White Police Officers

Some readers may wonder why these African Americans did not report white racial violence and terrorism to the local police. The reason is clear and disturbing: The police were white and as a rule were either on the side of the white attackers or winked at their violent actions. In addition, white officers themselves often engaged in violence and other brutality against blacks. In a recent interview, an older black respondent describes what happened to him around 1970 when legal desegregation was supposed to be coming to the South. He got into an argument in a restaurant with whites because he was with a white woman, and the white police officers who were called took him to an isolated wooded area: "They had taken me out to the woods to teach me a lesson....I was scared to death. I'd been slammed around, slapped, and beaten....When I told my father they had taken me out to the woods, they denied it...."[31]

Expressing similar fear, a black woman interviewed in another research study accents an important difference in the experiences of black and white women. After noting that whites feel safe among white officials, she recounts being in a car in rural Georgia: "[A] white woman and I were stranded in a ditch in her car. When some policemen came and helped us, she was relieved to see them but I was frightened."[32]

In most segregated communities, black experience with widespread police brutality, and the lack of police protection, generated yet more pain and fear. When those whites in authority collude in violent oppression, there is then no authority to whom one can turn—which makes the destructiveness and misery of oppression much worse. Such accounts show the ways in which the *government* and *legal institutions* of most white-dominated communities have historically provided yet one more set of buttresses for systemic racism. Moreover, many of these communities still have problems today with white law enforcement officers mistreating black residents.

Racial Violence and Imposed Segregation in the North

As with the case of employment discrimination, also in the areas of policing and housing, African Americans in the North faced much overt discrimination and informal segregation, often enforced by mob violence. During the late 1910s and early 1920s, from East St. Louis and Chicago to Charleston and New York, whites engaged in antiblack rioting and other collective attacks directed at new African American residents to these cities. White police officers often colluded in or winked at the white violence, or themselves engaged in police brutality targeting African Americans. Moreover, it was recurring violence against black civilians by white police officers, together with other racial discrimination, that set off hundreds of black community demonstrations and violent uprisings in northern cities during the 1960s and early 1970s. In many northern cities, white officers often used excessive force against black Americans thought to have committed crimes or to not be sufficiently conforming to northern patterns of racial deference or informal segregation.[33]

White northerners used violence and other discriminatory strategies to keep African Americans in segregated residential areas. They often adopted residential covenants prohibiting African Americans from buying or occupying homes in their communities. Even a Supreme Court decision in 1948 declaring that courts could not enforce such restrictive housing covenants did not stop their being enforced by banks and other private companies in all regions of the country. For many decades, until at least the 1970s, almost all white homeowners and real estate agents worked diligently to keep black families out of their neighborhoods. Much violence was used where other means did not keep black families out of white neighborhoods. For example, between the 1940s and the 1960s, whites in one major northern city, Detroit, formed some 192 community organizations designed to keep residential neighborhoods white. More than two hundred times, the white residents there used aggressive picketing and group violence, including arson, against black families to keep them out of historically white residential areas.[34] For the most part, moreover, the local and national mass media ignored this white violence until the mid-1950s. Whites in Detroit were not unique in the use of intimidation and violence against African Americans:

> Detroit's whites, like their counterparts in Chicago, Cincinnati, Philadelphia, and Trenton, resisted the African American

migration regardless of the size of the influx of the black new-comers. Elected officials in almost every major city grappled with public policies, from housing to antidiscrimination laws, intended to address the problems generated by racial conflict.[35]

THE MANY COSTS OF WHITE RACISM

In chapter 2 we saw some of the many costs of white oppression as de-scribed by those who had been enslaved. These heavy and undeserved costs continued during the legal segregation era. The racial hierarchy's sharp asymmetry in socioeconomic resources and in the rewards for hard work by individuals or families is unmistakable during the legal segregation era. Employment and other economic discrimination meant yet more unjust impoverishment for black Americans, whose wages and incomes were on the average far lower than those of white Americans. Unemployment, underemployment, and poverty were everyday reali-ties in all black communities—the intended result of centuries of racial oppression by whites. Moreover, the negative impact of this oppression extended far beyond impoverishment, for it also encompassed much damage done to the physical and psychological health of individuals and to the social health of families and communities.

Fear and White Intimidation

Most recounting of black life experiences under legal segregation re-flects much anguish and trepidation, either overtly or beneath the sur-face. Dr. Martin Luther King, Jr., once summarized the agony of being black: "Being a Negro in America means...trying to hold on to physical life amid psychological death."[36] King is thus arguing that being black in the United States, both in the past and in the present, has meant endur-ing lots of unnecessary grief and pain.

The psychological damage and death inflicted on black Americans in this segregation era has yet to be fully told. Many interviews with black Americans who lived under legal segregation include at least one comment along the lines of this statement from a man in his seventies:

> Now it is wonderful to be able to speak my opinion and say what I have to say. You see everything was bottled up for so many years, that I could not say what I wanted to say. "Yes sir, no sir, yes sir, no sir, Mr. White Folks." You see I don't have to do that no more....Back then I didn't have no voice. Back then you had to be humble...very humble. Because you didn't want them to come along and try to burn the house down and your family on

account of you.... You just couldn't prove it. If you try to live big, they would destroy you. The message was they didn't want you to make the money. You were living too high. [Whispers] You were living too high. You'd better not live too high. [Why didn't the community come together?] Scared! Scared. You want to know the truth, scared. They could get hurt. [Lowered voice] Definitely, get hurt.[37]

This older man vividly describes experiences under conditions of a type of racial totalitarianism where he had no voice and where the black community was necessarily fearful. Like other voices from the legal segregation era that we have listened to in this chapter, he speaks fearfully and graphically about white violence and the ways that black Americans had to defer to whites just to survive.

These accounts of official segregation in the United States remind a sensitive observer in some ways of accounts of Jews and others who suffered extreme discrimination and died in Nazi-controlled Germany. During legal segregation servility was enforced not only by the recurring terrorism of white supremacist groups, but also in the everyday actions of ordinary whites, including those who would never support Klan-type violence. Again we see the lasting effects of extreme racial subordination, for the last respondent still feels the pain and indicates his fearfulness even now, as we see in his manner of speaking. The many decades of official racial segregation thus continue to have a heavy impact today, and one can see the need for appropriate reparations in these accounts from living Americans of past and present racial oppression in the United States.

Varieties of Resistance: Surviving with Deferential Behavior

In another interview, a former domestic worker became nervous and tense as her interview progressed. She makes this poignant comment about her experiences under legal segregation:

During the time that I was coming up, we were always taught to always—especially to a white person—they would tell us always be obedient to them. "Yes sir, no sir, yes madam and no madam...." [Emphasized] That is the way I tried to bring my children up too. Always be obedient. Be obedient to them. Never be sassy. I tried to tell them, "I have been obedient, and I have listened to a lot of instruction that I got from my foreparents. I don't know how I would have brought you all up if I had not been obedient." My dad and my stepmom would always have us together, and he would talk to us about different things and how to be obedient…[to] white people during that time, "[or] they may find you dead somewhere."[38]

According to her interviewer, this respondent had much fear in her face. The still-present fear could also be seen in her reactions as she took hold of her grandsons sitting nearby, and said, "That is why I tell my grandbabies to always be obedient. That is what I tell them." And they listened to her with rapt attention.

The ever oppressive institutions of white-imposed segregation have always had a severe impact on the lives, feelings, and memories of those oppressed. Conspicuous here is the multigenerational impact—the ways in which oppression's lessons in one generation are transmitted to subsequent generations. This is an important aspect of the social reproduction of the system of antiblack racism over long periods. Substantial fear of whites is frequently evident in interviews with African Americans who suffered greatly during the many decades of U.S. apartheid. Their fearfulness is seen in their words and in expressed feelings and unconscious reactions. Systemic racism has routinely created its own type of posttraumatic stress syndrome, now for some fifteen generations of African Americans.

The Cave of Racism

The structuring processes of the total-institution framework of official segregation were life-consuming and overwhelming. The everyday experiences of black Americans were decidedly different from the experiences of their white tormentors and oppressors. This point about official segregation may seem obvious, yet it is missing in much of the mainstream literature, both popular and scholarly, on "race" in the United States. In an autobiography, the aging W. E. B. Du Bois reflects thus on decades of experience with legal segregation and offers this dramatic metaphor:

> It is as though one, looking out from a dark cave in a side of an impending mountain, sees the world passing and speaks to it; speaks courteously and persuasively, showing them how these entombed souls are hindered in their natural movement, expression, and development; and how their loosening from prison would be a matter not simply of courtesy, sympathy, and help to them, but aid to all the world. One talks on evenly and logically in this way, but notices that the passing throng does not even turn its head, or if it does, glances curiously and walks

on. It gradually penetrates the minds of the prisoners that the people passing do not hear; that some thick sheet of invisible but horribly tangible plate glass is between them and the world. They get excited; they talk louder; they gesticulate....They may scream and hurl themselves against the barriers, hardly realizing in their bewilderment that they are screaming in a vacuum unheard and that antics may actually seem funny to those outside looking in. They may even, here and there, break through in blood and disfigurement, and find themselves faced by a horrified, implacable, and quite overwhelming mob of people frightened for their own very existence.[39]

Rarely has any analyst reached this level of insightfulness about the imprisoning and psychologically devastating impact of comprehensive racial segregation—the forced hurling of oneself against recurring racial barriers for all those trapped endlessly in the "cave" that was, and still is, systemic racism.

CONTENDING AND COPING WITH SYSTEMIC RACISM

As Du Bois suggests, resistance is a *principal* feature of racial oppression as it has developed over centuries of U.S. history. We saw this clearly in the chapter dealing with the contending and coping strategies of those who were enslaved. Many of the strategies of resistance used under slavery were also used by African Americans responding to the everyday pressures and discrimination of the official segregation era. Here the resistance strategies and countering efforts continue to reveal the difficult and dialectical character of the ongoing black struggle against systemic racism.

Resistance Strategies: Concealing Feelings
and Other Internal Resistance

Interviews with African Americans who lived under legal segregation reveal that they constantly used an array of behavioral strategies to cope with and fight racial barriers. These included withdrawal, confrontation, humor, and sarcasm. Different situations called for different strategies. Anthropologist John Gwaltney interviewed a black woman who was born in Arkansas but was then living in the North. She explains how centuries of systemic racism have made African Americans justifiably suspicious and very cautious: "It was slaves and their children who had to be devious, subtle and complicated. Masters and their children kind of had to be simple people."[40] In dealing with white systems of oppression, African Americans have historically had to think out an array of strategies, such as hiding their thoughts and understandings from whites. Both slavery and official segregation called forth careful, subtle, and complicated strategies from the oppressed.

Another black woman remembers her mother's protective strategies during the long years of enforced segregation in North Carolina:

> My mother...used to say, that lady I work for is foolish enough to believe that I really like her. She said I'm not thinking about her one way or the other....And I learned, too, that I could smile on the outside.[41]

Similarly, a teacher in his sixties explains his forced role performance as a black man living under the comprehensive racist system of legal segregation:

> The rule of thumb was you never tell white folks what you thinking. Because they are going to use it against you, no questions about it. There was this whole coping skills that black men had. They call it shuffling, shuffling around, scratching their heads....I saw them doing it. "I don't know." "Yes sir." "I don't know." "I don't know sir." You know, but the white would come to you because they thought you had something to tell them. So the first thing you do was to deny it, but you couldn't say, "How dare you come to me and ask me this?" You had to take on the role of a buffoon to get this guy off of you because he could make life difficult for you. So, that's what you did and it worked. Once the white person left, you laughed. You know, it happened all the time. "Do you boys know so and so and so and so?" "No sir, never heard of him!"[42]

During this extremely oppressive and dangerous era, African Americans were frequently forced to hide their real thoughts from those whites likely to do them much harm. They were forced to pretend to be dumb or a buffoon to survive under the constant threat of white retaliation and recurring violence. Ironically, many whites, then as now, would say that they "knew their black folks" or that "their black servants liked them." Yet, it was usually the whites who were ignorant, naïve, and simple-minded about those they exploited and oppressed. Rarely have so many Americans been wrong so profoundly than the millions of white segregators who professed dogmatism in regard to knowing "their blacks."

Confrontational Strategies

Overt confrontational resistance was less common, but still significant. Defensive preparations were commonplace. Some black fathers armed themselves against the white "night riders" who marauded through black communities at night, often raping or shooting as they went. Black men sometimes fired back. Thus, one woman who grew up under legal segregation in Georgia notes how black men and women sometimes did fight back against terroristic violence:

> You had to take care of yourself. That is what dad always told us....Your parents would take you out to practice how to shoot. I was the oldest of six and when my mother and father had to go some place, they left me in charge of the children, and say keep the gun up so that no one would get it. And if I hear a noise my father said, put the children behind and shoot. Shoot the KKK. That is the way he brought us up. And I knew of a woman who told her daughter to shoot the KKK. And she did. She killed one of them on the porch. She shot one of them and they [left]. I said, thank you Jesus, Alleluia![43]

Sometimes, against the advice of their parents, young people openly resisted the indignities of legally imposed segregation. In this commentary, an older woman who worked in gas stations and hotels tells about her reaction when she was younger:

> I remember one day I said I am not going to the back of the bus. I was standing and the driver said "I am not going to move the bus until you go to the back." I said, "I am not going back there." And I didn't. We were in a black neighborhood and he couldn't do anything. I didn't go. I don't know, that day I just didn't care. But my father was very very scared.[44]

Such aggressive responses could lead to retaliatory white violence against black families.

Other responses to intense subjugation included leaving a region. Recall that by the late eighteenth century many enslaved black Americans were fleeing the more oppressive slave states to other states, including those in the North, using the largely black-maintained "underground railroad." In this manner, they often increased their opportunities, although they still faced large-scale racial discrimination wherever they went. Similarly, many black Americans who were chronically burdened by official segregation migrated to northern areas, especially during war periods, even as various laws in the South frequently made leaving and migration north very difficult. By going north, they typically reduced the overt racial discrimination they faced, but usually not as much as they had hoped.

Enabling Children to Survive and Resist

For centuries, black parents have played a central role in socializing their children for facing and countering the many racial barriers that they face over lifetimes. During official segregation, black parents had to begin this socialization early, for one mistake in interacting with whites, especially certain white men, could result in serious injury or death. White parents, in contrast, did not have to spend valuable time on teaching such defensive strategies for everyday racism. Dr. Martin Luther King, Jr., once described the difficult task of the black parent:

> [T]he moment comes when he must explain to his offspring the facts of segregation. My mother took me on her lap and began by telling me about slavery....She tried to explain the divided system of the South—the segregated schools, restaurants, theaters, housing; the white and colored signs on drinking fountains, waiting rooms, lavatories—as a social condition rather than a natural order.[45]

Next, his mother tried to explain that, in spite of this, he was "as good as anyone." Difficult lessons about contending with racial oppression often come with attempts to support the developing psyches of young black children. The difficult lessons have traditionally included much racial knowledge that African American parents and other adults have accumulated over a long period in contending with racial oppression. Gathering and passing along important information is one step in contending with and countering the everyday cruelties of systemic racism.

Black Americans who grew up under segregation report an array of important lessons taught by their mothers, fathers, and other relatives. This man notes that there were things black children in his family did not do when they were growing up in Alabama:

> [W]herever we went out of town, they took us. We never had to go to the bus station for anything. Until I got to be 10 years old, they didn't take me to buy shoes. They bought my shoes. And if they didn't fit, they'd take them back and get another size.[46]

He adds that his parents did the same for clothes, in order to not subject the children to the hostility or attacks of whites. Adult whites could be dangerous to black children's health, so black parents often took extensive precautions, in this case by using an avoidance strategy.

Most black children were taught to be careful. One woman's mother gave her this advice: "My mama told me to always keep my distance from white folks....She said you can't trust them...they will grin and smile in your face but they are not your friend. This is what I tell my children."[47] When the interviewer of this now-elderly woman went to her house, it was in the middle of a sunny day, yet the respondent's house was very dark, and her shades were drawn. In addition, she would not allow the tape recorder to be on, so this interview was recorded by hand. The brutal and far-reaching oppression of the official segregation period has a severe impact on her life *today*, and this woman is *still* very fearful of what whites might still do to her.

Relatives besides parents were important in teaching critical survival lessons. Key survival tools included an internal rejection of what the white racial frame constantly imposed on its targets. In the 1960s, James Baldwin gave this advice to his New York nephew about white people who discriminated routinely against him: "Please try to remember that what they believe, as well as what they do and cause you to endure, does not testify to your inferiority but to their inhumanity and fear."[48] Baldwin had honed well these internal survival tools, as we see in his many essays and novels insightfully analyzing racial oppression in various regions of the United States.

Some lessons from parents and other relatives have included confrontational strategies in the ongoing struggle to counter whites' oppression. For example, Dr. King also recounted the story of an encounter of his father, a leading minister who was himself a sharecropper's son, with a white police officer:

> A policeman pulled up to the car and said, "All right, boy, pull over and let me see your license." My father replied indignantly, "I'm no boy." Then, pointing to me, "This is a boy. I'm a man, and until you call me one, I will not listen to you."[49]

King then recalls that the police officer was so rattled by this aggressive response that he quickly wrote a ticket and left. King indicates that confrontational incidents like this taught him that the omnipresent segregation was irrational and unmistakably immoral. Clearly, such actions by his father taught him to be courageous in battling everyday discrimination.

Knowledge from Racism: Second Sight and Double Consciousness

Black Americans have accumulated great resistance knowledge as they have countered much racism from millions of whites over hundreds of years. This accumulated store of valuable knowledge has played an essential role in enabling most, both young and old, to survive the rigors and pain discriminatorily imposed on them. Writing from the heart of southern segregation around 1900, W. E. B. Du Bois probed deeply into the psychological impact of this total-institution framework. The black American is

> [b]orn with a veil, and gifted with second-sight in this American world—a world which yields him no true self-consciousness, but only lets him see himself through the revelation of the other world. It is a peculiar sensation, this double-consciousness, this sense of always looking at one's self through the eyes of others....One ever feels his twoness—an American, a Negro; two souls, two thoughts...in one dark body, whose dogged strength alone keeps it from being torn asunder.[50]

Born encircled by institutionalized racism, African Americans are consigned to a great struggle. One critical insight here is the "twoness" forced upon African Americans, a white-imposed racial identity versus an internal self striving to have an identity free of that racially imposed identity. Openly expressing one's true self, identity, and understandings was usually dangerous under official segregation, so the real selves of African Americans were generally unknown to most whites. Indeed, the history of African Americans is a long history of individual and collective striving against racism to express one's true self openly and without fear.

Recall from chapter 2 that the enslavement narratives reflect extensive black knowledge about white practices and institutions. Yet leading slaveholders would naïvely remark on how unreflective, ignorant, or irrational they thought enslaved people were. The contrasts between the black and the white views of slavery's oppression are great. The same is true for the legal segregation experience of black and white Americans. We will see in the next chapter how little white segregators and discriminators really understood about those they routinely subjugated and degraded. Writing in the early 1960s just before segregation began to crumble in the South, the savvy James Baldwin explained how such subjugation inadvertently created valuable resistance knowledge for African Americans:

> That man who is forced each day to snatch his manhood, his identity, out of the fire of human cruelty that rages to destroy it

knows, if he survives his effort, and even if he does not survive it, something about himself and human life that no school on earth—and, indeed, no church—can teach.[51]

By constantly countering this advanced human cruelty on the part of white Americans, most African Americans thus became quite knowledgeable and insightful about the character and contours of ongoing interracial interactions and about the panoply of burdens in the country's racist institutions.

African Americans, unknown to most whites, have commonly been major social theorists of their oppression. Thus, in one interview study, a black man nearly ninety years old made this probing comment about lessons gained from dealing with racist whites over many decades:

> The generality of black men is better than the generality of white men because the black men do not have to deny their civil natures. The best white men have told their brothers that they were wrong to live as they do....The decision to do wrong is a kind of chain too. They are prisoners and jailers too. To me, the knowledge that I am morally superior to white men is important.[52]

This man's deep insights have a prophetic ring, particularly his assessment of the historical consequences that today stem from long-term racial domination. In his penetrating view, oppression puts into question the morality of most whites. Like Frederick Douglass, he sees the damage done by systemic racism to whites, the heavy "chain" that "doing wrong" creates for the latter over centuries of time. Without a doubt, resistance to oppression begins in one's mind and must continue for a lifetime, however long that may be.

CONCLUSION

The importance and utility of the systemic racism perspective are again demonstrated in the many nuanced accounts of this chapter. Seen from this theoretical perspective, legal segregation from the 1870s to the 1960s was yet another manifestation of the country's longstanding and systemic racism. The ongoing structure of racial oppression during the legal segregation epoch was somewhat different in its details from that of slavery, but in fundamental ways it was similar. Again, the official segregation of the southern and border states and the informal segregation of the northern states were far more than a matter of white bigots abandoning supposedly egalitarian U.S. ideals and institutions, but rather they were about central economic, political, and other social institutions that were intentionally and systemically oppressive and antidemocratic. As under slavery, these institutions were highly exploitative, hierarchical, supremacist, and undemocratic. White elites, with their white subordinates, remained firmly in control of this post-slavery racial oppression. Routine racial domination continued to keep African Americans burdened down, attempting to subjugate them firmly, both physically and psychologically. Examining the everyday experiences of the black respondents in this chapter, we see that they, like their enslaved ancestors, regularly contended with violence and other coercion by white segregators attempting to enforce what was in effect a racially totalitarian system.

Throughout their nuanced accounts, those who suffered long and harshly under overt segregation provide insightful analyses of systemic racism. Collective memory is central to their accounts, as they make use of collectively gained knowledge from their communities in order to assess and survive the travails of official segregation. Like the enslaved Frederick Douglass, William Wells Brown, and Harriet Jacobs, they often examine the system of racism thoughtfully and deeply, again like social physicians with a sociological scalpel. Here, too, we see a theoretical framing of many racial issues from a level grounded in everyday experience. These conceptually sophisticated accounts describe the relations of subordination forced onto black Americans by white Americans, as well as the family and friendship relations that developed as they tried to negotiate and survive the legal apartheid of the South and the more informal segregation of the North. In these lucid commentaries, we observe unmistakably the group that does the racial oppression, the active white segregators and discriminators, as well as the targeted black group. Evident too is the enduring social reproduction process that constantly generates alienated racist relationships between the oppressed and the oppressors and embodies those relationships in the complex structures of systemic racism.

These eloquent respondents demonstrate that economic domination was central to U.S. apartheid, which indeed followed on the heels of the extreme exploitation of slavery. The economic exploitation of slavery was replaced under segregation by the near-slavery of sharecropping, tenant farming, debt peonage, and low-paid manual or domestic work. Almost all better paying jobs outside black communities were off-limits to African Americans. Whites generally benefited from higher wages, as well as from the exclusion of black workers from many jobs in workplaces and businesses. Segregation significantly reduced job competition for white workers. There was also an extensive and enforced system of racist etiquette that required African Americans to defer, often obsequiously, to whites in public and private settings. In the many areas of racial domination, whites also benefited greatly from the psychological wage of whiteness that gave them a strong sense of racial superiority like that of their white predecessors during the slavery period.

During the official segregation era, many whites routinely used violence, including beatings, lynchings, and property destruction, in order to keep black residents of rural and urban communities in their racialized "place." Such violence had material consequences and was experienced as physical and psychological terrorism by its targets. Such a severe impact is nowhere acknowledged in reflections on segregation in the accounts of whites we examine in the next chapter. The destructive impact of slavery on black families is replicated to a substantial extent under legal segregation. Rapes and attempted rapes of black girls and women by white men were commonplace, and many white men assumed they could take such coercive action with impunity. In the accounts segregated black female respondents, like the enslaved Harriet Jacobs and her many enslaved sisters, describe this added layer of oppression faced by black girls and women from recurring sexual violence at the hands of white men.

Moreover, without the support of extended families, however battered they might be, African Americans would not have survived slavery or legal segregation. White segregators generally miss—as did the famous enslavers Jefferson, Madison, and Washington—the great importance of family ties and support among African Americans. These families, as the black commentators show, were protective of their children and were training grounds where most black Americans were taught how to counter and cope with everyday oppression. The legal segregation accounts provide nuanced discussions of strategies of resistance, some parallel to the strategies of those enslaved. Some types of resistance to official segregation were defensive, as when African Americans used deception to conceal their feelings from probing employers or when they fled to hiding places to avoid violent whites. Concealing from whites their views about work or their desires for freedom likely had a liberating effect for the minds of many. Overt resistance included speaking out and, perhaps more commonly, fleeing to the North in hope of better treatment there. In the official segregation era, black resistance was still part of the dialectical character of racial oppression. Racial oppression routinely created patterns of protest and opposition, which in turn often generated a renewed countering and coercive response from whites.

As with those black Americans who were enslaved, those who were targeted by U.S. apartheid engaged in much thinking, reasoning, and planning. Such was required as everyday behavior just to survive the great burdens and costs of being rigidly segregated. In contrast, as we will see in chapter 5, during the legal segregation era, most whites rarely if ever perceived the black desire for, and insightful reflection on, freedom and liberty. During this period, black Americans continued to be major carriers of the celebrated U.S. values of equality and justice, much more so than most whites. Clearly, they thought a great deal about countering and resisting discrimination and about gaining freedom from oppression. They rooted their understandings and protest actions in deeply held, often intensely religious views of freedom and justice. One historian has underscored this point: "It is hard to imagine masses of people lining up for years of excruciating risk against southern sheriffs, fire hoses, and attack dogs without some transcendent or millennial faith to sustain them."[53] Their brave struggles in the 1950s and 1960s civil rights movement eventually liberated the entire society from the dead hand of official segregation.

During the slavery and official segregation epochs, many black Americans were able to develop a more insightful view of the present and future of systemic racism than virtually all white Americans. Black Americans developed deep insights into the impact of racism on black and white Americans. Writing about the troubled "souls of white folk," Du Bois made this sage comment about the state of racial segregation at the time U.S. government officials were working to bring peace after World War I:

> It is curious to see America, the United States, looking on herself, first, as a sort of natural peacemaker, then as a moral protagonist in this terrible time. No nation is less fitted for this role. For two or more centuries America has marched proudly in the van of human hatred—making bonfires of human flesh and laughing at them hideously, and making the insulting of millions more than a matter of dislike—rather a great religion, a world war-cry: Up white, down black; to your tents, O white folk, and world war with black and parti-colored mongrel beasts![54]

A white-controlled country in which thousands of African Americans had been brutally lynched and where millions of African Americans were severely oppressed was in his view in no position to be giving significant moral instruction to other countries around the globe.

The legal segregation era provided many painful contexts within which millions of African Americans had to develop deep insights about U.S. racism. Thus, even as he stood in the middle of a difficult but ultimately successful 1960s struggle against white segregationists, in the South and in the North, many of whom were trying to injure or kill him and destroy the civil rights movement, Dr. Martin Luther King, Jr., patiently explained why the social structure of official segregation had to be brought down. In reply to some moderate white clergy who counseled against more nonviolent protests as "untimely," in April 1963, King made this comment in a famous letter from the Birmingham jail where he had been imprisoned for protests against segregation:

> For years now I have heard the word "Wait!" It rings in the ear of every Negro with a piercing familiarity. This "Wait" has almost always meant "Never." We must come to see with the distinguished jurist of yesterday that "justice too long delayed is justice denied."[55]

5

LEGAL SEGREGATION:
THROUGH THE EYES OF WHITE AMERICANS

Directly or indirectly, Jim Crow segregation in the South, and its informal counterpart in the North, greatly affected the views and lives of most white Americans. During the decades from the 1870s to the 1960s, virtually all whites gained some racial privilege, varying degrees of economic assets, or access to social and cultural capital because African Americans were exploited, marginalized, or excluded. As they did during the slavery era, many whites in this period spent significant time interacting with African Americans. Thus, once again, we can ask: What generalizations did they make from this experience? What do their accounts tell us about the operation of systemic racism in the decades-long era of official segregation?

To answer these questions, I examine here the accounts and commentaries of numerous whites, both those with substantial power and those in the rank and file. These twentieth-century accounts and commentaries demonstrate not only the social fabric of whites' everyday lives at the individual level, but also how well-institutionalized racism remained in relation to white and black lives during this era. The lives and prosperity of the white majority were still rooted in or indirectly linked to the legal segregation system dominating southern and border

155

states or to the de facto segregation actively enforced in northern states. In chapter 4, I examined the experiential reports of African Americans about legal and de facto segregation that explicitly assessed most major dimensions of systemic racism. Interestingly, the white accounts and commentaries do not deal as explicitly or substantially with the array of dimensions of systemic racism. Generally speaking, these white accounts are much more limited in their revelations of how legal segregation worked on a quotidian basis.

As was the case for white slaveholders, a dimension of systemic racism often demonstrated in these accounts is the racist framing of the social world, a framing that includes the racial ideology substantially inherited from the slavery era. The framing of the world by whites who implement and maintain the system of racial oppression seems to require an ideology rationalizing oppression and legitimating the privileges and interests of whites as a group. In this era, white elites crafted and maintained not only extensive racial segregation—legally in southern and border states and informally in northern states—but also perpetuated and honed the white racial frame that defended white privilege and accented the supposed inferiority of those oppressed. As I will demonstrate, this white-racist framing of the societal world is extensive and reveals many links to earlier articulations of it by Jefferson, Madison, Washington, and others in the founding generation.

While those at the top of the racial ladder in U.S. society have generally played the greatest role in creating and maintaining this racist ideology, this construction and maintenance have taken place in ongoing interaction with the views and practices of most ordinary white citizens. The accounts from rank-and-file whites in this chapter reveal that the white-racist framing of the social world was popularly supported. While some commentators indicate, occasionally in detail, varying degrees of discomfort with racial segregation, like the slaveholders in chapter 3 they provide remarkably little analysis of the racialized institutions of legal segregation, particularly as those institutions shaped and benefited their lives and livelihoods, as well as those of their families and friends.

DEFENDING OFFICIAL SEGREGATION

Rewriting U.S. History to Legitimate Racism

Because racial oppression is foundational and systemic in the United States, most whites have been unable to see through the dominant legitimating ideology that has long defended it. Indeed, until the last decade or two, most white Americans in all regions of the country, including most historians, accepted the white southerner's view of the Civil War, of the Reconstruction era, and of the so-called Redemption period when the southern white elite took back power from democratic forces after Reconstruction.[1]

Interestingly, before the Civil War, many whites outside the South had complained of the excessive power, both economic and political, wielded by the southern elite, the white slaveholders—the societal control then called the "slave power." However, after the Civil War and a brief Reconstruction period, most whites in all regions soon came to accept not only the legal segregation imposed on African Americans in southern and border states, and informal segregation in the northern states, but also the racist ideas and myths often developed by southern whites to rationalize slavery and official segregation. During official segregation and for a time thereafter, the U.S. Civil War and Reconstruction were conceptualized mostly in terms of the often mythological southern white perspective. One scholar has summarized the matter thus:

> Having lost the trial of arms, the unrepentant South won the postbellum battle of ideas. From the early twentieth century until at least the mid-1960s, the general understanding of the causes of the war and the nature of Reconstruction was one provided almost entirely by pro-Southern historians. In the Southern revisionist account, the Civil War was a needless conflict, brought on by a tiny minority of fanatical and deluded abolitionists and by a "blundering generation" of politicians who failed to see that compromise was always within easy reach.[2]

For the most part, the white South also prevailed in its view of the need for rigid segregation of African Americans, at least up until the 1950s. Thus, included in the pervasive racist mythology was an extensive stereotyping of the supposedly "free" African Americans as still lazy, ignorant, dangerous, and threatening to whites, whose only option was to ruthlessly subordinate them in the racist system of Jim Crow segregation. In this ongoing racist ideology, legal segregation was necessary to "save" whites from the threats of black Americans.

Even today, many whites across the country still parrot many of the southern-derived myths about the history of slavery and legal segregation, views all too often associated with vigorous defenses of racial oppression in the U.S., past or present.

Southern Manifestos: Defending Racial Segregation

When racial discrimination in the United States is aggressively challenged or aggressively defended, we can often see better how it is actually structured and arranged. This is the case for official segregation. Beginning in the late 1950s, a slow movement to racial desegregation was forced on a mostly recalcitrant white South by an active, mostly black, civil rights movement and by the justice-oriented actions of a few federal agencies, including the U.S. Supreme Court in major desegregation decisions such as *Brown v. Board of Education* (1954). However, many whites in all regions were very disturbed by these pressures for and movements toward racial change. When African Americans stepped out of their traditional place in society, that action shook the foundation of white thought and white society.

Significantly, in a 1956 document officially known as the "Declaration of Constitutional Principles," and commonly called the "Southern Manifesto," most of the all-white southern delegation of U.S. senators and House members vigorously attacked the Supreme Court's 1954 school desegregation decision with this strong language: "The unwarranted decision of the Supreme Court in the public school cases is now bearing the fruit always produced when men substitute naked power for established law." Racially separate institutions, they further declared, "time and again, became a part of the life of the people of many of the States and confirmed their habits, traditions, and way of life."[3] This accent by some of the country's top political leaders on traditions and habits is an important element in their rationalization of systemic racism, and indeed in their white-centered orientation to the world. Amazingly enough, they then argued in this manifesto that white-black segregation "is founded on elemental humanity and commonsense, for parents should not be deprived by Government of the right to direct the lives and education of their own children." They, of course, meant *white* parents and children of the South, once again clearly revealing a racist framing that could only look at the societal world from the vantage point of white minds. There are many sincere fictions in their manifesto about the goodness and necessity of a racially segregated society, and indeed of the goodness of the white self. From atop the racial hierarchy, these white patriarchs do not seem to be aware of the extreme parochialism of their assertions, for a fifth of the southern population was African American at the time they wrote their defiant manifesto. The views of the latter receive no attention in the manifesto. This white-centered framing of the world is a clear indication of the distancing, separating, and alienating impact of systemic racism.

This white racial frame is narrowly constructed and extremely white centered. In the 1950s and 1960s, *Richmond News-Leader* editor James J. Kilpatrick took the position that the South had "a sense of oneness here, an identity, a sharing, and this quality makes the South unique." The South is a "state of mind." Significantly, he adds that a constant theme running through this state of mind is the "consciousness of the Negro."[4] Obviously, he really means the *white* southerner's state of mind. In his influential book, *The Southern Case for School Segregation*, Kilpatrick only notes briefly that when he speaks of the South he means the white South, adding that the reason is the "Negro South" is so "mysterious and incomprehensible to most white men."[5] Then he mostly ignores his own qualification and often writes paternalistically as though he is speaking for the entire South, white and black. In his commentaries and in similar antidesegregation sentiments by other white leaders of this era, the framing of issues is only in terms of the views and experiences of the white majority. At that point in southern history, there was no general "southern case" on any major racial matter, for most black southerners did not share this dreamy view of racial oneness, of a common southern identity, and of beneficent racial segregation. In the 1950s and 1960s, the majority of whites in the South and the North assumed the legitimacy of their racial position and did not view black Americans as people to be considered seriously for dramatically and comprehensively expanded economic, social, and political opportunities, much less for racial equality with white Americans.

As we observed in accounts from black Americans in the last chapter, this era of legal segregation was one that brought antiblack discrimination and exclusion not only in the economic realm but in most other societal arenas. Public accommodations were a major area of recurring discrimination. Thus, white business owners like the celebrated Lester Maddox, who later became governor of Georgia in part because of his stand against racial desegregation, aggressively defended their right to keep black customers out of their businesses. Writing in 1975, a decade after he closed his restaurant rather than integrate it, Maddox makes this comment:

> I believed then, as I do now, that it was my right under the Constitution to serve whomever I chose to serve in my place of business. I am a segregationist and I chose to operate my restaurant on a segregated basis. Because of this I was called a racist, although the words are far from synonymous. A segregationist is an individual—black, white, or any other color—who has

enough racial pride and racial integrity and love for his fellow
human beings to want to see all races protected and preserved.[6]

Like most whites of his era, Maddox presumes to speak for the social interests of black Americans without consulting them. Throughout
the 1960s, a great many whites, including influential political and business leaders like Maddox, remained vigorous supporters of racial segregation. While some later changed their public views, many others
remained intransigent well after the 1960s. Note in this comment the
distinction that Maddox makes between a "segregationist" and a "racist,"
which suggests that even someone committed to excluding black people
from public accommodations, and thus keeping them "in their place,"
did not want to see himself viewed as "a racist." Here is an example of
a sincere fiction in whites' racial framing of society, for many whites
wished to see even their discriminatory actions as something good and
not to be regretted.

In the numerous states with legal segregation, most of the white
leaders and most rank-and-file whites supported the rigid hierarchy of
segregation. In his first inaugural address as Alabama governor in 1963,
the influential George Wallace made a widely quoted commitment to
racial segregation that then represented the views of a majority of whites
in southern and border states, and large numbers of whites elsewhere as
well. Wallace first says that he is standing where the Confederacy was
born, then adds:

> It is very appropriate that from this Cradle of the Confederacy,
> this very Heart of the Great Anglo-Saxon Southland…we sound
> the drum for freedom.…I draw the line in the dust and toss
> the gauntlet before the feet of tyranny…and I say…segregation
> now…segregation tomorrow…segregation forever.[7]

In this white framing of the racial world "freedom" means, then as now,
the freedom for whites to stereotype and subordinate black Americans
and other people of color as whites see fit.

Maintaining whites' segregation from blacks was the prized goal
of many in the southern white elite into the late 1960s. Even after a
bombing on the University of Alabama campus near the dorm where
the only black student, Vivian Malone, was staying, Governor Wallace
replied to a request from a university administrator to help stop the
bombing by asking: How long would it take "to get the nigger bitch"
out of the university?[8] Significantly, he expressed no concern whatever for the white-terrorist violence or for the pain and safety of the
black student. Indeed, Wallace often referred to African Americans as

"niggers," and even called Senator Edward W. Brooke—the only African American in the U.S. Senate since Reconstruction—the "nigger senator from Massachusetts." Into the 1970s, even when he had come to accept desegregation and moderated greatly his "segregation forever" stance, Wallace would still talk privately in blatantly racist terms about "the big nigger vote" or about "nigger talk."[9]

Throughout their public discussions—and private comments, insofar as we have accounts—these white leaders showed little or no evidence of understanding the extremely oppressed lives of those across the still-rigid color line. Social alexithymia is quite evident throughout most white commentaries in this chapter.

Collusion in Official Segregation

For many Americans who look back on the official segregation era, the white insistence on rigid racial segregation, and white opposition to desegregation, are usually seen as distinctive of the South, while whites in the North are viewed as mostly supporters of dismantling racial apartheid. Yet, the majority of whites in northern states colluded in the persistence of official segregation in the southern and border states, and they also insured that informal racial segregation was the general rule in the North. Indeed, a majority of whites in the North shared many of the stereotyped views of white southerners about African Americans. This was true from the beginning of legal segregation in the South. In 1884, not long after legal segregation had begun to spread across the southern and border states, Albion Tourgee, a perceptive white abolitionist who had lived in the North and the South, noted that white northerners "have always reflected the Southern idea of the negro in everything except as to his natural right to be free."[10]

For most of the official segregation era, U.S. presidents were among those whites who held very negative views of African Americans. Just as legal segregation was beginning to spread to every nook and cranny of southern and border states, the supposedly "progressive" Theodore Roosevelt made it clear that he was obsessed with categorizing all people in terms of race. Over many years of racial analysis in his writings, Roosevelt accented "stronger" and "weaker" races, placing black Americans in the latter category as a "perfectly stupid race."[11] He saw blacks as "kept down as much by lack of intellectual development as anything else," indeed far more than "all the acts of oppression of white men put together."[12] These comments were from a president whom many whites actually saw as too liberal because he occasionally consulted with moderate black leaders like Booker T. Washington. However, the hypocrisy of such contacts could be seen in Roosevelt's expressed vision of the Republican party as a "white man's party."

Another "progressive" president and Princeton history professor, Woodrow Wilson, argued that U.S. slavery was a good civilizing process for black Americans and that Ku Klux Klan violence against black Americans had been necessary during the Reconstruction era. Wilson, who loved to tell racist "darky" jokes about black Americans, placed outspoken segregationists in his cabinet and viewed racial "segregation as a rational, scientific policy."[13] Until at least the 1970s, most subsequent presidents seemed to share some of these antiblack views. For example, President Harry Truman referred to the black member of Congress, Adam Clayton Powell, Jr., as "that damn nigger preacher," though he later would desegregate the U.S. Armed Forces.[14] About the time that the modern civil rights movement began, no less a figure than the esteemed military leader and president, Dwight D. Eisenhower, often revealed his racist views in private. He loved to tell "nigger jokes" and had racially segregated facilities on the train he used for campaigning as president.[15] Earl Warren, then U.S. Chief Justice, recounted that Eisenhower told him at a dinner in 1954 that white southerners opposing school desegregation were "not bad people. All they are concerned about is to see that their sweet little girls are not required to sit in school alongside some big overgrown Negroes."[16] By stereotyping ordinary schoolboys as "big overgrown Negroes," Eisenhower conjures up scary images of black boys and men (perhaps implying criminals) that we see in other white accounts. In his conversation, Eisenhower apparently did not note the painful impact on black boys and girls of the frequently violent white opposition to desegregation.

Likely putting his racist ideas into action, President Eisenhower gave passive support to white southerners' fierce opposition to legal segregation, especially in the public schools: "Not once during those six years [after the 1954 Brown decision] would Eisenhower publicly support the ruling; not once would he say that Brown was morally right, or that segregation was morally wrong."[17] Eisenhower took no public stand even in regard to the need for the federal government to enforce the Supreme Court's Brown decision. Here we see connections between racist practices in one area, such as in segregated education, and the supportive racist action or inaction in another institutional area, such as the federal executive branch. Such conspicuous connections illustrate the commanding role of government in creating and reinforcing the "race" category and the laws buttressing that categorization, a point underscored well by racial formation theorists like Michael Omi and Howard Winant.

Officials at all government levels—federal, state, and local—played an important role in supporting blatant segregation in the South and the North. Thus, the accounts of African Americans in chapter 4 indicate that local law enforcement authorities were often on the side of white segregators. And we see the racist thinking and action of *leading* members of Congress in the aforementioned "Southern Manifesto" and in the hostile reactions of southern governors like George Wallace to desegregation efforts. During the era of blatant segregation, these government officials helped to imbed racist thinking ever more firmly in many white minds and in white inclinations to take discriminatory action against African Americans.

WHITE VIOLENCE BEHIND SEGREGATION

Teaching Violence to Youth

When many whites talk about the official segregation era, they often reveal its white-dominated reality in an oblique fashion—such as in accounts that focus more on white settings and actions than on the experiences of black Americans. Thus, in his revealing autobiography of growing up white in the South, Melton McLaurin records the routine taunting and harassing of black youth and adults that white boys engaged in. White boys would often throw blocks of granite or shoot BB guns at black children.[18] McLaurin notes that the parents of these white boys rarely objected to such violently discriminatory behavior. Evidently, this parental inaction taught his friends that routine violence against black residents was acceptable. Such a parental response likely caused a hardening of the racist framing of the social world among white children, a framing of white superiority and black inferiority that might lead as they grew older to yet more violent attacks against black men and women, including the thousands of lynchings that took place during the Jim Crow era.

Enforcing Legal and Customary Segregation with Violence

The everyday norms of racial segregation were backed up by a constant threat of violence. If African Americans stepped out of line in a way that offended whites, the hierarchical structure of segregation was regularly maintained with the threat or reality of violence, often of an extreme kind. Many white men saw their racial-gender role as one of keeping black people subordinated in "their place." For example, in 1949 in Montgomery, Alabama, two black teenagers from New Jersey got on a public bus and sat in the front because they were unfamiliar with southern segregation laws. The white bus driver used his gun to force them off the bus and called the police, who kept them in jail for two days before they were released.[19]

Even a small slight to a white man or woman could end in injury or death for a black person. According to one white observer of southern patterns writing in the late 1950s, the racist code of etiquette prescribed that a black person should

> [n]ever assert or even intimate that a white person may be lying. Never impute dishonourable intentions to a white person. Never suggest that the white is of an inferior class. Never lay claim to, or overtly demonstrate, superior knowledge or intelligence. Never curse a white person. Never laugh derisively at a white person. Never comment upon the physical attractiveness of a white person of the opposite sex.[20]

Thus, when whites heard that a black man in one Mississippi county was violating this code with "big talk," ten of them went to his house, forced him out, and began shooting at him. When the man's cousin fired back in self-defense, the cousin was arrested and sentenced to jail time. Moreover, in 1946 in Atlanta, Georgia, a black military veteran called out to a black friend on a local streetcar, saying that his friend should "Straighten up and fly right." The white driver, thinking he had been the target of the remark, shot and killed the black veteran. When the driver was taken to court for a hearing, the white judge released him in a courtroom filled with threatening Ku Klux Klan members.[21] Whites could enforce racial customs with little concern for punishment.

One white man interviewed in Natchez, Mississippi, describes this response to a black man questioning his accounting record that showed some shoes had been bought:

> He claimed that he hadn't bought them but I told him someone must have bought them on his account....He got mad and said I was lying and I hauled off and hit him in the mouth and cut my finger. He then started to hit me and someone ran up and hit him. He turned to the other fellow and chased him down in the cellar. When the nigger came out of the cellar he was the bloodiest thing I ever saw, there must have been fifty people who took a poke at him.[22]

Black questioning of white bookkeeping was met with extreme violence at the hands of dozens of whites, and there is no sense here or in similar white recountings of the immorality and larger impact of such crimes of violence against African Americans.

Another white man in the same southern city describes extreme white violence targeting African Americans as more or less routine:

We often have to whip one of them around here who gets too uppity or insolent or does something....You may have noticed that tall yellow Negro....We whipped him one time till I thought he would die, we laid it on so.[23]

The whipped man's offense was to phone a white prostitute in the hearing of white men. In both cases, using extreme violence to "discipline" black residents was viewed as legitimate in the white-racist framing of society in many areas of the southern and border states. Violent enforcement of the normative environment was perpetrated by many whites, not just by a few deviants on the fringe of communities. This differential pattern of violence in the official segregation epoch, including beatings of African Americans for alleged "disobedience" or "insolence," was a societal reproduction of antiblack violence that began during the slavery era as a way of attempting to keep those oppressed from assertive protest and rebellion.

Vigilantism and Lynchings

In chapter 4, I discussed briefly the thousands of brutal lynchings perpetrated by whites against black Americans over the many decades of legal segregation—and occasionally since the end of that segregation in the 1960s. If the alleged violation by a black person of white understandings of custom or law was great enough, whites created vigilante groups that killed African Americans by means of bloody lynchings. Note too that many lynchings were unrelated to the actions of the black targets, but were just intended to show local black residents of an area that they must always stay in "their place."[24]

Lynchings often played out as an extremely bloody and sadistic ritual. For example, this white man's account from the 1940s involved a black man who was accused of trying to rape a white woman:

I ain't tellin' nobody just what we done to that nigger but we used a broken bottle just where it'd do the most damage, and any time you want to see a nigger ear all you gotta do is go to see old man Smith and ast him for a peep at one....Yes, ma'am, we done things I never knowed could be done and things I certainly ain't mentionin' to no lady.[25]

After being cut on, the black victim was burned alive, with this ending: "And then the groanin' got lower and lower and finely it was just little gasps and then it wasn't nothin' a tall." Then the mob tied him to a tree and left him there.

Such violent attacks on black Americans were not rare in southern and border states. When asked about lynchings in her southern town, one white woman recalls a typical 1916 lynching when she was young:

> Lynchings were not uncommon. In that the law was not always able to control them or they didn't try hard enough or something....I remember there had been a lynching and among the whites the story was that the blacks were going to come forward and show that they were not going to put up with this sort of thing. My father thought well there will be a war between the whites and the blacks....There were three colored men that these white men got together and they hung them. My father was very worried because he thought that the blacks would react to this and there would be real trouble...a young man came and took us to [another city]. But there wasn't any trouble.[26]

It is significant that the event that sparked this lynching of three black men (plus two black women, who are not even mentioned here) was a shooting of an armed white deputy sheriff who had banged on the door of a black man's house late at night. When the black assailant could not be found, a large crowd of whites lynched five other black residents, alleging they had helped him to escape.[27] In this interview, neither the white interviewer nor the white respondent discussed the extraordinarily threatening and painful impact of these violent actions on the local black community. We only get, once again, a sense of whites' concern for some black retaliation for the lynchings. To the present day, the southern area where the lynching took place is called "Lynch Hammock" and is still remembered for its violent past in the local black community.

WHITE MYTHS AND MISCONCEPTIONS

The Myth of "Good Race Relations"

White commentators present a number of interpretative themes in their white-centered framing of the racial segregation era. For example, in the "Southern Manifesto," the South's powerful political leadership asserted the hoary myth of "good race relations" in the South. As they announced, the pressure for racial desegregation

> is destroying the amicable relations between the white and Negro races that have been created through 90 years of patient effort by

the good people of both races. It has planted hatred and suspicion where there has been heretofore friendship and understanding.[28]

This "amicable relations" notion is one of the important sincere fictions that whites clung to vigorously under official segregation. The usually sincere mythology of white superiority included a number of related illusory conceptions. In his autobiography of growing up white in a North Carolina town, historian Melton McLaurin has commented on the contradictory character of whites' actions toward black residents. He has suggested that white arguments that whites

> …enjoyed warm personal relationships with individual blacks cannot be easily dismissed.…My experiences as a youth, however, indicate that whites believed blacks inferior but at the same time responded to them as individuals on an emotional level that contradicted, at least temporarily, their racist assumptions.[29]

What McLaurin misses here is that these constructions of "warm" relationships with black residents were only from a white point of view. It is likely that what whites saw as warm and kind treatment was frequently seen differently, indeed as paternalistic, if not threatening, by its black recipients.

In interview studies, many whites who lived under official segregation recall what they still see as the "good race relations" of that era. For example, in a recent interview, one white southerner in his seventies recalls the racialized patterns of farm life in positive terms:

> I was raised on a farm…and we grew vegetables and tobacco, corn, and things like that. We had a colored family living on the farm, and, they worked with us and helped us gather vegetables and tobacco and things like that…sometimes my father would trade with them on a half crop. They did the labor, and we furnished the fertilizer and seed and the mules to plow them with. Each year we made out a new contract, not in writing, but it was verbal. And they had colored kids, and usually a man and his wife, and the entire family worked in the field, as my family did.[30]

While he accents the friendly and cooperative relations, this man does allude in passing to the racial hierarchy in the rural scheme of economic exploitation. As we have also seen in chapter 4, the habitual exploitation of African Americans as sharecroppers, tenant farmers, and farm workers was characteristic of farming in the Jim Crow era and often took a form not far removed from similar arrangements under slavery.

Leading white planters perhaps benefited the most from this entrenched and routinized exploitation, as they insisted on getting much
low-wage labor. Indeed, one wealthy planter, Walter Clark, made a rare
acknowledgement of the heavy dependence of white planters on black
tenant farmers and laborers. Clark, then president of the Mississippi
Cotton Association, once put it this way: "Every dollar I own those
Negroes made for me. Our ancestors chased them down and brought
them here."[31] The relations of material exploitation were central to the
black and white experience in rural areas and thus created profit or other income for many whites, especially those in the upper and middle
classes. At the core of the relations of exploitation under legal segregation was continuing unjust enrichment (however modest that might
be for some working-class whites) for each new generation of whites
and a corresponding unjust impoverishment for each new generation of
blacks. What were portrayed as "good race relations" for and by whites
were usually extremely oppressive for blacks.

Interestingly, a white male respondent quoted previously also comments in his interview on everyday interactions between whites and
blacks in a farming area:

> So we all worked together, and we didn't have any problems
> at all. But things were hard. We didn't have much money. The
> main thing we worked for was food to keep ourselves going and
> sustain the animals and things that we had....But we had differ-
> ent families from time to time to move on our farm, and they
> did the same thing—we worked together. They were quite close,
> really, because we didn't have the facilities to travel around and
> that kind of thing. So it was a pretty close-knit situation. Dad
> killed a hog, he'd give them half of it or something like that...we
> just furnished the house. Then the trade, dad always called it
> the "half crop" situation. They would help us gather, and we
> would too, and dad would split the money with the tenants.
> And I don't know, it was tough living.[32]

He remembers the tough living for all, the "working together," and
his father sharing with the black family. His detailed portrait is one of
good relations where whites and blacks got along well, with no "problems at all." Again, there is no hint here of the extreme hardship that racial segregation imposed on black families, in addition to hardship that
went with difficult economic times, nor is empathy expressed for the
blatant discrimination and racialized pain they suffered in most areas
of their everyday lives. This is not unusual, for the mainstream white

framing of the world of legal segregation almost never includes any empathetic understanding of the devastating impact of the color line.

This respondent further recalls the variable patterns in socializing between white and black children:

> It really was, but as far as being real close with them, we didn't associate with them in that way, in activities....Yeah, yeah we played. Of course the larger we got, we didn't really associate with them very much, other than riding on the wagon, going and coming from the field and that kind of thing. As far as going down to their house, or the kids coming up to our house, it didn't happen.[33]

During the official segregation era, young white children were frequently allowed by their parents to play with young black children, typically on more equal terms than would exist as they got older. Just before puberty, however, these play relationships were usually ended by white adults. Virtually without exception, the racial hierarchy, with its barely hidden racial-sexual implications, was rigidly imposed by parents in these southern areas as the white and black children got older.

Learning the Color Line

In spite of its many brutal and bloody aspects, most older whites recall the era of legal segregation mostly in positive and neutral terms—in fact as not being especially burdensome for black Americans. Thus, one white woman near ninety, a member of an old plantation family, offers memories of blacks sitting at the back of the bus: "I don't think that the white people just were cruel to them and made them do that."[34] She then reiterates this point. Here we detect an inability on the part of a white person to remember, or apparently to understand, the cruelty of segregation's racist arrangements and strongly etched racial hierarchy. Her racist framing of that societal world includes an exonerating rationalization, for whites are viewed as good even as they discriminate against black Americans.

Many interviews with ordinary whites that touch on legal segregation seem to focus on what they remember when they were children or adolescents. Racist teachings by parents and other important adults imbed negative ideas and emotions in children, as we see in this account from a retired white-collar worker who details what her mother told her as a child in order to secure her obedience:

> The niggers would come in the night and steal us away and use us for their pleasure, that's what my mother told us.....I think

she must have done that to make us behave. It worked; she scared us to death. The first time I ever saw a colored person I just about had hysterics. And there he was, right in front of the door to the shop we were going shopping at. I remember him as an absolutely huge black man, menacing and very frightening. I burst into tears and would not go into that store.[35]

Interviewed some decades later, this woman added that she is still uncomfortable when near a black man. For systemic racism to persist, children must be taught by adults and their peers the white framing of the world; that is, how to be racist in their views and actions directed at racial outgroups. Childhood socialization is an integral part of the social reproduction process for a system of racism.

In the few interview studies that we have for whites who lived for a significant time under legal segregation, only a handful talk about their involvement in or enforcement of the extensive racial etiquette of segregation, especially as adults of any age. Instead, they tend to accent events during their younger years. For example, looking back on that era, one articulate white woman recounted an event after school in Miami in the 1940s, where all facilities were segregated, including the public schools. One day she decided to wave down a certain bus when she was going home from school. The white driver had a shocked look:

Every passenger on the nearly full bus was black, and all were looking at me....When I got home, I told my mother about the nice Negro lady and what the Negro man had said. My mother said, "Florida is a southern state, so it's segregated, and you got on a Negro bus."[36]

Apparently, like most white adults in this era, the child's mother did not discuss with her the impact of this racial segregation on black Floridians.

Another white woman has written about a summer when she was a three-year-old child growing up in the 1930s in southern Illinois, which was then segregated much like the South. Walking down the street, she saw black people coming toward her and stepped off the sidewalk to allow them to pass, but was reprimanded: "'You don't get off for them. They get off for you.'"..."'Why?'" I asked...."'Because they are coloreds.'" I returned to the walkway and craned my neck to see the people as they stepped onto the street. "Don't stare at those dirty people."[37]

For white and black children, the lessons learned about the way of responding to customary or legal segregation in settings such as public streets and accommodations were usually learned at a young age, here at

about three years old. Note that the rationale given to a white child includes negative, almost visceral stereotyping about black "dirtiness," yet
another feature of a racist framing of the world. Essential to being an oppressor under segregation, as under slavery, was an ingrained inability
to understand the intense anguish and recurring pain of those who were
oppressed. We see in the accounts of whites reflecting on their childhood experiences with official and informal segregation that part of the
process of training white youngsters to be antipathetic and alexithymic
involved teaching them not to identify with those oppressed. The oppressed others are "not like us," and are thus inferior and to be avoided.
White youngsters learn that African Americans are so different that they
need not empathize with them or their white-imposed problems.

Memories Critical of Segregation

Like a few Quaker leaders in the founding era, some whites were critical
of legal segregation during its long years, or at least look back on that era
sensitively or critically when they are interviewed today. For example,
reflecting on legal segregation, one white respondent who grew up in a
southern state today brings to mind his childhood:

> I will tell you some generalities from a perspective of a child,
> because you remember I was not an adult, and so anything that
> was done against African American people, I was not involved
> in anything. I was a child going to school…and growing up,
> everything was segregated. I remember water fountains that
> said "white" and "colored," and bathrooms that said "white" and
> "colored." That's just the way it was. And if you asked about [it],
> well "That's just the right thing to do. It's the right thing for the
> races to be separated." And a child doesn't question things like
> that. So you grow up, and all your life you hear that this is the
> way things have always been, this is the right way to do things,
> and it's not until you start getting close to adulthood that you
> may begin to question things. So these are the things that I'd
> heard from friends, relatives, and so forth.[38]

We get a sense here of the rigidity and normality of segregation's customs and laws, again viewed just from the white perspective. White adults
rationalized systemic racism with the moral language of what was "right
to do." This reflective respondent makes a point of noting that as a child he
was "not involved in anything" and suggests some things that were "done
against African Americans." White children were taught early about the
racial etiquette of everyday segregation, and most rarely questioned their

relatives and friends who taught them. Even now, most whites do not question their own collaboration in the segregative etiquette. This same respondent adds that segregative ideas and actions were

> ...a part of a lot of people's lives, but I was just insulated from it, and I think [for] most people in the South at that time, it was something that just didn't come up. The African American community did things their way, and the white people did the things they wanted to, and there just wasn't that much contact between [them]. It really didn't play a part of my life at all.[39]

Like most whites, especially children, he did not see at the time the white privilege all around him. Being a white child meant that the systemic racism seemed normal. His phrase "most people" refers, of course, to most white people, and blacks are of course not envisioned in the comment about racial issues not coming up when he was younger. Even where there is some critical sensitivity, it is almost always framed from the white point of view. In these white interviews, we sense a reluctance to talk about the oppressiveness of racial segregation, or the respondents' likely roles in enforcing that segregation when they were younger.

When interviewed today, some older whites will acknowledge, if usually briefly, that legal segregation was problematical or morally wrong. One southerner now in his sixties has recently recalled that

> the racial atmosphere was pretty bad, frankly. [Long pause] The general attitude was that African Americans were socially inferior, and their place was in the fields and doing domestic work and coming in the back door. One was not to sit down at the table and eat with them, none of that.[40]

Again we see that the racist etiquette was normative and insistent in its separating and alienating relations, with black Americans put firmly in "their place." This man certainly remembers the racial atmosphere as "pretty bad." His long pause suggests perhaps that he finds reflection on this oppressive past rather difficult even today.

In an insightful moment, another white southerner recently remembers his grandparents' actions and orientations during the official segregation era:

> And the irony of it was that they ran a...cleaning business here in town, and most of their help and most of the people that worked for them—they even had a black...cleaning business on the other side of the tracks, three blocks from them. And they had set those people up in business as a satellite operation. You

know…the irony of it is that they had such a great warmth. But it was like when they went home at night, they went home to their own world and their culture or whatever, and that crossing of the tracks thing…there was a disconnect there. And that maybe typifies a lot about this community, and maybe not just about us, but about so many communities in the South where you get that perspective of "Oh there's nothing wrong here. I don't dislike 'Johnnie May' or…or 'Elijah,' or whatever you know. They're good people…as long as they're over there, as long as we have this arm's length kind of relationship."[41]

These last sentences note the white adults' framing of the world, with its commonplace rationalizations of extensive segregation as friendly, normal, and natural. As long as African Americans kept to their alienated position of racial deference, whites usually felt secure, and the long-term structure of entrenched and pervasive segregation could be easily preserved. Each person, white or black, young or old, was supposed to know his or her place in the cruel arrangements of racial apartheid. We see how white adults maintained a thoroughly racist system with its harsh reality of separate and alienated social worlds and an elaborate racist etiquette for all. Whites who enforced this devastating and comprehensive segregation were usually "good" or "warm" people, especially to their kin and friends. Racial oppression was, and still is, executed and imposed by otherwise normal human beings.

Writing in 1949 at the peak of the legal segregation era, the outspoken liberal white southerner, Lillian Smith, once noted that, "From the day I was born, I began to learn my lessons."[42] The racial lessons were about systemic racism and its required etiquette. Her mother and father taught her how to pray at night and then how to keep black people in their place the next day. Thinking critically about the oppressiveness of segregation, Smith has provided an example of how these lessons were taught: One day, some white women saw that a new black family in their Florida town included what looked to be a white child, who was playing in front of a home in the black section. The whites grabbed the child, and Lillian Smith's mother took her in for a time. The child played, slept, and ate with the rest of Lillian's family until the town's whites discovered that they had made a mistake, for the phenotypically "white" child was indeed "black" under the white-racist rule that anyone with known black ancestry was legally "black." The child was quickly taken back to her original home in the black community. When the young Lillian asked why the child could not stay, her mother replied curtly: "You're too young to understand. And don't ask me again, ever again, about this!"[43] In Smith's account we again observe white children learning the racist etiquette and being reprimanded for asking a pertinent question about it.

In her pained recounting, Smith recalls having to tell her new friend that she could not stay because she was "not white," and then concludes thus:

> I knew my father and mother whom I passionately admired had betrayed something which they held dear. And they could not help doing it. And I was shamed by their failure and frightened....There was something Out There that was stronger than they and I could not bear to believe it.[44]

Smith was rare among whites of the era in her ability to sense that something was unjust and to perceive that the "Out There" of segregation was so overwhelming that even her honorable parents could not resist it. Later in life, she came to fully understand that the distorted structure "we have put around every Negro child from birth is around every white child also."[45] Very few southern whites ever verbalized the way in which the system of racism distorted the lives of whites as well as blacks.

Yet, even Smith, the liberal observer, does not comment on the great pain—even terror—that this "black" child was likely going through during her abduction from, and then too speedy return to, her family of origin. It was extremely difficult for whites to even begin to understand the conditions and experiences of black Americans, young or old, during the eras of slavery and segregation. In Smith's accounts of her life experience, we see much sympathy for the conditions of African Americans, but relatively little attempt to understand empathetically what life was like on the other side of color line. Social alexithymia seems to have affected virtually all whites living under the extreme social arrangements of Jim Crow segregation.

RATIONALIZING OPPRESSION: AGGRESSIVE ARGUMENTS AND POWERFUL EMOTIONS

Recall from chapter 1 that over the course of U.S. history, white Americans, and most centrally the white elites, have developed a strong racial frame to defend systemic racism and to assert that racial privileges for whites are earned and are thus meritorious. As part of this racial framing, whites in various social classes have constantly alleged the racial inferiority of those whom they oppress. This white framing includes much misinformation about and neglect of historical realities. Thus, virtually all U.S. high-school textbooks that discuss the legacy of

Thomas Jefferson view it as exclusively or primarily one of the great ideals of equality and "liberty and justice for all." However, there is another less noted, but at least as important, legacy of Jefferson: The extensive white racial frame, including an aggressively racist ideology, which Jefferson developed in the *Notes on the State of Virginia*, his letters, and other commentaries.

Recall that Jefferson's racist ideology rationalizes oppression by defining superior and inferior racial groups that allegedly deserve their places in society. White elites have maintained or refurbished the system of racism at each critical juncture in U.S. history, and they have usually been the central players in developing essential defenses and rationalizations for that oppressive system. This was certainly true for the legal segregation era. On occasion, white historians and other commentators have tended to exculpate the educated elites and to blame the development of racist categorizations mainly or entirely on ordinary whites. Thus, in his early 1900s book on the segregated South, prominent white journalist Ray Stannard Baker, considered a liberal, argued that the "tragedy of the Negro is the colour of his skin.... The human tendency is to class people together by outward appearances." He adds that the classification is "not so much drawn by the highly intelligent white man" as by the ordinary white person.[46] Here, as elsewhere in his book-length analysis, the otherwise perceptive Baker blames much of the problem of systemic racism on less-educated whites or on whites generally.

Visceral Rejections of Equality: Fears of "Mongrelization"

Nowhere is the hierarchical and alienated character of systemic racism more visible than in the extreme views that many whites have held, in the past and in the present, about "racial mixing." Strong ideas about and emotions against white-black sexual relations and marriage were evident as early as the mid-seventeenth-century colonial laws against such relationships. During the founding generation, white leaders were strongly opposed to such mixing. Benjamin Franklin, like Jefferson and numerous others, argued that white "amalgamation with the other color produces a degradation to which no lover of his country, no lover of excellence in the human character can innocently consent."[47] This view has long been a centerpiece of a racial framing of this society.

During the era of official segregation, powerful whites had the greatest ability to publicize racist stereotypes and understandings about this and other racial matters, though rank-and-file whites also circulated and extended the pervasive racist ideology. When they discussed official segregation and its everyday patterns, white leaders in the South and elsewhere periodically accented white superiority and related racist themes. Thus, during the 1930s Great Depression, one white member of the U.S. Congress made this comment about giving black Americans political equality: "Political equality means social equality and social equality means intermarriage, and that means the mongrelizing of the American race....I cannot and will not be a party to the recognition of the Fourteenth and Fifteenth Amendments."[48]

We observe here themes that white leaders and rank-and-file citizens, in the South and the North, frequently espoused during official segregation. Even the U.S. Constitution was not legitimate if it was interpreted to protect black civil rights. Here too is a great concern that political equality for African Americans will lead to "mongrelizing" the "American race." Sexual fears and stereotypes are just beneath the surface. Also conspicuous here in the white-racist framing is the notion that the "American race" is ideally white.

Two decades later, in the 1950s, the famous U.S. Senator James Eastland of Mississippi, then chair of the powerful Senate Subcommittee on Internal Security, strongly articulated a similar concern in this regard:

> I believe in white supremacy, and as long as I am in the Senate I expect to fight for white supremacy, because I can see that if the amalgamation of whites and Negroes in this country is permitted, there will be a mongrel race, and there will come to pass the identical condition under which Egypt, India, and other civilizations decayed....The cultural debt of the colored peoples to the white race is such as to make the preservation of the white race a chief aim of the colored, if these latter but understood their indebtedness.[49]

This white patriarch is openly supremacist and concedes no power to black Americans, who in his view are not really citizens. He views racial amalgamation as a threat to the purity of the white "race," which is seen as a white family. Similarly, after his first election as governor of Alabama in the 1960s, George Wallace told a teacher that children mixing in desegregated schools will "result in...intermarriage of the races, and our race will be deteriated [sic] to that of the mongrel complexity."[50] As late as the 1950s and 1960s, numerous white political and business leaders openly espoused a white supremacist viewpoint that expressed not only a substantial concern for racial "amalgamation," but also that such mixing would lead to a decline in "American civilization."

White Obsessions and Fears of Black Sexuality

One of the strongest stereotypes carried in the white racial frame has long been a grossly exaggerated, even wild, image of black male and female sexuality. This image has often been reproduced in recurring conversations and discussions among whites, as Melton McLaurin recounts in this incident when he was a young boy in a North Carolina town. A white man pointed out to him an older black man who was said by whites to be a "ladies' man," and McLaurin replied that the latter did not look the part. The white man continued:

> Well, boy, that just goes to show you that looks can be deceiving. They say that old devil's got a dick a foot long....Drives them nigger women wild, that's what they say. Them women practically stand in line to get some of it.

McLaurin adds that white men in this town linked this oversexed male imagery to another illusion, that of the "black rapist," who "personified the white man's belief, and his fear, that the secret desire of every black male was to ravish every white female."[51]

The stereotyping of black men as sexual threats to whites accelerated during the era of official segregation, probably as a way of rationalizing white violence, such as the commonplace lynchings, that targeted black men:

> Scholars agree that the most virulent racist ideology about black male sexuality emerged in the decades that followed the Civil War, and some historians have recognized that the lynching of black men for the alleged rape of white women was comparatively rare in the South under slavery.[52]

In addition, the gendered racism that most whites directed at black women routinely viewed them as having "jungle bunny" sexual desires and procreative abilities. White men viewed this as not only acceptable, but enticing. In his autobiography, McLaurin further notes some of the white men's salacious and vicious comments on black women that they would pass in the street: "That nigger'll fuck anything that walks, boy. Half the damned nigger women in this town's pregnant. That's the thing they do best, I reckon, have younguns. Niggers breed like rabbits, son."[53] White men often carried their speculations about black sexuality to this extreme level. Stetson Kennedy, who has written the best overview book on what legal segregation was like, reports this amazing comment that a white lawyer made to him when he was writing the book: "We must never put any restrictions on the sex life of blacks, because that is what keeps them too exhausted to protest about anything."[54]

Some scholars have suggested that this white male preoccupation with black sexuality, with its crude racist imagery, reflects deep psychological problems growing in part out of the white male role in the sexual coercion of black men and women during slavery and legal segregation.[55] Moreover, as I noted in chapter 3, for centuries most white men have viewed themselves as "virtuous republicans," as religious, moral, and civilized. Early white male colonists portrayed European Americans as rational, ascetic, and sexually controlled, while black Americans and Native Americans were stereotyped as uncivilized, hedonistic, irrational, and happy-go-lucky.[56] As was the case for the founding generation, white men who have expressed such views since that early era are likely reflecting the longings of whites for greater personal freedom, happiness, and hedonism in their own lives. Their views, of course, do not accurately reflect the dominant experiences and responses of most African Americans, for whom worry, sadness, pain, and grief have been the common experiences and emotions imposed by omnipresent oppression.

Indeed, for centuries now, many whites have revealed themselves as preoccupied with African Americans in ways suggesting deep antiblack feelings and major psychological obsessions. For example, Governor George Wallace, as one reporter who knew him has noted, was obsessed with racial issues: "I mean, it was race—race, race, race—and every time that I was closeted alone with him, that's all we talked about."[57] For centuries, many whites have been obsessed with blackness and have seen black people as not only inferior but as somehow alien, dangerous, or threatening to whites and whiteness. Indeed, whites' racial emotions have frequently trumped their reason when it comes to their intensely negative views of black Americans.

MORE NOTIONS OF BLACK INFERIORITY

As in the slavery era, during the legal segregation period specific antiblack stereotypes and prejudices were webbed firmly into an overarching white racial frame including not only an overtly racist ideology but also many assumptions about whiteness itself. Then as now, whites have usually been taught an array of stereotypes and the umbrella racist ideology encompassing them at a young age. Thus, in his autobiography, McLaurin discusses how he was taught early the key elements of the racial ideology asserting white superiority over blacks.[58] In this era, the psychological benefits of a sense of racial superiority, the psychological wage of whiteness, remained central to the racial framing of society.

This sense of white superiority could be found at all levels of U.S. society, including among its political leaders. As Governor George Wallace's biographer has summarized for the 1960s: While the patriarchal Wallace "tolerated 'good' blacks…Wallace, like most white southerners of his generation, genuinely believed blacks to be a separate, inferior race."[59]

Supposed Mental Inferiority

White Americans in all social classes have clung devotedly to negative images of black intelligence and mental processes now for several centuries. Viewing African Americans as racially inferior is a hoary way of defending segregation and other oppression as legitimate. We observed such views of the flawed intelligence of African Americans in the commentaries of the white founders. Later, in the twentieth century, white segregationists commonly perpetuated these old racist images in their speeches, writings, and laws. For example, in 1948 the Georgia Commissioner of Agriculture wrote a letter to the *Atlanta Journal* newspaper:

> The yellow people, the brown people and the blacks are mentally unfit for directors in our form of government. You can not change these natural and God-ordained mental processes.… When, and if, our voters' list contains a large percentage of voters of other than Caucasian stock, then our constitutional form of government becomes impossible and unworkable.[60]

A recurring commentary from whites during this era centers on the alleged lack of intelligence of African Americans. Here this supposed lack is extended to all people of color and linked to their continuing exclusion from voting and other aspects of the political process, a problem that lingers in some form for African Americans to the present day in several areas of the United States. Such white views suggest the often totalitarian character of southern governments in this era, where white government officials denied African Americans their basic political rights and where most whites did not see African Americans as deserving of the full array of civil rights of U.S. citizens.

Many whites linked this presumed mental inferiority to the aforementioned issue of racial mixing and amalgamation, as in this comment from a prominent Mississippi physician in the late 1930s:

> God didn't put the different races here to all mix and mingle so you wouldn't know them apart.…You know the Negro race is inferior mentally, everyone knows that, and I don't think God meant for a superior race like the whites to blend with an inferior

> race and become mediocre....I think I am right in saying that, and my attitude is Christian-like. There is just something about the different colored races that is a little bit abhorrent to me....I think that is the way with most white people.[61]

This man's defense of white supremacy, as in numerous similar commentaries in this era, is grounded in a strongly professed religion. Official segregation was seen by most whites as God-approved, if not God-given. Indeed, this man views his white supremacist views as "Christian-like." Like others we have quoted, his racist framing of the world goes beyond the cognitive level to a visceral, emotional level. People of color are evidently abhorrent to him, and in his defense he asserts that such feelings are commonplace among whites.

Alleging Cultural Inferiority

In the commonplace white view, alleged black mental inferiority has long been associated with alleged cultural inferiority. Some of the earliest European American images of Africans assert notions of cultural inferiority and the superiority of European "civilization." Continuing throughout the 1950s and 1960s, many whites extended the concept of racial inferiority to many areas of U.S. cultural life. For example, in his defense of racial segregation in the mid-1960s, the influential journalist, James J. Kilpatrick, is blunt about what he regards as the *common* white view:

> [T]he Southerner rebelliously clings to what seems to him the hard core of truth in this whole controversy: Here and now, in his own communities, in the mid-1960s, the Negro race, as a race, plainly is not equal to the white race, as a race; nor, for that matter, in the wider world beyond, by the accepted judgment of ten thousand years, has the Negro race, as a race, ever been the cultural or intellectual equal of the white race, as a race. This we take to be a plain statement of fact....[62]

A little later in his diatribe he adds more fuel to the fire:

> The South earnestly submits that over thousands of years, the Negro race, as a race, has failed to contribute significantly to the higher and nobler achievements of civilization as the West defines that term. This may be a consequence of innate psychic factors...the South prefers to cling to the characteristics of the white race, as best it can, and to protect those characteristics, as best it can, from what is sincerely regarded as the potentially degrading influence of Negro characteristics.[63]

Again, the words "South" and "the Southerner" refer only to whites. In his book, Kilpatrick includes numerous paragraphs that repeatedly assert the racial inferiority of black Americans. In his view, they have "not earned" equality and should thus be treated like troubling children and second-class citizens, because that is in fact only what they deserve.[64] In his concluding pages, he predicts that the South will probably have to desegregate higher education, employment, and public accommodations eventually, but that whites will likely keep a firm "separation of the races"—especially in public education, social clubs, and churches—for many years into the future.[65]

Significantly, nowhere in Kilpatrick's vigorous defense of racial segregation is there a single paragraph that examines the very high level of discrimination faced by millions of African Americans at the hands of millions of white segregators and oppressors. Not a single sentence shows any empathetic awareness of the painful and often shockingly brutal discriminatory experiences and unjust impoverishment of those forced to live across the color line. In addition, for all his professed understanding of the achievements of "civilization," Kirkpatrick reveals no knowledge of the advanced civilizations of Africa that existed prior to the European invasions of that continent, civilizations that are part of the distinguished, if often forgotten, heritage of African Americans.

IRONIC NOTIONS OF "HAPPY" BLACKS

Over centuries now, white Americans in all social classes have spent much time working out an array of rationalizations for the oppression of black Americans in most U.S. institutions. As a rule, whites have only seen what they have wanted to see in African Americans, and much in that view has been greatly distorted or simply mythological.

During the legal segregation era, whites continued to use the patriarchal language that had long been used to describe and assess the lowly position of black Americans in society. In a 1930s study of Natchez, Mississippi, almost all whites interviewed by the researchers had a negative view of black Americans, including the common opinion that they were "like children."[66] As official segregation gained strength in the late nineteenth century, many whites in the South and the North adopted a variant of the old slaveholders' paternalistic, and metaphorically patriarchal, perspective in dealing with now-free African Americans. Most white paternalists of the legal segregation era, however, had a somewhat different vision than that of slaveholders, for they viewed African Americans as growing children now responsible for their own futures, with little white help. Mostly what these more conservative whites would offer was moral exhortation and moral criticism. Even self-described "friends of the Negro," the white progressives (including President Theodore Roosevelt), viewed African Americans as "helpless wards," as children in need of liberal white paternalism.[67]

A related view common among whites was that blacks were happier and more carefree than whites. One white man interviewed in the Natchez research study expresses himself thus:

> I often think the Negroes are happier than the whites no matter how little they have. You always see them smiling and happy as long as they have a little to eat. One reason they are so carefree is that they have no morals to worry about and they don't have to keep up their good name.[68]

In this view, black Americans are better off because they look happy to this white man. He, like other whites, saw what he wished to see, not what was likely there. He does not consider the possibility that African Americans had to hide their true feelings from men like him lest they come to some harm at white hands. Also, according to his stereotyping, blacks are typically less moral than whites. Such accents on the immorality of the racial others once again signals how even segregationist whites wish to be seen as "virtuous republicans," as the carriers of morality in U.S. society.

Another white respondent, a man who like many larger white farmers was still called a "plantation owner" or "planter" during the official segregation era, speaks in a similar way about the tenant farmers he exploited:

> Speaking of slaves, the Negro is no longer the slave, but the planter is. We have to worry over the crop, over financing the tenant and everything like that, while he just looks to us to take care of him and hasn't a worry as long as he is fed.[69]

The contrast here between the white perspective and that of black farmers in chapter 4 is striking, for the latter often spoke of the extreme oppressiveness of tenant farming and sharecropping. Though the last two respondents imply that blacks sometimes had too little to eat, they do not extend this insight in an empathetic way. Apparently, they did not wish to really see the black impoverishment that was clearly in front of them.

One elderly white woman, a member of a Louisiana family that once owned a slave plantation, describes her memories of blacks being "happier" than whites because "nothing worried them."[70] Again we have the stereotyped opinion that black Americans are somehow worry free and thus better off than most white Americans.

Even whites who sometimes wrote critically of racial patterns during the legal segregation era accepted these stereotyped images of African Americans as happy and carefree, as in this 1940s account from the usually perceptive analyst Wilbur Cash: "But the Negro is notoriously one of the world's greatest romantics and one of the world's greatest hedonists…in the main he is a creature of grandiloquent imagination, of facile emotion, and, above everything else under heaven, of enjoyment."[71]

Cash echoes the views of earlier racist thinkers like Thomas Jefferson in regard to black emotion and pleasure seeking, although he disagrees with Jefferson's assessment of African Americans as lacking imagination. Similarly, in their 1940s analysis of the legal segregation era, the ostensibly liberal Swedish researcher Gunnar Myrdal and his U.S. associates wrote of African Americans as typically characterized by "aggressiveness…emotionality and spontaneous good humor." They are also seen as trying "much harder than do whites to get as much pleasure out of their work as they can." Having a "devil-may-care" attitude, African Americans "lack a strong cultural tradition" and possess a certain cynicism, both of which make them less inhibited and thus often "dangerous" to each other.[72]

When whites look at the racial world only from a *white* perspective, even a relatively liberal perspective, they commonly miss much of what is taking place in that world. This is conspicuous in their stereotyped, and often quite erroneous, assessments of black lives. As the black respondents in the previous chapter indicated, they frequently had to hide their true feelings and views—including their worry, pain, and anger—from whites of all persuasions. They had to play a masked subordinate role under official segregation, as under slavery, to protect their lives and to garner enough support for their families to survive. No perceptive white observer of the slavery or official segregation eras who even began to look at the world from the vantage point of the oppressed could have missed the very harsh and painful realities of black lives, and the need for concealing much in front of ever dangerous whites.

IMAGES OF DISEASE AND CRIMINALITY

Fear of Blackness As Disease

During the long era of official segregation, as well as before and after that era, whites often stereotyped African Americans in terms of disease and criminal imagery. Such imagery was well entrenched during the slavery era, as we have seen in the accounts of men like Madison and Jefferson. It seems to be linked to an animalization of those racial groups that must be considered inferior to whites in order for them to be exploited without guilt. In his autobiography, McLaurin has recounted his sudden reaction as a child, a reaction made with "bolts of prejudice," to realizing he had just put his mouth on a basketball needle lubricated with saliva by a black child:

> The realization that the needle I still held in my mouth had come directly from Bobo's mouth, that it carried on it Bobo's saliva, transformed my prejudices into a physically painful experience....These black germs would ravage my body with unspeakable diseases, diseases from the tropics.[73]

Common to much white stereotyping then as now are these themes of "black germs" and Africanized diseases, stereotyped images that have such a strong emotional loading that they can make whites themselves ill. While the account does not mention it, it seems likely that such images of African diseases came not only from parents and peers but also from the media, such as Hollywood's many Tarzan movies with their extremely racist stereotyping of Africa and Africans.

Allegations of Criminality

Assertions of black criminality date back to at least the early slavery era of the mid-seventeenth century. Such accusations were also commonplace during official segregation, as we have already seen in some comments above. In his field study of early-twentieth-century segregation, the liberal journalist Ray Stannard Baker wrote what has been considered, especially by later white analysts, to be a fair evaluation of southern racial patterns. Yet, in his book-length analysis, Baker only occasionally describes with accuracy the racial hostility and discrimination faced by black southerners. Instead, he focuses on such issues as the poverty of African Americans and on the "problem of race mixture." While sympathetic to black southerners' problems, Baker has great difficulty in looking at issues from anything but a white perspective:

> Many Southerners look back wistfully to the faithful, simple, ignorant, obedient, cheerful, old plantation Negro and deplore his disappearance....That Negro is disappearing forever along with the old feudalism and the old-time exclusively agricultural life....And the new Negro...doesn't laugh as much as the old one. It is grim business he is in, this being free, this new, fierce struggle in the open competitive field for the daily loaf. Many go down to vagrancy and crime in that struggle; a few will rise.[74]

Baker describes the longing of "southerners" here, but he writes only from a white viewpoint, for he too means white southerners. This white longing is said to be for blacks to be docile like they supposedly were on the slave plantations. In the process of describing the impact of urbanization in the South, Baker develops racist stereotypes of blacks as being susceptible to "vagrancy and crime." One irony of such white commentaries on black vagrancy and petty crime is that southern white politicians implemented numerous laws designed to prevent black tenant farmers and sharecroppers from ever leaving the farms of the often highly exploitative whites for whom they labored. If they tried to leave the slavery-like conditions, they were defined by the law as "criminals." Baker writes much about what he calls the "low-class Negro":

> This worthless Negro, without training or education, grown up from the neglected children I have already spoken of, evident in his idleness around saloons and depots—this Negro provokes the just wrath of the people, and gives a bad name to the entire Negro race.[75]

Even though he explicitly says that the number of such men in black communities is small, like many other whites then as now, Baker appears to be excessively preoccupied with this group of men. Significantly, no white commentators or respondents examined for this chapter seemed to understand that problems of black vagrancy and street crime in this era were often linked to the fact that almost all black men and women had long been excluded by white discrimination from decent-paying jobs—and often from any jobs, especially during recessions—in virtually all areas of the economy.

Even in his chapter on antiblack lynchings by mobs of white criminals, Baker seems preoccupied with black criminals:

> Lynching in this country is peculiarly the white man's burden....All the machinery of justice is in his hands. How keen is the need, then, of calmness and strict justice in dealing with the Negro! Nothing more surely tends to bring the white man down to the lowest level of the criminal Negro than yielding to those blind instincts of savagery which find expression in the mob. The man who joins a mob, by his very acts, puts himself on a level with the Negro criminal.[76]

Although clearly horrified at the white lynchings, Baker draws a ludicrous parallel between the savagery of the white lynch mob and the supposedly similar actions of typical black criminals. This parallel is inaccurate in that most black crime then involved violations of vagrancy and farm tenancy laws, petty theft, prostitution, gambling, and similar crimes. Such law violations do not in any way compare with the violent savagery of the thousands of white mobs that attacked and killed black men and women, usually with impunity, during the legal segregation period. The usually perceptive Baker is looking at lynching solely from the white point of view and thus calling on potential or actual white lynchers not to behave like the so-called criminal Negro. Baker seems unable to evaluate lynchings simply as ghastly white violations of human rights in themselves.

Into the 1960s and 1970s, white southern leaders articulated similar concerns about black disease and black criminality. For example, after his election as governor of Alabama, George Wallace told a teacher that blacks were inherently criminal, that a "vast percentage of people who are infected with venereal disease are people of the Negro race," and that blacks are prone to the "most atrocious acts of…rape, assault, and murder."[77] In his views, the unreflective Wallace was likely representing a large body of white opinion, in the South and in the North.

CONCLUSION

Throughout these white commentaries we observe direct or indirect evidence of the important dimensions of systemic racism laid out in chapter 1. We observe the active agency of whites in maintaining the racial hierarchy and its associated set of economic, social, and political burdens. Coercively placed on African Americans, such burdens were well institutionalized in this legal segregation era and were a continuation of previous oppression in the form of economic exploitation and unjust impoverishment, as well as of the legal enforcement of these realities. As in the slavery period, legal segregation involved whites' seeking and preserving a great and significant array of material and psychological benefits for themselves, their families, and their communities.

As was the case for the white founders, most elite whites in this period are generally supportive of thorough racial segregation, and they are mostly negative in their views of those oppressed by this U.S. apartheid. They continue to be indispensable figures in honing and maintaining this racism. We see exceedingly strong support for racial segregation among southern and border state members of Congress and governors, all of whom were white. Such support shows the direct and critical linkage between government action and other aspects of the imposed racial segregation. Not surprisingly, rank-and-file whites usually followed the lead of those in the elite. Legal segregation was characteristically maintained by violence or threat of violence on the part of white men in both groups. Indeed, several white interviewees seem matter-of-fact about the regular use of brutal violence to keep black Americans firmly in their subordinated "place" in society. The significance of social alexithymia for sustaining social oppression seems all too evident in these callous and vicious commentaries.

We human beings have a distinctive ability to acquire much knowledge from our parents and other predecessors and to pass that acquired knowledge down to the succeeding generations. The white collective memory as to how to "do racism" is central to the accounts of segregation from white leaders and ordinary citizens quoted in this chapter. Especially in the more recent interviews, whites looking back on the official segregation they grew up in—and probably participated in as young adults—tend to view themselves as just children who were not directly involved in maintaining segregation and its etiquette. They remember segregated buses, water fountains, rest rooms, and social lives for adults, but virtually nothing about the severe impact of segregation on African Americans. Like most whites, they seem to be buying into the image of "good race relations" that white political leaders took great pains to insist were characteristic of the South up to the 1960s. Only exceptional whites, like the courageous Lillian Smith in the 1940s, were able to analyze candidly and critically the oppressive character of these racial relations during legal segregation era. Indeed, Smith paid a heavy price for her honest writings in the form of social ostracism and recurring threats of violence from white men, especially for her outspoken views against segregation.

Much commentary by the whites in this chapter reflects the maintenance and further development of the white racial frame that have long been central to most whites' orientation in the racialized world of U.S. society. This frame includes racialized emotions and images, as well as the rationalizing ideology that asserts white superiority and black inferiority. This ideology persists from the slavery past, with mostly modest changes, as part of whites' collective defense of racially imposed oppression. Whether expressed by ordinary whites, or even by educated analysts like Wilbur Cash and Gunnar Myrdal, stereotyped views of African Americans are often a continuation of earlier views of leaders like Thomas Jefferson, James Madison, and George Washington.

An array of sincere fictions about white superiority and black inferiority protect what many of these whites perceive to be a God-ordained racial hierarchy. African Americans continue to be stereotyped as especially emotional, jovial, and carefree in their approach to life, even by relatively liberal white observers. Stereotypes of criminality and vagrancy are common among whites seeking to rationalize segregation, as well as by a few whites who are uncomfortable with that segregation. Of great concern to numerous whites in this apartheid era is racial mixing, so-called mongrelization, which they fear will come with extensive desegregation. Connected to this fear is a commonplace stereotyping of black men as oversexed or dangerous, or of black women as oversexed or animal-like in sexual abilities. Most of the white understandings of racial segregation are framed entirely from a white perspective, one often using a type of patriarchal language. Once deeply imbedded in white minds, the racist ideology remained a strong force that shaped white actions across an array of institutional and geographical settings. As they did under slavery, these racist ideas helped to legitimate making African Americans—human beings—into "things" to exploit and oppress.

Legal segregation and its rationalizing ideology had significance far beyond those specific states where it was enshrined in its worst manifestations. That racist ideology was not limited to southern whites, for much of it was shared by a majority of whites across the United States. During the 1950s and 1960s, a majority of whites across the country still viewed African Americans as racially inferior or as a threat to their jobs and communities, particularly as the latter migrated north in large numbers to escape the extreme oppression of southern areas. Near the end of the legal segregation era in 1963, one major opinion survey found that a majority of whites *nationwide* agreed with blatantly stereotypical statements about African Americans, such as they "tend to have less ambition," "smell different," and "have looser morals." In addition, half of these white respondents said they would object to a black family next door, and most were opposed to a close friend or relative marrying a black person.[78] Official segregation had more than sufficient human energy to keep the white racial frame, with its ideological racism, "in motion by its own further unfolding."[79]

Though whites usually did not see it, legal segregation had a severely negative impact on whites in the southern and border states. Reflecting on systemic racism during this era, W. E. B. Du Bois once commented about its impact thus: "It was a triumph of men who in their effort to replace equality with caste and to build inordinate wealth on a foundation of abject poverty have succeed in killing democracy, art and religion."[80] During the entire legal segregation era, southern politics was, on the whole, much less democratic in its everyday operations than in many other areas of the United States. During legal segregation, most black voters were not allowed to vote, and southern political oligarchies developed across the South to protect that segregation, thereby reducing the political power of ordinary whites as well as of blacks. Because of these strong political oligarchies, arch-conservative southern governments usually provided considerably less support for such things as public health programs and public education for all southerners than did many governments in other regions. Indeed, the negative consequences of the long era of relatively autocratic and racially conservative governments can be seen even today in the low ranking of many southern states in regard to such government support programs.

Ironically, white workers have also paid a significant price, in the short run and the long run, for their commitment to the oppression of African Americans and other Americans of color. By insisting on racial privilege and historically rejecting most attempts at multiracial labor organizations, white workers thereby helped capitalists to fashion a U.S. (and worldwide) labor system grounded first in slavery, and then in legal segregation.[81] Once this highly racist and segregated system of labor was in place, white workers found themselves in great difficulties. By creating weak and segregated worker organizations, white workers, though racially privileged, eventually found themselves as having much less power to resist the antiworker decisions of corporate executives of the internationally mobile U.S. corporations. The current weakness of the U.S. union movement is rooted in this old racist history.

6

CONTEMPORARY RACIAL REALITIES: THROUGH THE EYES OF AFRICAN AMERICANS

Over the decades of legal segregation, beginning in the early 1900s, a gradually expanding civil rights movement put pressure on the white elite to make changes in systemic racism. The black civil rights movement periodically created political and legitimation crises for the elite. During and after the two world wars, African Americans accelerated their fight against racism, as W. E. B. Du Bois once underscored:

> Slowly they beat upon public opinion and then entered the courts. The courts dodged and evaded with every subterfuge, but they faced inevitably clear decisions unless the principle of democratic government was to be completely surrendered in the presence of world war in which we claimed to lead democracy.[1]

Moderates in the white elite were ever more concerned about the image of the United States during and after both world wars in the twentieth century, for they had long heralded aggressively the ideals of freedom and democracy against undemocratic enemies overseas.

Some civil rights progress became possible in the decades after World War II because of the Cold War with the Soviet Union. As Du Bois early noted, "It was simply impossible for the United States to continue to lead a 'Free World' with race segregation kept legal over a third of its territory."[2] Internationally, struggles with the Soviet Union over the minds of people around the globe, most of them people of color, forced the U.S. elite to increasingly emphasize the ideals of freedom and democracy. Thus, the Department of Justice submitted a supportive amicus brief in the 1954 *Brown v. Board of Education* case. The brief discussed the need to improve the international image of the United States by removing such "existing flaws in our democracy" as racial discrimination, and it included a statement from the U.S. secretary of state arguing that discrimination provides "unfriendly governments the most effective kind of ammunition for their propaganda warfare."[3] These new political conditions insured that the concerns of the black-generated civil rights movement would be considered seriously at the highest levels of white decision making, albeit temporarily. Concern over political legitimacy internationally led many whites, especially in the elite, to abandon support for official racial segregation. Another reason for increasing white support for some change was that the wartime eras—including the world wars, wars in Korea and Vietnam, and the Cold War—required substantial mobilization of black workers and soldiers for U.S. success.[4] Thus, in the periods of U.S. history when some significant racial change does take place, the political and international interests of the white elite have generally been more important in generating change than their commitments to racial equality and justice.

During the Cold War period of the 1960s, three civil rights laws were passed, the first major civil rights laws since the nineteenth-century Reconstruction period. No longer could whites legally exclude African Americans from business, employment, health care, leisure, and educational institutions. With new doors opening up, many African Americans sought to enter them. Exerting great personal and collective efforts, many succeeded in making some advances in the economy, education, housing, and other institutional arenas. Yet, they have made these advancements against much continuing exploitative and exclusionary discrimination at the hands of many whites, discrimination that today takes subtle, covert, and blatant forms. Today, many gains of the 1970s and 1980s, as we will see, have more or less ended, as whites have backtracked and generated a backlash against feared large-scale change. Indeed, even given these earlier advances, many African Americans and other Americans of color view the United States as now moving backwards in regard to remedying continuing racial oppression.

AFRICAN AMERICAN ACCOUNTS
OF CONTEMPORARY EXPERIENCES

In this chapter, I assess the voiced experiences of African Americans in contemporary settings across the United States. During the decades of the legal segregation era, especially after 1900, many African Americans moved to northern and western areas of the U.S., which is one major reason that systemic racism is so visible across the country. Today, as in the past, most black Americans are still forced by economic necessity to labor for white employers and alongside white workers. Both groups frequently participate in discrimination against African Americans in regard to hiring, promotions, or an array of job conditions. Grounded in the social patterns created by slavery and legal segregation, the hierarchical and asymmetrical relations between white and black Americans in workplaces and many other public arenas have persisted to the present day. These asymmetrical relationships generate, or relate closely to, an array of socioeconomic and sociopolitical structures that perpetuate and maintain everyday discrimination.

The black respondents here discuss the complex realities of racial oppression in a reputedly "free" U.S. society. One does not have to speculate about the experiences of those who live under contemporary racism, for if we look at recent research we can find a substantial number of pointed and accurate accounts from those who have suffered for varying periods under contemporary racism. I draw here on many interviews done in recent research projects that I or my students have conducted, as well as from other recent research projects. Once we have examined the contemporary experience with racial oppression from the viewpoint of those oppressed, we will examine in the next chapter the views on African Americans and discrimination held by whites, both members of the elite and ordinary whites. Once again, by examining the racialized experiences of black and white Americans comparatively, we can add interpretive layers to a general theory of systemic racism.

When African Americans assess the reality of being black in institutions controlled by whites, they speak not just in abstract concepts but recount in specific and often graphic terms the oppressiveness of routinized encounters with whites. These real-life accounts from black women and men offer us not only a window into their personal microlevel experiences, but also insight into the ways in which the broader structure of racial oppression impinges on and shapes many aspects of their everyday lives. The systemic character of contemporary racism constantly reveals itself in these everyday accounts of life in the United States.

THE PAST STILL BURDENS THE PRESENT: THE BOTTOM LINE OF CENTURIES OF OPPRESSION

One striking aspect of the contemporary black reports on discrimination and its impact lies in the importance of the past and collective memories of that past. One sage black professor, now retired and in his late eighties, has explained why current discrimination has such a negative impact on African Americans. Even one "nigger" epithet hurled at a person can have a very significant effect, he notes, because such a term "brings into sharp and current focus all kinds of acts of racism" that he, his family, and his friends—as well as his ancestors—have had to endure over the centuries.[5] One specific incident with a racist epithet can act as a magnifying glass, bringing into sharp focus a person's awareness of the many different kinds of past and present racism targeting African Americans.

In interview studies of nearly one thousand black and white Americans, my colleagues and I have found that black Americans in all walks of life are usually very aware of, and sensitive to, the multifaceted reality of everyday racism for themselves, their families, and other African Americans. They are on the average much more conscious of the reality and importance of the country's highly racialized past, both the recent past and the distant past, than are white Americans. James Baldwin once noted that "People are trapped in history, and history is trapped in them."[6] This is true for all Americans, yet black Americans tend to have more of a sense of the historical traps and often understand well the connections between present-day racial discrimination and the past of slavery and official segregation. Most can see beyond present-day expressions of racism to the historical process underlying that racism. In contrast, if forced to consider that past, many whites like to push the eras of slavery or segregation as far back into the distant past as they can. They express this attitude with statements like "slavery happened hundreds of years ago," "my family never segregated any lunch counters," or "blacks should get over it, forget the past, and move on." In contrast, for African Americans that oppressive past is so much a part of their present-day experience with white-generated and white-maintained racism that they cannot ignore it. Clearly, significant collective remembering by blacks and significant collective forgetting by whites are both aspects of a still highly racist U.S. society.

Today, racial oppression remains *systemic*. As in the past, it is not something superficial that is appended to an otherwise healthy U.S. society. This oppression typically takes the form of racial discrimination—that is, differential treatment by whites of black Americans and other people of color—in an array of major institutional areas, including employment, housing, education, health care, recreation, politics, policing, and public accommodations.

The bottom-line data on centuries of white-on-black oppression are not difficult to find, though our schools and the mass media rarely analyze their deeper significance. Numerous recent research studies have shown time and again the reality and consequences of continuing antiblack discrimination by whites. Basic statistics on white-black differences in life chances and experiences suggest just how much racial inequality remains. Currently, for example, the unemployment rate for African Americans is more than twice the unemployment rate for whites, a ratio that has stayed at or near that level for all the decades since such figures were first tabulated. Similarly, median black family income today is still only about 58 percent of median white family income, a percentage that is worse today than at the end of legal segregation in the 1960s. Today the poverty rate for African Americans is about 24 percent, about three times the white rate. An even larger percentage of the next generation of black Americans—the children—live in poverty. Perhaps most indicative of the way in which unjust enrichment and unjust impoverishment have been reproduced over many generations is the *huge imbalance in the wealth* of average white and black families.[7]

As a result of these huge income and wealth inequalities, white Americans are much more likely to own homes than black Americans. Generally speaking, black Americans also face higher rents, higher property tax rates, higher prices in many local stores, higher interest rates, and poorer social services than do whites.[8] They also face discrimination in shopping and public accommodations. Recall from the preface the recent report of the New Jersey citizen action group indicating a state and national pattern of black and Latino car buyers being quoted substantially higher finance rates than comparable white car buyers.[9] In terms of health, African Americans have an infant mortality rate two and a half times as high as that for whites, a ratio higher than it was in the 1970s. Black death rates are generally more than twice the rates of whites for such diseases as hypertension, kidney disease, diabetes, and septicemia.[10] Perhaps most telling is the disturbing reality that African Americans live much shorter lives than whites, with a life expectancy differential of nearly six years. This shorter life expectancy is a severe personal, family, and community consequence of centuries of oppression.

In his last book, published near the end of the legal segregation era, Dr. Martin Luther King, Jr., reaches a verdict on this society that would need to be changed only a little to fit today's inequality data:

> When the Constitution was written, a strange formula to deter-
> mine taxes and representation declared that the Negro was 60
> percent of a person. Today another curious formula seems to
> declare he is 50 percent of a person. Of the good things in life
> he has approximately one-half of those of whites; of the bad he
> has twice those of whites.[11]

King concludes from these inequality data that there remains a huge
"gap between existing realities and the goal of equality" and that
African Americans

> proceeded from a premise that equality means what it says, and
> they have taken white Americans at their word when they talked
> of it as an objective. But most whites…proceed from a premise
> that equality is a loose expression for improvement.[12]

Here, too, he would need to change these conclusions but little to fit
today's situation of continuing racial oppression, whose systemic and
often devastating reality most white Americans are not interested in
changing significantly.

ECONOMIC DOMINATION: DISCRIMINATION AND EXCLUSION

Economic domination can involve direct economic exploitation or it
can involve exclusion or marginalization, which are attempts to decrease
economic competition and thereby increase white advantage. Whites
who are employers often benefit from direct exploitation in terms of
lower wages or redefined jobs for black workers. Estimates from the
Urban Institute indicate that black workers today suffer more than $120
billion in lost wages annually because of various kinds of employment
discrimination, dollars that stay in white employers' hands.[13] This takes
the form of differential pay and the discrimination that comes from
channeling black workers qualified for better jobs into lesser jobs that
whites will often not prefer or accept.

It is also significant that white businesses garner some $500 billion
annually from black customers, dollars that flow to the benefit of white
business owners because of fewer black business owners—which is also
a consequence of large-scale racial discrimination over recent decades.[14]
White workers benefit not only from less job competition because of
the excluded, segregated, or marginalized African American workers—
which increases whites' job chances and incomes—but also from the
economic multiplier effects of black customers having to spend most of

their consumer dollars with businesses that employ only (or disproportionately) white workers and that thus help to keep white communities
economically vibrant. White workers and business owners also benefit
from continuing white-race privilege, the psychological wage of whiteness. This latter advantage is less tangible, as it is a matter of perceived
racial status and the psychological sense of being racially superior, yet it
remains a very important reason why many whites still labor to preserve
racial discrimination in the economy.

We should note that economic exploitation involves stealing the labor and the energy of those who are racially subordinated to enrich unjustly the exploiters. This economic theft of labor and energy is just one
aspect of a broader theft of energy that stems from the system of racism.
In one probing interview, a veteran black professor who has taught at
a major historically white university summarizes racism's impact on a
black person's energy:

> If you can think of the mind as having one hundred ergs of en-
> ergy, and the average man uses fifty percent of his energy deal-
> ing with the everyday problems of the world…then he has fifty
> percent more to do creative kinds of things that he wants to do.
> Now that's a white person. Now a black person also has one hun-
> dred ergs; he uses fifty percent the same way a white man does,
> dealing with what the white man has [to deal with], so he has
> fifty percent left. But he uses twenty-five percent fighting being
> black, [with] all the problems being black and what it means.[15]

One can view racial oppression as a vampire-like system for exploiting
and draining the energies of those targeted for oppression in many areas
of society. This reality began with slavery and has continued to the present day. In this sage respondent's estimate, African Americans still must
use half their creative energy over their lifetimes to deal with the imposed
reality of just being black in a still racially oppressive United States.

Business Discrimination Backstage

Whites express racial prejudices and stereotypes both in frontstage areas,
the more public arenas, and in backstage areas with white friends, peers,
or relatives. In recent decades, however, many whites have learned to
reserve much overt expression of blatantly racist views and stereotypes
to these backstage arenas. With the end of legal segregation have come
opportunities for African Americans and other Americans of color
to do business in areas once off limits to them. However, as they have
moved into various economic sectors, including that of small business,

they have frequently encountered new racial barriers, many of which are subtle or covert.

In its many negative forms, economic discrimination remains central to the black experience, as this owner of a small consulting firm in a major city explains: "We learn the rules of the game, and by the time we have mastered them to really try to get into the mainstream, the game becomes something else...."[16] The relations of oppression have changed somewhat, because African Americans have officially been freed, by the 1960s civil rights laws, from the near-slavery of legal segregation. Over the last few decades, they have been allowed by whites to enter new business arenas, yet major racial barriers remain for most African Americans seeking to build a business. Central to modern racial oppression is whites' changing the rules of the business or other societal "games" for their own benefit. The racial hierarchy described for earlier eras remains conspicuous today. Whites, who control most large banks, other business enterprises, and key government agencies, routinely set up subtle and covert barriers that, with little fanfare, impede or block entirely the economic progress of other Americans of color.

In her interview, the aforementioned consulting firm owner continues by describing an attempt at racial exclusion as she attempts to do business with a major city government. She says that she now has a contract with that city government, but that getting it was very difficult because she was competing with big white-controlled accounting firms that usually get such contracts.

We might note here that big U.S. corporations are not nonracial enterprises, for in important ways most are "white" corporations. Capitalism in the United States has been, from the beginning, a white-crafted and white-oriented economic system imbedded in white-made business laws. A great many of the large U.S. firms got their start when African Americans were entirely excluded from starting such businesses. Because of centuries of slavery and segregation, African Americans never had the chance to get into the business game at a time and with the resources that would have enabled them to compete fairly with whites then and in subsequent years. Moreover, white-controlled firms, whether founded before the end of legal segregation or more recently, often have had a clear edge in many such contract negotiations, because firms owned by African Americans have typically been disproportionately small, have had difficulty in raising capital because of banking discrimination, and thus have had difficulty in competing effectively.

This brave entrepreneur continues with an account of what happened in her struggle to secure the contract. The professional evaluation panel had decided that she had the best program and track record and ranked her first, but this was not enough, as she continues:

> And the director of their department made a very racial statement, that "they were very sick and tired of these niggers and these other minorities because what they think is that they can come in here and run a business. None of them are qualified to run a business, especially the niggers."[17]

She was told this by a white employee who had heard the white director's comments in private. She then notes that the director had planned to reject her covertly, not by openly expressing his view. She had gotten all the votes from the professional panel, yet he was still going to block her application.[18] Significantly, she did not allow the "backstage" racism, which she only learned about fortuitously, to make her bitter or to end the matter. She continued the struggle for the contract by fighting back aggressively. She let everyone know that she knew the director's racist views and eventually got the contract.

Clearly, many white government officials, like many white executives in the private sector, are much more comfortable dealing with white-owned firms than with those owned by people of color. Today, as in the past, this sense of comfort with other whites is part of the white racial framing of the world. Many whites hide their real views and feelings in public, yet express them openly just off the public stage. This black entrepreneur learned of the racist thinking of a key white official by accident, but was savvy enough to use it to head off the imposition of another racist barrier to her doing business. In her longer account, she speaks several times about how she had to be intensely "competitive" and "fight" and be "smarter" in order to get the contract. Her account, like those of most other black Americans recounting interactions with powerful whites, is dialectical, as black Americans move to counter and outflank, where they can, the discriminatory actions of whites. Even when as here there are successes in this dialectical struggle, great energy must be wasted just to do everyday tasks that are required to make a living against white-imposed discrimination, everyday tasks ordinarily involving no racial barriers for whites.

The "Plantation Mentality": Whites in the Workplace

Black Americans face much discrimination as employees in historically white workplaces. This is true whether they are blue-collar or white-collar employees. Recall from the preface that studies in Milwaukee, Chicago, and Boston have found that blacks applying for listed jobs were much less likely than comparable white applicants to be called back—a signal of white employers likely being influenced by stereotypes of black men and women in screening for hiring.[19]

Once in a historically white workplace, black employees frequently encounter racial discrimination that signals the racial legacy of slavery and legal segregation. Connecting events to the past of systemic racism seems helpful in interpreting recent racial events. For example, black Americans frequently cite what they view as the current "plantation mentality" of many white Americans, especially those whites with power in organizations. In a recent lawsuit against Microsoft, the world's largest software company, one group of black employees has accused the company's management of having just such a "plantation mentality," by which they reportedly mean racial hostility and discrimination in the hiring, promotion, and pay of black employees.[20] We see a similar perspective in this commentary from a black entrepreneur about how black women and men are treated by many whites in workplaces:

> I think it goes back to the slave mentality times too, black women being easier to deal with but yet more capable of being controlled....I think the demise of black women is that the white, male, Anglo-Saxon power structure feels as though it can manipulate black women. And with black men it's better to castrate them at the beginning and not let them in as a player and that way you eliminate the competition.[21]

She draws on extensive experience with whites to reach her nuanced evaluation. The contemporary white racial framing of workplace settings, in her view, reflects the "slave mentality times." The old racial frame is still present because white discriminators with power in organizations and institutions have made it so. In the past, as now, whites have gendered much of their racial discrimination and thus controlled black women and black men in somewhat different ways. Black men are viewed by whites as more threatening, and thus commonly suffer harsh discrimination (for example, rejection or "castration") if they do not defer sufficiently to the whites in power. In many cases, black women are controlled more by paternalistic or other sexist manipulation, though they too face much racial discrimination.

Indeed, in the black experience, many white managers and other white employees still harbor old racist stereotypes of black men. Drawing on substantial experience, a black female counselor offers these comments about white fear in the workplace:

There is some hesitancy, or some fear, of black men. And I think it's unfounded, but I also think it's crazy....And I didn't believe that until recently when I saw the fear in a white group when a black man came in....And I've watched it over the years at concerts and workshops. It's just that their body language changes when a black man comes in.[22]

In previous chapters, we have seen that this image of the dangerous black man is central to the dominant white racial frame and its ideology, and it seems to underlie much white fear of black Americans since well before Thomas Jefferson's time. This sense of danger may have originated from white fears of black Americans trying to free themselves from enslavement and legal segregation. Significant in these commentaries from black women is that they have observed much white behavior and drawn some acute sociological insights. Both they, and the black men they describe, are targets of psychological violence, or threats of such violence, on the part of whites in the contemporary workplace.

The "slavery mentality" of whites shows up in a variety of work settings. In this next account, a black law enforcement officer explains his attempt to help a white woman who was involved in a serious family dispute:

I got on the property and it was an older white female. The house was an old cracker-barrel-type house, the wood and so forth, had dogs in the yard, and a fence around it. She had a problem with her niece, and it was a personal family thing. And I came and she told me to get off her property. That she needed a real deputy, that I was black, and so on. And she tried to sic her dogs on me....Oh, she was furious....And she had the old mentality that black people were below and beneath them.[23]

Such aversion and rejection on the part of whites is a common experience for African Americans who work in historically white settings. In all social classes, many whites prefer to deal with other whites, with whom they appear to be more comfortable. Avoidance racism is one aspect of the "old mentality" that has long viewed blacks as beneath whites in the societal pecking order. Even those whites not consciously aware of such thinking often react aversively to those who differ from them in skin color, even those sent to help them. By so doing, whites assert a collective whiteness and their individual participation in that whiteness, and they thereby remind themselves that in U.S. history total black deference was once the omnipresent reality. When racial patterns change, however modestly, many whites appear to have a nostalgic desire to return to the more restrictive racial order of earlier eras.[24]

The white racial framing of the world routinely appears in historically white workplace settings. It commonly leads to exclusionary discrimination or resistance to efforts at desegregating organizations along racial lines. One's employer or one's subordinate can generate problems. For example, many whites do not like having black supervisors or managers over them, as in this account of a black school administrator in the North. She first recounts that she once supervised a white man who did not like his subordinate situation, then adds:

> Now, I'm having the same problem because I have another, a white woman who's scheduled to come into our program and she has a doctorate also....They still have the plantation mentality, the plantation mentality is alive and well.[25]

Again we see the interpretation, honed by some experience and linked to the past, that there is a "plantation mentality," the white framing that reflects a centuries-old, alienated racial order imbedding white privilege and black disadvantage. This mentality clearly cuts across gender lines, as it is reflected in the responses to her by a white man and a white woman. Asserting the old plantation hierarchy, consciously or unconsciously whites expect to be giving directions to African Americans, and not the reverse. Racist practice and response have become habitual and normal.

Favoring Whites in Promotions and Evaluations

Today, as in the past, economic discrimination includes preferential treatment for whites. Whites often sermonize to black Americans that they should "get a good education," quit "relying on affirmative action," and "work hard" without preferences the way whites supposedly do. Yet this white framing is a fantasy view of the world, for preferential discrimination favoring whites has, as we have seen in previous chapters, long been the everyday reality in historically white workplaces. White managers still control most levels of most larger businesses, and they often make choices favoring whites over others. In this case a black bank employee on the East Coast reports how he and a white friend started working for a bank at the same time with similar degrees from the same college:

> We both went in for management training. They put him in management training, and put me on the teller line, and told me it would be better for me to start off as a teller and work my way up from the bottom, whereas they automatically put him on the management training.[26]

In his interview, this respondent describes numerous examples of workplace discrimination, which he notes has hardened his will to succeed in his career. Whites frequently speak of the difficulty of finding a good job because of affirmative action giving too many positions to people of color. Yet, as in this case, much more often the problem is the reverse, for whites are the ones who actually get the racial preference. Given the continuing racial hierarchy of the U.S. workplace, with whites in most positions of power to hire and promote, in larger organizations this result is unsurprising, though it is often hidden in the oxymoronic public rhetoric of "reverse discrimination." Such rhetoric is not systemically challenged because whites control most of the public and intellectual discourse of the country.

Much racial favoritism for whites seems to involve a social cloning whereby whites prefer and choose yet other whites to fill positions traditionally held by whites. Favoritism often proceeds along critical white "old boy" (less often, "old girl") networks. An example of this racial favoritism is given by a black officer in a historically white police agency:

> I've faced a lot of opposition toward promotion. I've been up for lieutenant eleven times, and I've been passed over even though I've passed every exam....I was just recently transferred back to [an old post] where I have [whites] who are my junior, people that I had recruited that have been promoted and that are now my supervisors. They have less education, they have less time in grade, they have less experience as an officer, but now they're my supervisors. So, I've faced much opposition, simply because I'm very outspoken.[27]

A highly qualified black man finds himself in a situation commonly reported by black employees in similar organizations, one where whites that he recruited are promoted over him. When racial issues come up, whites often speak of their workplaces as meritocratic, yet most historically white workplaces have built-in mechanisms that routinely favor whites and continue to reproduce systemic racism therein.

In most accounts of workplace discrimination, we get a strong sense of how much of everyday life involves a struggle with white discriminators. The tension in white-black interactions is felt in many such accounts. This is especially true when it comes to evaluations for work performance. Black employees often face opposition from whites who are thinking in blatantly stereotypical terms. Here a sales account manager describes the reaction of her white supervisor to her excellent job performance:

I had gone into my evaluation interview anticipating that he
would give me a "VG" (very good), feeling that I deserved an
"outstanding" and prepared to fight for my outstanding rating,
knowing my past experience with him and more his way toward
females. But even beyond female, I happened to be the only
black in my position within my branch....And he and I had had
some very frank discussions about race specifically....So I certainly knew that he had a lot of prejudices in terms of blacks.[28]

In spite of her great performance, however, he only gave her a "G"
(good) rating, not even the VG she expected. She then recounts that she
had kept and prepared carefully a list of her many accomplishments,
which she presented to him. Still, he rejected her arguments, though
he later changed his mind and gave her a better evaluation. The dialectical character of the white-black struggle is again conspicuous here.
A white supervisor had previously expressed negative views of African
Americans, probably views central to the commonplace white racial
frame that assumes the legitimacy of white privilege and power. This
white male manager seems to have felt that whatever he did she would
just have to accept. Power, as they say, corrupts, and racialized power
seems to be extraordinarily corrupting.

This manager was apparently unprepared for her to challenge
strongly his actions, yet another example of the resistance that African
Americans must be constantly prepared to exhibit if they are to succeed. Indeed, in a variety of workplaces, African American employees
report that they must routinely keep careful records in order to counter
recurring white discrimination when they can. A critical aspect of the
operation of racial oppression today, as in the past, relates to ongoing
individual and community resistance by African Americans and other
people of color to that white-imposed oppression.

Hostile Workplace Climates

Those African American employees who have moved successfully into
jobs and careers in historically white institutions often face much more
than particular instances of racial discrimination such as we have just
discussed. In mostly white workplaces, especially those where there have
been relatively few black employees historically, they typically encounter
a hostile racial climate, one that is designed to permanently marginalize
them or even to drive them out.

In many cases, ongoing racist commentaries by white employees and
managers, including periodic comments using painful racist epithets
that recall for black Americans centuries of antiblack violence, remain

commonplace in historically white workplaces. Other white actions include the re-creation of negative images, such as hangman's nooses or objects made up to look like stereotypical images of black Americans. Blatant racism is by no means inconsequential in many workplaces, as a college-educated black clerk makes clear in this thoughtful account of working twelve years with white men who kept telling her she should quit and go home:

> When I refused to leave, they started to [put up]…racial photographs, pictures, drawings, writings on a calendar and things of that nature to try to intimidate me into leaving.…It's sexism, racism, because I've heard the Mexican-American guys called "wetbacks," "Olympic swimmers," "taco benders." I've heard the blacks called "niggers" and "boys" and "spooks."[29]

Many aspects of a racist framing that go back at least to Jefferson's time are evident here. Asserting the racial hierarchy and attempting to drive her out of "their" workplace, her white coworkers articulate notions of black incompetence and spout a litany of racist epithets for blacks and for Mexican Americans. Her fellow employees put up racist, sexist, and pornographic pictures to harass her. We also see gender discrimination (taking "a man's job"), and thus a situation in which a black woman is a target for racist and sexist abuse. Her list of blatant actions is long in her interview, and she does not even mention many of the lesser types of discrimination that, like other black employees, she undoubtedly experiences. There seems to be no attempt by these white men to understand life across the imposed color and gender lines. Yet, in spite of the hostile racial climate, she resists. In her longer interview account not excerpted here, she accents her constant struggle to maintain her dignity and to fight back. She refused to leave in the face of intense opposition and, in line with the old black commitment to justice, took her case to the federal Equal Employment Opportunity Commission.

Unmistakably, such racist actions by whites generate heavy costs for their targets, yet these costs have seldom been systematically documented. In a recent interview, a black professional discusses an incident involving fellow employees outside the workplace, including reactions to racist comments:

> I have felt extremely upset, anger, rage.…One incident that comes to mind happened in a social setting. I was with…my former boss and some coworkers and a [white] man who ran, like, a federal program. And we were having dinner, and he made a comment, and he had been drinking heavily. And he

referred to black people as "niggers."….And as soon as he said it, he looked in my face. And then he turned beet red, you know? And I said, "Excuse me, what did you say?" And he just couldn't say anything. And then my boss, my former boss, intervened and said, "Now, you know, move his glass, because he's had too much to drink."[30]

Whites commonly excuse racist incidents, especially when they happen in public, with lines such as "he was just joking" or "he had too much to drink." Many whites, including well-educated and prominent whites, seem unwilling to acknowledge the serious and damaging reality of such racist incidents, as well as their widespread character across society. The costly impact of such racist incidents on this professional is clear; she recounts her well-remembered anger at such racial discrimination, which doubtless comes on top of hundreds of similarly racist actions by whites in recent years. She resists by challenging the white speaker. Repeatedly, in these many accounts we observe the dialectical character of racist incidents that force the human targets to be on guard and prepared to counter racist actions at any moment of the day. While desegregation has allowed numerous African Americans to move into jobs in historically white institutions, they still face and counter racial barriers virtually every day.

Black employees must be prepared to resist at a moment's notice. In this recent account of a workplace incident, a black police officer discusses the racial climate:

I reported and was told that I'd be riding with another [white] officer who was going to show me around. There was another trooper in the [highway] median and as we…pulled over into the median to see that trooper to talk, he looked over and saw, you know, that there was another new trooper there. And he said it as a joke, but it wasn't funny at the time. He used the word "nigger." "Oh, that's just what we need, another fucking 'nigger,'" you know, and laughed, and they laughed and carried on. And I looked, and they could see I wasn't laughing.[31]

He adds that fellow officers often told racist jokes, which joking helps to create a hostile racial climate for black employees in a variety of workplaces. Blatantly racist commentaries by whites in public seem to have gradually declined in many workplaces between the 1960s and the 1990s, but more recently they appear to have increased again. In this account, we have not only the powerful racist epithet used openly, but also the commonplace "joking" way that whites often express such overtly racist sentiments. The supposed joking gives whites a certain plausible deniability, so that if they are called on their racist commentaries, they can respond, "Oh, I was only joking." Such joking, at a minimum, signals to the racial "outsiders" that they are unwanted. Clearly painful and damaging for African Americans, this joking commonly involves an instructive form of bonding among many whites, especially among men, inside and outside their workplaces. By exchanging racist views, these whites reiterate and reinforce the racist categories of "white" and "black" in everyday settings, and thus the system of racial oppression as well.

Another black officer notes the comments of his white partner as they are patrolling in a police car and pass an apartment complex:

> We passed some black people who were out in the yard of this apartment, and he…goes, "Now, those people there, I would consider them 'niggers.'"…[H]e didn't think that I would even take exception to it. "Well, you know, guys like you and these other guys on the police department" and he named some people in the community, "I don't consider them that way, but people like that, drinking and all, I would consider them 'niggers.'"[32]

We see here a racial framing of an urban world, for negative views of ordinary African Americans loom large in the white officer's commentary on those he characterizes with racist epithets. The white officer, this respondent notes later, did not see the incident as "a big deal," a clear sign of the social alexithymia that seems widespread in many historically white workplaces. Clear, too, in these accounts of workplace discrimination is the social reproduction process that generates an alienated racial relationship between the oppressed and the oppressors.

Analyzing the incident, this black officer later notes that he protested the white view of people at an apartment complex. He must deal not only with a crude racist ideology that stereotypes working-class African Americans as lazy and immoral, but also with a white assumption that a black person employed in a historically white institution would not be offended by such an exhibition. Resistance is often part of these accounts by black Americans of their workaday experiences.

EVERYDAY DISCRIMINATION: HOUSING AND PUBLIC ACCOMMODATIONS

Systemic racism frequently shapes and disrupts the lives of African Americans outside their workplaces. The American dream is often placed beyond their reach by the routine operation of racial discrimination in most sectors of U.S. society. At the top of the list of things promised by the American dream to those who work hard is a decent apartment or house in a pleasant neighborhood. Like whites, black Americans greatly value this promise. For them, as for most Americans, housing is more than a place to live, for it represents pride of ownership and a visible indicator of accomplishments.

Discrimination in Housing

Blatant denial of access to a decent home is perhaps the most basic of the discriminatory constraints facing black Americans seeking housing in formerly white areas. In all regions of the country, white landlords and homeowners frequently cooperate with white real estate agents in excluding blacks from historically white residential areas. Thus, a dentist in a large city discusses such a discriminatory experience. He begins with a call from a supportive real estate agent who said she had found a house he might be interested in. They went to see it, after which his agent contacted the white owner, an insurance company executive:

> She conveyed an offer; he countered. I countered; he accepted it. I signed the papers; we sent them to him. We never got them back. The real estate owner that she [the salesperson] worked for was totally uncooperative with assisting her. Days went by; weeks went by; over a month went by.[33]

His real estate agent confronted the white owner of the firm, but he would not help resolve the white executive's discriminatory behavior. Then the respondent wrote a letter to the president of that executive's insurance company explaining the situation and that neither he nor his real estate agent could understand the white executive's long delay in responding. He also sent a copy of his letter to the NAACP.

This likely discrimination involves white attempts to avoid selling to a black person, a type of exclusionary and avoidance discrimination. The personal and family consequences of such actions, repeated millions of times each year in the United States, are often serious. Racial discrimination in the housing market means an economic loss, such as in the form of blacks having to pay higher house prices and higher monthly payments just to get a home. Prepared for such an incident, this professional took planned and aggressive action to deal with the discrimination, and he adds in his later account that the general legal counsel of the large company responded to his complaint and made sure that he was treated fairly by their executive. His experience is not unusual. Recent housing audit studies, using black and white testers who inquire about places to rent or buy, have found high levels of housing discrimination against African Americans in numerous U.S. cities.[34]

Once a black person finds housing in a building or neighborhood that is racially integrated, the discrimination may continue, as in this case reported by a young black woman when she went to borrow the vacuum cleaner from a white couple that had just moved into the building. The husband starts to give it to her, but his wife looks him in the eye

> And raises her eyebrows and says, "Remember, it's broken." Then he says, "Oh." Right then I knew, I shouldn't even try to deal with them. My encounters with them thus far have included a nasty encounter regarding my poor parking, refusing to answer the door when I needed help and quick stares when I am nearby. They (or she) have a problem with race, and they did not even need to tell me. I know by their actions.[35]

Today, much white hostility is communicated by what black Americans sometimes call "the stare." Some analysts have discussed this type of discriminatory action on the part of whites as "subtle," and thus as much different from discrimination in the past. Yet, one has to question just how subtle this discrimination really is, for its targets clearly see the discrimination and feel significant pain as a result.

Discrimination in Public Places

For most people, everyday living requires much movement across many public arenas. Although Jim Crow segregation was finally ended in the late 1960s, today African Americans still face much racial discrimination in public places. They face an array of humiliating types of discrimination. In one interview account, a law professor explains an incident involving a white sales clerk in a store that he knows routinely accepts checks from white customers:

> People were looking, and she said, "Oh, well, we're just not able to take checks" and all that. And I said, "Oh, that's all right, I understand." And I said it with the kind of English and the kind of dignity that she would think should be reserved for whites, and I said it in the most logistic voice I had. I said, "I understand exceedingly well." I said it just that way....And that's my point, there's so much wrapped up in the approach that I have. It allows me to get practical results. I understand the larger issues.[36]

Such rejection of checks or credit cards in white-owned stores is commonly reported by black shoppers interviewed in recent research studies, and again there are clear energy and economic costs attached to having to deal with this recurring discrimination in favor of whites.[37] The professor does not accept the discrimination quietly but speaks up in a way indicating that he knows what is actually taking place. In his interview, he had noted previously that he often wishes he could say to whites, "Hey, you're not fooling me, I know that this is racism, it's just bigotry, and that's all it is." Not only does he resist the discrimination, but he also takes action that reinforces his sense of dignity. In his interview he makes quite clear that he, like most African Americans for several centuries, has thought out carefully what whites are doing and how he should respond. The stereotyped image of reasonless, irrational African Americans so central to much white thinking is strongly refuted by many of these accounts of black coping with contemporary discrimination.

Black students regularly report racist incidents at the hands of whites near their college campuses. For example, one such student describes an incident as he was walking down a street near his historically white campus in one of the country's most diverse cities:

> And out of the blue comes this [white] guy driving in a van. He had one of those, you know, loudspeakers on the van, and he's like, "Is that a nigger with a white girl?" You do not understand how hard it was for my girlfriend to keep me from running and pulling him from the window of that truck because I knew he had to stop at the stop sign.[38]

Here a young black man is suddenly and unexpectedly targeted with a severe racist epithet, and the racial humiliation is heightened by the presence of his girlfriend. Thinking from within the white racial frame, like their ancestors over many generations, whites often demonstrate their great distancing of and alienation from black Americans in this manner. As we have seen earlier, most whites seem to feel that much of the space of the United States is indeed "white space," which whites are entitled to control. In most spaces like this one near a historically white university, black Americans are often seen as racial intruders. This white man's hostility was caused by the dreaded presence of an interracial couple, yet another linkage of his racist framing to past thinking by whites about interracial relationships since before Thomas Jefferson's day. This oppressive action again generates the desire on the part of the black target to respond strongly.

In an interview for a national project on the experiences of middle-class African Americans, a black humanities professor was eloquent and perceptive about the commonplace ecological pattern to racial discrimination faced by African Americans in public places and various other social settings.[39] She explained that when she is with friends at home, she is protected against most racism, and even at her university, her status as a professor gives her some protection against some racism. Yet, when she is out in public, especially in her ordinary clothes in stores, she faces much discrimination because most white strangers only see her as a "black" woman. Her analysis explicitly conceptualizes a spatial ecology of racism. As she describes her daily journeys, her encounters with racial problems vary greatly depending on the social setting. To my knowledge, no theorist of racial discrimination has explored this existential and spatial ecology of discrimination. Yet, it is a critical dimension of everyday life for African Americans, both today and in the past. We see this in the enslavement accounts of Frederick Douglass, William Wells Brown, and Harriet Jacobs, as well as in the accounts of the black respondents interviewed about life under legal segregation. They, too, were protected from at least some of the many ravages of white oppression when they were sheltered with family and friends and were usually least protected from white assaults of various kinds when out in the sphere of white strangers.

ENCOUNTERING RACISM: SCHOOL SETTINGS

White Actions and Black Reactions

Systemic racism often becomes obvious in the lives of white children and of children of color at a relatively young age. Indeed, black children learn early that whites of all ages insist on a white framing of what is, even for children, a racially hierarchical world. Several recent books by the mothers of black children have given numerous examples of how this works in everyday life.[40] A few field studies have also provided similar accounts. Working with the author, graduate student researcher Debra Van Ausdale spent eleven months in a multiracial daycare center. One day, the children were making a handprint poster by choosing colors in response to a teacher's request to pick a color that "looks just like you do." One three-year-old black child, Taleshia, selects a pale pink color to use as her hand color for the poster. Robin, a four-year-old white child questions Taleshia's choice: "She's not that color. She's brown. Look, Taleshia." Robin compares her light-skinned arm next to Taleshia's dark-skinned arm, adding a little later that "She's just not pink, can't you see that, she's black." "Look," she says to Taleshia. "You are brown! See? I am pink." Taleshia ignores her. Robin adds strongly, "Taleshia needs to be brown." When asked if she wants to be brown, Taleshia shakes her head "no," saying "I want that color" and points at the pink bottle. Soon Peggy, a three-year-old white child, comes over, and also informs Taleshia that she is not pink, saying "You can't have that color." Taleshia insists, "I want this color," and touches the pink bottle.[41]

One need not speculate long on why Taleshia chose the pink poster paint, for the palms of her hands were indeed that color. However, most whites seem to see African Americans only as "black," though in common usage this word refers just to a darker shade of brown than most whites are. The themes of racial imposition, plantation mentality, and resistance that we have seen in the adult accounts of discrimination by whites appear here as well. A young black child is learning to resist the imposition of white understandings on her. She is aware of her identity and of her body's various colors, and she refuses to allow controlling white children to define her. Even at three and four years old, white children have already accepted white society's color coding and lost some ability to see across the color line to the desires and understandings of a black child. Seeking enlightenment or at least more information, the white children could have asked Taleshia about her choice, but, already exhibiting the sense of white superiority and privilege, they insist that the black child is making the wrong choice. This inability to understand or empathize across the color line, an essential aspect of systemic racism, clearly begins at an early age, as many other examples of white children's behavior in Van Ausdale's field research also show.[42] In a thoroughly racist society, black children face many challenges in gaining respect for who they are.

Black students often continue to face challenges from white peers once they are enrolled in historically white colleges. One student recently gave us this account of his semester at a historically white college in the Midwest:

> This is one of those sad and angry nights for me. Tonight marks the third time since the beginning of the school year that I've been called a nigger by a bunch of white students on a...weekend....At first I used to wonder where they actually take the time in their heads to separate me from everyone else by the color of my skin. I used to just blame alcohol consumption for their obvious ignorance and racist attitudes, but I have since stopped trying to make excuses for them....I don't understand how such a system of hate could exist....Sometimes it seems that if I am around all white people, then I become nothing more than a token black "exhibit" for their amusement. I guess that even I have to be careful not to judge all based on a few bad examples, which more often than not is the fate of many

in the black community today. The saddest thing however, is that these people, these college students are supposed to be the supposed crème de la crème, the future business and political leaders.[43]

The level of reflection is again remarkable as this student not only reacts emotionally to recurring racist epithets but also sorts out carefully his thoughts in this journal entry prepared for us. In the past, he has tried to explain whites' racist actions as ignorance and drunkenness, but has stopped. Feeling sometimes like a token on exhibit, he still cautions himself not to stereotype all whites because of those who discriminate against him. Very sharp is his final reflection on the troubling racist behavior of the country's future, and supposedly well-educated, white leadership.

Moreover, at all levels of education and indeed throughout the society, the white racial framing of society includes a hierarchy of beauty that is usually taught to children at an early age. Today, black Americans, and especially girls and women, still face much racist imaging and commentary in the mass media and in advertising that suggest that black bodies are ugly, or are not as beautiful as other bodies. The racist character of dominant body imaging goes back at least to the eighteenth century, during which era Thomas Jefferson penned his famous characterization of white as beautiful and black as ugly—a characterization articulated by other founding fathers such as Benjamin Franklin, who spoke too of increasing the "lovely white" people in this country.[44]

A black honors student at a historically white university in the southwest here underscores the difficulty of growing up black and female in this environment. She explains that her parents drilled into her that she was beautiful,

> that my blackness was a beautiful thing, that the fact that I braided my hair was fine, that I didn't have a perm was fine. But when you're like, nine, ten, eleven, you tend not to listen to your parents, and you tend to listen to everything else…and all society which is white…with *Teen* magazine and *Seventeen* magazine flung in my face all the time, Barbie dolls flung in my face all the time, soap operas with all these white folks with blonde hair and blue eyes.…[45]

Showing significant resistance to conventional white beauty models, this student's parents taught her that being black was good, that her skin and hair were beautiful. Societal pressure on children not to listen to their parents in this regard is strong, for young girls of all backgrounds are drawn to media images around them, as well as to the image of the Barbie-type dolls with which they often play. One resource used by parents and others to counter these negative images stems from the black collective memory of past responses to such racism, a collective memory that often accents strongly alternative and positive aesthetic values and images.

Discrimination by White Teachers

Recall from the preface the Florida study that found that black students with unusual names averaged lower scores on tests and got fewer recommendations to gifted classes than their siblings with less distinctive names, apparently because exotic-to-whites names brought the former children less help from their teachers.[46] In ostensibly desegregated public or private school settings, black children today face an array of racial problems set for them by many whites, including teachers, students, parents, and counselors. We just examined some evidence of this at a multiracial preschool. Similar racial problems are created for children of color at all levels of public and private education across the United States. For example, in a focus group discussion with other African Americans about the impact of discrimination, a dental assistant discusses an incident involving her girlfriend's daughter at a private elementary school:

> She's in a Christian school. And the [white] teacher told the kids that black...children are born with their sin. And the little girl went home, and she asked her mother, she said "I just wish I was white." And she's only nine, she's nine. And [the] little girl had said what the teacher had said. And she said "Black people were born of sin, let's pray for the black people." And now the little girl is really scarred, but you don't know how scarred, and that she is scarred. And that kind of stuff makes you angry.[47]

The impact here goes well beyond the young girl suffering in the immediate setting, for her mother and mother's friend likewise suffered negative consequences from the white action. The teacher seems to be alluding to something like the old racist story of the biblical Noah condemning his son Ham's supposedly black descendants to be the servants of the supposedly white descendants of Noah's other sons—an indication of how racist thinking and religion have often been intertwined in some variations of the dominant racist ideology. Reflecting the white propensity to act on that ideology, this teacher, however unknowingly, inflicted significant psychological harm on the child and on people in her social network. The mother's friend is justifiably concerned and angry at the costly impact on a black child, who now wants to be white. This is the reaction of some black children in early encounters with systemic racism, as they are seeking to get out from under the pain of white oppression.

Note, too, the importance of family ties here, as in the earlier accounts of African Americans dealing with slavery and segregation. Collective responses to racial discrimination are usually honed in friendship and kinship networks. In her further account not quoted here, this respondent adds that such racist commentaries have an impact on white children as well, by reinforcing their sense of racial superiority. The white racial frame is learned by white children as much by observing adults as by their direct teaching.

African American students in historically white colleges and universities similarly face an array of racist barriers as they try to earn their degrees. They report differential treatment—an array of blatant, covert, and subtle discrimination—by white staff members and professors, as in this report about a social science professor from a black student at a large predominantly white university:

> I had a professor; I guess she just had it out for me. She didn't like me at all. But anyway one day we were talking about black stereotypes, and you know how they say like, "They're criminals and always wanting to rob people." So after class I wanted to talk to her. And a girlfriend and I were standing waiting for her, so she's coming out of the class, and she's all like "Oh, what?" And I say, "Can I talk to you, whatever?" And she's like, "Oh, I thought you wanted to rob me or something."[48]

Here a white professor makes a comment that conjures up the common white image of black criminality, outside a class where there had been some discussion of this matter. Perhaps the professor considered her offensive comment a joke, although the fact that the student had negative encounters with her before suggests that at best this was a lame try at humor. Whatever the teacher's intention, the impact was negative, and some time later the stereotype is remembered by the student. Apparently unreflective responses by many whites in interactive settings with blacks suggest how imbedded in the white mind various old stereotypes and prejudices actually are. They are entrenched enough in the white framing of society that even well-intentioned whites may not realize how much damage such racialized banter may cause in interactions with African Americans and other people of color.

Differential treatment in colleges and universities can take a variety of forms. Another black student at a historically white university reports a problem repeatedly cited by black students across the country:

> I wrote a paper in a humanities course about how Africa was a civilization long before other civilizations....I know other people who wrote, you know, similar things...black issues... and the teachers like really got on them for that paper....I don't know what it is about the teacher but they really come down on you for...attempting to write papers, something, you know, that has to do with topics...that's black. If it's controversial, it's not good...if you write some papers...you get B's, B+'s, A's. And then all of a sudden you write this paper on Africa, and you get a C-. You're like "what!" How did this happen? Or you know when they try to invalidate your material...."You can't say this, you can't do this."...If I wrote about how great Abraham Lincoln was, I probably would have gotten an A.[49]

Here the mistreatment takes the form of differential grading and a likely attempt at channeling a student to research subjects preferred by whites. Central to this account is the desire of a black student to be creative, in effect to pursue new knowledge beyond the limits of the usual historical framing of the world by whites. One of the liberating aspects of a college environment should be the opportunity to explore a range of provocative issues, and black students who come into white institutions are often eager to use college resources to explore subjects of concern to them or their communities. Among these are topics of Africa and African history, which whites operating from the conventional white racial frame often have trouble seeing as legitimate for student attention and research.

Ironically, much white stereotyping in the media and political arena portrays African Americans as uninterested in education, as unwilling to seek educational achievement. Nothing could be more in error, for education in general and education about the African and African American cultural background is very important in the black community. Conveying a widely held view, a teacher in a southern city gives this overview:

> That you have to strive for the best and accept nothing less in you, and to get to that point, you have to know your culture, you have to know your history. I try to get them to love reading, to thirst for getting knowledge outside of the classroom. I try to stress to them that their education is the only thing an-

other person can't take away from them, that their education is on them.[50]

Periodically, there is discussion in the white-controlled mass media about African Americans taking more responsibility for their own communities. This discussion is usually led by white Americans or their conservative black acolytes. Yet, within their communities and churches, African Americans have long discussed the family values of personal and collective responsibility and have pressed within the limits of their resources to see that their children have full access to education.

Patterns of Racism: More School Research

The major problem here is not with black families, but the well-institutionalized racism in U.S. educational institutions. Today, most school districts remain very segregated in racial terms, and those predominantly composed of children of color typically get *much less* in per capita funding than those that are predominantly white.[51] Within the schools there are yet more problems. One recent Applied Research Center study examined twelve large public school systems and discovered that, in the North and the South, in towns and cities, black students and other students of color generally fared much worse than whites. The researchers concluded that students of color face accumulating racial profiling in their schools, where their color is often used to "pull them over" from regular progress to a good education.[52] In most or all of the school systems reporting data, black students were much more likely than white students to be pushed out (or to drop out) of school, much more likely to be suspended or expelled, and much less likely to be channeled to advanced classes. Schools for students of color often did not have a proportionally representative group of teachers of color, and few school districts had programs of multicultural training for their teachers. The researchers conclude,

> If racial equity were a required course, most U.S. public school systems would receive a failing grade. Data collected in a dozen school districts around the country confirm what residents of communities of color already know: the public schools consistently fail to provide the same quality of education for students of color as for white students.[53]

Moreover, while black high-school and college graduation rates have risen significantly over the last few decades, because of great efforts by black young people and their parents, the economic return for a given year of added education remains much less for blacks than it is for whites.

THE MANY COSTS OF CONTEMPORARY RACISM

Historically, as I have noted previously, unjust impoverishment in terms of economic resources is one of the great costs of systemic racism as it has unfolded over the centuries of this country's history. Yet, historically and today, the loss of economic resources is only one of the major consequences of racial oppression. In his last book, written as official desegregation was beginning to replace official segregation, Dr. Martin Luther King, Jr., wrote that, if white racism is to be eradicated, then the white person "must begin to walk in the pathways of his black brothers and feel some of the pain and hurt."[54] In the commentaries on everyday experience with racism so far presented in this chapter, I have already illustrated some of the individual pain for African Americans that stems from their dealing with whites' racist attitudes and discriminatory actions. In this section, I review briefly some additional costs of everyday racism.

Stress and Physical Health

One such cost is the impact of the stress that comes from dealing with recurring discrimination on one's physical health. For example, in a recent midwestern focus group, a savvy African American nurse notes that, when she was dealing with discrimination at the nursing home where she works, she was diagnosed as having high blood pressure.

> When I turned into the driveway, I got a major headache. I had this headache eight hours until I walked out that door leaving there....I went to the doctor...and he said, "[Her name], you need to find a job because you do not like where you work." And within myself I knew that was true. But also within myself I knew I had to have a job because I had children to take care of. But going through what I was going through wasn't really worth it because I was breaking my own self down....It was constant intimidation, constant racism, but in a subtle way. You know, but enough whereas you were never comfortable. And then I finally ended up on high blood pressure pills because for the longest, I tried to keep low.[55]

This poignant commentary demonstrates the damage done by constant, if sometimes subtle, discriminatory actions in a nursing home

setting. The negative psychological impact, indeed the psychological violence, of behavioral racism is coupled with a negative physical impact, in
this case serious headaches and increased hypertension. Discrimination
in the workplace continues the pain and difficulties of the racist past,
a past-in-present reality from which there is no escape for her because
of her family commitments. Significantly, and contrary to some white
stereotyping, most black accounts of coping with discrimination are set
within important, usually supportive family contexts. No matter what
the costs, many African Americans are unable to change their jobs when
faced with persisting discrimination because of the need to support their
families. Clearly, systemic racism creates a prison-like environment in
the workplaces of many African Americans.

Moreover, when African Americans seek out health care for
stress-related and other physical illnesses, they often face discrimination. One recent survey of racial discrimination in U.S. health care institutions listed study after study that show racial discrimination in medical
care. The researchers report several studies showing that black patients
with heart and renal diseases do not get as good medical treatment as
comparable white patients. They add that other researchers have found

> that quality of care was lower for black Medicare beneficia-
> ries than for others hospitalized for congestive heart failure or
> pneumonia…older African American women receive mam-
> mography less often than socioeconomically and demographi-
> cally matched European American women…nonwhite (mostly
> African American) pneumonia patients were less frequently
> admitted to intensive care units than similarly ill and similarly
> insured European American patients.[56]

They continue with a list of similar findings. In addition, they suggest
that controls for other factors like income do not eliminate the pattern
of racial inequality and discrimination.

Chronic Energy Loss

In many black reports of everyday discrimination, we sense its
energy-draining character. Just trying to fit into the white workplace
and similar historically white social worlds remains highly problematical for most African Americans. A few years back, for example, a very
talented black journalist, Leanita McClain, committed suicide. She had
won major journalistic awards and was the first black person on the
Chicago Tribune editorial board. The reasons for her suicide are likely
complex, but one factor looms large in her own accounts of her expe-

rience in the white world of large newspapers: countering often discriminatory whites and pressures to conform. Reviewing her life, one person close to her has noted the conformity to white ways that is faced by black employees in historically white workplaces: "To fit in, black women consciously choose their speech, their laughter, their walk, their mode of dress and car. They trim and straighten their hair." In such white-dominated situations, like their ancestors during slavery and legal segregation, black Americans must "learn to wear a mask."[57] The pressures to conform to a white-imposed self and thus to conceal one's real self—the double consciousness accented by W. E. B. Du Bois—often lead to stress-related illness or worse, as in this case.

Recall, too, the commentary of the black professor who once taught at a major historically white university in regard to his having to use half of his lifetime allotment of creative energy to deal with the omnipresent racial hostility and discrimination from whites. Unmistakably, racial oppression in the United States is a complex system that routinely exploits and drains the energies of those targeted by it. This agonizing and painful reality began with slavery and has continued through legal segregation to the present day. African Americans are still, to use Frederick Douglass's apt term, the "slaves of society" and typically must use much creative energy over their lifetimes in dealing with just being black in the United States. The continuing reality of this energy loss flatly contradicts notions in the common white view of U.S. society as "no longer racist."

Systemic racism steals personal energy that could be put to good use not only for personal development, but also for family and community development. The racial oppression encountered by an individual thus has great consequences for that person's significant social groups and networks. We see the family and community cost of energy loss in this account from a black teacher, who speaks about community activities after work:

> We had started a minority action committee which is still in existence, with the school district. And…it's very hard to get people after they've fought all day—in a sense, that have enough energy to come out and support an effort like that where it is needed. We know the racism is out there, we know we need to fight for our kids—that was the main thrust of it when we came together.… And we endeavored to do something about it, but, as I was saying, we were just so drained, it just never got off the ground.[58]

Dealing with racism in the workplace during the day makes it difficult to summon adequate energy to deal with both family and community matters after work. In an ever accumulating and domino-like impact, the energy-draining character of racial discrimination in one social arena often has a very negative impact on activities in other social arenas.

Racial discrimination's cumulative impact is well described in one assessment by a retired black professor who worked in many areas of the country over many decades. In his interview, he explains how whites generally do not understand the impact of one racist event or discriminatory action on African Americans, for even liberal whites tend to see these actions as isolated events. As he puts it, whites do not know that most of the time African Americans endure lives of "quiet desperation" that are constantly punctuated by hundreds of everyday incidents of racial oppression that crash in just because they happen to have a different skin color. They endure much of this oppression with dignity and without making a public display of their anger.[59]

Even those whites who sympathize with and support a black friend who has suffered a discriminatory event frequently miss the accentuated and lasting impact of one such painful event. One reason is a factor cited earlier in this chapter—the way in which a present instance of discrimination brings up and focuses memories of past and recent oppression, including racist atrocities. Another reason is that one particular instance of discrimination is only one in a long line of hundreds or thousands of such instances. Each discriminatory act is not isolated, but part of a "litany of daily large and small events" that constantly remind African Americans of their "place" in society. Again we see that for African Americans the past is always intrusive, because the still racialized present is in many ways an extension of the racially oppressive past. In addition, the refusal of most whites to openly remember and fully accept the bloody past of oppression is harmful to them and to the larger society, in part because that social amnesia makes it easier for racism to continue.

RESISTING RACISM: THE ONGOING STRUGGLES

In numerous accounts above, we have seen the assertive resistance to racial discrimination that African Americans often undertake. Workplaces are among the most common places where they must demonstrate and hone their best racism-countering strategies and tactics. Thus, we observed the strategy of a sales manager who struggled greatly with her openly racist and sexist supervisor for a fair evaluation of her excellent sales performance. To do this, she had to keep and present careful records of her performance to counter his anticipated negative and prejudiced reaction to her performance. We also observed how another black female employee had to counter extreme racist epithets and comments at her workplace by enduring and then finally having to take her case to the federal Equal Employment Opportunity Commission. We saw as well how a black police officer had to counter verbally the racist epithet and conceptualization applied by a white officer to some black Americans at a local apartment complex.

Wherever it is implemented, such active resistance by black Americans can have major consequences, for those who speak out against the discrimination that they and others face often get labeled as "difficult" or as "not team players." We see this response in a recent account from a veteran law enforcement officer with decades of service:

> Some people used to say I was a troublemaker, I said, "Troublemaker, how? What have I done to cause trouble? Because I won't let you say 'nigger' in front of me? That's a troublemaker? Because I won't let you treat people wrong, that's a troublemaker?"[60]

Here the sense of constant struggle, and the asserted courage to fight back whatever the cost, are evident. Those who face mistreatment at the hands of whites usually prepare in advance a variety of resistance strategies, some of which can be costly in terms of lost promotions and other lost workplace rewards, not to mention in terms of personal energy and health costs.

Across a great array of ages and societal settings, African Americans must today be prepared to counter recurring racist attitudes, practices, and other impositions from whites. Such attacks can come in most any place and at any time. In previous accounts, thus, we observed how a young black child had already learned from interactions with whites that she had to stand her ground, in this case in a multiracial daycare setting where a white child imposed her white understandings of colors and identities on the black child. In another account, we saw how a college student's parents had taught her to resist conventional beauty models and to hold her own skin in high esteem. In contending with racism, African Americans frequently accent the importance of family settings and support.

Indeed, the discussions of family support in the interviews cited above are typical of hundreds of interviews that my associates and I have conducted over many years. In numerous interview studies, African Americans have spoken strongly and poignantly about the importance of kinship, and indeed of a family-centered spirituality, in dealing with problems of racism. An example of this perspective is presented by a black psychologist:

Black people are more spiritual....We believe in relationships. I don't know whether it was African tradition, all I know is what happened in America you had a lot of extended families, where there was a lot of love and concern and helping and working with, and trying to do for each other, and not for ourselves. And see the white man's situation is very selfish, everything for him, whatever it takes for that one person to have power.[61]

Extended families typically provide some backup in dealing with everyday racism. The respondent continues in her longer commentary by noting that African Americans just do not need the high incomes that so that so many whites have and by accenting the point that African Americans like to share with their families and friends more than do whites. She thus offers a collective perspective underscoring the moral assets and advantages of being black in a highly materialistic United States.

One of the ironies of much white commentary on African Americans today is that whites are so far off the mark in evaluating black families—which most whites likely see as weak, disorganized, or "broken." While black communities do have significant family problems, they are no greater than those for white communities, especially communities of comparable socioeconomic circumstances. Indeed, in some important ways, African Americans have stronger family values than whites, and they also typically have strong family networks. A female professional stresses the centrality of her family network:

Somehow when I share with my family, which is what I have done all of my life, it seems to dissipate. And I get feedback, and I get the kind of support I need to handle the problem effectively. So, that's the first place I go.[62]

Later, she adds more on the family support system for all types of decisions: "I have a very, very, very large support group too." Her family network is stretched across the United States, and she uses the phone and mail to garner family and friends' input on decisions about a range of personal and family matters.

Numerous scholars have examined black families in recent years, and have found them to have many strengths for which they seldom get credit in the white-controlled media or in the speeches of white politicians. For example, in a recent book, the scholar Robert Hill has detailed the major strengths of African American families. At the top of his list is the importance of kinship bonds, which have for centuries been central to the resistance of African Americans to racial oppression and to survival and success in spite of that oppression. These kinship linkages are found not only in the communication and sharing of personal and racial problems of all kinds noted by the last respondent, but also in a range of kin-related decisions, such as bringing the elderly into one's nuclear family, the constant reliance on extended family networks, and the informal adoption of children in distress whether they are technically kin or not.[63]

CONCLUSION

The importance and utility of the systemic racism perspective are well demonstrated in these poignant and revealing accounts from contemporary African Americans. Continuing oppression by a diverse array of whites in the contemporary era is yet another socially reproduced manifestation of the country's age-old racist foundation and structures. While racial oppression is today different in certain details from that of legal segregation, it is similar in many fundamentals. Today's racial oppression is still much more than a matter of scattered bigots abandoning supposedly egalitarian institutions, but rather it is about major economic and political institutions systemically imbedding racial inequality and discrimination against African Americans, as well as against other people of color. As under slavery and legal segregation, major historically white institutions remain substantially exploitative, racially hierarchical, and rather undemocratic. White elites, with their immediate white subordinates, continue to be firmly in control of major U.S. organizations and institutions. Systemic racism continues to keep African Americans heavily burdened.

In chapter 7, we will hear a discourse from white Americans that often denies that racism is still devastating for Americans of color. Yet, in this chapter, all major aspects of systemic racism are discernible in the contemporary accounts of the racial hostility and discrimination faced by African Americans in their everyday lives. The racial hierarchy and its alienated and alienating racial relationships remain firmly in place. The white male elite is still at the top, with a white "labor aristocracy" below that elite class position but still holding onto the public and psychological wage of whiteness. The largest groups of people of color are still on the lower rungs of the U.S. racial ladder. Racial inequalities remain obvious. The unjust enrichment of whites is still clear in this racialized system of privilege, as is the reality of unjust impoverishment for African Americans whose ancestors first faced that impoverishment. We see a continuation of white discrimination and racial domination in its many guises, ranging from lesser job and other economic opportunities for African Americans to an array of racialized barriers for them in schools, politics, health care, and public accommodations.

Implicit, too, in many of the accounts provided by African Americans in this chapter is the persisting and somewhat refurbished white racial frame and the associated ideology that still rationalizes discrimination targeting Americans of color, an ideology that will be quite evident in the next chapter. In addition, across most of these experiential accounts is evidence of the ongoing racial struggle, one in which African Americans must constantly maintain a repertoire of resistance strategies to use in their struggles against everyday racism. Collective memory is central to their accounts, as black Americans continue to make great use of multigenerational knowledge from their communities in order to survive continuing discrimination, both blatant and subtle, at the hands of whites of all ages. The accounts here offer nuanced discussions of the common strategies of resistance to racism, some of which closely track the strategies of those enslaved and legally segregated in earlier eras. Much of this ongoing resistance to systemic racism is necessarily defensive, such as when African Americans conceal their feelings from discriminatory employers or when they try to avoid interaction with certain whites in their workplaces. Yet other reported resistance to everyday racism is considerably more aggressive and confrontational.

Like many contemporary black writers and commentators, the brilliant feminist author, bell hooks, has often recounted the painful ordeal of racism in the United States today. In an opening section of her book, *Killing Rage*, she notes the racial hostility she has faced in her daily rounds. On one fateful afternoon, she and a black female traveling companion hailed a cab in New York City, which began a string of negative and discriminatory events: "The [white] cabbie wanted us to leave his taxi and take another; he did not want to drive to the airport. When I said I would willingly leave but also report him, he agreed to take us." Once at the airport, she continues,

> We faced similar hostility when we stood in the first-class line at the airport. Ready with coupon upgrades, we were greeted by two young white airline employees who continued their personal conversation and acted as though it were a great interruption to serve us. When I tried to explain...I was told by the white male that "he was not talking to me."[64]

An intense discussion followed with the white employees denying that their inaction had anything to do with "race." hooks and her colleague resisted the discrimination assertively. After calling for the employees' supervisor, who listened and apologized, hooks and her companion finally got the necessary service, though as they left, the white employee had a "gleam of hatred" in her eyes. Once on the plane, her friend was called over the loudspeaker to the front of the plane. She was accused by the white flight attendants of trying to sit in a first-class seat not assigned to her, although she was in her correct seat with an incorrect boarding pass earlier given to her by the white airline employees. Her friend's explanation was ignored by the flight attendants, and a white man sat in her seat, with just a brief apology to her friend who was moved to another seat. The white man did not speak up and intervene on behalf of the black woman, but just occupied his seat. Sitting next to him, hooks argued with him about why he did not do the right thing and speak up. Thus, for hooks and her friend, the afternoon involved a string of racist incidents, which called forth a strong resistance. Yet, the bottom line in the final analysis, as she notes, was one of "killing rage."

In the current era of systemic racism, individual and collective resistance continues to be part of the ongoing, often dialectical character of racial oppression. In its quotidian operation, this oppression regularly creates new forms of black resistance, as it has now for nearly four centuries.

7

CONTEMPORARY RACIAL REALITIES:
THROUGH THE EYES OF WHITE AMERICANS

For a brief time in the 1960s and the early 1970s, some influential members of the white elite, including major politicians and journalists, responded to the civil rights movement and strongly supported new civil rights laws. One major reason for this response, as I suggested previously, had to do with the international struggle with the former Soviet Union for the hearts and minds of the world's people. While numerous white leaders seem to have supported civil rights changes mostly for political and pragmatic reasons, a few reconceptualized U.S. racial relations in relatively critical terms. For a short time, their interpretive discourse abandoned the blaming of black Americans for racial problems, and some even adopted a language that included some terms from the civil rights movement itself, like "white racism" and "institutional racism."

Thus, the final report of President Lyndon Johnson's 1968 presidential Commission on Civil Disorders dramatically concluded that "Our Nation is moving toward two societies, one black, one white—separate and unequal" and minced no words about white responsibility:

Discrimination and segregation have long permeated much of American life....White society is deeply implicated in the ghetto. White institutions created it, white institutions maintain it, and white society condones it....White racism is essentially responsible for the explosive mixture which has been accumulating in our cities since the end of World War II.[1]

According to this candid report, one key ingredient in this white-imposed racism is "Pervasive discrimination and segregation in employment, education, and housing, which have resulted in the continuing exclusion of great numbers" of African Americans from economic advancement in the society.[2] For a time, some prominent white analysts in universities, the media, and government interpreted the oppressive employment, education, and housing conditions of black Americans as generated by institutionalized discrimination on the part of whites, and some members of the elite in and out of government action pressed for some significant race-conscious remedies for this discrimination. Even President Lyndon Johnson began to adopt occasionally the "we shall overcome" language of the civil rights movement.

However, this candid discourse on racism and apparent support for dramatic antidiscrimination intervention in the society soon evaporated. Such intervention to end discrimination had never been fully accepted by a *majority* of the white elite or of rank-and-file whites. By the 1970s and 1980s, most influential whites had—not surprisingly given the inertial impact of the country's long racist history—taken the view that the "two societies" verdict of the 1968 Commission was much too harsh. To take one example, journalists writing in a major 1988 *Newsweek* article argued that "mercifully, America today is not the bitterly sundered dual society the riot commission grimly foresaw."[3] If they had ever been used, critical terms like "white racism" and "institutional racism" were eliminated from virtually all white media analysts' and major politicians' vocabularies, as well as from those of the majority of white academics and other researchers working on racial matters.

Indeed, since the 1970s and 1980s, the white racial frame has reasserted its ancient blaming of black individuals, communities, values, and culture for the society's racial problems. Such a strong accent on the old framing has helped most whites to feel better about the continuing, and massive, racial inequalities in society. Operating in the antiblack tradition going back to the seventeenth century, this racially conservative language has interpreted white-black issues mostly as problems of black culture and community, accenting such terms as the "black underclass," "black family pathology," and "black gangs and drugs." From its earliest days, this blame-the-victim discourse has operated to disguise the underlying reality of systemic racism and to prevent a society-wide understanding of the central role of systemic racism in everyday problems of black Americans. Significantly, in recent years many whites, including members of the U.S. Supreme Court,[4] have added to their racial framing of this society the new notion that white men are victims who are facing significant "reverse discrimination" as the result of government programs allegedly going too far in addressing traditional racial discrimination.

In this chapter, I explore the racial views of white Americans, both those in the elite and those in the rank-and-file. I assess specific commentaries from many whites who reflect on racial matters in the United States. I again ask, What lessons have whites taken from their racial experiences, including much contact with the mass media and their limited contacts with Americans of color? What generalizations and conclusions do they reach?

In their commentaries on racial issues, we see that these white Americans are still especially focused on African Americans, who for most whites remain the archetypal and most troubling racial group. A majority of whites seem to view contemporary racial matters, including the continuing necessity of the racial hierarchy, substantially in terms of the character, actions, and reactions of African Americans. In most of these white accounts, as in earlier white accounts for the slavery and Jim Crow eras, we find relatively little discussion of whites' racial power and privilege or even of their everyday personal interactions with Americans of color. Instead, we mostly find an array of often stereotyped reflections and generalizations that are in numerous ways linked to the centuries-old white framing of the societal world. While some whites do indicate discomfort with racial discrimination, like earlier slaveholders and segregationists, most offer remarkably little analysis of, or negative reactions to, the realities of contemporary racial oppression—particularly in regard to how these racial realities continue to benefit their lives and those of families and friends. Even as racial understandings and inclinations pervade most nooks and crannies of their lives, in most cases white Americans fail to see the heavy, enduring, and still systemic reality of contemporary racism.

WHITE RACIAL FRAMING: THE WHITE FOUNDERS' LEGACY

Nobel Prize winner Toni Morrison has sagely called for research on the "impact of racism on those who perpetuate it. It seems both poignant and striking how avoided and unanalyzed is the effect of racist inflection on the subject."[5] Not only are racist practices still pervasive in all major historically white institutions, but they are still perpetuated and fostered by the racialized conceptions and habits of white Americans. Central to the persistence of systemic racism into the present day is the organized set of racialized habits that whites consciously or unconsciously express in their everyday attitudes and actions in U.S. society. These habits include the racialized framing of the social world that most use extensively, a frame that imbeds an array of racist stereotypes, images, and emotions that are to a significant degree survivals of centuries-old antiblack and prowhite thinking. As we will see in this chapter, this white racial frame also incorporates background notions and deep racial assumptions. As a result, most whites ordinarily interpret interracial situations and events in terms of this frame—and not in terms of searches for new social data or of careful and rational calculations on racial matters.

By repeating elements of this racial frame, integrating items within the frame, and applying the learned emotions, stereotypes, and imagery in various types of discriminatory action, whites guarantee that this frame persists and remains difficult to counter. Particular cognitive or emotional items in this racial frame tend to resist substantial evidence countering them because of how deeply they are imbedded in white minds.

Today, as in the past, the well-entrenched frame that the majority of whites use in making sense out of important racial matters seems to be a metaphorical extension of the patriarchal model. African Americans are still often viewed as dependent beings, even as children who should follow the lead of their white "elders." From this perspective, "American society" still means whites, and "moral values" mean white-preferred values. A majority of white Americans view the continuing racial hierarchy of white over black as legitimate because they believe whites are culturally and morally—and still, for many, biologically—superior to African Americans and other Americans of color. As I have demonstrated for earlier eras, whites have developed within this racial frame an ideology defending white privilege as meritorious and accenting the inferiority of African Americans and other Americans of color. White elites are especially important in crafting and perpetuating ideological and structural racism, as they were in previous historical epochs.

Some researchers play down the strength of these white views, arguing that the majority of whites mostly hold suspicions and uncertainties, rather than firm negative views, about African Americans.[6] Yet much research using surveys, in-depth interviews, and journals contradicts this view—including much data from the private arenas of white interaction examined later in this chapter. In thinking about racial matters, the majority of whites today make much use of the old stereotyped views of African Americans. Thus, one recent national survey found that 58 percent of whites interviewed still admitted to a stranger, a pollster, that they held stereotypical images of African Americans such as these: African Americans are lazy, aggressive, or violent; prefer welfare; or are always complaining. One third publicly admitted that they held two or more of these stereotyped views.[7]

Stereotyping African Americans as Less Intelligent

Since well before Thomas Jefferson's time, large numbers of white Americans have also clung devotedly to the image of black Americans as somewhat or much less intelligent than whites. Then and now, many whites have been taught such stereotypes at a young age. In a recent interview, a leading corporate executive defends the view that black Americans have less intelligence than whites as scientifically demonstrated:

> Dr. Shockley, inventor of the transistor who did substantial sociological research showed that, matched on a variety of variables—blacks are born differently—on standardized intelligence tests...It's very socially unacceptable to say blacks are not as smart as the whites, are not as smart as the Asians, but there's a lot of research pointing to the fact that it is the case. And the liberals cannot accept that on a critical basis because it violates the empirical philosophical ideals that everybody has to be equal and that the reason for differences is caused by environmental and cultural factors.[8]

While a majority of white Americans no longer openly espouse this viewpoint in opinion surveys—probably trying to give a socially desirable answer to a pollster—a majority likely harbor some version of this negative image in their minds. For example, very large numbers of whites have had favorable reactions to racist books done by conservative white researchers, such as the 1990s bestseller, *The Bell Curve*, which sold more than a half million copies. The white authors, Charles Murray and Richard Herrnstein, sought to prove that black Americans (and Latinos) were less intelligent than whites because they tended to have lower average scores than whites on those paper-and-pencil tests called erroneously "IQ-tests," white-crafted tests that actually measure only a limited array of learned skills and not some global "intelligence."

Many white Americans mix their negative views of black Americans with images of white innocence in regard to racial conditions in the United States. Take this example of a white college student's reply to a question about her first experience with black Americans, in this case black children in her school:

> I switched from a...school which had no blacks to a public school, and I was thrown in the middle of a bunch of apes, no I'm just kidding....And I don't know, my parents have always instilled in me that blacks aren't equal....[9]

In her interview, this well-educated woman continues in this vein, making negative comments about African Americans of various ages as unequal to whites and periodically using the "ape" imagery for black Americans, the white-generated animal imagery that goes back to at least Thomas Jefferson's time.

Then, at the end of her interview, she adds: "I don't consider myself racist. I, when I think of the word racist, I think of KKK, people in white robes burning black people on crosses and stuff, or I think of the skinheads or some exaggerated form of racism." Some educated whites still make public use of strongly negative antiblack imagery. Also clear here is the strategy that many whites use to deflect concern over their racist commentaries or actions, one that insists that "I am not racist." Such statements of denial are common among white Americans, particularly those seeking to assert a view of themselves as ostensibly "colorblind."[10] They often defend such statements by citing whites they know who are even more racist in their thoughts or actions. In addition, like their predecessors in earlier eras, whites doing racist stereotyping today frequently make the othered human beings into nonhuman "things" (for example, "apes"). Today racial oppression still has more than sufficient energy to keep such racist stereotyping in play throughout most of U.S. society.

Persisting Stereotypes of Laziness and Criminality

In their highly racist framing of this society, early white leaders like Thomas Jefferson and George Washington accented what they saw as a weak work ethic among black Americans, and this ideological legacy can be seen in many white commentaries in public and private today. Against much evidence to the contrary,[11] many whites in all social classes persist in viewing African Americans from a racial frame that accents them as having much weaker work values than do whites. Thus, one white professional, when asked in a major study, "What do you think blacks need to do to become truly equal?" replies this way:

> For them to be as successful as we are, they are going to need to adopt our values. Be a part of our system or whatever....like wanting the money but not wanting to actually show up, being

reliable. The basic things we try to teach clients, or a high school kid about work, you know, like you need to be there, you need to work hard, so I guess it is the work ethic.[12]

There is a strong white assumption that black Americans today still do not have the same work values as whites and do not fit well into the workplace system, a view that dates back in white thinking now for centuries in spite of the centrality of much black labor in actually building up this society economically.

Similarly, a corporate executive develops this generalization from his experience in hiring:

To generalize is very difficult, but if you had to take a hundred blacks from one place and a hundred whites, I would think very often the blacks aren't working as hard....Whites have a tendency more to be more concerned about keeping their job because welfare is not such a stigma to the blacks as it is to the whites.[13]

From this traditional white frame, black Americans do not work as hard as whites because they do not see being on public welfare as having the same negative stigma that whites do. In this view, unemployment is not so much a structural problem as a problem of individuals personally not choosing to keep a job or not choosing to work hard.

Images of lazy public welfare recipients have been such standard fare in white thinking about African Americans that few are aware that historically whites have usually been the majority of public aid recipients. When a white educator is asked about programs to compensate African Americans for discrimination, he changes the subject this way:

There is this welfare system that enables young mothers...who can't support their children to have children anyway.... [it] encourages poor people to have children, and they don't have to work....I don't think you need to have money so much, just have some values towards certain types of things, like education or intellect, or something like that. Instead of, you know, just loafing, and watching TV, and getting welfare. And you know, getting fat, and being angry, and taking your anger out on robbing people, and killing people.[14]

Here is a mixture of racial and class stereotypes, including not only the image of lazy welfare recipients having too many children, but also the images of them getting too fat, having little concern with education, and committing crimes. The respondent also moves from the welfare imagery to stereotypes of black criminality. This imagery has an ancient pedigree. During slavery and legal segregation, whites often stereotyped African Americans in terms of images of disease and criminality—consistently ignoring the role of whites in generating highly stressful socioeconomic conditions for black Americans that might lead to such disease or crime or indeed the many serious crimes, such as violent interpersonal attacks and lynchings, perpetrated by whites against blacks.

Hoary stereotypes of black deviance or criminality are seen in much contemporary framing and interpersonal discussion among whites, as in this report by a black student of his white friend's reaction to a possible trip to a store:

> When he realized it was nearly 5 o'clock, he told me that we weren't going to be able to go…because he had to leave for a Tae Kwon Do class.…He laughed and told me that he would've been able to go to…but his Tae Kwon Do class was in the "ghetto" in a bad part of town. Then in a sarcastic voice he said, "I want to go early because I don't want to go in the ghetto and the black guys punk me because I'm probably going to have the best car in the whole block." Then he lowered his voice and said, "I would try to fight them but I don't think Tae Kwon Do would be a good weapon against a block full of people that probably all have guns." I looked at him kind of puzzled, because his statements implied a lot of things about black neighborhoods, then I said in a still voice, "Wow, so you think everyone over there owns a gun?" And he replied in a sarcastic voice, "Only the people that can afford it."…When he saw that I actually took offense to his comment, he began to laugh and said in a relaxed voice, "You know I was just playing."[15]

This revealing incident shows a high degree of stereotyping about criminality and violence in black communities on the part of the white student, the respondent's reputed "friend." Apparently, many whites still feel comfortable engaging in overtly racist commentaries or performances even in the presence of black acquaintances and friends. Here is a classical stereotype in the white racial frame, that of "dangerous black men." This stereotype seems to conjure in the white mind an array of connected ideas, such as the idea of taking precautionary action when going near black men or of reporting black men as perpetrators of crimes when they are not (as in numerous white hoaxes).[16] That the stereotyping here was done intentionally is signaled by the fact that the white student actually lowered his voice in making the comment. But there is more than stereotyping here, for the common white racial framing of society includes emotions and inclinations to action. The white student reveals certain emotions, first in the sarcastic tone of his racist remarks and in his backtracking with a laugh and a comment that he was "just playing." Some type of joking response to being called on one's racist remarks seems common among white Americans. This white student also demonstrates an action inclination in that his stereotyping has led him to conclude that he should arrive in the area early for self-protective reasons.

In addition to possessing images of black criminality in their minds, many white Americans prefer to ignore or do not understand the criminality that whites, including white authorities such as police officers, often engage in against African Americans. For example, as he thought about a scene where some elderly African Americans were welcoming the not guilty verdict in the case of O. J. Simpson, one well-educated white professional concluded that, "There's a lot of [black] parents who probably were subjected to police brutality or harassment when they were young, who still remember that [and] still have resentment."[17] He recognizes the impact that police malpractice has had on African Americans, but consigns it only to the past.

However, police brutality remains a serious problem for African Americans today, and it is almost entirely a white-on-black crime. In an analysis of 130 police-brutality accounts in numerous major cities, sociologist Kim Lersch found those targeted for this malpractice were almost always African Americans or Latinos. People in these two groups made up 97 percent of the victims of brutality, while the overwhelming majority (93 percent) of the offending officers were white.[18] Such data, together with the absence of an outcry against these events from the white population, suggest that whites in cities across the country either support or tolerate excessive police violence against people of color. Such instances of brutality, as well as more common police harassment and profiling just short of overt violence, are part of the ongoing process not only of subordinating African Americans generally, but also of sustaining the racial segregation of residential communities by pressuring black Americans to stay out of traditionally white areas. From the beginning of slavery onward, being seen as "out of place" by whites has been potentially dangerous for black Americans.

Deep White Fears: Interracial Sex and Marriage

Fear of increased social contacts and intimacy across the color line has motivated racist commentary by whites since the colonial period, as we saw in the previous accounts from whites living in the slavery and Jim

Crow epochs. Today, many whites' negative views of African Americans are linked to the concern that the latter might transgress the color line in regard to interpersonal intimacy. This is especially clear in the case of interracial dating and marriage, where a primary concern of many whites is protecting and perpetuating "white" families.

In one interview study of white women on the West Coast, the researcher reported significant white resistance to interracial dating and marriage. A white female respondent makes this comment about her husband's attitude toward their son dating a black person:

> And on the racial issues…it's hard for him not to accept our son's girlfriend, who's Jamaican, in a personal way—he really likes her. But just to accept the fact that his son, the only person carrying his name, is going in such a new direction. His children might be biracial. That just doesn't feel good to him.[19]

Even whites in reputedly liberal areas, such as northern California in this case, often harbor negative feelings about cross-racial dating and marriage. Assessing a question about how he would view interracial dating and marriage on the part of his children, a medical professional recently put it this way:

> To be perfectly frank, I would rather that my grandchildren be white. I have a tremendous amount invested in my identity as a white person,…and I have a tremendous amount of emotional energy and psychic energy invested in being a white person.[20]

Relatively rare is such an overt verbalization of the importance of whiteness to a white person's view of himself and his descendants. For most whites, this understanding seems present but is usually left unstated. For them, substantial energy is indeed invested in white identity construction and maintenance, however unconscious that effort may be.

Interracial dating and sex provoke very strong reactions from many whites, as in the case of a businessperson who reacts to a hypothetical question offered by an interviewer, one asking how he would feel if an adult child were to date or marry a black person:

> I'd be sick to my stomach. I would feel like, that I failed along the way. I'd probably take a lot of the blame for that. I would feel like probably I failed out on the job along the way or they would not have those tendencies to do that. I'd feel like I probably failed as a father, if that was to happen. And it's something that I could never accept.…It would truly be a problem in my

family because I could never handle that, and I don't know what would happen because I couldn't handle that, ever.[21]

Not only are the white business leader's emotions visceral in the literal sense, but he links his patriarchal views and inclinations to his important family network. His role as a father would be a failed one if his children were to cross the color line in regard to intimacy. In numerous commentaries in this chapter, we observe some white men to be assertive carriers of very negative attitudes and inclinations in regard to interracial marriage and dating. White men seem to work hard to protect their family networks against intrusions of what they frame as undesirable racial "others."

Sincere Fictions of White Selves and White Civilization

A majority of white Americans hold to a racial frame that includes much more than negative thoughts, images, and feelings directed at racial out-groups. These views and feelings are rooted deeply in a related view of white Americans' superior position in the racial hierarchy of the country, and indeed of the world. From the seventeenth century to the present, white Americans have had the advantaged hierarchical position in terms of privileges, resources, and opportunities. Most whites still learn this sense of racial group position at an early age.

Whiteness is centrally about prizing white beauty, values, opinions, stereotypes, and culture. In the Revolutionary Era, numerous white British founders felt that the presence of non-British immigrants, including enslaved Africans, was problematical for the long-term future of the country. Recall that in the eighteenth century, Benjamin Franklin suggested that, because "the number of purely white people in the world is proportionably very small," the new country should not "increase the sons of Africa" but rather the "lovely white and red."[22] Other famous leaders, such as presidents Thomas Jefferson and James Madison, speculated about or worked for the export of black Americans, if they were to be freed, to geographical places outside of North America as a way of whitening the country.

Today, many whites are still concerned, along the lines of Franklin's ideas, with darker-skinned immigrants decreasing the demographic dominance of whites in the U.S. population. This contemporary white concern about immigrants from Latin America, the Caribbean, Asia, and Africa is often aggressively coupled with a strong prizing of the virtues of whiteness. Not only rank-and-file whites, but also prominent white officials and leading commentators, have recently made clear how concerned they are about a United States that is not predominantly white. The ongoing trend toward a multiracial, multicultural society makes them very fearful.

For example, a former advisor to presidents and U.S. presidential candidate Patrick Buchanan has insisted that "our Judeo-Christian values are going to be preserved and our Western heritage is going to be handed down to future generations and not dumped on some landfill called multiculturalism."[23] For him the "Western heritage" here is presumptively white European, as he has made clear in another comment about immigration:

> If we had to take a million immigrants in, say, Zulus next year or Englishmen, and put them in Virginia, what group would be easier to assimilate and would cause less problems for the people of Virginia? There is nothing wrong with us sitting down and arguing that issue that we are a European country, English-speaking country.[24]

Again, the U.S. is envisioned as fundamentally a white European country, and Zulu immigrants, who are black Africans, are seen as much less capable of assimilating than some English immigrants. Yet, in his racist framing of the world, Buchanan neglects the fact that African Americans currently make up a large percentage of the Virginia population and would thus provide a social context within which African immigrants could be incorporated at least as easily as European immigrants. African Americans have been in North America since 1619, much longer than have many European groups. Certainly, Buchanan's own group, Irish Catholics, mostly came to North America well after African Americans, who had been here in substantial numbers for more than a century when large groups of Irish Catholics came.

Some leaders in the U.S. business community have asserted similar nativist views. Take the example of *Forbes* magazine editor Peter Brimelow. In his book, *Alien Nation*, he asserts that "the American nation has always had a specific ethnic core. And that core has been white." Some decades back, most Americans "looked like me. That is, they were of European stock. And in those days, they had another name for this thing dismissed so contemptuously as 'the racial hegemony of white Americans.' They called it 'America.'"[25] Brimelow, himself an immigrant from Great Britain, argues that new darker skinned immigrants from Latin America, Asia, Africa, and the Caribbean constitute a major threat—a future "alien nation," instead of Brimelow's own prized future of an overwhelmingly white and European country.

While Buchanan and Brimelow are more aggressive in openly and publicly presenting their nativist views on these matters than many other whites, the essence of their views is widely shared. Thus, Samuel Huntington, the influential Harvard University professor and onetime presidential advisor, has argued that if multiculturalism ever becomes central in the United States, this country might join the former Soviet Union "on the ash heap of history."[26] In his view, previous nativist worries about European immigrants assimilating to the core culture in the early twentieth century were unwarranted, but today the situation is one where numerous immigrant

> groups feel discriminated against if they are not allowed to remain apart from the mainstream....They deny the existence of a common culture in the United States, denounce assimilation, and promote the primacy of racial, ethnic, and other subnational cultural identities and groupings.[27]

Huntington mainly has in mind darker skinned immigrants who are not European in origin, such as those from Latin America, Africa, Asia, and the Caribbean. Significantly, however, he does not discuss the pervasive racial hostility and discrimination often faced by these immigrants and their children, usually at the hands of the white Americans whom he deems to be exemplars of "civilized" people. Such racial hostility clearly creates barriers to full and fair societal incorporation for new immigrant groups of color.

In all these analyses, there is a strong suggestion that certain cultural traits of people of color are quite undesirable and substantially inferior. As many whites have shifted in the contemporary era from the older dominant views of people of color as biologically inferior, they have emphasized increasingly that the latter are culturally inferior. This latter notion is not a new addition to the white racial frame, for whites have accented the cultural inferiority of African Americans and other Americans of color from at least the seventeenth century forward.

Many white political, economic, religious, and academic leaders, as well as many rank-and-file whites, strongly prefer a future United States that is overwhelmingly white. This is even the case for the prominent science fiction writers and leading moviemakers who prepare widely circulated books and widely distributed movies for the general public. In recent research, Victor Romano has analyzed contemporary science fiction movies—such as *Gattaca, Minority Report*, and *A.I.*—and found that a racist formula is typically employed in creating these futuristic movies:

> Whites play all major characters (a token black is OK, but no Latinos). Whites compose the vast majority of the population, despite the fact that they will likely be the minority. People of

color should not be cast in roles that would have great power. Interracial dating/marriage has no place. There is usually some new form of life that is feared or revered.[28]

In contrast, today some 30 percent of the U.S. population is currently made up of Americans of color, who will likely be the population majority by about the middle of the twenty-first century. Yet today most white moviemakers seem to be dreaming of a mostly white future.

Children as White Supremacists

As we have seen in previous chapters, the continuing sense of the superiority of whites and of white-generated cultural forms is often learned early. Not only do white children acquire negative stereotyping of racial outgroups at a young age, they also learn and practice being "white" at that early age. For example, in a study of a multiracial daycare center undertaken by Debra Van Ausdale and Joe Feagin, on one typical afternoon, Renee, a four-year-old white child, was pulling Lingmai, a three-year-old Asian child, and Jocelyn, a four-year-old white child, in a wagon on the daycare center's playground. After pulling a while, Renee let go of the wagon handle, and Lingmai picked it up, ready to pull the wagon herself. But suddenly Renee asserted, "No, No. You can't pull this wagon. Only white Americans can pull this wagon." When Lingmai attempted to move the wagon nonetheless, Renee, with hands on hips and frowning, again asserted that only "white Americans" could do the wagon pulling.[29]

This and numerous similar incidents at the daycare center suggest that many white children early on learn not only negative views of outgroups, but also strongly positive views of whiteness and white identity. Renee has learned that U.S. society, and indeed global society, is made up of whites and racialized others. She clearly positions "American" with "white" in interacting with the child of an Asian international college student. Whiteness is already central to her identity and is coupled with a condescending ordering around of a child of color that she viewed insistently as not a "white American."

LEARNING RACIST THOUGHT AND BEHAVIOR

The Critical Role of Networks: Family and Friends

Racialized learning in childhood lasts a lifetime. For the eras of slavery and Jim Crow segregation, we have relatively modest information on how this socialization of children worked in everyday settings. In chapter 3 on the Revolutionary Era, we did get a little insight into the impact of slavery on children from Jefferson's comment that white children on plantations routinely see the ways in which the "commerce between master and slave is a perpetual exercise of the most boisterous passions." Jefferson expresses considerable (if brief) concern about slavery's impact on white children, although not on black children. Unquestionably, white children were affected by slavery and learned racist orientations from other children and from adults, then as now.

Adults also socialize other adults. Leading whites like Jefferson, Madison, and Washington regularly interacted with other whites of all classes, and it is likely that in such settings they too exchanged ideas, images, and stereotypes from the white racial frame that was already well-developed in the revolutionary era. Likewise, during the legal segregation era, white political and business leaders joined in pressing the racial frame on whites young and old, as in the infamous "Southern Manifesto" from influential southern political leaders. In chapter 5, we saw some childhood racial socialization in the rank-and-file white accounts of the legal segregation era. There we glimpsed the often vigorous ways in which white parents and other white adults insisted that children learn well the social norms and customs of official segregation.

One advantage of researching systemic racism in the contemporary era is that we have more interviews with white Americans, both leaders and the rank-and-file, in regard to how and where they have learned their racial views, images, emotions, and practices. These lessons about "race" are routinely taught to many millions of young white Americans. For example, one white woman in her twenties explains an earlier childhood lesson about racial matters this way:

> I'm playing with my black paper dolls, having a good time. Then somebody comes to visit my parents, and they saw these dolls. And they say, "Oh, you let her play with nigger paper dolls? You let her do that?" Later, when this person leaves, my parents come over, and it's "She bought nigger paper dolls! What's with her!?" And they took my paper dolls away. To this day there's this little something in me that, I want those paper dolls back.[30]

In spite of civil rights laws and related social and political changes enacted since official segregation ended in the late 1960s, many white adults still think in terms of blatantly racist ideas and use overtly racist language to other adults and children, although often they reserve their openly racist comments for private settings with friends and relatives. Drawing on the white racial framing of society, they continue to pass along racist views to their children.

Children themselves are creative in using racially stereotyped ideas that they learn from relatives, friends, and the mass media. We have seen examples of this creative performance in previous discussions of a multiracial daycare center study by Van Ausdale and Feagin. One of the first situations involving a child making a racist remark was noticed early in that study. One day, Van Ausdale observed a white three-year-old, Carla, who was about to lie down for the resting time. Carla moved her cot, saying, "I need to move this." Asked "why?" by the teacher, Carla replies: "Because I can't sleep next to a nigger," pointing to Nicole, a four-year-old black child on a nearby cot. "Niggers are stinky. I can't sleep next to one." Little Carla already knew much about racial issues, including the painful racist epithet and the age-old stereotype with which it is associated. Here she applies the stereotyped image to a situation where it is likely that she has never seen it applied before—and thus she is not simply imitating adult behavior. Later, at a meeting of daycare center staff and Carla's parents, the staff members insisted Carla did not learn that word at the center. Both her parents said they did not know where she got the word, but Carla's father did remark: "I'll bet she got that from Teresa. Her dad...he's a real redneck."[31] If her father is correct, Carla got the tools for her racist toolkit from her friend or her friend's father—again, an indication of the importance of social networks in the racial learning process.

Over time, a majority of whites of all ages mostly accept the dominant racial frame and conform to many or most of the significant prejudices and stereotypes of white relatives, friends, teachers, or coworkers. Negative views of Americans of color, as well as positive interpretations of white identity and privilege, enable whites to become full-fledged members of the white social networks and groups in which they spend much of their lives. Most racial knowledge is localized, learned, and shared in such social groups. Commonplace racist ideas are part of shared beliefs and understandings that often "exist in the mind at the nonreporting level."[32] While some individuals may have a distinctive take on a few pieces of their racialized knowledge, most of these bits of individual knowledge are extensions or elaborations of group knowledge. Important social networks are the sites for reproduction and repetition of racial stereotypes, images, and emotions. Recall the sage conclusion of Maurice Halbwachs, who explained that one cannot find such bits of knowledge "preserved in the brain or in some nook of my mind to which I alone have access: for they are recalled to me externally, and the groups of which I am a part at any time give me the means to reconstruct them, upon condition, to be sure, that I turn toward them and adopt, at least for the moment, their way of thinking."[33] Fictions about and images of racial ingroups and outgroups connect directly to ongoing networking efforts that reinforce and legitimate individual understandings.

Racial Performances: The Network Setting

Ongoing pressures from those in relevant social groups and networks pressure most people to learn, use, or elaborate their individual bits and pieces of racialized knowledge. Perhaps the most important of these networks are those of friends and relatives. In a recent research project, Leslie Houts and I have examined how whites think and act in regard to overtly racist language, ideas, joking, and other behaviors as they move from public arenas to private networks of friends and relatives. We have gathered more than six hundred journals from white college students in which they recorded for a few weeks the various events and incidents taking place around them that entailed some racial issue, image, or understanding.[34]

Unmistakable in these relatively brief journals from generally well-educated white Americans is the harsh and enduring reality of blatantly racist stereotyping and action, much of it accented or performed within their important friendship and kinship networks. In one recent account, for example, a white college student in the Midwest provides details on certain discussions and performances that occur when he gets together with his network of five white male friends:

> When any two of us are together, no racial comments or jokes are ever made. However, with the full group membership present, anti-Semitic jokes abound, as do racial slurs and vastly derogatory statements. Jewish people are simply known as "Hebes", short for Hebrews....Various jokes concerning stereotypes that Jewish people hold were also swapped around the gaming table....These jokes degraded into a rendition of the song "Yellow," which was re-done [in our group] to represent the Hiroshima and Nagasaki bombings. It contained lines about the shadows of the people being flash burned into the walls.

Here there seems to be no reluctance to engage in joking and songs that are openly and blatantly racist. After his listing of these racist acts and commentaries, he records yet more racist joking that is shorn of any subtlety:

> A member of the group also decided that he has the perfect idea for a Hallmark card. On the cover it would have a few kittens in a basket with ribbons and lace. On the inside it would simply say, "You're a nigger." I found that incredibly offensive. Supposedly, when questioned about it, the idea of the card was

to make it as offensive as humanly possible in order to make the maximal juxtaposition between warm- and ice-hearted...no group is particularly safe from the group's scathing wit, and the people of Mexico were next to bear the brunt of the jokes.[35]

This interactive, repetitive racist performance seems critical not only for learning and doing the status-role of "white man," but also for white male bonding and maintaining critical social networks. As children and as adults, whites typically learn racialized frames for viewing the world within vital personal networks such as these. Here the presence of an all-male social group creates a rather distinctive dynamic, for this student notes in his account that such racist joking and performances only take place when there are several friends together in one social setting.

Given the thousands of such accounts of racist thought and action that we have recently gathered from just a few hundred white college students, we can strongly suggest that many, if not most, young whites do not enter new interracial situations with open and tolerant minds, minds untarnished by racist socialization in backstage settings. Their minds seem to be shaped substantially by socialization within their important social networks. Most performances like these seem to be ritualized drills in which some whites lead other whites in developing and reinforcing hostile understandings of, and proclivities toward, racial outgroups. This ritualistic behavior not only helps to create and perpetuate white-centered groups with similar interests but also to reinforce, communicate, and perpetuate an array of white-framed inclinations and privileges.[36]

Societal developments in regard to civil rights, as well as a greater black presence in historically white organizations since the Jim Crow era, have made it less socially acceptable for whites to be openly racist in public settings. For that reason, it appears, many whites now reserve most of their openly and blatantly racist commentaries and performances for the more private, whites-only, family and friendship settings. Most whites are doubtless aware of this hiding of openly racist performances by themselves or by other whites, although they rarely talk openly about it. In another research study by the author, a perceptive white respondent consciously notes how this deception operates in the white families he knows:

> Most white families like to say that they're not prejudiced. They like to say that they don't discriminate, that they want true equality, that they want all these things, but if you ever put them to the test there is a lot that would back off. A lot of whites

still, the majority I'd say, will say the right, politically correct things at the right times, but behind closed doors, or with their friends, their small circle of friends, will be extremely bigoted in their comments.[37]

This respondent assesses the situation as one where whites are inclined to present themselves as egalitarian in public, yet remain extremely bigoted behind closed doors. From his own experience, he suggests that their public actions are likely to be quite different from their private actions.

In these backstage settings, whites often reveal how they might exhibit or hide their real racial views. In another journal that Leslie Houts and I gathered, a white female college student in the Midwest discusses returning to meet her old high-school friends:

I went over to the Smith farm this afternoon around dinnertime. I went to a small farm school, graduated with 42 kids, all white and mostly farmers. The farmers that I graduated with are all racist, everyone knows this—it's not a secret. Todd asked how school was going and then asked when I was going to let them come down and visit. I said, "I don't know guys, one of my suitemates is black, you would have to be nice to her." All the guys said, "Black!?!" Like they were shocked that I could actually live with someone of another color. Then David said, "Now why would you go and do that for?" Then they agreed that nothing would be said if they came to visit and then started to talk about some fight they had gotten into with some black kids in town.[38]

In the social setting she describes, only her white friends were present. Evidently, they expected the respondent to have acted on their racist views and thus to have rejected a black roommate, a type of exclusionary racism reminiscent of the Jim Crow era. Significantly, the journal account shows that these young white men seem to realize the difference between the backstage and the frontstage, for they suggested that they would not say anything to the black woman should they meet her in a public setting at the college. Once again, we see the way in which genuine interracial relationships in this society are likely foreclosed by an alienating and alienated racial framing of society.

RESIDENTIAL SEGREGATION
AND SOCIAL ISOLATION

Today, as in the past, systemic racism continues to manifest itself spatially. There is a distinctive spatial ecology to racial segregation, albeit a more informally determined pattern in the present era. Research analysis using 2000 census data on thirty of the largest U.S. metropolitan areas has demonstrated that there is much continuing residential division along racial lines. On the average, fully two-thirds of the white (or black) residents of these thirty metropolitan areas would have to move from their present residences in order to create proportional desegregation in residential housing arrangements in those cities.[39]

Racial Isolation

Great social isolation is signaled by this large-scale residential segregation of our towns and cities. As they did under legal segregation, most whites today live in what might be termed the "white bubble"; that is, they live their lives generally isolated from intensive equal-status contacts with African Americans and most other darker-skinned Americans. This is true for all age levels. One key to understanding much white thinking about racial matters is the fact that most live in the type of social isolation that generates or reinforces separating and alienated relationships between whites and black Americans, as well as between whites and many other Americans of color.

Most white adults have little equal-status contact with African Americans, except perhaps for a few coworkers and retail clerks. In one interview, a white college student suggests that most whites develop a limited knowledge of African Americans from within encapsulated residential areas:

> Most white people feel, I think, detached from blacks in the sense that they are kinda in their own world and blacks are kinda in their own world. You look at them through a looking glass and say, "Hmm, isn't that interesting what that black family's doing or what that black couple's doing, or what those black teenagers like to listen to, or like to dance, how they like to dance." And things like that. But they don't really identify that well or aren't that close with them totally.[40]

He uses the metaphor of the looking glass, of whites examining African Americans always at a significant and alienated distance—which makes real understanding and empathy difficult if not impossible.

The absence of equal-status experiences with black families because of intentionally segregated neighborhoods and communities contributes materially to white unfamiliarity with black Americans. In Chicago, several journalists did some interesting field research on the impact of residential segregation on cross-racial attitudes. They interviewed Chicagoans in two adjacent working-class suburbs, one predominantly white and one predominantly black. Whites were found to be very isolated and mostly living out their lives "without ever getting to know a black person." In both communities, there were fears and suspicions of the other group. However, the source of the fears varied significantly. The black suburbanites were "fearful because much of their contact with white people was negative," while "whites were fearful because they had little or no contact" with similar black Chicagoans.[41]

Residential segregation does not stand alone as a societal problem, for it has many structural impacts. Residential segregation reinforces, even creates, segregated schools, religious organizations, recreational facilities, and workplaces. All such segregated organizations in turn reinforce residential segregation—and thus reinforce white isolation from and stereotyping of people of color. Indeed, because of the racial ecology of everyday life, the majority of blacks spend much more time interacting with whites than the majority of whites spend interacting with blacks. Most black Americans have to work, shop, or travel with large numbers of white Americans, whereas relatively few whites do the same with significant numbers of black men and women. White views of blacks are thus not likely to be grounded in equal-status contacts, but instead reflect the age-old white racial framing of society. The sense of white superiority is reinforced by the continuing process whereby the majority of whites grow up and live lives that are for the most part residentially separated from black Americans and other darker-skinned Americans.

The Window in the White Bubble: The Racially Biased Media

One of the windows looking out of the racial isolation in which the majority of whites live is that of the mass media, such as mainstream television and talk radio. Most whites spend not only much time in their important social networks but also a great amount of time with the mass media. However, the mass media do not have much of a broadening effect for most whites, who often learn, or have reinforced, from the media numerous negative impressions and images of Americans of color. Media programs—comedies, other fictional programs, and local news programs—frequently imbed an array of racial images that are often negatively stereotyped in subtle or blatant ways, and these are important in the perpetuation of systemic racism. Two scholars suggest that

> the mediated communications help explain the tenacious survival of racial stereotypes despite a social norm that dampens public admission of prejudice. And they help explain the pervasive White ambivalence that shrinks from open prejudice but harbors reactive fear, resentment, and denial that the prejudice itself widely exists.[42]

Pervasive media communications undergirding the white racial frame help to explain how racial stereotypes persist even when there are some societal norms against such stereotyping. The mainstream media offer a limited range of accounts of the lives of African Americans—mainly conventional stories about entertainers, sports figures, and criminals. In the media arenas of music, comedy, and sports, black Americans are exploited for the purpose of white entertainment. Only occasionally do black professional or business figures make the local or national news, especially in a positive and sustained way. Relatively rare are fictional television stories or accurate news presentations of ordinary working-class and middle-class African Americans who do not fall into these conventional categories, particularly stories where they are major and positive figures. One research study found that when national news magazines portray the typical U.S. adult or child, such as on their front covers, they usually feature white adults and children. In this manner, the mostly white-controlled mass media teach all Americans that the most valid or most typical "American" is still white.[43]

Media research reveals that local television news stories on African Americans are much less likely to accent their achievements and societal contributions than are stories about whites. Local news shows also tend to present, disproportionately, whites as victims of crimes and blacks as victimizers. Not surprisingly, thus, heavy reliance on the whitewashed media for information leads most whites to very mistaken notions on racial matters, such as the common white misconceptions that African Americans are one-third or more of the U.S. population or make up most of the violent criminals who attack whites.[44] Without a doubt, this substantial reliance on biased media presentations facilitates and supports stereotyping and insensitivity about black Americans and other Americans of color.

In effect, most of the communications networks that make up the mass media are part of a larger white-dominated societal networking system. Given that most whites have little recurring, sustained, and equal-status contact with African Americans and other dark-skinned Americans, their views of such groups are significantly reinforced or created by white-generated media images. As communications researchers have noted, "Lacking much opportunity for repeated close contact with a wide variety of blacks, whites depend heavily on cultural material, especially media images, for cataloguing blacks."[45]

WHITE OPPOSITION TO RACIAL CHANGE

The black-led civil rights movement and subsequent civil rights laws ended legal segregation. Under pressure from this civil rights movement, white politicians, business leaders, and government administrators—in private and public organizations, in the South and the North—abandoned most types of legally protected racial discrimination and set up some limited remedial programs. These programs, including some called "affirmative action," occasionally placed white men in situations where they might pay some price, usually modest, for desegregating workplaces and other public settings that had historically been all white, and commonly all white male, in composition. More competition for jobs and other positions that had historically been white was not welcomed by the majority of white Americans, especially once these efforts spread outside the officially segregated southern and border states.

Negative Responses to Affirmative Action

By the 1970s and 1980s there was a backing off on serious desegregation commitments among many whites across the society. Most whites, as Dr. Martin Luther King, Jr., pointed out, had come to believe the self-deceptive fantasy that U.S. "society is essentially hospitable to fair play and to steady growth toward a middle-class Utopia embodying racial harmony."[46] Over the next few decades, most desegregation and other racial remedy programs were weakened or phased out as a more conservative white perspective regained full control in many major public and private institutions. Today, this retrenchment from racial desegregation of U.S. society is quite substantial, and it resembles the white reactionary backtracking in the nineteenth century that took place after the Reconstruction era. After Reconstruction, the white elite replaced slavery with the near-slavery of legal segregation, much to the long-term detriment of the entire society.

One reason that this backtracking from full societal desegregation came so quickly to this country is that at no point during the civil rights era of the 1950s and 1960s were majorities of the white elite and

rank-and-file whites ever committed to an aggressive effort to desegregate all historically white institutions. Indeed, for less than a decade,
enough whites in the elite and rank-and-file supported some desegregation for areas that had practiced legal segregation long enough for
that legal segregation to collapse. However, most whites never had any
commitment to go beyond this modest desegregation to a full racial integration of the major institutions of the society. In recent years, even
modest efforts at affirmative action, virtually all of which had been
crafted initially by elite white men, have been reduced or abandoned by
later groups of more conservative elite white men. Thus, a recent survey of employers in major cities found that less than half made any use
of affirmative action programs or of Equal Employment Opportunity
legislation in their hiring. Very few, just one in twelve, ever made use
of fruitful outreach efforts associated with diversifying employment,
such as recruiting employees from public schools and state employment
agencies.[47]

From the time of their first being proposed in the 1960s, comprehensive and aggressive affirmative action programs have been opposed
and questioned by a majority of white Americans, including those in the
political and business elites.[48] The character of this questioning can be
seen in this recent interview with a white professional who is opposed
to affirmative action:

> Because I wouldn't like to have a physician taking care of me who
> didn't have the appropriate background, nor would I want to be
> defended by a lawyer who…did not have the educational back-
> ground to really have earned his way into law school, nor would
> I want my accountant to be someone who passed his accoun-
> tancy examination because he got an extra 10 points because he
> was a black person or a green person or a purple person.[49]

In this case, the concern, a common one among many whites, is with
allegedly unqualified people of color who are brought into positions
of professional performance, yet this is a complaint that is usually not
backed up with evidence. This negative casting of active programs aimed
at racial change reflects what is essentially a mythological view that has
been generated in the white-run mass media. The evidence indicates
that Americans of color are in most cases qualified for the jobs for which
they are hired. In many cases, indeed, they have to be better qualified
than their white peers just to get hired or promoted.[50]

One aspect of the contemporary era that is often noted by whites is
the increased presence of African Americans as entertainers, athletes,
and politicians, especially in the mass media. Amazingly enough, this

relatively new presence, together with various other instances of modest or token desegregation, have convinced many whites that African Americans are now roughly equal to whites in many important institutional areas. Note, for example, this pointed commentary by a well-educated white male professional:

> They are equal; they do not need to become equal....Progress has been made in the laws and in jobs. And there are thousands and thousands of blacks who are making twice as much money as I am making and have better jobs than I have.[51]

This man then brings forward the case of Bill Cosby to illustrate the commonplace notion among whites that many blacks are more successful than average whites are. Exaggerations and distortions of progress on racial matters by the white-controlled mass media buttress this type of misinformed white view. Thus, one research study of the popular television series that made Cosby so visible (and which is still shown in reruns today) found that most whites who were interviewed liked the black family portrayed in the show, yet many of them did not change their view of African Americans as a result. They held fast to the view that African Americans were generally lazy and that they could succeed if they worked harder like the black family on the television show. For many whites, Cosby's television shows demonstrated that, while some black people can do well, most do not. For them, thus, the Cosby television show was cited to "prove the inferiority of black people in general (who have, in comparison with whites, failed)."[52]

Recent surveys show that most white Americans live with an array of myths about black success in various areas of this society. One national survey asked about white and black access to health care, education, jobs, and good incomes, and found that seven in ten whites viewed the average black person as having access that was equal to, or better than, that of the average white person in at least one of these four major areas.[53] About half of the whites interviewed held two or more erroneous beliefs in regard to these important white-black comparisons, and nearly a third were wrong on all four questions. In contrast, data from many research studies (see chapter 6) show that in not one of these institutional areas have African Americans achieved anything like real equality with whites.[54] Most strikingly, most whites interviewed in the aforementioned survey felt that black Americans generally had socioeconomic opportunities equal to or better than those of whites. Yet, in reality African Americans are a long way from socioeconomic parity with whites. This notion of a still very discriminatory and racially hostile society now being good for African Americans seems to be a contemporary manifestation of the age-old white-racist view of "good race relations," the view that was so widespread among whites during slavery and legal segregation.

Today, it appears from numerous research studies that white men as a group are more openly critical of affirmative action programs, and indeed of racial change, than white women as a group, although a majority of the latter are also opposed to comprehensive racial change. Perhaps encouraged by right-wing talk show hosts, conservative ministers, conservative media pundits, and people in their kinship and friendship networks, many white men view themselves as "victims" of something they call "reverse racism" or "reverse discrimination." In an interview conducted by one of my students, a white respondent described his racial-gender category this way:

> As a white male, I feel like I'm the only subsection of the population that hasn't jumped on the victim bandwagon. And I feel from a racial perspective, as the white man, I have been targeted as the oppressor, and frankly I'm getting a little tired of it, because I haven't done a whole lot of oppressing in my life.[55]

One societal change evident during and since the civil rights movement of the 1960s has been the increase in public and academic discussions of the role of white men in racial discrimination, however gingerly this may be broached in much of the mass media and in other historically white institutions. This questioning of white male power and privileges by people of color is new for white men who have never encountered significant challenges to their top hierarchical position and power. Not viewing themselves as seriously implicated in racial oppression, they often refer to themselves (or their families) as "not being privileged" or "not being powerful." Indeed, many view themselves as victims of the remedial programs that they see as unfairly benefiting Americans of color—who, in their uninformed view, are no longer victims of racial discrimination.

Given this strong white male perspective, one can understand why so many of the remedial programs aimed at racial discrimination have been eviscerated or abandoned over the last few decades. One can also understand a number of other major phenomena as well, including the dramatic rise in influence of the Republican party among working-class and lower-middle-class white men who might otherwise be attracted to the Democratic party.

Reshaping U.S. Politics: The Racial Past and Present

The past of systemic racism has become the present of systemic racism, with some significant changes, generation after generation. In the contemporary era, the changes in systemic racism since the 1960s civil rights movement and civil rights laws have been far fewer than most African Americans and other progressive Americans had hoped for. Significant progress on civil rights and racial desegregation for a brief period from the mid-1950s to the late-1960s has been followed with stagnation or backtracking, especially as the pressures of the civil rights movement have been reduced. Since the 1970s, we have seen ever more substantial white backtracking on, even overt resistance to, the tentative commitments of the 1960s to some significant racial desegregation. Indeed, about the same time that the Kerner Commission report accented the problem of "white racism" and the last major civil rights act was enacted in the late 1960s, the country saw a reinvigorated conservative political movement designed to stop projected racial change and to roll back numerous changes that had taken place. This mostly white political movement has gained great national political power in the period from 1968 through the early 2000s. The dominance of a racially conservative Republican party in U.S. politics in this period has been directly linked to the negative response of many white Americans to modest national efforts at the racial desegregation of major historically white institutions.

Thus, in the 1968 presidential primaries, the segregationist governor of Alabama, George Wallace, had substantial political success in the South and the North. Wallace garnered 14 percent of the total vote nationally, including a significant number of white votes in northern states. Indeed, nearly ten million Americans voted for Wallace. While Wallace is now mostly remembered as just a southern segregationist, he did play an extraordinarily important role nationally in creating the potent political combination of white racial fears of the civil rights movement and racial desegregation, white longings for a less multiracial country, and right-wing economic thinking, a combination that helped to generate the white conservative political resurgence that has taken place between the late 1960s and the early 2000s.[56]

Building a White Political Party

By the late 1960s and early 1970s, these factors had stimulated the movement of many working-class and middle-class whites, in the South and North, away from their traditional home in the Democratic party into an aggressively pro-white Republican party. Since the 1960s, thus, the

Republican party has increasingly become the party representing the barely disguised racist goals of the majority of white Americans who fear major racial change in U.S. society. For that reason, elected politicians from the Republican party, virtually all of them white, have led in intentionally weakening or destroying government programs aimed at significantly reducing racial discrimination and inequality in this society.

A leading Republican activist, Ralph Reed, has commented on the future of the Republican party in a revealing manner. Reviewing the past and future of the party, Reed has suggested that, "you're going to see a new Republican party that is still primarily white and that is fiscally and morally conservative, but that also is attempting to project an image of racial tolerance and moderation."[57] Apparently, Reed and most of his white colleagues want the Republican party to be overwhelmingly white, but they also want their party to look good, that is, to "project an image of racial tolerance." Image, not reality, seems to be a primary concern. Today, the Republican party is the omnipresent guardian of whiteness in this society, while still trying to appear nonracist to Americans of color and to a global community that is mostly not white. This façade is created by token appointments of a few Republicans of color to visible political positions.[58]

Interestingly, since the 1932 presidential election, in which the Republican party lost to Franklin Roosevelt, the Republican party has moved away from the party of Abraham Lincoln that had for decades supported civil rights reforms and thereby garnered the votes of most black Americans to one that is subtly or covertly antiblack in some of its major political positions and, for that reason, now draws a remarkably small percentage of black voters in most elections.[59] With the presidential campaign of Barry Goldwater in 1964, the Republican party intentionally abandoned the concerns of black voters for a strategy openly targeting what have been seen as the primary interests of a majority of white voters. This explicitly pro-white political strategy has put emphasis on the interests of whites in suburbia and the southern states. Code words such as "quotas," "states' rights," "busing," and "crime in the streets" have been substituted for the more explicitly racist terms of the days of legal segregation. Texas Senator John Tower, one of the first Republican senators in the South since Reconstruction and a force in the remaking of the Republican party, was until his death a major leader in this pro-white political effort in the South and nationally. This was evident in his opposition, as an overt segregationist, to the 1954 school desegregation decision, the 1960 and 1964 Republican national platform proposals favoring civil rights, the 1964 and 1965 civil rights acts, and numerous other civil rights laws.

Initially developed by Barry Goldwater and other white conservatives in the 1960s, this white-interests strategy could be seen in the famous Republican "southern strategy"—that is, a strategy aggressively
seeking southern white Democrats with overtures to their racial concerns. The white conservatives' strategy secured a victory in keeping a
key civil rights plank out of the 1964 Republican platform. Although
the party lost nationwide in 1964, the racist southern strategy did work
regionally in capturing a majority of white voters in five traditionally Democratic southern states and in winning over those states on a
permanent basis for the Republican party. The southern strategy was
reinvigorated and effectively used by Richard Nixon in 1968 and 1972
to win the first two presidential elections for the Republican party
with that racialized political strategy. This political approach was celebrated in Kevin Phillips's *The Emerging Republican Majority*, a book
that became the "Bible" of many in the Republican party in the 1970s
and 1980s.[60] Phillips explicitly argued that Republicans did not need
appeals to "urban Negroes" and to other progressive "vested interests"
to win nationally.

Once elected, President Nixon, who frequently used the words "nigger," "jigaboo," and "jigs" in his various phone calls, brought in conservative white officials strongly opposed to enforcing the civil rights of
African Americans and other Americans of color. Nixon instructed his
officials to weaken enforcement of most federal court school desegregation orders, removed numerous strong civil rights advocates from federal government positions, and pressed the FBI to go after civil rights
activists and groups. Nixon regarded government social programs as
not benefiting black Americans in part because they were "genetically
inferior to whites." While sometimes supporting limited civil rights
measures and periodically courting moderate black leaders and some
black voters—usually for calculated political purposes such as forcing
Democratic officials to pay attention to black voters and to further identify that party with blacks—Nixon worked with Republican party op-
eratives to buttress the political strategy of securing white voters in the
South and the suburbs of the North.[61]

The neosegregationist strategy targeting southern and suburban
whites was also used effectively in the Ronald Reagan and George H.
W. Bush campaigns of the 1980s and early 1990s. Reagan began his
presidential campaign asserting strongly a states' rights doctrine, and
he intentionally picked Philadelphia, Mississippi—the town where three
young civil rights workers had been lynched in the 1960s—to make this
symbolic appeal to southern white voters. Once in office, Reagan and
his associates sought aggressively to dismantle further federal civil rights

enforcement efforts, including severely weakening the U.S. Commission on Civil Rights and Equal Employment Opportunity Commission and attacking affirmative action programs, all to please white voters and constituents. The FBI and other agencies were used to intimidate and reduce voter registration and turnout campaigns on behalf of southern voters of color.[62]

Moreover, when Reagan's vice president, George H. W. Bush, undertook a run for president, he ran a campaign "so implicitly racist that it appeared suited to a prior century."[63] In his 1988 campaign, Bush and his advisors conducted an infamous advertising campaign that used visual images of a disheveled black rapist, from his opponent's home state, to intentionally scare and effectively recruit many white voters to the Republican party. The campaign intentionally targeted white voters with an aggressively stereotyped and racialized message of violent crime.[64] Not surprisingly, Republican strategists used *no* images of the most common rapist in the United States, the white male rapist. Once in office, Bush and his white associates extended the Reagan rollbacks of government equal opportunity and affirmative action efforts, even attacking new civil rights legislation as a "quota bill." Bush gave speeches attacking multiculturalism and, in a cynical political move, appointed the arch-conservative black judge Clarence Thomas to the Supreme Court.[65]

After losing elections in the 1990s to the moderate Democrat William Clinton, the Republican party succeeded in electing George W. Bush as president in two consecutive elections (2000 and 2004). In both, the Republican party focused heavily on securing white voters in the South and in northern suburbs, and some Republican officials sought to restrict black voting in several key states such as Florida. Once in office, this President Bush sought to reduce federal enforcement of civil rights laws and to end most affirmative action efforts. A draft report of the U.S. Commission on Civil Rights summarized the first George W. Bush administration's civil rights record thus:

> President Bush seldom speaks about civil rights, and when he does, it is to carry out official duties, not to promote initiatives or plans for improving opportunity. Even when he publicly discusses existing barriers to equality and efforts to overcome them, the administration's words and deeds often conflict....In his first three years in office, the net increase in President Bush's requests for civil rights enforcement agencies was less than those of the previous two administrations. After accounting for inflation, the President's requests for the six major civil rights

programs…amount to a loss of spending power for 2004 and 2005.…While judicial and legislative achievements of the 1960s and 1970s largely broke down the system of segregation and legal bases for discrimination, the effects persist and hamper equal opportunity in education, employment, housing, public accommodations, and the ability to vote. President Bush has implemented policies that have retreated from long-established civil rights promises in each of these areas.[66]

Still the White Party: Democracy in Decline?

At one time centered in the states of the East and upper Midwest, today the Republican party is, as a result of its recent political remaking, now centered in the South, parts of the Midwest, and the Rocky Mountain states. In recent political campaigns, the Republican party has continued to be what some call the "white party," the one aggressively representing white interests, albeit in disguised language. In elections between 1992 and 2004, the Republican party got a remarkably small percentage (8–12 percent) of black voters, and a minority of most other voters of color. Since the 1960s, the southern states have increasingly become states divided between a Republican party that is overwhelmingly white and centered politically in predominantly white areas such as city suburbs versus a Democratic party that is multiracial and multiethnic and centered politically in rural and urban areas heavily populated by people of color. Indeed, just over half of all black voters are still in the southern states, where they are effectively disenfranchised when it comes to state and presidential elections because they are consistently outvoted by whites who vote heavily for the Republican party and against any political candidates seeking aggressively to further desegregate U.S. institutions.

Not only has there been only a handful of black delegates at recent Republican party conventions, but the Republican National Committee has had few black members. The percentage of black delegates at national party conventions has oscillated up and down, between 1.0 percent and 6.7 percent since 1964. (These percentages compare with Democratic party percentages now at about 20 percent.)[67] Service at the highest decision-making levels of the Republican party has in the last few decades been almost exclusively white. Thus, in late 2004, there was only one African American from the fifty U.S. states (plus a black member from U.S. Virgin Islands) among the 165 members of the Republican National Committee. This compared to the 97 black members on the Democratic National Committee, more than one fifth of the total membership at about the same time. In addition, most of the black Americans in positions within state Republican party organizations are involved in minority outreach programs, in contrast to the far more numerous black members of state Democratic party organizations, where most are active outside these minority outreach programs.[68] In addition, as of late 2004, all black members of the U.S. Congress, and something like 98 percent of the 9,000 black officeholders at all government levels across the United States, were members of the Democratic party.[69]

This highly segregated pattern of political party interests and participation has characterized U.S. politics now since the civil rights movement of the 1960s. In the southern and border states, the Rocky Mountain states, and numerous states of the lower Midwest, white voters now tend to vote overwhelmingly for the Republican party in presidential elections, and for that reason some people now explicitly refer to the party as the "white party." The Republican party has brought about its political resurgence since the major losses in presidential elections of the early and mid-1960s by explicitly using a politics of "race" that works mainly because the racist legacies of slavery and legal segregation have persisted aggressively into contemporary U.S. society. Few white analysts in the mainstream media or academia have analyzed the dire consequences of this huge racial divide for democracy in the United States.

CONCLUSION

Systemic racism today is clearly different in some important ways from slavery and legal segregation, but in certain fundamentals—including continuing white-on-black domination and persisting racial inequality in wealth and privilege—it is broadly similar to the racial oppression of the past. Contemporary racism is still much more than a matter of scattered white bigots discriminating against other people, but rather is about central U.S. institutions that still remain racially discriminatory and quite inegalitarian. As under slavery and legal segregation, U.S. economic, political, educational, religious, and media institutions remain dominated by whites, racially hierarchical, often exploitative, and chronically undemocratic.

Though periodically challenged, whites today remain firmly in control of all major historically white institutions. This oppression continues to keep black Americans and other Americans of color down, attempting to subordinate them materially, physically, and psychologically. As with slavery and legal segregation, we see today an extensive set of racialized burdens coercively placed by whites on their racial targets.

These burdens are well institutionalized and include economic discrimination, unjust impoverishment, legal enforcement of subordination and segregation, attempts at family destruction, and a thoroughgoing racist ideology set in a white framing of society. The relations of racial domination linger on as central to the black and white experience and persistently generate privilege, income, or wealth for most whites. At the core of the relations of domination under contemporary racial oppression is yet more unjust enrichment for new generations of white Americans, coupled with a corresponding unjust impoverishment for yet new generations of black Americans. In addition, the accounts of white and black Americans in this chapter and the previous chapter suggest how racially generated economic inequality continues to shape in major ways the actions of local, state, and federal governments and the legal system in the United States. The continuing lack of adequate (or any) black representation at the highest political levels—such as the presidency, the U.S. Senate, Supreme Court, and state governorships—is just one of the major signals of how pervasive white domination and racial discrimination remain in the United States.

Today a dominant discourse among the majority of white Americans denies that racism is still systemic and devastating for African Americans and other Americans of color. In spite of the support a majority of whites have given to some racial desegregation since the late 1960s, a substantial majority of whites have also made clear their deeper commitments to an age-old racist system that maintains most racial inequality and most white power and privilege in this society. By the 1970s, indeed, there was much discontent and backlash among whites in business, government, the media, and academia in regard to the civil rights laws and affirmative action remedies put into place just a few years earlier. There was also much white discontent over the growing numbers of African Americans seeking to move into traditionally white institutions and neighborhoods. Since the 1970s the majority of white Americans have revealed their support of the traditional foot-dragging approach on societal desegregation—of the approach of making as little change in historically racist institutions as is possible under the circumstances of blacks' and others' protest and resistance. The decline of the 1960s civil rights movement facilitated this resurgence of white racial protectionism and a reinvigorated racist language (for example, "reverse discrimination") designed to stall progress toward further desegregation of society, or even to roll back some desegregation that was well underway.

White racism today remains "normal" and deeply imbedded in most historically white institutions. Every such institution is still substantially whitewashed in its important norms, rules, and arrangements.

Yet, given the accounts in this chapter, it seems likely that a majority of whites cannot see just how whitewashed their historically white organizations and institutions really are. Historically white institutions were created, and have mostly been maintained ever since, by white Americans, especially by those with major influence and power. These historically white institutions are, as Americans of color quickly realize once they are inside them, very white in their everyday norms, customs, and deep structures.

As was the case with most whites in earlier eras, a majority of whites today reveal a high level of social alexithymia. They rarely or never understand what daily life is like across the color line or understand the human impact of whites' discriminatory actions. Recently, at a large workplace, a white supervisor harshly criticized some employees for their mistakes at their jobs by using highly racialized language. According to a union newsletter, the manager suggested that "those responsible should be chained to a pickup and dragged down the road, and that he knew a couple people in Texas who could do the job, but they'd have to get out of jail first."[70] This was a reference to the brutal lynching of a black man in the late 1990s in Texas. This white supervisor had black employees working under him, who likely endured significant pain because of the harsh commentary. The reality and horror of violent lynchings persist in the individual and collective memories of African Americans because historically they, as a group, have experienced many thousands of such violent white attacks.

Essential to being an oppressor today, as it was under slavery and Jim Crow segregation, is an inability to understand the recurring suffering and pain of those who are racially oppressed. Thus, we have observed in the accounts in this chapter white children taking part in antiblack oppression at a rather early age. In such cases, they are effectively in training to be more antipathetic and to not identify with those oppressed. The subordinated racial others are "not like us" and thus are racially inferior. While whites who hold strongly to the white racial frame and its stereotyped interpretations of black personality, values, and subculture doubtless function well in most of their social lives, clearly they have lost contact with the social reality around them to some degree. When it comes to many racial matters, they cannot see what is actually in front of them.

8

REPRISE AND ASSESSMENT: THE REALITY
AND IMPACT OF SYSTEMIC RACISM

In order to understand systemic racism well, one must listen carefully to the accounts of experience with systemic racism given by African Americans. Beginning with the autobiographical accounts of Frederick Douglass, William Wells Brown, and Harriet Jacobs, we have encountered deeply penetrating sociological analyses of the system of white-on-black oppression that has developed in this country for centuries. These enslaved black Americans assess the bloody and exploitative world of enslavement with much insight and authority. Like the accounts of later generations, their narratives recount painfully and poignantly how systemic racism involves an array of concrete burdens placed on them and other black Americans by white Americans, including those in the elite and ordinary working people. Unambiguous in the autobiographical accounts is the highly coercive dimension of racial oppression.

The black accounts of racial oppression, as well as the white accounts defending it, indicate clearly that such oppression is not a modest accretion on an otherwise healthy social system, but rather is a systemic reality central to a very unhealthy society. Systemic racism is the United States, and the United States is systemic racism. This is true of this society today, and has been true for several centuries. A careful examination of the historical and contemporary realities of this oppression reveals remarkable continuities in institutionalized oppression over many generations. This country's major institutions have long involved social arrangements that are racially exploitative, hierarchical, white supremacist in rationale, and undemocratic in operation. Especially when seen from the black perspective, the continuities over the centuries are obvious, well institutionalized, and extraordinarily inhumane. Ridding U.S. society of systemic racism will require large-scale efforts, going well beyond the pathbreaking civil rights movement of the 1960s, to bring massive changes in all historically white institutions.

For the three broad periods we have analyzed, the black and white accounts indicate unmistakably that racial oppression has been operative in every major nook and cranny of this society for centuries. This is indeed a white society, where most institutions, even the majority of public spaces and places, are controlled by whites, and thus they are in practice white institutions, spaces, and places. In the U.S. case, racial oppression is influential in or integral to every major institution, even those such as the family, which predate its emergence. This racial oppression has been part of society for so long that it has often been difficult for whites even to perceive it consciously, as their commentaries show. Indeed, what most contemporary whites can now clearly see as racial oppression—such as slavery and legal segregation—was seen by earlier whites as the normal operation of healthy institutions, which were necessary for protecting the power and privileges of their "white race" against the threat of "lesser races." Indeed, missing from almost all the experiential accounts of slavery and legal segregation provided by whites who lived in those eras, as well as from most accounts of racial matters provided today by whites, is an in-depth analysis of systemic racism or a deep sensitivity to its broader significance for society.

Let me now summarize some key points and link them to some broad issues about how systemic racism operates today.

BUILDING A GLOBAL RACIST ORDER

African American Enslavement: Building an International System of Racism

Central to white-on-black oppression from the beginning has been the harsh reality of economic exploitation. By the early eighteenth century, the British colonies were well grounded in a wealth-generating economic system substantially centered around the use of enslaved labor and the sale of enslaved black Americans and of slave-produced products.

The accounts of those enslaved, as well as of leading slaveholders, presented in this book reveal the bloody and exploitative reality that is the foundation of this society.

These accounts of everyday experience with systemic racism are provided by individuals who were at the center of a global racist order that was also a global capitalistic order. The Atlantic slave trade, colonial slavery, and modern capitalism emerge together in the same period of world history. W. E. B. Du Bois eloquently summarized this historical point of intersection and reinforcement:

> Modern world commerce, modern imperialism, the modern factory system and the modern labor problem began with the African slave trade. The first modern method of securing labor on a wide commercial scale and primarily for profit was inaugurated in the middle of the fifteenth century and in the commerce between Africa and America. Through the slave trade Africa lost at least 100,000,000 human beings, with all the attendant misery and economic and social disorganization. The survivors of this wholesale rape became a great international laboring force in America on which the modern capitalistic movement has been built and out of which modern labor problems have arisen.[1]

Early capitalism was thus in part a "capitalism with chains." The first large-scale, globally oriented capitalism in human history was substantially centered in the Atlantic slave trade and the trade in the agricultural products produced by millions of those enslaved in the North American, South American, and Caribbean colonies. In this process, major commercial firms, shippers, ship builders, banks, and insurance companies were created or expanded; they became the centers for capital accumulation and circulation through which modern capitalism thrived. The "modern West," indeed modernity itself, emerged with the genocide targeting indigenous peoples and the enslavement of Africans as a substantial part of its base.

This African slavery was envisioned by its European and European American originators and perpetrators as part of a global system of wealth generation. Indeed, at the zenith of U.S. slavery in the first half of the nineteenth century, many in the white slaveholding elite saw their economic system of African slavery as necessarily spreading aggressively across both American continents and around the globe.[2] The demand for enslaved labor in North and South American areas spurred the opening up of much of Africa for intensive and brutal European exploitation, anticipating the later nineteenth-century colonialism in most of Africa. European imperialism had by the late 1800s reached most of the globe and indeed created something approaching a global racist order in which Europeans and European Americans were increasingly dominant and which had severe negative consequences for many of the world's societies. Among other things, this European colonialism and imperialism carried the ideology of white supremacy across the globe.

The colonialization of what would become the United States was important not so much for the precious metals sought by early explorers but rather for the production by enslaved African Americans of major agricultural products and for the opening of new markets for European goods. This international trade in slaves and slave-produced products, as well as in supplies and other products sold to slaveholding farmers and planters, spurred the expansion of the world market, and thus of wealth for capitalist elites and their acolytes in Europe and North America.[3] In the North American colonies, enslaved black Americans produced tobacco, sugar, indigo, rice, cotton, and other products that were sold to consumers or processed in manufacturing plants in New England and Great Britain. This processing of raw materials contributed greatly to the growth of manufacturing in these areas, and thus to what became known as the "Industrial Revolution." Great inventions, like the improved steam engine of James Watt, often came in slave-linked agricultural or manufacturing industries.[4] Increasingly, new manufacturing and manufacturing-related enterprises were created, at least in part, from the great profits circulating from slavery-linked agricultural and commercial operations. By the eighteenth century, British dominance in the Atlantic economy, to a substantial degree, came off the bloody backs of enslaved African workers in the North American and Caribbean colonies. Slavery was thus a central part of the "foundation of Atlantic capitalism."[5]

Legal Segregation: Slavery Unwilling to Die

An essential feature of the North America slavery system was that white men were fully in charge of its development and evolution from the beginning. When the U.S. was developed out of the European American colonies, its institutions were also shaped by powerful white men. Often viewed in godlike imagery, the founders created and shaped a society incorporating their concern for white control, power, and privilege. Moreover, this elite, though full of white southerners, included influential men from all regions. Those whites in charge of the society's major institutions in the seventeenth and eighteenth centuries have been succeeded, generation after generation, in a type of social cloning process, by white men much like them.

More than two centuries of black slavery were finally ended by a bloody Civil War. After a brief Reconstruction period, during which there were lost opportunities for major changes in systemic racism, both white leaders and the white rank-and-file worked diligently to see that the oppressive realities of slavery would persist in the form of official segregation in the South and legal or informal segregation in the North. The benefits to whites of slavery were maintained in the near-slavery of legal segregation by coupling oppression firmly to the negative "badge" of skin color that whites had long assigned to African Americans. The modern world's developed understanding of "black" and "blackness," as attached to certain physical characteristics, largely comes out of the slavery period, and these physical markers have made later incarnations of racial oppression possible. Whites have used these socially invented racial markers not only to designate "black" people for oppression, but also to identify "whites" who typically benefit from the many racial privileges handed down from the past or still generated in the present.

Among the essential features of slavery were extortion of labor for personal profit, unjust impoverishment of those enslaved, the racialized hierarchy with its alienated relationships, the political protection of the economic exploitation, the rationalizing of oppression by means of a racist ideology and a white-racist frame, and recurring resistance by enslaved African Americans. All of these features were continuing aspects of racial oppression during the years of legal segregation from the 1880s to the late 1960s. For the large majority of African Americans still resident in the southern and border states, and some areas of certain northern states, most aspects of daily life were riddled with racial oppression in the form of legally segregated jobs, housing, public accommodations, schools, and policing. Beyond this legal segregation there was extensive informal and customary segregation in virtually all areas of the United States.

Contemporary Racism: Slavery Still Unwilling to Die

The legal segregation apparatus was dismantled only in the late 1960s, much more recently than many Americans realize. With the 1960s civil rights laws coming into effect, African Americans were finally freed from this near-slavery of official segregation. On the surface, much would seem to have changed. At the time, however, many white Americans openly resisted these changes and persisted in overt and blatant discrimination in many areas, while national opinion surveys showed that the majority often did not support the government-generated changes taking place. Thus, in one 1966 national survey some 70 percent of the white respondents felt that black Americans were moving too fast in trying to secure equal rights, and far less than half (just 35 percent) felt that black Americans were justified in protesting discrimination by means of public demonstrations. Just 4 percent of whites supported giving compensatory preferences for jobs to black workers because of a century of job discrimination.[6]

During the 1960s, there was a period of overt support among many white leaders and many rank-and-file whites for some racial desegregation in regard to voting, juries, and public accommodations, and there was even majority support among whites for getting rid of legally segregated schools (mainly in the South).[7] However, the majority of whites made it clear that they desired only limited change, and they continued to assert openly their commitment to white power and racial privilege, including a strong opposition to ending racial inequalities by aggressive government action. By the late 1960s and early 1970s, the assassination of Dr. Martin Luther King, Jr., and the weakening of the civil rights movement, permitted a resurgence of overt white protectionism with its pro-white, antiblack, anti-affirmative action language designed to stall or reverse progress toward large-scale desegregation of societal institutions. Eradicating legal segregation was enough for most whites. Aggressively eradicating informal discrimination and redressing the continuing legacies of past oppression were considered inappropriate by a majority of whites, as they still are today.

Evaluating the contemporary United States, we see that systemic racism has in some ways changed significantly from the racialized patterns of slavery and legal segregation, yet in certain fundamentals—such as the enduring racial hierarchy, persisting white-imposed discrimination, and white privilege and advantage in all major institutional areas—systemic racism today remains rather similar to the systemic racism of earlier eras.

ASSESSING MAJOR DIMENSIONS OF RACIAL OPPRESSION

Systemic racism is not some unfortunate appendage to society that is now largely eliminated. Racial oppression persists as foundational and integral to society in the present day. Whites continue to target African Americans and other Americans of color for much racial stereotyping, hostility, and discrimination in all major historically white institutions. Moreover, systemic racism has a huge impact even beyond the more obvious and overt racial discrimination that we see everyday, for there is also much subtle and covert discrimination. Major U.S. institutions are so deeply racialized that the racial bias is often difficult to perceive, particularly by white Americans. Economic, political, legal, educational, and social welfare institutions are racialized even when they do not appear on the surface to be so. These major institutions would be rather different in many ways, small and large, if there had been no history of large-scale racial oppression in the United States.

The many black and white accounts examined in previous chapters provide substantial support for a systemic racism perspective on the past and present of this society. Recall Figure 1 in chapter 1, which diagrammed the key dimensions of systemic racism. I will not review here all these dimensions, but rather will emphasize a few issues that we can now assess more deeply after having listened to many black and white accounts from the major eras of oppression. I emphasize here issues in regard to economic exploitation and discrimination, the costs of systemic racism, the white racial frame and the racial ideology, black resistance, and government protection of systemic racism. I conclude by looking at the related issues of the impact of systemic racism on U.S. foreign policy and on other Americans of color who later came into a well-entrenched system of white-on-black oppression.

Remember, too, that each dimension of racial oppression is linked directly or indirectly to every other dimension. One can separate important dimensions of racial oppression for analytical purposes, but in the everyday world they cannot be separated, for they generally occur in concert with one another.

Dimensions of Systemic Racism: Economic Exploitation

A central lesson from the extended analysis in this book is that racial oppression involves the social construction of a material reality. For all historical eras, central to the racial burdens of African Americans have been economic exploitation and the accompanying unjust impoverishment at the hands of white Americans. This racialized exploitation has always involved hierarchical social relationships, with an exploiting class and an exploited class. From slavery days to the present, these social relationships have been alienating and alienated, separating basically similar human beings so that the former group can exploit the latter.

For the slavery era, Frederick Douglass discussed how the labor of those enslaved generated much in the way of privileges and wealth for white families. The autobiographical accounts of those enslaved reveal how numerous whites, not just slaveholders, benefited from the large-scale enslavement of black Americans. From the beginning of systemic racism, both whites in the elite and ordinary white workers and their families have benefited from and worked diligently to maintain that oppressive system. From slavery to the present day, white workers have profited from the "public and psychological wage" of whiteness—the economic, status, and other privileges that stem from being defined as "white," whatever one's social class might be. As a white journalist wrote in 1886, "The white laboring classes here are separated from Negroes... by an innate consciousness of race superiority which excites a sentiment of sympathy and equality on their part with classes above them...."[8]

In the past, as now, white workers have generally supported the national and international economic and political goals and actions of the white elite. Wherever workers of color have been superexploited by this country's capitalists, white workers have usually approved, and the latter have only occasionally sought a *strong* relationship with workers of color here or overseas. Indeed, with the full support of the white working class, the United States and other capitalist nations saw to it that most of the world's workers, as W. E. B. Du Bois noted, "became the basis of a system of industry which ruined democracy" and often resulted in economic depressions and imperialist wars.[9]

Many whites who today say that their ancestors "never owned any slaves" have indeed gained significantly over many generations from the fact that those white ancestors often traded with slaveholding farms and plantations or worked in various occupations, reserved for whites only, that were generated by or linked to the economically dynamic and expansive slavery system. For more than two centuries, the economic exploitation of African Americans under slavery directly and indirectly generated many economic opportunities and assets, as well as much social capital, for white Americans, which were usually passed along in some form over many generations of white Americans. In addition, these subsequent generations of whites have profited, often handsomely, from the continuing racial exploitation, segregation, and other discrimination targeting black Americans during the eras of legal segregation and of contemporary racism.

Reporting on the official segregation era, the many black voices we have heard in previous chapters suggest from personal experience how economic domination was central to that period as well. Slavery's economic exploitation was generally replaced by the near-slavery of sharecropping, tenant farming, debt peonage, and erratic and low-paid manual or domestic work for most black workers. This economic exploitation was buttressed by an omnipresent and innervating etiquette of deference to all whites and with recurring white violence. During legal segregation, whites continued to garner the psychological wage of whiteness in the preferences they got for good educations and better-paying jobs and in their access to other economic assets such as home owning. Most got a significant basket of life-sustaining privileges just by being white.

Today economic opportunities and assets still follow the color line, with whites having far more access to such than do African Americans. No longer does economic exploitation take the form of the actual ownership of African Americans, yet there is much economic discrimination and domination of African Americans by whites by means of such institutionalized arrangements as job channeling, discriminatory wages, hostile work climates, and discrimination in mortgage loans and home buying. The continuing consequences of past and present racial oppression are seen in the huge and persisting racial inequalities in annual income and in wealth, for individuals and for families. Recall that the median black family income today is less than 60 percent of the median white family income, a percentage that is worse than it was in the 1960s. The black poverty rate is three times the white rate. The median household wealth of black Americans is less than one tenth of the median household wealth of whites.[10] Absent centuries of racial oppression, these socioeconomic indicators should be roughly similar for both racial groups. Indeed, if slavery had been abolished early and replaced with a truly just and free society, economic discrimination and inequality along racial lines would not exist today. When it comes to matters of economic opportunities, and especially persisting income and wealth inequality along the color line, the racialized past is indeed a persisting and intricate part of the racialized present.

The Social Reproduction of Racial Oppression and Inequality

How is the societal system of racial oppression and inequality reproduced as a whole? For systemic racism to persist across a great many generations, it must reproduce all the necessary socioeconomic conditions and the supportive institutional mechanisms. The social inequality routinely reproduced over the centuries involves disproportionate control by whites of major economic resources and of the educational, political, and ideological resources necessary to subordinate racial groups such as African Americans.

A central argument of this book is that white-on-black oppression and its accompanying inequalities have been socially reproduced by the actions of white individuals and small groups set within critical institutional and community frameworks. Once members of a group are racially privileged, as whites were from the extensive exploitation of African Americans in slavery and legal segregation, they typically pass on that privilege—in the form of money capital, social capital, and/or cultural capital—to their descendants, over one generation after another. This family transmission of privilege and resources is strongly supported by an array of societal institutions. The ability or inability of individuals and families to transmit important asset-generating resources from one generation to the next is highly dependent on the support of major institutions. Reproduced over time are these racially structured institutions, such as the economic institutions that persistently exploit and discriminate against black labor and the legal-political institutions that protect that oppression. In every generation, major organizational and institutional structures protect the highly racialized enrichment and impoverishment that are central to U.S. society.

Recall that the median wealth of black families is now substantially less than one tenth of the median wealth of white families and has declined relative to that of whites over the last decade. This great wealth imbalance has many significant consequences, generally including far less access for black families as a group to such items as home ownership and good college educations for their children. When individuals receive substantial assets from significant relatives, they can use them to build up yet more resources and wealth to pass to their own children and grandchildren. This societal reality reveals the major, multigenerational impact of centuries-old racial oppression. Thus, generally speaking, racial inequality today is substantially the result of centuries of racial inequality in individual and family opportunities, resources, and assets.

The Many Costs of Systemic Racism

A major theme highlighted by the black accounts of experiences with systemic racism is that they have paid, and still pay, a very heavy price for racial exploitation and domination by whites. We have just noted the huge and continuing economic losses for African Americans. Today, as in the past, African Americans suffer not only in economic terms, but also in terms of personal, family, and community health. Personally, they have suffered physical and psychological stress and harm from societal oppression, and black families and communities have suffered much loss of material assets and of individual and group energy in their omnipresent and recurring struggles with racial oppression. The array of losses from long centuries of oppression is dramatic and greatly in need of major redress.

One aspect of the costs of oppression needs to be accented—the centuries of white-on-black violence. Too often in contemporary white analyses of racial matters the emphasis is on black crime and violence affecting whites, yet by far the greatest violence over the long course of U.S. history has come to Americans of color at the hands of whites. Some of the white violence that African Americans have faced has been psychological, but much white violence has been physical. In most recent discussions by whites of U.S. history, far too little attention has been given to the bloody and violent character of white-on-black oppression, especially during slavery and legal segregation. As we have observed in both white and black accounts, during the slavery and official segregation eras whites regularly, even casually, used violent actions—beatings, rapes, lynchings, and property destruction—and the threat of such violence to keep black workers and their families in their subordinate "place." Indeed, white Americans invented the violent—and often gun-oriented—traditions that are so distinctive of this society in the process of violently enslaving millions of African Americans over more than two centuries of modern human history. In addition, one of the bloodiest wars in human history, the Civil War, was started and pursued by white southerners seeking, in substantial part, to preserve their ability to enslave other human beings by violent means. The Civil War was soon followed by the development, again by whites, of violent means of subordinating the now-free African Americans under the emerging form of systemic racism called legal segregation. This development involved the creation of white terrorist groups such as the violent Ku Klux Klan, which is currently the world's oldest terrorist organization and which is still legal and operating in the United States.

Reviewing the autobiographical accounts of those enslaved, we observe how white concerns for profit and control constantly threatened and affected black families. Extreme family disruption and destruction were routinely inflicted on black families as part of whites' quest for financial gain, sexual exploitation, and social control. During the slavery and legal segregation eras, rape and other sexual violence perpetrated by white men were a constant threat for black women. During both eras, African Americans suffered attacks by whites on their persons and their property for becoming relatively prosperous or just for speaking out against racial discrimination. In response to the omnipresent psychological and physical violence, black extended families played a central role in enabling their members to survive oppression, a role that continues for these families to the present day.

In the contemporary era, elite whites and ordinary whites have rarely engaged in the overt use of physical violence to oppress African Americans directly, but they have frequently allowed or encouraged white police officers to engage in brutality and other coercive mistreatment of African Americans—malpractice in urban and rural areas that today continues the nearly four centuries of using physical violence to harass and subordinate black Americans.[11] Moreover, today many millions of white men and women, in all classes and most age groups, often engage in an array of discriminatory actions that do material harm to, and involve psychological violence against, African Americans who must venture, as part of their everyday lives, into historically white workplaces, businesses, schools, health care facilities, recreational facilities, and public accommodations.

The White Racial Frame and the Racist Ideology

Slavery, legal segregation, and contemporary racism have been central to shaping the ways that elite and rank-and-file whites have come to think, feel, and act in regard to themselves, to black Americans, and to other Americans of color. Centuries of this oppression have had a profound generating and shaping effect on most whites' character structure and on the commonplace white framing of the world. The white racial frame is an organized set of racialized ideas, emotions, and inclinations that is closely linked to habitual discriminatory actions, all of which are expressed in the routine operation of this society's racist institutions. This racial framing assists whites in their cognitive and emotional understandings of a racially constructed society. It has, in its turn, been central to rationalizing and reinforcing slavery, legal segregation, and contemporary oppression targeting African Americans and other Americans of color.

Since the seventeenth century, as part of their white framing of society, elite whites have often conceptualized this society metaphorically as a sort of plantation controlled by powerful white "patriarchs," and they have sold this view of society to the rank-and-file whites whose privileges come from their interstitial position between the elite at the top and people of color at the bottom of the hierarchy. Originally, the key developers of the white frame were slaveholders, merchants dealing with the slave trade or slave-produced products, bankers, and associated ministers, teachers, and politicians; over time, the slaveholding elite was replaced in the maintenance of the oppression ideology by manufacturers and other industrialists, as well as by new types of commercial entrepreneurs, bankers, teachers, media figures, and politicians. Over many generations now, these white economic, political, religious, and educational leaders have been central to the creation, maintenance, and reworking of systemic racism and its complex array of constituent social institutions.

Consider how the white and black accounts of experience with systemic racism reveal the early development and subsequent enhancement or alteration of the white racial framing of this society. The white vision of the societal world, with its enduring images and ideas, sits deeply in the white mind. For centuries, one essential ingredient of this framing has been a legitimating racist ideology—one that strongly asserts the superiority of white Americans, white families, and white culture, together with the inferiority of black Americans, black families, and black culture. Showing some stability over time, the positive views of whites and whiteness and the negative views of blacks and blackness have mostly persisted as habitual generalizations over many generations of white Americans.

Prior to North American colonialization, Eurocentric and proto-racial thinking was already evident in regard to Africans in European slave-trading countries such as Spain, the Netherlands, and England. Overseas colonialism was supported by a sense of European supremacy, though this view was initially a strong sense of religious and cultural superiority rather than of biologically oriented "race" superiority.[12] As European-fostered slavery developed, leading European philosophers and political thinkers, such as Immanuel Kant and David Hume, contributed to the development and legitimization of an extensive antiblack ideology and helped thereby to rationalize more fully the enslavement of African Americans. Leading whites in the North American colonies were perhaps the first to develop extensive written versions of a fully developed white-racist ideology, as we saw in Jefferson's extraordinary *Notes on the State of Virginia*. Their strongly articulated concept of "race," the concept of groups differing socially and culturally because of deep biological variations (beyond skin color), is one of the most important and devastating ideological inventions of modern Western civilization, a broad concept honed vigorously in this era by slaveholders, their hirelings, and their intellectual minions.

For centuries now, elite and rank-and-file whites have collectively developed a distinctive defense of the oppression imposed on African Americans. Antiblack stereotypes and related views have been key expressions of an overarching and increasingly developed antiblack ideology accenting cultural and biological inferiority. Whites have long held numerous sincere fictions about whites and whiteness, including color-coded stereotypes about the superiority of white morality, beauty, reason, and work efforts. For centuries, these sincere fictions have been asserted and presented visually and verbally. One of the common white notions has been that white relations with blacks have consistently amounted to "good relations." For whites, this has usually meant that blacks, such as those who were enslaved, were properly deferential and stayed in their subordinated "place," and that significant change was demanded only by outsiders or troublemakers. Also buttressing the notions of whites and whiteness during the slavery era were common, negative, and emotionally accented views of those they enslaved. African Americans were denigrated as less than adult human beings and were stereotyped for their supposed inferiority. This view of African Americans and other Americans of color being less than fully adult human beings has been essential to the idea of "race" in this country since the days of slavery.

During the legal segregation era, these positive fictions about whites and whiteness, as well as the negative views of African Americans, persisted and were asserted by whites at least as publicly and overtly as they had been during slavery. During both the slavery and segregation eras, African Americans were widely and routinely stereotyped by whites as, among many other things, lazy, emotional, carefree, oversexed, and immoral in their approach to life. These views were more than cognitive, for they were typically emotionally loaded and visually imbedded in the white-racist framing of society.

Today, these traditionally negative images of African Americans are still quite alive among white Americans, though they are often more subtly presented by most whites discoursing in public settings and the mass media. Even today, the typical white mind, deep down, seems to be pervaded with important images, emotions, and stereotypes of whiteness and blackness. Generally, thus, antiblack images, emotions, and stereotypes are more pervasive and invasive in the majority of white minds than the racialized images, emotions, and stereotypes that whites hold in regard to any other racial group. Indeed, they are often so invasive that they spill over into numerous other thought and action patterns. Nonetheless, one significant change since legal segregation is the declining willingness of many white Americans to assert the historically common negative stereotypes and images of African Americans in most public settings. Social conformity and social correctness now seem to incline a majority of whites—but by no means all—to make many of their negative public commentaries on African Americans or other Americans of color in more subdued or subtly racist terms. However, the majority of whites, continue to articulate a significant array of the conventional and blatantly antiblack stereotypes and prejudices in numerous private settings—that is, backstage with white relatives, friends, and acquaintances. The open expression of traditionally racist notions in private, and the blatantly racist comments uttered in public settings by a significant minority of whites, signal that some of what many African Americans call the "old plantation mentality" remains significant in a majority of white minds today.

The persisting white racial frame, with its entrenched racist ideology, functions to legitimate continuing racial discrimination and inequality.

For centuries, this white frame has operated to hide or disguise the injustice of oppression by insisting, among other things, that oppressed groups are in various ways "not like us," but instead are culturally, socially, and racially inferior. While most whites who have accepted the stereotyped interpretations of black personality, values, and subculture doubtless have functioned well in other areas of their lives, clearly they have to a significant degree lost contact with the reality of most black lives and communities—perhaps revealing a common sort of "social psychosis." Without this distorting and legitimating racist ideology, as Wahneema Lubiano has noted, the "United States' severe inequalities and betrayal of its formal commitments to social equality and social justice would be readily apparent to anyone existing on this ground."[13] Indeed, as in the past, ideological racism today remains "a distorting prism that allows the [white] citizenry to imagine itself functioning as a moral and just people while ignoring the widespread devastation directed at black Americans particularly, but at a much larger number of people generally."[14]

In every historical era, collective forgetting by whites has been critical to the perpetuation of oppressive institutions and the white frame that rationalizes them. For the most part, whites have repressed the historical memory of much of the society's long centuries of oppression or have developed, individually and collectively, an intentional ignorance of that oppression. This repression of history and trained ignorance of oppression have been critical to living comfortably as a white person in a still-racist society, to the present day. As a result, whites of various educational attainments still pass along much ignorance and misinformation about, and misrepresentation of, the country's long history of group oppression.

The white accounts examined for the slavery era offer relatively little in the way of information about the impact of slavery on whites themselves. In contrast, whites looking back on official segregation seem to comment more on daily life from the white viewpoint. They recall riding in segregated buses, living in segregated housing, using segregated water fountains and rest rooms, and encountering segregation in their social lives. They often remember this era with some discomfort or even significant regret for its obvious unfairness or immorality, yet very few demonstrate more than a superficial sense of the significant impact of official segregation on the lives of black Americans, even those with whom they came into regular contact.

Since the days of slavery, most whites have revealed a rather high level of social alexithymia, the sustained inability to relate to and understand the suffering of those who are oppressed. As they have developed or participated in oppression, most whites seem to have lost much of their human propensity for empathy, especially across group lines. For centuries, this social oppression has both required and constantly bred a lack of empathy and recognition of the full humanity of Americans of color. Today, most whites still do not "see," or do not wish to see, the impact of institutionalized racism or to recognize its determinative role in everyday life. A substantial majority persist in denying that white racism is systemic, commonplace, and devastating for its targets. The widespread denial of the reality of contemporary racial oppression is part of the age-old white racial framing of society. Indeed, the commonplace character of the denial of racism's foundational reality was revealed when I recently did an Internet search using a leading search engine. Extensive searching of billions of Internet websites found no references whatever among white commentators to language indicating a serious in-depth discussion of racial oppression as a critical and continuing part of the *foundation* of the United States.[15]

The Dimension of Black Resistance

Social oppression affects every major aspect of the lives of those targeted by it, whether its form is slavery, legal segregation, or contemporary racism. This totalizing reality is too often forgotten in current public and scholarly discussions of historical or contemporary oppression. Resistance under such circumstances often has to be subtle, covert, and enshrouded in requisite fear and necessary caution. Nonetheless, those who are the targets of omnipresent oppression are almost always more than "victims," for they fight back as best they can; and they and their families most often survive or thrive under the most difficult conditions. Dialectically over time, their resistance frequently shapes how whites react and buttress the system of racism—in an ongoing process of response and counterresponse. They remain agents even as they are subordinated and savaged in a racist type of Procrustean bed.

In combating oppression over time, African Americans have used an array of countering strategies. They have engaged in slave revolts, fleeing oppression to other areas, work stoppages, boycotts, sit-ins, legal challenges, and nonviolent or violent civil disobedience. They have used overt and confrontational tactics as well as covert and subtle efforts. In the accounts of African Americans in previous chapters, we have observed their constant strategizing about and implementation of resistance, a persistent resistance that in turn shaped white responses and thus the character of continuing oppression. From the earliest days of slavery, most whites have been fearful of black resistance. The resistance to enslavement by African Americans constantly shaped the way that white slaveholders arranged their economic and social institutions, their militias and slave patrols, their enslavement laws, and much of their government organization. Indeed, if those enslaved had really been "contented" like whites often contended, "slaveholders would have been less likely to respond violently, to restrict freedom of speech and to require political conformity."[16] Such was also the case under legal segregation, as whites created relatively autocratic institutions in order to keep African Americans firmly in their "place," at the same time limiting how democratic the country could be for all Americans, including whites. This white fearfulness and response to black protest and reaction to oppression have reappeared periodically since the black civil rights movement helped to bring an end to legal segregation in the 1960s.

One of the mechanisms important to the social reproduction of systemic racism, as well as for the reproduction of resistance, is collective memory. In all the eras we examined, black Americans discuss or allude to the importance of young people being taught about white-on-black oppression. Older black Americans recount or imply the importance of collective memories indicating lessons, for young and old, on what past oppression was like and on how to respond when it crashes into an individual's or a family's life in the present. Unquestionably, whites' individual and collective rationalizations are central to the social reproduction of oppression over time, and blacks' individual and collective memories of resistance are critical to countering that pernicious reproduction.

One strong conclusion suggested by the black accounts of experience with slavery, segregation, and contemporary racism is that the black family has had much greater importance in the survival of black Americans than many white scholars and other commentators have acknowledged. Typically, the white racial frame accents the negative features of black families, imagery that has been significant in much scholarly analysis for decades. Even whites in close contact with black families over many years have often been unable to perceive what was obviously in front of them—the very strong ties of love and affection that made the family difficulties created by systemic oppression such a central concern for African Americans since the days of slavery. Indeed, for centuries, black families have been protective of children and critical training grounds where most learn how to counter and contend with everyday oppression.

One little-known aspect of black responses to systemic racism is conspicuous in the black accounts. In all eras, we find an immense amount of reasoning, thinking, and planning, often at a profound and agonizing level, that black Americans have had to engage in for survival—and, where possible, for thriving. Their recurring experience with oppression has generally required them to give much thought to whites and their dangerous actions, as well as to countering measures to be taken against such actions. Large investments of mental energy for such purposes are not required for whites, who thus have much more energy for other important undertakings. For the most part, probing reflection on the meaning of slavery, legal segregation, and contemporary racism has been the required province of African Americans. They have often reflected on the meaning of oppression and of liberty, including freedom of person and free speech, and when possible they have given written and organizational expression to that reflection.

Moreover, over more than two centuries, numerous black commentators have been eloquent in their examination of the negative impact of institutionalized racism on the entire society and on whites themselves, including the impact of oppressive institutions on whites' character and political ideals. These probing black analysts have generally been far more insightful than most white commentators on U.S. racial matters. With rare exceptions, leading whites have not examined critically the benefits or liabilities of systemic racism for themselves or the larger society. In regard to racial matters, the sociological intelligence of white Americans is on the average far inferior to that of black Americans. I will return to these resistance issues in more detail in the next chapter.

THE GOVERNMENT AND SYSTEMIC RACISM: THE FAILURE OF U.S. DEMOCRACY

From the beginning, this country's much-praised "democratic" political institutions have been greatly shaped by, and integral to, the societal foundation of white-on-black oppression. In the first two centuries of development, whites' understandings of freedom for themselves and their implementation and understandings of slavery emerged together in the society. Indeed, the white American revolutionaries purchased their independence from Great Britain to a substantial degree with profits off the bodies and labor of enslaved African Americans.[17] Directly or indirectly, the white revolutionaries used profits from the slavery-centered economy to help in supplying an army, in gaining French government assistance, and in otherwise waging war against a powerful Great Britain. Virginia slaveholders provided much of the leadership for this revolution, wrote the Declaration of Independence, shaped the U.S. Constitution, and were most of the presidents for the first three decades of the new country's existence. About this time, white Virginians also owned 40 percent of all enslaved black Americans, and they had an essential and innovating role in making black enslavement central to the new country's economy.[18]

During the slavery period, no less figures than U.S. presidents, Supreme Court justices, and congressional leaders crafted or reinforced the extensive system of white-on-black oppression that extorted trillions of dollars (in current dollars) of arduous labor from those enslaved. Indeed, this country's capital city is located in Washington, D.C., mainly because of the decisions of a few powerful slaveholders, including President George Washington—who also, like other early presidents, was concerned about preventing enslaved African Americans from running away and about presiding over a President's house staffed in part by enslaved African Americans.[19]

The U.S. Constitution and Undemocratic Political Institutions

The political buttress for economic exploitation of African Americans was generated or reinforced in numerous provisions of the U.S. Constitution—including the sections counting slaves as three-fifths of a person (for the purpose of white congressional representation), giving Congress authority to suppress slave insurrections, preventing abolition of the slave trade before 1808, and requiring the return of runaway slaves. Nowhere in this Constitution is there a recognition of the humanity or rights of those enslaved African Americans who were doing much of the arduous labor that created the booming economy of the new nation at the time of its founding.

The famous "three-fifths" clause, called the federal ratio, was put into the supposedly democratic Constitution to enhance greatly the political power of whites in the major slaveholding states. The provision gave the major slaveholding states significantly more votes in the U.S. House and in the electoral college (which chooses the president) than they otherwise would have had. In the long term, the federal ratio was more significant than the fugitive slave or slave trade sections because it gave the South enough extra votes to guarantee that slavery would not be abolished. Without these extra votes in Congress, slavery would have been banned in Missouri, President Andrew Jackson would have failed to pass his 1830 Indian Removal Act, and the Kansas-Nebraska bill would not have become law.[20] Other major legal efforts in the interests of slaveholders would likely have stalled in Congress as well. The extra representation also gave the southern states effective control of many key positions in Congress, such as Speaker of the House and chair of the Ways and Means Committee. White southerners secured control of the Democratic Party caucus and held a majority of high civil-ser-

280 • Systemic Racism

vice posts in the government.[21] In 1843, former President John Quincy Adams spoke to Congress and pointed out that the United States was not a democracy because it was substantially controlled by a few thousand slaveholders.[22]

To the present day, the antidemocratic elements of that U.S. Constitution hamper efforts to further democratize the United States today. Slavery interests at the constitutional convention played a significant role in creating a relatively undemocratic political body, the U.S. Senate, in order, as James Madison put it, "to protect the people against the transient impressions into which they themselves might be led."[23] Under the Constitution's antidemocratic provisions, U.S. senators were elected by state legislators (until 1914), not directly by voters, and they served staggered six-year terms so a majority could not be replaced in one election; and they also served longer terms than members of the more democratic U.S. House.[24] Each state, no matter its population, got two senators. Thus, at one point, six southern states had 12 senators, six times the number for the state of Pennsylvania, which had about the same population as all those states together. The U.S. Senate has generally been a white male club, remaining heavily white and male to the present day. In addition, Senate rules have historically been important in helping conservative senators maintain the racist system. By the 1840s, the Senate's seniority rule gave control of major committees to the dominant party's senior members, who were often southerners. Also useful for the preservation of racial oppression, including slavery and official segregation, was the absence of a rule to stop Senate debate—replaced only in 1917 by a weak rule permitting an end to debate if that was approved by two-thirds (later 60 percent) of those present and voting.[25]

The leading political scientist Robert Dahl has noted that after more than two centuries the U.S. Senate

> has unquestionably failed to protect the fundamental interests of the least privileged minorities. On the contrary,...[it] has sometimes served to protect the most privileged minorities. An obvious case is the protection of the rights of slaveholders rather than the rights of their slaves.[26]

Moreover, using Senate rules, the minority of southern senators blocked every significant piece of civil rights legislation between the 1870s and the 1964 Civil Rights Act.[27]

After the brief Reconstruction era ended in 1877, racist white southerners, often members of the old slaveholding elite, regained their disproportionate representation in the U.S. House. Because of the Thirteenth Amendment (1865), the federal ratio was no longer a part of the U.S. Constitution, but now all the black population (not just three-fifths) was counted in determining how many political representatives the white South had in the U.S. House. White southerners got representatives based on a population count that included all African Americans, yet most of the latter were blocked by violence-backed discrimination even from voting. Thus, the white southerner marched "to the polls with many times as much voting power in his hand as the voter in the North."[28] Once again, the constitutional tradition, this time as interpreted by the undemocratic U.S. Supreme Court (which has allowed barriers to black voting for many decades, indeed in some areas to the present day), protected systemic racism. During this legal segregation era, very strong support for the oppression of African Americans came from almost all southern members of Congress, southern governors, and other major southern politicians—all of whom were white because of the overt white suppression of black voters.

Another important political doctrine that has protected white power and privilege is the hoary doctrine of "states' rights." The idea of states' rights became part of the U.S. Constitution for reasons having to do with much more than protecting slavery, but once it was firmly in place it became essential in the protection of slavery over a half century. States' rights as a principle of U.S. federalism early came to mean that southern whites could implement and protect the enslavement of African Americans without interference from other states or the federal government.[29] Scholar and former Civil Rights Commission chair, Mary France Berry, has summed up this governmental protection:

> The British theory of federalism, the division of power and responsibility between the central and local governments, which arrived in America with the first colonists, has become a handy philosophical tool for maintaining white superiority. Federalism as a policy has been advanced to explain national noninterference when state agencies refused to protect nonconforming blacks from white violence intended to keep them in their place.[30]

The Reconstruction era reforms attempted after the Civil War failed in part because they were interpreted by judges and other officials as violating the states' rights doctrine built into the Constitution. Similarly, the same states' rights doctrine protected the system of state-mandated racial segregation from much federal challenge, during the long years from just after Reconstruction to the mid-1960s. The use of federal government "power to prevent white southerners from using their state governments to mistreat black southerners not only offended racial sensitivities but also clashed with traditional conceptions of the American federal system."[31]

From the first decade of U.S. independence, whites have always dominated the U.S. government, and leading white officials have mostly operated to protect the political-economic interests of whites and thus the status quo. Berry has summed up the result of this control:

> Though the Bill of Rights, the Civil Rights Act of 1866, and the Fourteenth Amendment purport to protect individuals in their lives, liberties, and property, these ringing phrases have in fact afforded little protection to black people as a group. Law and the Constitution in the United States have been a reflection of the will of the white majority that white people have, and shall keep, superior economic, political, social, and military power, while black people shall be the permanent mudsills of American society.[32]

In themselves, the U.S. Constitution and other national documents proclaiming "justice" and "equality" have done little to bring justice and equality for African Americans (as well as for many other Americans) over the long course of U.S. history. Instead, only the vigorous and organized protests of African Americans and their white allies, such as in the abolitionist movement of the mid-1800s and the civil rights movements of the 1950s and 1960s, have forced white members of the elite to make important concessions in the direction of "liberty and justice for all." Without these organized movements, the changes toward less racial oppression would likely never have been implemented. Moreover, unless these formerly excluded groups have continued the political pressure, the new laws asserting fairness have usually been, at best, weakly enforced by white authorities.

Political representation is another indicator of racial power in the United States. Given the omnipresent reality of racial oppression, since the founding of the United States in the 1780s—when every fifth American was African American—not one African American has ever served in the highest elected positions such as president, vice president, Speaker of the House, or leaders of major political parties in Congress. Only two have ever served on the Supreme Court, and only five have ever served in the U.S. Senate. Today, this racial exclusion and marginalization persists in the twenty-first century, a continuing political legacy of "slavery unwilling to die." The United States is not even close to being the political democracy often heralded today across the globe by its top officials and its media commentators.

More Political Impact: U.S. Foreign Policy and Antiblack Racism

The ever perceptive observer of U.S. government action, sociologist W. E. B. Du Bois, once offered a remarkably prescient analysis of the impact of the white South's racist attitudes and practices on both U.S. history and the history of the entire world:

> Democracy in the South and in the United States is hampered by the Southern attitude....The [white] South does and must vote for reaction....A solid bloc of reaction in the South can always be depended upon to unite with Northern conservatism to elect a president. One can only say to all this that whatever the South gained through its victory...has been paid for at a price which literally staggers humanity. Imperialism, the exploitation of colored labor throughout the world, thrives upon the approval of the United States, and the United States gives that approval because of the South.[33]

Du Bois wrote these words in the 1930s near the high point of official segregation in the United States, yet his words remain on target to this very day. Democratic change in the United States, Du Bois noted, has a difficult path, for "Across this path stands the South with flaming sword."[34]

A good illustration of Du Bois's argument can be seen in U.S. foreign policy since 1800. For more than two centuries now, U.S. foreign policy has been infected by systemic racism. White men at the helm of the government have constantly shaped U.S. foreign policy with little input from African Americans or other Americans of color. The foreign policies of the United States have often exhibited a white arrogance and know-it-all orientation that preaches whites' political views to, and often imposes them upon, the majority people on the planet—who have for centuries been people of color.

Soon after he took office, President Thomas Jefferson, a Virginia slaveholder, worked to overthrow the modern world's only successful slave rebellion, which had begun in August 1791 when enslaved Africans overthrew the French and took control of the country of Saint Domingue (now Haiti). Like many white slaveholders, Jefferson was very fearful that the liberty ideas of the Domingue "cannibals," as he crudely stereotyped them, would spread to enslaved African Americans, and he met with the French to try to help them regain control. When the black population there won its war of liberation from France and set up its own government, President Jefferson worked to end trade with the country and to undermine its economy and new black government.

Political independence and a rights revolution were, in his and other white U.S. officials' minds, for whites only.[35]

A little later, another slaveholding president from Virginia, James Monroe, asserted what has been called the "Monroe Doctrine," a U.S. government view that all the Americas were off limits to further intervention by European governments. This doctrine strongly implied white American dominance of the Americas and all their peoples. Not long after the Monroe doctrine was articulated, in the 1840s, a doctrine of "manifest destiny" was asserted and circulated by influential white Americans seeking to develop the United States further into an imperialist and colonizing power much like numerous European countries. According to this expansive and openly white supremacist view, the U.S. government had a goal to change the world in "accordance with its own self-image," which included an ever expanding invasion of other lands so that the "civilizing influence" of the "white race" could have its beneficial impact.[36] The first great expansion involved the taking of northern Mexico by military force in the 1840s, and this was followed just a few decades later in a war against Spain in which the U.S. government took over control of the Philippines and Puerto Rico, suppressing indigenous independence movements by people of color in that imperialistic process.

The U.S. government also annexed Hawaii in 1898, which one prominent member of the U.S. Congress described as a step "in the onward march of liberty and civilization" and the "conquest of the world by the Aryan [white] races." He added that the "reign of the Aryan, with justice, enlightenment, and the establishment of liberty, shall penetrate to every nook of the habitable globe" and that the "onward march of the indomitable race that founded the Republic" could not be prevented.[37] In addition, the U.S. government often dealt violently with the Native American societies that were increasingly in conflict with the many white invaders (the so-called "settlers") immigrating into what is now the western United States. "The same theories of race used with respect to blacks were applied" to Native Americans, who were also viewed as a "decayed, degenerate, and inferior race" in need of the "relentless progress" of European American civilization.[38] All racial groups but whites from northern Europe were viewed by whites as alien, inferior, and uncivilized. These racially inferior groups were seen by whites as not ready for freedom and equality, for they were lesser "races" that needed to be treated like dependent children or as "savages."

In recent decades, this whitewashed approach to U.S. foreign policy has persisted; barely disguised in much U.S. foreign policy is a strong and assertive sense of (white) American cultural or racial superiority. For example, during the Ronald Reagan administration of the 1980s,

Reagan and his conservative advisors openly backed the white-racist government of South Africa, which enforced with great violence a racial apartheid system, and the conservative Reagan even vetoed congressional attempts to impose tough economic sanctions on the racially oppressive and extremist South African government.[39]

Today, the systemic racism of the United States, with its firm racial hierarchy, now has impact and influence across the globe, as white Americans have become what Amy Chua calls the "world-dominant minority, wielding outrageously disproportionate economic power relative to our size and number."[40] This power is wielded not only by leading U.S. politicians, but more importantly by U.S.-based multinational corporations, which are clearly among the most powerful white-controlled organizations on the planet. The economic and political operations of U.S. multinational corporations, backed by closely linked high federal government officials, have created increasingly huge wealth gaps on a global scale, gaps that mostly privilege white groups and mostly impoverish and subordinate peoples of color.

U.S. government intervention overseas is now linked to protecting the expansion of multinational corporations overseas, although the rhetoric is often broader and imperialistic. Many U.S. government officials have viewed U.S. military or economic intervention overseas as a "civilizing" operation rationalized in the sanitized language of bringing "freedom" or "U.S. democracy" to the world. For example, in a major address to the German parliament, President George W. Bush defended his invasion of Iraq as

> defending civilization....America and the nations in Europe are...heirs to the same civilization. The pledges of Magna Carta, the learning of Athens, the creativity of Paris, the unbending conscience of Luther, the gentle faith of St. Francis—all these are part of the American soul....These convictions bind our civilization together and set our enemies against us.[41]

This all-European view is only a revised version of the earlier white "plantation mentality" with its framing of a world in need of European-like civilization and military redemption. "Civilization," for most U.S. political and business leaders, is still white and European, and U.S. foreign policy thus remains in the thrall of the still omnipresent white racial frame.

Incorporating Other People of Color into White-on-Black Oppression

From its first century onward, whites of European descent have imposed on all residents of this society a white-supremacist social and ideological reality initially developed for destroying or excluding indigenous peoples and for exploiting extensively African and African American labor. Central to this European American domination has been a well-established group-status continuum and a legitimating conceptual frame. As whites have historically viewed and shaped this society since at least the eighteenth century, the prevailing racial hierarchy and racial status continuum run from "highly civilized" whites at the top to "uncivilized" blacks at the bottom, from high intelligence to low intelligence, from privilege and desirability to lack of privilege and undesirability. As Lewis Gordon has put it, U.S. racism is centrally a white-on-black phenomenon "with enough semiotic flexibility to mask itself as living 'beyond' such a dichotomy....One is black the extent to which one is most distant from white. And one is white the extent to which one is most distant from black."[42] For whites, new non-European groups brought into the United States since 1800 have been positioned in the white mind and in the white-dominated social structure somewhere between these two ends of the continuum. For centuries, whites have incorporated each new non-European group within this racial ladder and continuum of oppression. Each non-European group has been incorporated more or less according to the determinations of elite white decision makers and their supportive minions. The key to understanding what happens to any immigrant group coming in this society is that white Americans, especially those in the elite, have always controlled the general placement of such a group in this age-old ladder of racialized oppression.

After the United States was officially created in the late eighteenth century, Mexican Americans became the first new non-European group of size that was incorporated into the relatively new white-dominated United States. During the mid-nineteenth century many whites sought, by means of a substantial military intervention, to incorporate a huge area of northern Mexico as part of the inexorable "manifest destiny" of the United States to expand westward. If people of color were brought in during that process, these U.S. imperialists felt that was necessary and that "inferior races," such as Mexicans, would gain the benefits of supposed civilization in that process. However, yet other whites opposed such annexations on similarly racist grounds. Always operating from the white-racist frame, whites viewed the Mexicans in much the same way as they had blacks. Thus, one white Texan told the famous planner Frederick Law Olmsted, who visited there, that Mexicans are "as black as niggers and ten times as treacherous." Mexicans, Olmsted noted, allied themselves "with the Negroes."[43] Stephen F. Austin, a major white colonizer of Texas who gave his name to the state capital, viewed Mexicans as a "mongrel Spanish-Indian and negro race."[44] During congressional debates over annexing Mexican territory, prominent southern Senator John C. Calhoun argued that the United States had never "incorporated into the Union any but the Caucasian race....Ours is a government of the white man."[45] From this widely accepted white perspective, the "colored and mixed-breed" Mexicans were unacceptable in an allegedly free United States.[46] It is significant that both those whites who defended the seizing of Mexican territory and those who opposed it used similar racist arguments. All these whites operated from within the white frame with its firm view of European American supremacy that had been honed for centuries in regard to the one group of color so firmly at the center of the white-dominated society and prevailing white mindset—the archetypal African Americans. This white racial frame has long included both sincere fictions of the white self and of white superiority, as well as negative views of racialized outgroups. When a new group is incorporated into this country, thus, whites again and again accent white superiority vis-à-vis that group and view new non-black people of color much as they have the blacks they had so long oppressed.

The character of the reception and oppression faced by each new non-European group entering the system of racism has varied somewhat depending on time of entry, region of entry, size, socioeconomic capital, and physical characteristics. All entering non-European groups have not shared exactly the same fate, but in all cases the dominant white group, and especially the elite within it, has determined the rate and character of a group's incorporation into society, including the racialized definition of that group and its position on the racial ladder.[47] For the most part, powerful whites have controlled the major ways in which all U.S. racial groups are seen within the white racial frame and how they are generally treated in the society's public institutions and spheres in terms of racial discrimination and other racial oppression.

White elites or their agents have frequently recruited new immigrant groups to supply needed workers for the U.S. economy (for example, nineteenth-century Chinese and Japanese immigrants and early-twentieth-century Mexicans), or they have encouraged immigration to solve a refugee problem created by imperialistic military interventions by the U.S. overseas (as in the twentieth-century cases of Filipino, Korean, and Vietnamese immigrants). After the immigrants' arrival, those whites in power have seen to the socioeconomic placement of all immigrant groups somewhere between the white and black ends of the racialized hierarchy of political-economic wealth and power, as well as somewhere on the corresponding racial group-status continuum.

The white-racist conceptual frame, with its anchoring antiblack imagery, has incorporated negative images of other non-European

Americans with ease. In part, this is a matter of a transfer of numerous traditional antiblack stereotypes to recent immigrant groups of color, such as the majority of Latin Americans and Asians. Like black Americans, they too have suffered stereotyped images of being uncivilized, criminal, devious or untrustworthy, or threatening to whites. Over time, whites have honed and imposed somewhat different stereotypes for these more recent immigrant groups of color, images that have sometimes differed from those of African Americans, at least in emphasis. For example, in the case of Latin American and Asian immigrants—both those who entered in the mid-nineteenth century and those who have arrived in recent decades—many whites have responded with views of these immigrants as culturally "alien," "foreign," and threatening to Anglo American culture and society.[48] Even here, however, these negative images of foreignness have precedents in early white views of enslaved African Americans and decimated Native Americans as uncivilized, strange, and foreign.[49] From the early decades of the country to the present, most European Americans have viewed non-Europeans from within an interpretive frame that persistently defines them as uncivilized compared to European Americans, and as somehow alien and lesser human beings. For centuries now, most non-Europeans have been viewed by European Americans as alien to the dominant culture.

Today the white racial frame remains very much in evidence and operation in the United States. Most whites grow up as children in a society that is still presented to them by parents, peers, or the media as a more or less racialized world. They learn positive images and understandings of whiteness and white superiority, as well as ways to evaluate outgroups that are not white in blatantly or subtly negative terms. In this dominant framing of the society, black Americans typically remain the paramount "other" against whom "white" and "whiteness" are explicitly or implicitly defined. Today, black Americans still anchor in a majority of white minds the bottom of the racial hierarchy and group-status continuum. For that majority, they remain a primary threat to whiteness and white privilege, which threat may be felt or asserted consciously or unconsciously. Black Americans also remain for many whites the archetype of the "inferior colored race." For centuries, young white minds have regularly developed within this context of a vigorous white-on-black framing of society.

With the recent large-scale immigration from Latin America and Asia, this visualization and interpretation of U.S. society as overwhelmingly white-on-black in its racial structure and oppression may be changing somewhat in white minds. Still, recent research shows us that much antiblack thinking is still being passed along to white youngsters who

continue to define themselves (and whose parents and grandparents define them) as "white" Americans and who continue to accept willingly
white norms and decisions in historically white institutions. Moreover,
the racial status continuum on which non-European Americans are
placed today by still-dominant whites remains mostly anchored in
whiteness versus blackness. For example, this is clear from major research on the racialized conversations, discussions, and actions that a
majority of whites still engage in, especially in private settings with their
white friends, acquaintances, and relatives. Research that Leslie Houts
and I have done indicates that whites still do a great deal of backstage
and frontstage interaction with other whites that features convention-
ally racist views and ideas about African Americans.[50] Thus, a substantial majority of the white students at numerous colleges and universities
in our 2002–2003 research rely on centuries-old stereotypes of African
Americans in their backstage interactions and commentaries about
racial matters in the United States. About three quarters of the thousands of accounts that these 626 white college students gave us about
racist incidents and events they experienced actually involved African
Americans as targets of negative comments, with only about 10 percent
of the accounts targeting Latinos and the rest targeting various other
groups such as Asian Americans, Jews, and Arabs. While other groups
of color are periodically targeted in this racialized interaction among
whites, African Americans continue to hold the central place in regard
to racial matters in settings where white relatives, friends, and acquaintances routinely gather, even in areas of the United States with relatively
small proportions of African Americans in the local populations.

In addition, research that Eileen O'Brien and I have done with influential white men indicates that a majority of these men think of "race"
in U.S. society as centrally a matter of white-black relations, and they,
too, are just beginning to grapple with the meaning of the significant increases in the numbers of other people of color, once again usually from
within the traditional white-on-black framing of the society.[51] Indeed, it
is the minds of powerful whites—who are mostly men over forty years
of age—that are in many ways the most important in terms of decision
making affecting all people of color, because they are the ones in charge
of most major U.S. organizations. In terms of incorporating and racially
identifying new groups of color, the institutional decisions of members
of the white elite and its immediate white subordinates usually make
the greatest difference in people's lives over the long term, especially in
public settings.

African Americans were the only people of color that the majority of
white Americans had significant encounters with until the period from

the 1970s to the 1990s. There were exceptions in earlier decades, such as for whites who lived in south Texas, in a few large cities in California, or in Miami and New York City, but until recently most whites have not encountered significant numbers of non-black Americans of color because these groups were small or regionally concentrated. Even today, the majorities of the Latin and Asian American groups are first- or second-generation Americans. This demographic fact is one key to understanding the relative recency of much white imaging and accentuated negative discussion and action directed toward these non-black Americans of color.

From the time of their first entry into the new United States in the mid-nineteenth century, Latin American and Asian immigrants and their children have been positioned, again most influentially by powerful whites, somewhere on the racialized ladder below whites—with a substantially negative evaluation on the social dimensions of superior/inferior and insider/foreigner.[52] Thus, Latin American and Asian immigrants and their children, unlike earlier European immigrants by the second or third generation, have not been allowed by whites to assimilate structurally and completely into the extant white society.

Some of the identity struggle of new immigrants of color has involved struggling and trying to define themselves in ways that counter socially imposed white definitions. However, if you are a person of color in this society, you are limited in what you can do about the white-imposed definition of your racial identity in the everyday worlds outside your home and local community. At home or in the local community, with friends and relatives, you are likely to be able to identify racially more or less as you wish—but usually not with white employers, white police officers, white teachers, or other important white decision makers. Non-European immigrants and their children often face a white-imposed identity that may conflict with the identity that they prefer. There is much contemporary research on racial-ethnic identities that assesses how racial-ethnic groups come to see themselves in society, but relatively little identity research so far focuses in detail on the *externally imposed* racial-ethnic identities and their great societal consequences.

In recent years, some analysts have suggested that whites are selecting, or may soon select, *certain* Latin and Asian American groups for a "near white" or "honorary white" status, especially as whites sense the need for political allies or coalitions in a country that will in a few decades have only a statistical minority of whites in the population.[53] However, being categorized by whites as nearer the white than the black end of the racial ladder and status continuum will not likely mean that white-chosen Latin or Asian Americans will get the full privileges of whites or that they will even be viewed as "white" by most whites. Americans of color who are courted by whites for a white-dominated political coalition are likely to remain second-class citizens in white eyes and in persisting discriminatory treatment by whites in major institutions.

What groups are today seen as "white" by whites? There is much exaggeration in mass media and some scholarly discussions suggesting that some groups of color are now seen by large numbers of white Americans as already "white." However, this view is likely erroneous. I recently gave a questionnaire to 151 white college students asking for them to place a long list of U.S. racial-ethnic groups into "white" or "not white" categories. Very large majorities (86–100 percent) indicated that the following groups were "white" in their view: Irish Americans, English Americans, German Americans, Polish Americans, and Italian Americans. In contrast, not one of the 151 students listed African Americans as white, and only one listed Haitian Americans as white.[54]

In addition, overwhelming majorities of these white students classified all listed Asian American groups (such as Japanese Americans and Chinese Americans) as not white and also classified all listed Latino groups (such as Mexican Americans and Puerto Ricans) as not white. No more than 12 percent of these well-educated whites felt that any of these Latino or Asian groups could be categorized as white. Middle Eastern groups were also listed as not white by overwhelming majorities of these students. These college-educated whites are clearly operating with the traditional racial status continuum in mind when they place various U.S. groups into racial categories. African Americans are the only group firmly and clearly at the bottom of the racial ladder for all the white students, and northern European groups are firmly at the top of that ladder for most of them, with other European groups currently close to that top rank for most as well. In addition, for most of these whites, all groups of color are viewed as much closer to the black (or non-white) end of the racial continuum than to the white end. In these educated, mostly young, white minds, no group among the many groups of color is as yet significantly "whitened." It seems likely from these data that large percentages of white Americans are not yet incorporating groups of color into a white or near-white category in their minds.

In historically white workplaces and other such societal institutions, the racial identities of members of subordinated groups are largely determined by whites there, especially by those whites who are decision makers. How whites view a group's identity usually shapes what happens to them in public institutions, especially in regard to access to key white-controlled resources and opportunities. The white racial mindset consistently looks at racial identity from a distinctive perspective honed over centuries of racial oppression.

Moreover, whites are collectively so powerful that they pressure all new immigrant groups, including immigrants of color, to collude in the white-racist system by adopting not only general white ways of doing and speaking, including the English language, but also the white racial frame and its view of the racial hierarchy of U.S. society. Immigrants from all countries are pressured to accept the white racial frame, with its antiblack ideology and underpinning, in order to assimilate to whites and within a white-dominated society. Thus, cognitive scientist Otto Santa Ana has noted the strong white pressures on Latin Americans to "attempt to become white." Not only are Latin Americans pressured to reject Spanish and all things Latino, but they are also expected to accept the old white racial hierarchy that especially deprecates the "darker or more 'Indian'-looking Latinos."[55] In this way, whites are pressuring Latin American immigrants and their children to substantially reject themselves, their relatives, and their communities if they wish to be accepted—albeit then only to a degree—by whites who still control most of the society's major institutions.

CONCLUSION

The United States has long stood, especially in white minds, as a symbol of liberty and justice for the world community. The conventional phrase "liberty and justice for all" is asserted millions of times each week, especially by U.S. schoolchildren, even though it is far from the societal reality. For most white Americans, this conventional phrase is interpreted to be what currently exists—the weakly democratic, strongly hierarchical, white-dominated institutions of U.S. society. No country's leaders have insisted more on liberty and justice for other countries, yet at the same time have created or permitted such a huge discrepancy between these ideals and the lived reality of their own country, now indeed for centuries. While the U.S. political system is freer and more democratic than many other political systems, it is not as free or as democratic as numerous countries in Europe. The white elite that has led the United States for its entire history has mostly been composed of people who are not committed in practice to full liberty and social justice for all Americans. Thus, the formerly enslaved Frederick Douglass could ask, in an 1852 speech at a Fourth of July celebration, this poignant question:

> What, to the American slave, is your 4th of July? I answer, a day that reveals to him, more than all other days in the year, the

gross injustice and cruelty to which he is the constant victim. To him, your celebration is a sham…your denunciation of tyrants, brass fronted impudence; your shouts of liberty and equality, hollow mockery.[56]

Today, as in the past, the people of the United States live under a banner of liberty and justice that is only a hypothetical ethic not well realized in practice. In the face of this ethic, hypocritically, the white elite, as well as most rank-and-file whites, have constantly generated and regenerated an extensive system of racial discrimination and other racial oppression. Racial discrimination and informal segregation remain widespread, and racial oppression remains systemic. Every major historically white institution remains substantially white in its subtle norms, overt rules, and internal social structure. These institutions are, as most Americans of color quickly realize once they are inside them, very white places in terms of their everyday operations. What keeps these institutions racialized is the great array of white norms and privileges that most whites work aggressively to maintain or extend.

There is a societal cycle to the reproduction of systemic racism. Each new generation inherits a hierarchical structure of racial inequality from its parents and grandparents. Each new generation becomes more or less firmly positioned in the prevailing racial hierarchy with its greatly unequal allocations of resources, power, and privilege. Most whites assume that the contemporary incarnation of systemic racism is natural and normal. The longer those who are privileged live with their inherited and well-institutionalized privileges, the more comfortable they become with them. As they have in that past, most whites today view their social privileges and assets as their birthright—if, perhaps, eroding because Americans of color are now regularly challenging white privileges and trying to move into areas of society from which they were long excluded. Indeed, that perspective is a major reason why large-scale remedial actions designed to break down the discriminatory legacy of past oppression have not been implemented by the federal government on a society-wide basis. Aggressive action to eliminate the institutionalized racial discrimination and inequalities persisting from the days of slavery and legal segregation is something that most whites have never supported. When African Americans and other people of color challenge whites' unjustly gained social privileges, resources, or positions, the latter frequently defend them vigorously and resist strongly. Indeed, this recurring defensive action tends to reinforce whites' rationalizing of the system of racial discrimination and inequality and their antagonism to challengers of that system.

Recall, too, that the white racism of the United States now has spread across the globe, as white Americans have become the "world-dominant minority." As a result, people of color across the globe, who make up 80 percent of the world's population, are increasingly challenging this domination.

9

EPILOGUE: REDUCING AND ELIMINATING SYSTEMIC RACISM

A central problem of the United States today is that the system of racial oppression is still unwilling to die. The leading abolitionist Frederick Douglass lived long enough to see the legalization of extensive segregation for African Americans. In an 1889 address, he provided an appropriate metaphor: "While we have no longer to contend with the physical wrongs…of slavery…We have…to contend with a foe, which though less palpable, is still a fierce and formidable foe. It is the ghost of a by-gone, dead and buried institution."[1] The ghost of slavery has now lingered for many decades since Douglass made that comment. Several decades later in the 1930s, W. E. B. Du Bois accented a similar theme, describing fully entrenched segregation as a "new slavery" and concluding that support for real democracy had "died save in the hearts of black folk." Recall, too, that, a half century later, as the United States began to move from legal segregation to contemporary racist patterns, Justice William O. Douglas again picked up on this theme of slavery constantly reproducing itself. As he phrased it in a late 1960s Supreme Court decision, contemporary racial discrimination is still "slavery unwilling to die."[2]

Nearly a century and a half ago, many whites rejected slavery, yet not the racialized mindset and commitment to white privilege that characterized that slavery era. In a recent book two scholars of slavery, James Horton and Lois Horton, summarize the impact of slavery today:

> Its legacy remains in the history and heritage of the South that it shaped, in the culture of the North where its memory was long denied, in the national economy for which it provided much of the foundation, and in the political and social system it profoundly influenced. Slavery and its effects are embedded in the national culture and in the assumptions and contradictory ideals of American society....Although it is troubling to consider, it is nonetheless true that slavery was, and continues to be, a critical factor shaping the United States and all of its people. [3]

Clearly, today the United States is by no means a country that is liberated from the continuing impact and negative consequences of slavery.

In this epilogue, I examine briefly some ideas and possibilities for going beyond this slow, often backtracking, incrementalism in regard to racial change and aggressively eliminating many of the contemporary burdens and disabilities stemming from the racialized slavery tradition once and for all. Such solutions should help to move the United States toward a truly democratic multiracial society for the first time in its history.

BLACK RESISTANCE: LESSONS FOR CHANGE

Central to the economic and political foundation of the United States is the U.S. Constitution. Two of the major white leaders discussed in earlier chapters, George Washington and James Madison, were central figures at the 1787 Constitutional Convention, the first as president of the gathering and the second as the "father" of the Constitution that came out of the gathering. They and their colleagues worked to create a Constitution that would protect the entrenched system of oppression centered in racial slavery. Over more than two centuries since, the Constitution they constructed has frequently been interpreted and used by powerful whites in all branches of government to buttress that racial oppression and to divert or suppress racial change.

Nonetheless, on occasion, the founding documents have been taken up by some Americans seeking to bring significant change in the system of racism. The rhetorical ideals of human equality in the Declaration of Independence and of social justice in the preamble to the U.S. Constitution have been seized upon by later activists and freedom fighters who have sought to bring significant societal change. They have expanded these concepts of equality and justice far beyond what the white founders had in mind, even to the point of envisioning new founding documents.

Contrary to some historical and contemporary opinion, white Americans as a group have not been the strongest carriers of robust ideals of liberty, equality, and social justice for U.S. society. For several centuries now, the strongest commitment to these ideals among long-term residents of this country has probably been that of black Americans. Since well before the founding of the United States, black Americans have been at the forefront of those pressing strongly and organizing aggressively *within this country* for these ideals to be put into practice. In every generation, black Americans have pressured white Americans to implement fully the age-old ideals of liberty, equality, and social justice.

Thus, without the recurring struggle of African Americans, this society would likely be less democratic than it currently is, and there would be less hope for a much more democratic future. Given the archetypal position of African Americans in U.S. history, their centrality in the struggle for a democratic United States should not be surprising. Without their involvement in numerous important historical events, the U.S. Constitution and federal court decisions interpreting and extending it would likely have changed in a more democratic and egalitarian direction much more slowly. From the Reconstruction Amendments of the 1860s and 1870s to the 1960s civil rights acts, from *Brown v. Board of Education* (1954) to *Grutter v. Bollinger* (2003), black Americans have provided the impetus for many civil rights laws and court decisions from which Americans of all racial and ethnic backgrounds, not just black Americans, have greatly benefited. In the case of the United States, expanded civil rights is substantially a gift that black Americans have given to the entire country.[4]

Precedents for New Founding Documents

Even a brief critical reflection on the founding political documents of U.S. society and on how they were made can lead one to the view that these undemocratically generated documents are in great need of comprehensive revision, if not complete replacement. African Americans have long been in the forefront of individual and collective efforts to further democratize the founding documents. The African American revolutionary, Lemuel Haynes, fought for the American cause and wrote the first known essay by an African American, a strong anti-slavery essay in which he argued that tyranny "was lurking in our own bosom" and that an African American "has an undeniable right to his Liberty."[5] An early attempt to significantly update and revise the Declaration of

Independence was undertaken in 1829 by a courageous black Bostonian, the abolitionist David Walker. In his widely circulated *Appeal to the Coloured Citizens of the World*, Walker quotes the famous phrase "all men are created equal" from the original Declaration, and then adds this penetrating comment directed at white Americans:

> Compare your own language above, extracted from your Declaration of Independence, with your cruelties and murders inflicted by your cruel and unmerciful fathers and yourselves on our fathers and on us—men who have never given your fathers or you the least provocation!...I ask you candidly, was your sufferings under Great Britain, one hundredth part as cruel and tyrannical as you have rendered ours under you? Some of you, no doubt, believe that we will never throw off your murderous government and "provide new guards for our future security."[6]

The brilliant and heroic Walker was convinced that African Americans had to force themselves to be included in a more comprehensive version of the Declaration's asserted ideal of equality. He felt that African Americans would eventually throw off the "murderous" system of oppression then taking the form of racial slavery. For his efforts and revolutionary stance, Walker had a bounty put on his head by slaveholders, and he died relatively young and in mysterious circumstances, perhaps murdered by slaveholding interests. Significantly, if whites had heeded Walker's appeal for major change, the United States could early have become a much freer and more democratic society.

Three decades later, African Americans made up a substantial majority of the first group of Americans to propose a U.S.-oriented Constitution that asserted racial equality. In May 1858, the white abolitionist John Brown, working with the black abolitionist Martin Delaney and other black and white abolitionists, set up a little-known antislavery meeting in Chatham, Canada, an area with a substantial free black population, many of whom had roots in U.S. slavery. Nearly four dozen blacks and whites met in this safe town to formulate a new constitution that would govern a growing band of armed revolutionaries fighting for an end to the bloody slavery system. Looking forward to a free and egalitarian U.S. nation, their *Provisional Constitution of the Oppressed People of the United States* had this remarkable preamble:

> Whereas slavery, throughout its entire existence in the United States, is none other than a most barbarous, unprovoked and unjustifiable war of one portion of its citizens upon another portion—the only conditions of which are perpetual imprisonment

and hopeless servitude or absolute extermination—in utter disregard and violation of those eternal and self-evident truths set forth in our Declaration of Independence: therefore, we, citizens of the United States, and the oppressed people who, by a recent decision of the Supreme Court, are declared to have no rights which the white man is bound to respect, together with all other people degraded by the laws thereof, do, for the time being, ordain and establish ourselves the following provisional constitution and ordinances, the better to protect our persons, property, lives, and liberties, and to govern our actions.[7]

Brown, Delaney, and the other delegates envisioned self-governing guerilla groups, operating from mountainous areas of the East Coast, that would recruit more of those who were enslaved and develop guerilla resistance that would help to end U.S. slavery. Their revised declaration of independence stated that

We therefore, the Representatives of the circumscribed citizens of the United States of America, in General Congress assembled…Do in the name, & by the authority of the oppressed Citizens of the Slave States, Solemnly publish and Declare: that the Slaves are, & of right ought to be…free…And that as free and independent citizens of these states, they have a perfect right, a sufficient and just cause, to defend themselves against the Tyranny of their oppressors.[8]

To my knowledge, this constitution and declaration of independence are the only ones in U.S. history to be debated and ratified by representatives of the racially oppressed black residents of the United States, with their interest in liberty, equality, and justice clearly in mind. Once again, if white Americans had heeded such early declarations of liberty and justice, this country might well have been spared the hundreds of thousands of deaths that soon were to result from an extraordinarily bloody Civil War and would likely have had a much different racial history, to the present day.

Black Men and Women: Forcing Constitutional Change

Black Americans fought against their enslavement for centuries. The constant black resistance to enslavement, the thousands of blacks involved in hundreds of slave conspiracies to revolt and in actual revolts, the hundreds of thousands of black runaways, the hundreds of thousands of black Union soldiers and Union support workers—all these black men, women, and children made slavery's eventual death inevitable.

Perhaps most importantly, about 200,000 African Americans served in the Union army and navy during the Civil War, and another 200,000 to 300,000 served in civilian roles supportive of the military efforts. Most of these men and women had been enslaved in 1861, but a few years later were fighting for their permanent liberty. During the first two years of the war, the sentiments of most northern whites, including President Abraham Lincoln, were that the Union had to be restored, but that abolition of slavery was not a principal goal of the war effort. After the general order to recruit black soldiers belatedly came down in May 1863, and with the help of influential leaders like black abolitionist Frederick Douglass and white abolitionist George Stearns, large numbers of black Americans were recruited for numerous military units. These courageous soldiers provided the military strength needed at a time of serious manpower shortage—a shortage that was due in part to northern whites resisting the new draft law. In addition, tens of thousands of enslaved (or formerly enslaved) men and women spied for Union forces, destroyed Confederate facilities, or fled the plantations to the North. The withdrawal of much black labor played a major role in the demise of the slaveholding Confederacy. Without the slaves' abandonment of the southern economy and their large-scale military service, the Union cause would likely not have seen victory—a point that President Lincoln himself made late in the war. Without that Union victory, the U.S. would likely have had a dramatically different subsequent history than that which has taken place.[9]

The heroic efforts and many sacrifices of millions of enslaved and free African Americans made morally necessary and politically likely the pathbreaking and liberating Thirteenth, Fourteenth, and Fifteenth Amendments to the Constitution. Du Bois once underscored this:

> It was the rise and growth among the slaves of a determination to be free and an active part of American democracy that forced American democracy continually to look into the depths....One cannot think of democracy in America or in the modern world without reference to the American Negro.[10]

In spring 1864, the first attempts to pass the Thirteenth Amendment abolishing slavery failed in the U.S. House. However, as Union armies won more victories—with the substantial aid of formerly enslaved southerners—the Congress finally passed the amendment in January 1865.[11] This momentous amendment to the U.S. Constitution, ratified by enough states by December 1865, reads as follows: "Neither slavery nor involuntary servitude...shall exist within the United States, or any place subject to their jurisdiction."

Blacks' constant commitment to, and indeed strong conceptualization of freedom, made its expansion all but inevitable. Continuing black pressure for recognition as U.S. citizens soon brought fruit. In July 1868, the extraordinary Fourteenth Amendment was finally ratified by enough states. It explicitly included, for the first time in U.S. constitutional history, a phrase with the word "equal":

> All persons born or naturalized in the United States and subject to the jurisdiction thereof, are citizens of the United States and of the State wherein they reside. No State shall make or enforce any law which shall abridge the privileges or immunities of citizens of the United States; nor shall any State deprive any person of life, liberty, or property, without due process of law; nor deny to any person within its jurisdiction the equal protection of the laws.

Moreover, in February 1870, the Fifteenth Amendment was ratified by enough states to become part of the U.S. Constitution. It asserted that "The right of citizens of the United States to vote shall not be denied or abridged by the United States or by any State on account of race, color, or previous condition of servitude." All three Reconstruction amendments included specific provisions giving Congress the ability to enforce them with appropriate legislation. While all three had been strongly opposed by many whites in the North and South, after much effort they were passed and finally made black Americans real citizens of the United States with, at least on paper, important civil rights.

Marking a glacial change in constitutional history, these new provisions brought the idea of equality into the U.S. Constitution for the first time, and they remain the only provisions of the Constitution that deal explicitly with dismantling aspects of the country's racist political and legal foundation. U.S. residents celebrate widely the Fourth of July as the birth of this nation. Yet December 18, 1865, is arguably the date of the real birth of a nation committed substantially, if still rhetorically and haltingly, to human liberty and democracy. That was the day that the Thirteenth Amendment freeing all enslaved Americans was finally ratified.[12] This legal action would not likely have taken place without the active resistance to oppression by African Americans, who thereby played a central role in bringing their own eventual liberation. At base, it was not Abraham Lincoln's famous Emancipation Proclamation that brought an end to slavery, but rather the very active efforts of those African Americans who had been enslaved.

White Action and Official Segregation

Significantly for the country's future, the antislavery white legislators who composed and fought for the Thirteenth Amendment in the U.S. Congress understood it to mandate an end not only to slavery but also to the "badges and incidents" of slavery. ("Badges" referred to indicators of racial rank, while "incidents" referred to heavy burdens accompanying enslavement.) Senator Lyman Trumbull, an Illinois Republican, authored and introduced the Thirteenth Amendment on the floor of the U.S. Senate in 1864. Two years later, when he and his colleagues sought passage of a comprehensive 1866 Civil Rights Act to eradicate those "badges and incidents" of slavery, Trumbull aggressively defended the view that this Thirteenth Amendment gave Congress the authority to

> destroy all these discriminations in civil rights against the black man, and if we cannot, our constitutional amendment amounts to nothing. It was for that purpose that the second clause of that amendment was adopted, which says that Congress shall have authority, by appropriate legislation, to carry into effect the article prohibiting slavery.[13]

Today the Thirteenth Amendment, as well as the Fourteenth and Fifteenth Amendments, should still be read as exerting significant pressure for the eradication of the many vestiges of slavery that appear in the guise of contemporary racism.

Unfortunately, white reactionaries on the U.S. Supreme Court soon derailed the original goals of the Thirteenth and Fourteenth Amendments to end the badges and incidents of slavery. In the *Slaughterhouse Cases* (1873) the Court construed the critical "privileges and immunities" clause of the Fourteenth Amendment extremely narrowly and effectively killed that amendment in regard to protection of the then-endangered rights of newly freed black Americans. Moreover, after Congress passed the 1875 Civil Rights Act updating the 1866 act, the Supreme Court ruled in the *Civil Rights Cases* (1883) that this law was unconstitutional because, in the white judges' minds, it went beyond the Thirteenth and Fourteenth Amendments to prohibit racial discrimination in public accommodations by private individuals.[14] In this case, the majority of an unelected Supreme Court overturned a critical civil rights law passed by an elected Congress to implement the old U.S. ideals of liberty and justice. In his dissent to this Supreme Court decision, Justice John Marshall Harlan argued for the civil rights law's constitutionality, noting that the court majority itself had even recognized that the thirteenth amendment established freedom; that there are burdens and disabilities, the necessary incidents of slavery, which constitute its substance and visible form; that congress, by the act of 1866, passed in view of the thirteenth amendment…undertook to remove certain burdens and disabilities, the necessary incidents of slavery, and to secure to all citizens of every race and color…those fundamental rights which are the essence of civil freedom;…and that legislation, so far as necessary or proper to eradicate all forms and incidents of slavery and involuntary servitude, may be direct and primary, operating upon the acts of individuals, whether sanctioned by state legislation or not.[15]

This was the first federal judicial decision to raise the issue of the social reproduction of slavery over time—in this case in the form of societally imposed segregation—and to assert prominently that there were continuing racial badges and incidents of slavery that could be seen conspicuously in that segregation. Yet in this decision most of the judges firmly supported racial segregation that was privately imposed by white discriminators.

A little more than a decade later, moreover, an openly racist Supreme Court decided to support state-mandated segregation as well, in direct contradiction to the intentions of the lawmakers who added the Reconstruction Amendments to the Constitution. In *Plessy v. Ferguson* (1896), the Court upheld the legality of government-imposed, racially segregated facilities for white and black Americans, reasoning fallaciously that white racism was natural and that "legislation is powerless to eradicate [whites'] racial instincts."[16] As one historian has concluded, "Northerners finally let the Fourteenth and Fifteenth Amendments lapse into impotence in terms of human rights and let states' rights override them."[17]

More Racial Change: The Civil Rights Movement

In the late nineteenth and early twentieth century, various governments at the local, state, and federal levels—backed by a white male Supreme Court—developed a structure of extreme racial segregation that persisted until, yet again, African Americans themselves organized effectively to counter and eventually overthrow that legal segregation. Within a few years of the *Plessy* decision, in 1909, several black and white Americans, including W. E. B. Du Bois and Ida B. Wells-Barnett, organized the National Association for the Advancement of Colored People (NAACP). Over the next few decades, and often led by the NAACP, an increasingly vigorous civil rights movement gradually put more pressure on white leaders for significant changes in systemic racism.

From the 1920s to the 1960s, the efforts of the NAACP and other African American organizations to desegregate historically white universities and other historically white institutions pressed the Supreme Court to rule in favor of fairness and equality. These desegregation cases, and especially the famous 1954 *Brown v. Board of Education* decision, have been hailed as pioneering decisions by brave white justices seen as way out in front of the country's citizenry.[18] Yet, these white justices were not ahead in reasoning or action of most African Americans. Indeed, black parents had brought the *Brown* case because of great concern for their children's education.

Extensive organizing and voting by increasingly large numbers of black Americans were substantially responsible for the white elite's growing but very belated concern to take action against legal segregation. Like previous black efforts against systemic racism, the civil rights movement of this era brought significant changes to the racial patterns of the United States. Black civil rights groups grew in number and strength, and by the end of World War II the NAACP alone had one thousand local organizations. Black colleges and churches provided much of the membership and leadership for local and national civil rights organizations. And many black veterans returning from World War II, a war ostensibly fought for "freedom," joined the organized efforts against the official segregation still operational in southern and border states.[19] In addition, during the 1930s–1970s cold war period, the desire of the white elite for maintenance of U.S. political legitimacy internationally in the face of many demonstrations and protests from hundreds of thousands of black Americans was central to the success of that civil rights movement. Without aggressive pressuring from black Americans and their leadership, the white elite would not likely have moved toward racial desegregation. Once again, black civilians and soldiers had forced white leaders to further democratize U.S. society.

For a brief period, major court decisions like *Brown*, together with continuing nonviolent civil rights protests against segregation, were taken by numerous white legislators and judges as the moral authority to end much state-created segregation. As a result of the civil rights movement and changes in federal courts resulting substantially from that movement, Reconstruction Senator Trumbull's conclusion that the Thirteenth Amendment provided authority for Congress to eradicate discrimination against black Americans was included in a major 1968 housing discrimination case. In that case, a lucid Supreme Court majority argued that the continuing impact of slavery could be seen in current antiblack discrimination. Continuing discrimination by whites was asserted by the court majority to be a "relic of slavery" and "slavery unwilling to die."[20] A few years later in a federal appellate case, Justice John Wisdom accented the continuing authority of the Thirteenth Amendment: "When a present discriminatory effect upon blacks as a class can be linked with a discriminatory practice against blacks as a race under the slavery system, the present effect may be eradicated under the auspices of the thirteenth amendment."[21]

Also important in this era were the positive actions of white members of Congress who felt pressure from the black-led civil rights movement and its international supporters, as well as, for northern members of Congress, from growing numbers of insistent black voters in the North. Under this pressure, they passed major civil rights laws prohibiting discrimination in employment, education, voting, and housing. Once again, the determination of black Americans to be free and equal forced the white leadership, as well as rank-and-file whites, to rethink what U.S. democracy means and to make some concessions in the direction of expanding that democracy, an expansion ultimately benefiting whites as well as African Americans and other Americans of color.

THE CHALLENGE TODAY: BRINGING MORE CHANGE

Occasionally, over the decades since the Civil War, a majority of whites have accepted some significant racial changes, but their view of permissible changes in systemic racism has generally been limited in time and extent. Periods of dismantling certain aspects of systemic racism have lasted only a decade or so, and then have been followed by decades of whites' backtracking on change commitments and of resurgent racial oppression. This was true for the era after Reconstruction and has been true as well for the period since the civil rights movement of the 1960s and 1970s.[22] Today, as in previous centuries, the majority of whites remain opposed to private or government action aimed at bringing substantial changes if those actions mean a surrender of significant white power and privilege. Du Bois once described the key barrier to change thus:

> The chief obstacle in this rich realm of the United States, endowed with every natural resource and with the abilities of a hundred different peoples…to the coming of that kingdom of economic equality which is the only logical end of work is the determination of the white world to keep the black world poor and themselves rich.[23]

While today the majority of whites no longer routinely assert openly racist ideas in public arenas, they still hold racist images, stereotyping, and proclivities in their minds, which are frequently expressed backstage with relatives and friends. Indeed, most whites have never been strongly committed to comprehensive desegregation of major historically white institutions.

People typically think and reason in terms of entrenched interpretive frames and the metaphors and stereotypes associated with them. They usually do not think critically about the frames themselves, but accept those that they have inherited from their predecessors. Thus, imbedded in the minds of the white men who made the U.S. Constitution was an extensive white-superiority framing of their social, political, and legal world, a framing that they played a central and long-term role in enhancing and sustaining. Similarly, the powerful white men (and a few white women) who succeeded them over subsequent generations, such as those serving on federal courts and in federal and state legislatures, have enhanced and sustained a broadly similar white framing of society. Today, as in the past, this white racial framing is deeply imbedded in white minds and is often hidden from conscious view, which makes significant change slow and difficult.[24]

The Persisting White Racial Frame

As we have seen in previous chapters, the white framing of society encompasses much more than certain negative attitudes directed against African Americans and other Americans of color, although racial prejudice and stereotyping are the emphasis in most of the relevant social science literatures. This white racial frame involves a very large set of negative prejudices, stereotypes, images, ideas, notions, propensities, interpretations, and action orientations that whites learn and use to make sense of the racial world around them. The many racial bits of the frame constitute a more or less integrated whole designed to interpret and perpetuate the racial status quo. To understand the white racial frame, and to change it, one must understand that it is an integrated whole that is learned and reinforced in white social networks over lifetimes. The white racial frame is deep in most white minds because of the early socialization of whites into this framework in primary social networks and persists because it is constantly presented and reinforced in all major historically white institutional settings.

Recently, demographic trends have presented new challenges to the white racial frame of this society. Since about 1970, the substantial immigration of people of color from Latin America, Asia, and the

Caribbean has changed the demographic makeup of U.S. society in a more populous and racially and ethnically diverse direction. Over the next generation or two, whites will become a statistical minority of the population in most U.S. cities and states, as they currently are in half the country's larger cities and in the states of California, Texas, New Mexico, and Hawaii. No later than about 2050, African Americans, Latinos, Asian Americans, and Native Americans will be the new majority of the U.S. population. Increasingly, whites are becoming aware of these major demographic changes, yet the majority seem to fear a more multiracial future where they will be the minority of the population and, eventually, of voters and political officials. The majority of whites seem to look at these changes from within the white racial frame and thus cannot visualize a United States that is highly diverse in racial terms, minority white, and more democratic and egalitarian.

Negative white views of this increasing racial-ethnic diversification are in line with the racist thinking of Thomas Jefferson and other white founders. These white founders and their minions could not conceive of a United States in which white and black Americans were racially integrated within the same communities and living on egalitarian terms. That is one reason why the founders and rank-and-file whites often pressed for the export and overseas colonialization of the African Americans who might be freed from slavery. Similarly, during the legal segregation era, a very negative view of a racially integrated society was conspicuous in the "segregation forever" discourse of a great many whites, including the white leadership of the South. Today as well, positively envisioning and valuing a racially diverse and minority-white society seems to be difficult for the majority of whites, given that their thinking about such matters still typically involves an application of the conventional white-racist framing of society.

A Reinvigorated Social Justice Frame

Today, antiracism activists can aggressively counter this conventional white racial frame with one that accents racial justice and equality, taking these old ideals out of the realm of dusty rhetoric and placing them in a reinvigorated antiracism frame. To bring significant change, thus, antiracism activists must focus constantly and assertively on displacing or replacing this white framing and the racial inequality that it buttresses and defends. There is nothing in principle about human minds (brains) that makes this major conceptual change impossible. In recent decades, both social science research and neuroscience research have shown that human beings can learn and unlearn a great deal at any age, including as they grow older.[25]

Efforts to counter and change the white racial frame can be undertaken for all ages, but such efforts are especially important for children. Currently, the substantially segregated U.S. educational system colonizes young white (and other) minds with the white racial frame. If we are to dismantle the system of racism, this educational system must be dramatically reformed so that it is reasonably integrated along racial lines and, most especially, provides all the country's teachers and youth with the tools to recognize clearly, analyze critically, and replace substantially or completely the white frame with its many racial stereotypes and other bits of racialized misinformation, emotions, and inclinations to discriminate. By the time white children are in school, most already hold negative views of Americans of color. Their stereotyped views must be directly challenged and replaced in a new array of required school courses. At an early age, students everywhere need to be taught in schools and other settings just how to break down and critically analyze the many racial-ethnic stereotypes of this society. In addition, teachers and other change agents can insist actively and constantly on African Americans and other Americans of color being viewed seriously as equal and valuable members of society from whose creativity all can benefit.

An accurate racial and ethnic history of the United States should now be provided to all children, and indeed all adults, so that they can understand not only the origins and realities of systemic racism but also the many contributions to the society of all groups of Americans. Historian Howard Zinn has accented the power of information and its dissemination through social networks. Individuals speaking out frequently with accurate information on systemic racism can be a start toward significant racial change. No one is born thinking critically about the oppressive realities of the society around them. Each person who learned to think critically did so in response to education of some type, in response to new societal information:

> There was a moment in our lives (or a month, or a year) when certain facts appeared before us, startled us, and then caused us to question beliefs that we strongly fixed in our consciousness—embedded there by years of family prejudices, orthodox schooling, imbibing of newspapers, radio, and television.

Given this reality, then, one action concerned individuals can take for change is "to bring to the attention of others information they do not have, which has the potential of causing them to rethink long-held ideas."[26]

Throughout this book, I have suggested the importance of making critical historical facts better known to the people of this country. Thus, one cannot view U.S. history, or indeed contemporary U.S. society, the same after taking seriously the historical data on Sally Hemings or Ann Dandridge, black members of the Jefferson and Washington families. Nor can one have the same view of the possibility of ending slavery, and thus the very foundation of systemic racism, in the 1790s after learning that numerous white slaveholders, including the powerful Virginian Robert Carter III, knew what was the just action to take and freed those African Americans whom they had enslaved. Unlike better remembered white founders, these powerful whites had the courage to live up to the then heralded ideals of liberty and justice in this regard. The implications have been clearly stated by historian Andrew Levy. He has argued that the more one reads of the courageous actions of whites like Carter who acted against slavery, at substantial personal cost, "the more one feels a sense of fury that the whole thing—the Civil War, Jim Crow, the Ku Klux Klan, two hundred years of relentless bitterness and division—could have whimpered and died in the Potomac tidewater."[27] Indeed, the American revolution for equality could truly have taken place in the eighteenth century if whites had followed the moral leadership of the white and black abolitionists.

Of course, many whites and others will never change their racial framing of the society when confronted with the historical or contemporary facts, but there are many who can begin to rethink their positions if only they encounter the new information that is necessary to begin that journey. So, a key task for people seeking to be change agents is to spread the historical and contemporary information about racial matters as widely as possible.

Long ago, in a letter to a white correspondent, Frederick Douglass noted that his correspondent's use of the phrase "the Negro problem" was "a misnomer. It were better called a white man's problem....What the future of the Negro shall be, is a problem in which the white man is the chief factor."[28] One important step in this racial reframing is to get whites and others to recognize and name the racial "problem" accurately. The problem of racism has always been, most centrally, a white problem. To reframe is to also understand that racial discrimination is more than a societal "problem." As the white southern writer Lillian Smith dared to say in the 1940s, racial discrimination is a "cruel way of life for which, if we wish to survive as a free nation, a new way of life must be envisioned."[29]

Ironically, both injustice and justice have long been rhetorical concerns of this country's leaders and of many people in the general population. At its national birth, "to establish justice" was asserted as a principal goal by the authors of the U.S. Constitution. Defending the new Constitution in *The Federalist Papers*, James Madison wrote about justice:

> Justice is the end of government. It is the end of civil society. It ever has been, and ever will be pursued, until it be obtained, or until liberty be lost in the pursuit. In a society under the forms of which the stronger faction can readily unite and oppress the weaker, anarchy may as truly be said to reign, as in a state of nature where the weaker individual is not secured against the violence of the stronger.[30]

Ironically, there was no better example at that time of a political system in which the weaker group was not secured against violence from the dominant group than the slavery system. Yet, nowhere did Madison reflect seriously and at length on the massive injustice in which he was inextricably involved as a major slaveholder.

Today, we must go beyond the limited conceptions of founders like Madison and recapture social justice for a thoroughly egalitarian conceptual framing of U.S. society. We must specifically and repeatedly use this language of social justice in pressing for an end to racial oppression and for a great expansion of human rights within a supportive societal structure. Most Western analysts have viewed social justice in individualistic terms. For example, sharpening ideas in the tradition of political liberalism, philosopher John Rawls argued that a just society is built on two principles: (1) Everyone in that society has an equal right to the broadest system of equal liberties possible without harming the rights of others; and (2) any social or economic inequalities that exist must be such as to benefit the least advantaged in the society and must be attached to societal positions that are open equally to all people.[31] Today, systemic racism flagrantly violates both these principles. Equal liberties do not exist where there is still widespread discrimination in employment, housing, public accommodations, and schooling, and where the substantial socioeconomic inequalities of this society are neither beneficial to disadvantaged Americans of color nor the result of an equality of opportunities.

In building a just society, moreover, we must go beyond individualistic conceptions of social justice to a group conception, for racial oppression involves group subordination and differentials. Social justice necessitates "explicitly acknowledging and attending to group differences in order to undermine oppression."[32] Racial injustice involves social institutions that privilege one racial group over another. Racial justice thus means the ending of this unjust privilege and enrichment for white Americans and unjust disadvantage and impoverishment for black Americans. For social justice to be implemented for the United States, the material reality of unjust impoverishment and unjust enrichment must be dramatically altered. Social justice also entails an elimination of the societal structures that make existing inequality possible. An elimination of inequality and injustice must involve ending racial domination at every level of the society and in all its constituent organizations.

Associated with this ideal of social justice are the age-old ideals of human freedom and human equality. In regard to racial matters, the implementation of real freedom must mean, at a minimum, that people from all racial groups have the ability to develop themselves and their families to the fullest without having to face institutionalized discrimination. All significant group restraints and barriers to opportunity and achievement should be removed. In addition, authentic social justice in regard to racial matters involves more than formal equality; it involves significant and substantive equality across the color line. As Dr. Martin Luther King, Jr., once pointed out, when African Americans went from demanding fair treatment to a demand for real equality, most white supporters abandoned the black rights movement.[33]

If we take these ideals seriously, large-scale reparations are clearly due a number of racially oppressed groups, including reparations for the genocide against Native Americans and for the extensive enslavement and official segregation of African Americans. Racial equality necessitates a fair distribution of societal goods across all racial groups ("distributive justice"). In addition, racial equality must also mean that this society is itself substantially restructured to insure that people in all racial groups get a truly equal opportunity to secure those resources and to participate without racial barriers in all major U.S. institutions, including key political institutions.[34]

Reframing for Social Justice: Antiracist Whites

Numerous black leaders and writers, from Frederick Douglass to Martin Luther King, Jr., have noted that, while many whites are somewhat uncomfortable with racial discrimination, relatively few are willing to pay the price for its elimination in society. One challenge for a reinvigorated antiracism movement is to mobilize and increase significantly the number of whites who are questioning and displacing the white racial frame and who are willing to pay a substantial price for significant racial change in this society. Taking even the first significant steps is difficult for most whites because that involves a serious commitment to be and act differently, and that commitment includes giving up title to at least some white privileges and advantages.

Historically and in the present, a small minority of whites have moved away from the white racial frame in the direction of a social justice frame. Recall Quaker leader John Woolman, who in the mid-eighteenth century spoke out forcefully against slavery and about its negative impact on both blacks and whites.[35] He saw clearly that a white-racist framing of society was being generated. As he wrote, placing black Americans in the "ignominious title, slave, dressing them in uncomely garments, keeping them to servile labour...tends gradually to fix a notion in the [white] mind, that they are a sort of people below us in nature."[36] A few decades later, while considering the role of white northerners in slavery, Henry David Thoreau proclaimed that one white man standing against slavery could make a difference:

> I know this well, that if one thousand, if one hundred, if ten men whom I could name—if ten honest men only—ay, if one honest man, in this State of Massachusetts, ceasing to hold slaves, were actually to withdraw from this co-partnership, and be locked up in the county jail therefor, it would be the abolition of slavery in America. For it matters not how small the beginning may seem to be: what is once well done is done forever.[37]

Historically, and often working with African Americans, a few courageous whites have abandoned some or much of the white-racist framing of society and instead emphasized a strong social justice perspective. As we have just noted, a few white slaveholders early on took steps in this direction by freeing enslaved African Americans. By the 1850s, large numbers of white abolitionists were working with black abolitionists to challenge the slavery system. Later, during the official segregation era, more brave whites joined many even braver blacks in protesting racial oppression. Recall white writer Lillian Smith who, even as a child, dared to question the racist structures of the South into which she was being socialized. Many whites eventually joined with large numbers of African Americans in the black-led protests and demonstrations of the 1960s that helped to bring down legal segregation.

In recent years, modest numbers of whites have continued to participate actively in antidiscrimination action and organizations. Some have reframed their racist view of society by participating in civil rights movements, while other whites have been able to do this social justice reframing from reading and thinking on their own or from interactions with individual Americans of color who educate them to the reality of systemic racism. There are numerous recent examples of this type of change. For example, in a recent interview study in the South, one white woman showed more than just sympathy in regard to racial discrimination, for she spoke out critically about police actions leading to the death of a black man in a local jail. Her comment stimulated local officials to call her husband to try to quiet her:

> I was saying to my husband at that time, if I have begun looking out my front windows…if I felt intimidated—I mean, these were two times my husband is being admonished to have me shut up—if I felt intimidated—and you can tell from our environs [upper-class neighborhood] that we have the wherewithal not to feel at mercy to someone—what about someone who doesn't have means? What about someone who can't call on attorney friends? What about someone who wouldn't have people? That goes beyond intimidation, to me. That goes into terror…it's incomprehensible to me the fear that must set in some people, the feeling of powerlessness. I can't even imagine it. I think it's a terrible climate…I've always felt that if I were born black, I would have been a radical. And I'm not sure that I'd have had the strength of character to overcome hatred. Because I believe that if I'd been born black and I'd had children, that seeing the unfairness, or unkindnesses, that they were probably met with daily, or the false assumptions, I just don't know if I could have handled it.[38]

This woman has reflected critically and deeply on the meaning of being black and white in society and has taken some action to bring change locally. Her interpretive framing of society clearly reflects an accent on social justice and racial equality.

Only a small minority of white women and men in this society have shown a willingness to consistently assess racial discrimination and other racism as unfair and as a violation of the old ideals of social justice and fairness, and only a few have taken action to protest discrimination locally like this woman. Typically, moreover, these protest actions are often first steps and do not yet reveal a comprehensive perspective on systemic racism and on the organized action needed to thoroughly desegregate and democratize the society.

Just a few have made antiracist action central to their everyday lives. Thus, in another interview study, a white female professor was actually forced out of a teaching position because of the strong stands that she regularly took on matters of racism. As she notes, her antiracist stance and actions drove a serious wedge between me and the rest of the faculty, and that I believe seriously impacted my career and my willingness to stay at that institution.... [The department] wrote me this letter that no one signed. "Dear [name],...We believe that you will never publish things that we accept"—because everything I was doing about race stuff.... "We believe that you are a bad fit for this institution.".... And I had to say, am I going to stay and make a fight of this, or am 1 going to pack it in?...It was the relationship [I had] with the students of color, it was my stand on those issues, it was always wanting to teach those courses and be involved in those issues, it was replacing half of the white supervisors in the clinic with African American supervisors, when the white supervisors...were very popular. But where were we going to find black mentors, for our black and white students?[39]

Clearly, for this professor a social justice frame accenting racial fairness and egalitarian action has trumped the traditional white frame of racial matters. Her actions to reject or restructure apparent institutional racism in her college got her into difficulties with other white staff members. In such cases, it is easy for numerous white faculty members and administrators to claim that their views of an antiracist white professor "not fitting in" are not racially motivated, yet they do reveal excuses for supporting white-framed business as usual at the college. One major challenge is how to create more white Americans whose framing of the racial world has changed like these whites and how to provide support for such people in institutions that remain inhospitable not only to Americans of color but also to whites who move away from the white-racist framing of society and take serious actions to dismantle it.

Bringing Institutional Change

How do we bring change to the thinking and actions of large groups of white Americans and thus to the contemporary structures of racial oppression? Historically, two key factors have loomed large in regard to the successful forcing of significant racial change. One critical factor in progressive change in the past has involved large-scale antiracist organization and action. Over some fifteen generations now, as we have often seen in previous chapters, African Americans through their declarations and their actions have probably been the most important carriers of values of liberty and justice for this society. For African Americans, these have been much more than rhetorical ideals. Mass nonviolent action by black and white abolitionists helped to bring down slavery, and mass nonviolent action by blacks and their white supporters during the 1960s helped to bring down legal segregation.

There are major lessons to be learned from past organizing to reduce or dismantle systemic racism. Just before he was assassinated in 1968, Dr. Martin Luther King, Jr., insisted that large-scale nonviolent demonstrations would still be required in the future, on an ongoing basis, to constantly counter and eventually eliminate racist institutions in the United States. He suggested that nonviolent antidiscrimination demonstrations needed to be supplemented with much other organization against local forms of racial oppression—efforts such as electing political leaders of color and fighting discrimination in housing.[40] Such organization is difficult, but change in racial discrimination will not come without much more of it, today as in the 1960s.

A major challenge today is how to organize effectively for racial change. Concerned antiracist activists from various racial and ethnic groups, and from all walks of life, must come together to organize a social movement that will insist on the full array of human rights for all U.S. residents, and indeed for all people on earth. We need numerous organizations across all sectors of society working to reinvigorate the centuries-old antiracism effort and to eliminate the contemporary versions of slavery's racialized "badges and disabilities." Central to these efforts will doubtless be challenging all aspects of the dominant white racial framing of society, including its underlying assumptions and constituent arguments. Everywhere, this racist framing and the actions that spring from it must be replaced with a reinvigorated justice-and-equality frame and the associated modes of action.

A second important factor involves the international context. During the civil rights movement from the 1930s to the 1970s, the U.S. government was competing aggressively with the former Soviet Union for the allegiance of many countries whose populations were not white, and the negative publicity generated by legal segregation and whites' racial violence in the United States hampered that effort to win international respect and cooperation.[41] Antiracism struggles have been the most successful when the international political context has pressured white officials in the U.S. to take some action against systemic racism.

Today, the international context is increasingly supportive of the struggle for broader human rights for racially oppressed Americans, as well as for those racially oppressed in other countries. Most of the world's countries have now signed the United Nations Convention on the Elimination of All Forms of Racial Discrimination. The U.S. government held off for many years, but finally ratified this treaty in 1994. Now the U.S. government makes reports to the United Nations over-

316 • Systemic Racism

sight committee that watches over the Convention. Responding to this international pressure, a recent U.S. government report to this oversight committee claimed, with significant misrepresentation of the actual situation, that the U.S. government was "adamantly opposed to racism in all its forms and manifestations and was fully committed to being a world leader in the cause of human rights."[42] Significantly, the official rapporteur for the United Nations and various members of the United Nations committee were rather critical of the U.S. report. They raised significant questions about continuing racial discrimination and hate speech in the United States and about the declining enforcement of U.S. civil rights laws by a conservative Supreme Court and by increasingly conservative federal agencies.[43] Today, international pressure continues to bear down on the U.S. government to implement its own civil rights laws and to expand those laws in conformity with international treaties against discrimination and international treaties accenting broad human rights that have been signed by the United States.

In recent years, moreover, major international conferences, some with thousands of delegates from dozens of countries, have been held to examine and protest racial oppression across the globe. In August 2001, a major World Conference against Racism, Racial Discrimination, Xenophobia and Related Intolerance was held in Durban, South Africa. At this major conference, with at least eight thousand participants, officials from numerous international organizations and human rights activists from many countries strongly criticized continuing racial discrimination in the United States. Unfortunately, the U.S. government did not send a high-level delegation to this conference and withdrew from the conference early.

To the extent that U.S. political leaders can be pressured to become much more sensitive to this international criticism of U.S. racism, that pressure can have a significant effect on the enforcement and expansion of antidiscrimination laws within the country. Indeed, one type of action that a reinvigorated human rights movement in the U.S. could undertake is to aggressively highlight the importance of this international context for U.S. political leaders. Indeed, for several decades now, black civil rights activists have tried to get United Nations agencies to look into racial oppression in the United States. International pressure is likely to increase in the future as whites, including white Americans, become an ever smaller minority of the total world population, yet remain unfairly in control of a disproportionate share of the world's critical economic, mineral, and energy resources—a condition largely resulting from centuries of Western colonialism and imperialism, which have long been rationalized in racist terms.

A NEW CONSTITUTIONAL CONVENTION: REAL DEMOCRACY IN PROCESS AND STRUCTURE

Given that the central problem of U.S. society today is still systemic racism, it follows logically that a U.S. Constitution that was created in part to buttress white-on-black oppression should be a major target for substantial reworking or replacement by those involved in a reinvigorated human rights movement. One goal of this human rights movement should be to provoke a major reconsideration of the founding documents and of the currently weak democracy in the United States.

In previous writings, I have suggested the great need for a new constitutional convention for the United States. Let me recapitulate and extend that argument here.[44] The U.S. Constitution, made in 1787 under the leadership of men with a strong economic interest in slavery, aggressively and substantially reinforced white-on-black oppression in the new United States. With just a few amendments added since that time, this very outdated Constitution remains the country's legal, political, and moral foundation. At the original Constitutional Convention there were no African Americans, no other Americans of color, and no white women; not one of their number participated directly, or by means of elected representatives, in constructing the political constitution under which they and their descendants have had to live now for centuries.

Today, such a skewed representation at a constitutional convention would never be accepted as legitimate or democratic if it were held in some country being pressed by the U.S. government to implement political democracy. For that reason, one can raise the reasonable question as to why the current U.S. population majority must endure a Constitution into which their ancestors had no input whatsoever. In no era has a new constitutional convention been held in the United States to replace this substantially undemocratic document with one created by the representatives of all Americans. Recall that the major actions of the Chatham Convention, whose majority was composed of black Americans and which had to meet outside the United States, were a declaration of independence and constitution that would bring expanded liberty and real democracy to the United States. It is well past time for a new constitutional convention to be convened at which African Americans, Native Americans, other Americans of color, and white women are fully and proportionately represented.

If the United States is to ever become a more complete and developed democracy, there must be another constitutional convention at which all groups of Americans are fairly represented. Of all the civil rights and human rights that people deserve, perhaps the most important is the right to play a major role in determining the political norms, rules, and structures under which they live. A formal right to vote is not enough for a democracy to exist; this formal right must be supplemented by political institutions that facilitate active participation in the political decisions that shape people's lives. Some might fear that a constitutional convention under the current conditions of white male domination of society might lead to an even less democratic document,[45] but in my hypothetical scenario the new constitutional convention will not take place unless those who debate and write the new constitution are indeed representative of all sectors of the U.S. population. No other arrangement will create the necessary participatory conditions for full and open debates on matters of concern to all sectors of the population.

A truly representative assembly would insure that, for the first time in U.S. history, the white majority hears much discussion of, and faces pressure to take seriously, the group interests and rights of all Americans. Such an assembly will be diverse enough that many decisions on constitutional provisions will require a consideration of the originally excluded interests of Americans of color and of white women. As with the first convention, the debates will likely be vigorous and educational, not only for delegates, but for the country as a whole. These debates would likely remove the smokescreen disguising the undemocratic reality of this society and show unequivocally how racial, gender, class, and other forms of oppression operate to the detriment of a majority of Americans.

What specific substantive issues might be discussed and debated at such a convention? The egalitarian and democratic ideals associated with the Bill of Rights and the 1960s civil rights laws could well be starting points for important discussion at this new convention. Significantly, the U.S. Constitution lacks an economic bill of rights, a point constantly made by civil rights leaders since the 1960s. Few Americans know that in his 1944 State of the Union address to Congress, the most revered U.S. president of the last century, President Franklin D. Roosevelt, asserted the great need for an "Economic Bill of Rights" for the United States:

> This Republic had its beginning, and grew to its present strength, under the protection of certain inalienable political rights....As our nation has grown in size and stature...as our industrial economy expanded—these political rights proved inadequate to assure us equality in the pursuit of happiness. We have come to a clear realization of the fact that true individual freedom cannot exist without economic security and independence....We have accepted, so to speak, a second Bill of Rights under which a new basis of security and prosperity can be established for all—re-

gardless of station, race, or creed. Among these are: The right to a useful and remunerative job in the industries or shops or farms or mines of the nation; The right to earn enough to provide adequate food and clothing and recreation;…The right of every family to a decent home; The right to adequate medical care and the opportunity to achieve and enjoy good health; The right to adequate protection from the economic fears of old age, sickness, accident, and unemployment; The right to a good education.[46]

Here Roosevelt not only greatly expands the country's constitutional Bill of Rights to include an array of economic and related social rights, but also insists that they be for all people regardless of social station, race, and religion, the latter also a major advance in political goals for the United States.

Significantly, most of these rights articulated by Franklin Roosevelt soon became part of the United Nations' Universal Declaration of Human Rights, whose drafting in the late 1940s was overseen by Eleanor Roosevelt. Since that time, several very important United Nations documents on human rights have since expanded that Declaration's scope. Today, this United Nations Declaration and associated human rights covenants represent a growing international consensus on the broad array of human rights necessary for a socially healthy society. These United Nations agreements have represented international responses to, as Judith Blau and Alberto Moncada suggest, "genocide, oppressive labor practices, the antiapartheid movement, national independence movements, liberation movements of colonized people, and atrocities committed against civilians" and to the "civil rights movement in America, the feminist movement, and the newly empowered voices of indigenous groups and landless peasants."[47] The United Nations response to these movements has been to develop important human rights statements and covenants that go well beyond traditional U.S. conceptions of individual rights to strong assertions of social, economic, environmental, and cultural rights.

An official call for a new U.S. constitutional convention should indicate that the deliberations would be grounded in respect for the diversity of U.S. heritages and cultures and for full human rights as laid out in these pathbreaking United Nations human rights agreements. Clearly, the ideals of racial equality and racial justice imbedded in the Thirteenth, Fourteenth, and Fifteenth Amendments, should be central in discussions of a new U.S. Constitution.

Such a constitutional convention is of course only a first step. A truly democratic constitution would become the political basis on which to build an array of institutions designed to effectuate and perpetuate over the long term full democratic participation and representation in U.S. society. One necessary institutional change is the development of more democratic political bodies, including the replacement of the undemocratic U.S. Senate by a governing body elected on the basis of population (not state boundaries) and the replacement of the Supreme Court by a high court whose composition is more reflective of, and shaped more directly by, the American people. This latter step would be very significant, since from the first decade the meaning of the U.S. Constitution has been what this unelected and unrepresentative group of judges (usually all white men) has said that it is. Currently, this Supreme Court is the most powerful, least democratic political (indeed, legislative) body at the federal government level. Many legal and political analysts have argued that the U.S. Constitution is not frozen in time and that it has on occasion been reinterpreted, especially by the Supreme Court, in a more progressive and democratic direction.[48] Yet, we have always had an unelected and undemocratic Supreme Court that decides on the most important constitutional interpretations—almost always in line with the interests of the white elite at a particular time in history. For a time in the mid-1950s, and again in the late 1960s and early 1970s, the high court moved significantly in the direction of reducing racial segregation in this society, but by the mid-1970s the court, with more conservative Republican appointments, was backing off on the earlier commitment to racial desegregation in this society. Indeed, over the last few decades it has become a bastion of racial retrenchment and has allowed racial resegregation in schools and other societal arenas, especially if white officials do this backtracking with subtlety.

Significantly, there are political systems in other countries that operate in a fairer and more democratic fashion than the less democratic and less representative system that currently operates in the United States. While no country implements the United Nations' Universal Declaration of Human Rights and its associated civil, political, social, and economic rights covenants fully, there are numerous countries that implement major provisions of these agreements better than the United States.

For example, one key provision of United Nations human rights documents is the charge for governments to dismantle and redress racial discrimination in their bailiwicks. Following this perspective and mandate, the Canadian government and numerous European governments have put into effect explicit legal protections for certain remedial programs that are designed to end racial-ethnic discrimination. Thus, if one examines the current constitutional systems of Canada and the United States, one finds significant differences in the laws aimed at eradicating racial discrimination. In 1982, the Canadian political leadership added a provision to the Canadian Constitution that firmly protects affirmative action ("positive discrimination") programs.[49] In contrast, the U.S. Constitution does not explicitly protect active government programs to eradicate past discrimination. Indeed, the U.S. Supreme Court, which decides what the U.S. Constitution means, has in recent years knocked down several major affirmative action efforts and sometimes accepted oxymoronic notions of "reverse discrimination" against whites, thereby weakening the U.S. commitment to substantial equality along racial lines. Moreover, in recent years, the Supreme Court of Canada has interpreted the Canadian Charter of Rights and Freedoms as substantially expanding equality for all Canadians in major directions rejected by the U.S. Supreme Court—such as by finding that "racist and anti-Semitic hate propaganda produces and reinforces social subordination from segregation to genocide."[50] Operating from this human rights perspective, Canada's high court has outlawed much hostile hate speech.

In the U.S. case, a new and strongly democratic constitution—with broad citizen participation in its inaugurated institutions and with recurring citizen activism on behalf of human rights—seems to be a major guarantee of the much heralded ideals of "liberty and justice for all." From this base, contemporary Americans can build the egalitarian democracy that the best democrats in the founding generation of Americans had envisioned.

CONCLUSION: A RENEWED ETHIC OF "OTHERS PRESERVATION"

The reality of systemic racism in U.S. society is that the white majority—including most white decision makers in local, state, and federal governments—have never listened seriously to the pained voices and oppression-honed perspectives of African Americans and other Americans of color. Only by bringing in and attending to the perspectives and experiences of all Americans can the United States expect to meet the many challenges of an unknown, but certainly difficult, societal future. A great expansion of social and political democracy will make much essential knowledge finally available for the long-term improvement of still-fledgling democracies like the United States. It is well past time for whites, including white leaders, to listen carefully to, and heed the often sage advice of, African Americans and other Americans of color. Throughout this book, we have seen the remarkable and profound insights of African Americans into an array of important social justice and equality issues for people in this country and abroad. We have encountered concrete visions of a socially healthy United States and, indeed, of a socially healthy world.

Listen to Dr. Martin Luther King, Jr.. In his final book, King suggested that all human beings have inherited a "great world house" in which we must find a way to live together without so much major conflict:

> From the time immemorial human beings have lived by the principle that "self-preservation is the first law of life." But this is a false assumption. I would say that other-preservation is the first law of life precisely because we cannot preserve self without being concerned about preserving other selves.[51]

No present-day society would exist but for the contributions to human knowledge, insight, and advances that people in many other societies have made in the present and the past. Moreover, all life today is interdependent. Not only is this true ecologically, but it is also true in social and political terms. For example, the existence of nuclear weapons in a few countries is a threat to the entire planet's survival, and current racial and ethnic tensions might at some future point trigger a nuclear holocaust. Colonialism, imperialism, and multinational capitalism have resulted in the concentration of wealth in the hands of a few—and very disproportionately whites of European background. They are unjustly enriched while many are unjustly impoverished. In the long run, this unjust inequality does not work for humanity and its survival. Thus, we need to put this first law of life at the center of a new ethic of rights and responsibility: the law of others preservation. Without preserving others, we cannot in the long run preserve ourselves and our posterity.

No person is an island; all residents of the United States are part of the same deeply troubled society. All will thus benefit, yet to varying degrees, from a large-scale change in racial oppression, as well as from change in the often related oppressions of class and gender. Major racial change will mean that whites will lose much in the way of racialized power and privilege. Still, the payoff for them and for the entire society is large, for real liberty, justice, and equality are impossible without major changes in the racially oppressive structures of this society. Indeed, this planet will not survive much longer if we continue to rely so heavily on the white men now at the helm for key ideas, policies, and actions in regard to the world's ecology, economy, and politics. Systemic racism has killed not only people, but many important human values, scores of excellent ideas, and countless innovations and inventions. One need not be melodramatic to suggest that the survival of the planet likely depends upon the speedy elimination of racial oppression and other major social oppressions.

Eradicating racial oppression, indeed even partially dismantling it, will not be easy. The history of human rights movements in the United States teaches the key lesson that change requires much effective organization by those who are racially oppressed, assisted by supportive whites who are committed to implementation of social justice ideals. Large-scale participation by those who are targets of systemic racism will be required for significant change to occur simply because most whites will not acquiesce in major changes in systemic racism without great pressure from those who suffer at their hands. This is a sad but obvious lesson one gains from reviewing the long struggle of African Americans and other Americans of color against oppression. For major change to take place, those who are oppressed must organize and protest effectively and with great persistence. The history of the modern civil rights movement is certainly one of individual black Americans standing up against systemic racism, individuals like Rosa Parks in Montgomery, Alabama, refusing to move back in a bus. Yet in these cases, heroic black individuals were typically able to succeed in such protests only because their efforts were backed by many others who were organized and willing to work for change.

Historical reflection suggests that it is usually the oppressed who must organize to force large-scale changes in systems of oppression. Thus, to reduce or eliminate systemic racism now and in the future, African Americans and other Americans of color must again organize collectively and effectively to create more egalitarian social, economic, and political institutions, and thus to finally implement the longstanding U.S. ideals of freedom, liberty, and justice. Certainly, this does not mean that white Americans who support racial justice and equality can sit back and wait. They, too, must organize aggressively and effectively to bring change in white racist thinking and practice, including change in the institutionalized features of U.S. racism. This is by no means an easy task, for the systemic reality of racism means that it is deeply entrenched in society. Attacking it will take a huge effort by many people of all backgrounds. Eternal organization, like eternal vigilance, is still the price of human liberty.

As human beings working in this anti-oppression effort, we can assert publicly and forcefully a much better image of this society's future and of the world's future, and then work to reach that fair, just, humane, and egalitarian image. In the founding generation, the revolutionary democrat Tom Paine wrote in *Common Sense* that the goal of the revolution was "to begin the world over again." He argued that the "birthday of a new world" was near. Imagine such a new and better world. Suppose that at any point in our centuries-long descent into the racialized hell that whites have long been creating, social justice had gotten the organized support and reinforcement that it needed. Suppose that the U.S. government insisted on real political and economic freedoms for all people in the United States and around the globe. Further suppose that the U.S. eliminated racial oppression in its sphere of influence and educated all residents to their highest potential. Suppose, too, that the U.S. used its wealth and power to raise up all the people on earth to their fullest potential. Suppose, too, that modern science and technology were used to raise all the world's families to good health and prosperity rather than just the affluent few. This view is indeed just a dream, yet even a partially realized dream sought after aggressively by all those committed to real democracy would be far better than the fundamentally oppressive present.[52]

NOTES

PREFACE

1. Henry Wiencek, *An Imperfect God: George Washington, His Slaves, and the Creation of America* (New York: Farrar, Strauss, and Giroux, 2003), 84–85, 284–285.
2. Ibid., 72–79, 301–305.
3. James Baldwin, *The Fire Next Time* (New York: Dell, 1962–1963), 20.
4. J. A. Rogers, *Africa's Gift to America* (St. Petersburg, Fla.: H. M. Rogers, 1961), 216.
5. *Jones v. Mayer Co.*, 392 U.S. 409 (1968).
6. Edmund S. Morgan, *American Slavery, American Freedom: The Ordeal of Colonial Virginia* (New York: Norton, 1975), 387.
7. John Stuart Mill, *On Liberty*, 4th ed. (London: Longman, Roberts & Green, 1869), 17.
8. Frederick Douglass, "The Nation's Problem," in *Frederick Douglass: Selected Speeches and Writings*, ed. P. S. Foner and Y. Taylor (Chicago: Lawrence Hall Books, 1999), p. 739.
9. Josephine Louie, "We Don't Feel Welcome Here: African Americans and Hispanics in Metro Boston," Harvard University Civil Rights Project, (research report, Harvard University, 2005), i–iii.
10. David Wessel, "Racial Discrimination: Still at Work in the U.S.," *The Wall Street Journal Online*, at http://www.careerjournal.com/myc/diversity/20030916-wessel.html (ret. May 26, 2005). Summary of study by Devah Pager.
11. Ibid. Summary of study by Marianne Bertrand and Sendhil Mullainathan.

12. "University Of Florida Economist Finds That Black Children's Names Hinder Their Educational Development," *The Journal of Blacks in Higher Education Weekly Bulletin*, at file:///C:/Documents%20and%20Settings/ User/Local%20Settings/Temporary%20Internet%20Files/Content. IE5/85CF0Z0V/noname.htm#story5 (ret. May 26, 2005). Summary of study by David Figlio.

13. New Jersey Citizen Action, "New Report Highlights Impact of Hidden Practice of Auto Finance Markup on New Jersey Consumers," Press Release, February 23, 2005, at www.njcitizenaction.org/craautofinancpress.html.

14. "Mental Health Care Doesn't Meet Standards, Study Finds," Research Matters, Harvard University, at www.researchmatters.harvard.edu/story. php?article_id=108 (ret. May 26, 2005); "Minority Patients Face Barriers to Optimum End-Of-Life Care," *Research Matters*, Harvard University, at http://www.researchmatters.harvard.edu/story.php?article_id=361 (ret. May 26, 2005).

15. "Net worth" means assets minus debts. "The Racial Wealth Gap Has Become a Huge Chasm that Severely Limits Black Access to Higher Education," *The Journal of Blacks in Higher Education*, at http://www.jbhe. com/news_views/45_racial_wealth_gap.html (ret. March 15, 2005).

16. See Julian Borger. "Bush Team Tries to Pin Blame on Local Officials," *The Guardian*, September 5, 2005, at http://www.guardian.co.uk/ print/0,3858,5277736-103681,00.html.

17. Sharon Rush, *Loving across the Color Line: A White Adoptive Mother Learns about Race* (Lanham, Md.: Rowman & Littlefield, 2000), 173–174.

CHAPTER ONE

1. Henry Fairlie, "The Art of Revival; Washington Diarist—Ex-Presidents," *New Republic*, 6 May 1985, 42.

2. Trina Williams, "The Homestead Act—Our Earliest National Asset Policy," paper presented at the Center for Social Development's symposium, *Inclusion in Asset Building*, St. Louis, Missouri, September 21–23, 2000; on earlier giveaways, see James W. Oberly, *Sixty Million Acres: American Veterans and the Public Lands before the Civil War* (Kent, Ohio: Kent State University Press, 1990), 162–163.

3. For example, Neil J. Smelser, William Julius Wilson, and Faith Mitchell, eds., *America Becoming: Racial Trends and Their Consequences*, vol. I (Washington, D.C.: National Academy Press, 2001), 12–19 and passim; William G. Bowen and Derek Bok, *The Shape of the River: Long-Term Consequences of Considering Race in College and University Admissions* (Princeton, N.J.: Princeton University Press, 1998); and Richard T. Schaefer, *Racial and Ethnic Groups*, 9th ed. (Upper Saddle River, N.J.: Prentice-Hall, 2004), 4–6 and passim.

4. See, for example, Richard Alba and Victor Nee, *Remaking the American Mainstream: Assimilation and Contemporary Immigration* (Cambridge, Mass.: Harvard University Press, 2003), 1–67, 287–291, and passim.

5. See, for example, Smelser et al., eds., *America Becoming*; and Schaefer, *Racial and Ethnic Groups*.
6. See the articles in Smelser, et al., eds., *America Becoming*, vol. I and II.
7. See ibid., vol. I, 9.
8. See, for example, William Julius Wilson, *When Work Disappears: The World of the New Urban Poor* (New York: Knopf, 1996), xx–xxi.
9. See the articles in Smelser et al., eds., *America Becoming*; David A. Hollinger, *Postethnic America* (New York: Basic Books, 1995), 167 and passim; and Bowen and Bok, *The Shape of the River*, 5–14 and passim.
10. Michael Omi and Howard Winant, *Racial Formation in the United States: From the 1960s to the 1990s*, 2nd ed. (New York: Routledge, 1994), vii.
11. Ibid., 55.
12. Ibid., 55–59.
13. Ibid., 70.
14. Ibid., 157. For a recent statement, see Howard Winant, *The New Politics of Race* (Minneapolis, Minn.: University of Minnesota Press, 2004).
15. I draw herein on some ideas from systems theory, but do not accept the general framework. See http://pespmc1.vub.ac.be/SYSTHEOR.html (accessed November 18, 2004).
16. Richard Van Alstyne, *The Rising American Empire* (New York: Norton, 1974), 1.
17. Ibid., 6–7.
18. Neal Salisbury, *Manitou and Providence: Indians, Europeans, and the Making of New England, 1500–1643* (New York: Oxford, 1982), 3–11; Omar Swartz, *The Rule of Law, Property, and the Violation of Human Rights: A Plea for Social Justice* (Marano di Napoli, Italy: Foxwell & Davies Italia srl., 2004), chapter 3.
19. Quoted in John Collier, *Indians of the Americas*, abridged ed. (New York: Mentor Books, 1947), 115.
20. See Marimba Ani, *Yurugu: An African-Centered Critique of European Cultural Thought and Behavior* (Trenton, N.J.: Africa World Press, 1994), 476–481 and passim.
21. Quoted in John Collier, *Indians of the Americas*, 115.
22. See Donald E. Lively, *The Constitution and Race* (New York: Praeger, 1992), 4–5.
23. Russell B. Nye, *Fettered Freedom: Civil Liberties and the Slavery Controversy 1830-1860* (East Lansing, MI: Michigan State College Press, 1949), 34.
24. J. Sakai, *Settlers: Mythology of the White Proletariat* (Chicago: Morningstar Press, 1989), 8–9.
25. For example, when people are asked to think about the category "bird," they rarely think of an ostrich but more likely of a sparrow or crow. George Lakoff, *Women, Fire, and Dangerous Things: What Categories Reveal about the Mind* (Chicago: University of Chicago Press, 1987), 8–86.

26. Frederick Douglass, "The United States Cannot Remain Half-Slave and Half-Free," in *Frederick Douglass: Selected Speeches and Writings*, ed. P. S. Foner and Y. Taylor (Chicago: Lawrence Hall Books, 1999), 657–658.

27. Charles Gallagher, "Miscounting Race: Explaining Whites' Misperceptions of Racial Group Size," *Sociological Perspectives* 46 (2003): 381–396.

28. Winthrop D. Jordan, *White over Black: American Attitudes toward the Negro*, 1550–1812 (Chapel Hill: University of North Carolina Press, 1968), 95.

29. W. E. B. Du Bois, *Darkwater* (New York: Humanity Books, 2003), 56.

30. Olaudah Equiano, "The Interesting Narrative of the Life of Olaudah Equiano," in *Afro-American History*, ed. Thomas R. Frazier (New York: Harcourt, Brace, & World, 1970), 18, 20.

31. I am indebted to Melvin Sikes and Hernán Vera for comments here. See also, Iris Young, *Justice and the Politics of Difference* (Princeton: Princeton University Press, 1990), 49.

32. Quoted in James L. Huston, *Calculating the Value of the Union: Slavery, Property Rights, and the Economic Origins of the Civil War* (Chapel Hill: University of North Carolina Press, 2003), 1–2. I also draw here on Lerone Bennett, Jr., *Forced into Glory* (Chicago: Johnson Publishing, 2000), 215–224.

33. Huston, *Calculating the Value of the Union*, 29. The data are on pp. 27–28.

34. The current value of the labor cost depends on the estimated rate of interest over intervening years. All figures are in 1983 dollars, and the studies are cited in David H. Swinton, "Racial Inequality and Reparations," in *The Wealth of Races: The Present Value of Benefits from Past Injustices*, ed. R. F. America (New York: Greenwood Press, 1990), 153–162.

35. See J. A. Rogers, *Africa's Gift to America* (St. Petersburg, Fla.: H. M. Rogers, 1961), 69.

36. Patricia Williams, "Alchemical Notes: Reconstructing Ideals from Deconstructed Rights," *Harvard Civil Rights and Civil Liberties Review* 22 (1987): 415.

37. The report is summarized in Carole Collins, "U.N. Report on Minorities: U.S. Not Measuring Up," *National Catholic Reporter*, 18 June 1993, 9.

38. Robert Blauner, *Racial Oppression in America* (New York: Harper and Row, 1972); and Eduardo Bonilla-Silva, "Rethinking Racism: Toward a Structural Interpretation," *American Sociological Review* 62 (June 1997): 465–480.

39. Theodore Allen, *The Invention of the White Race: The Origin of Racial Oppression in Anglo-America*, vol. II (London: Verso, 1997), 252–253.

40. Ibid., 258.

41. Ben Simpson, "Ben Simpson: Georgia and Texas," in *Lay My Burden Down*, ed. B. A. Botkin (Chicago: University of Chicago Press, 1945), 75.

42. Quoted in Hortense J. Spillers, "Mama's Baby, Papa's Maybe: An American Grammar Book," *Diacritics* 17 (Summer, 1987): 68.

43. Kevin Johnson, "ACLU Campaign Yields Race Bias Suit," *USA Today*, 19 May 1999, 4A; "ACLU Report Blasts Racial Profiling," *Boston Globe*, 3 June 1999, A15.

44. "Hate Crimes," CBS News, http://www.cbsnews.com/stories/2004/11/22/national/main657048.shtml (accessed November 28, 2004).

45. Blauner, *Racial Oppression in America*, 41.

46. A. Leon Higginbotham, *In the Matter of Color* (New York: Oxford University Press, 1978); A. Leon Higginbotham, Jr., *Shades of Freedom: Racial Politics and the Presumptions of the American Legal Process* (New York: Oxford University Press, 1996); Roy Brooks, *Rethinking the American Race Problem* (Berkeley: University of California, 1990); and Roy Brooks, *Integration or Separation? A Strategy for Racial Equality* (Cambridge: Harvard University Press, 1996).

47. Antonio Gramsci, *Selections from the Prison Notebooks.*, ed. and trans. Q. Hoare and G. N. Smith (New York: International Publishers, 1971), 324.

48. I blend in this definition the ideas of Lakoff, David Snow, and Rob Benford. See George Lakoff, *Don't Think of an Elephant: Know Your Values and Frame the Debate* (White River Junction, Vt.: Chelsea Green Publishing, 2004), 16–25.

49. Charles R. Lawrence, "The Id, the Ego, and Equal Protection," *Stanford Law Review* 39 (January, 1987): 323–324.

50. Shankar Vedantam, "Many Americans Believe They Are Not Prejudiced. Now a New Test Provides Powerful Evidence that a Majority of Us Really Are," *Washington Post*, 23 January 2005, W12; and Associated Press, "Racism Studies Find Rational Part of Brain Can Override Prejudice," http://www.beliefnet.com/story/156/story_15664_1.html (accessed November 28, 2004).

51. Joe R. Feagin, *Racist America: Roots, Current Realities and Future Reparations* (New York: Routledge, 2000), 113–116.

52. I draw here on Hernán Vera and Joe R. Feagin, "Human Empathy," University of Florida research paper, 2005. What needs most to be explained is not the reality of human empathy and solidarity—the problem often stated by Western philosophers—but rather how this empathy for others gets destroyed and how human beings develop anti-empathetic inclinations essential to racial oppression. Vera was the first to suggest this alexithymic terminology.

53. For many white adults and children, one might even go farther in characterizing much of their perspective on racial matters as close to a "social psychosis." Traditionally, individual "psychosis" is defined something like this: "A severe mental disorder in which contact with reality is lost or highly distorted." While most whites who accept the often wildly stereotyped notions and images of black personality and values that I will document in later chapters are likely able to function well in their social lives, at least with other whites, they evidently have lost contact with actual racial realities, at least to some degree. They cannot "see" the everyday realities of the African Americans who may be near or around them.

Since so many whites share this racist perspective, we might label it a type of "social psychosis."

54. I draw here on George Lakoff and Mark Johnson, *Philosophy in the Flesh: The Embodied Mind and Its Challenge to Western Thought* (New York: Basic Books, 1999), 292–310. I am indebted to Hernán Vera and Nijole Benokraitis for helping me think through the patriarchal family model. Today, a more nurturant family model exists in tension with this strict-father patriarchal model. This nurturant-parent model accents a hopeful societal world, treating others in the family fairly and in an egalitarian manner, caring for others with empathetic understanding, making sure others have full opportunities, and emphasizing cooperation, trust, and open communication. This summary of the nurturant model of George Lakoff is from http://www.rockridgeinstitute.org/projects/strategic/nationasfamily/npworldview (accessed November 1, 2004).

55. In a famous revolutionary pamphlet, *Common Sense*, Tom Paine noted that "Britain is the parent country," but had failed as the parent because its governing abuse led people to flee Britain and to reject British government control in the colonies. Many American revolutionaries shared his view. See "A Rhetoric of Rights: The Arguments Used in the 'American Conversation' in the Era of the Revolution," E. Pluribus Unum Project, Assumption College, at http://assumption.edu/ahc/1770s/coreargs.html (11/1/2004).

56. Anthony S. Parent, Jr., *Foul Means: The Formation of a Slave Society in Virginia, 1660–1740* (Chapel Hill: University of North Carolina Press, 2003), 200.

57. Lakoff and Johnson, *Philosophy in the Flesh*, 292–310.

58. Theodor Adorno, Else Frenkel-Brunswick, Daniel Levinson, and R. Nevitt Sanford, *The Authoritarian Personality* (New York: Harper, 1950), 385–387.

59. Herbert Aptheker, *American Negro Slave Revolts* (New York: International, 1943), 12–18, 162.

60. Vincent Harding, "Wrestling toward the Dawn," *Journal of American History* 74 (1987): 719. I draw here on Gary B. Nash, *Race and Revolution* (Madison, Wisc.: Madison House, 1990), 77.

61. Peter Linebaugh and Marcus Rediker, *The Many-Headed Hydra: Sailors, Slaves, Commoners, and the Hidden History of the Revolutionary Atlantic* (Boston: Beacon Press, 2000), 228.

62. Nash, *Race and Revolution*, 78–79.

63. See, for example, the comments of African Americans in chapter 4.

64. Derrick Bell, *Silent Covenants: Brown v. Board of Education and the Unfulfilled Hopes for Racial Reform* (New York: Oxford University Press, 2004).

65. In recent generations especially, home ownership has been the major source of wealth for middle-income white Americans.

66. "Net worth" means assets minus debts. "The Racial Wealth Gap Has Become a Huge Chasm that Severely Limits Black Access to Higher Education," *The Journal of Blacks in Higher Education*, at

http://www.jbhe.com/news_views/45_racial_wealth_gap.html (accessed March 15, 2005).

67. Thomas M. Shapiro, *The Hidden Cost of Being African American: How Wealth Perpetuates Inequality* (New York: Oxford University Press, 2004), 31.

68. Ibid., 63–65.

69. Maurice Halbwachs, *On Collective Memory*, ed. and trans. Lewis Coser (Chicago: University of Chicago Press, 1992), 38, 52.

70. Karl Mannheim, *Ideology and Utopia* (London: Routledge and Kegan Paul, 1936), 3.

71. See "Collective Memory," *The Brain from Top to Bottom*, McGill University, at http://www.thebrain.mcgill.ca/flash/a/a_07/a_07_s/a_07_s_tra/a_07_s_tra.htm (accessed July 12, 2004).

72. Tzvetan Todorov, "The Evil that Men Do," *The UNESCO Courier*, at http://www.unesco.org/courier/1999_12/uk/dossier/txt01.htm (accessed July 12, 2004).

73. Feagin, *Racist America*, 105–135.

74. For an earlier and broader version of this argument, see Joe R. Feagin and Eileen O'Brien, *White Men on Race: Power, Privilege and the Shaping of Cultural Consciousness* (Boston: Beacon, 2003), chap. 1.

75. Hernán Vera and Andrew Gordon, *Screen Saviors: Hollywood Fictions of Whiteness* (Lanham, Md.: Rowman & Littlefield, 2003), 192.

76. Ashraf H. A. Rushdy, *Race and Family in Contemporary African American Fiction* (Chapel Hill: University of North Carolina Press, 2001), as quoted at http://uncpress.unc.edu/chapters/rushdy_remembering.html (ret. August 27, 2004).

77. *City of Richmond v. J.A. Croson Co.*, 488 U.S. 469 (1989).

CHAPTER TWO

1. Like all autobiographical accounts, the authors may sometimes combine various experiences into a single composite account, and sometimes they may put their own actions in a more favorable light than was the case. In any event, many other sources of data on slavery corroborate these enslavement accounts.

2. Frederick Douglass, *Narrative of the Life of Frederick Douglass, an American Slave Written by Himself Entered, According to Act of Congress, in the Year 1845* (Clerk's Office of the District Court of Massachusetts, 1845), http://www.pinkmonkey.com/dl/library1/digi009.pdf (ret. March 10, 2002), 60–61.

3. Ibid.

4. Merriam Webster, http://www.m-w.com/cgi-bin/dictionary?book=Dictionary&va=torture (ret. June 21, 2004).

5. Frederick Douglass, *My Bondage and My Freedom* (New York: Humanity Books, 2002 [1855]), 135.

6. Ibid., 71.

7. Robin Blackburn, *The Making of New World Slavery: From the Baroque to the Modern, 1492–1800* (London: Verso, 1997), 584.
8. Douglass, *My Bondage and My Freedom*, 85–86.
9. I am inspired here by the analysis of Hortense Spillers, "Mama's Baby, Papa's Maybe: An American Grammar Book," *Diacritics* 17 (1987): 68–78.
10. Douglass, *My Bondage and My Freedom*, 185.
11. Frederick Douglass, *Narrative of the Life of Frederick Douglass, an American Slave Written by Himself* (New York: Library of America, 1994 [1845]), 65.
12. Douglass, *My Bondage and My Freedom*, 282.
13. Ibid., 320.
14. Ibid., 374.
15. Ibid., 135.
16. Ibid., 170.
17. Ibid., 178.
18. James W. C. Pennington, *The Fugitive Blacksmith; or, Events in the History of James W. C. Pennington*, 2nd ed. (London: Charles Gilpin, 1849), iv–vii, as reproduced at http://www.gutenberg.org/dirs/1/5/1/3/15130/15130-8.txt (accessed April 14, 2005).
19. Yuval Taylor, "Introduction," in *Frederick Douglass: Selected Speeches and Writings*, ed. P. S. Foner and Y. Taylor (Chicago: Lawrence Hill Books, 1999), xi.
20. William Wells Brown, *From Fugitive Slave to Free Man*, ed. William L. Andrews (New York: Mentor Books, 1993), 34.
21. Ibid., 30.
22. Ibid., 33.
23. Ibid., 36.
24. Ibid., 67–68.
25. Ibid., 46.
26. Ibid., 45.
27. Ibid., 59.
28. Ibid., 64–65.
29. Ibid.
30. Ibid., 72.
31. Ibid., 77.
32. Ibid., 67–68.
33. Ibid., 88.
34. Ibid., 85.
35. Ibid., 86–87.
36. Ibid., 80.
37. Elizabeth Fox-Genovese, *Within the Plantation Household: Black and White Women of the Old South* (Chapel Hill: University of North Carolina Press, 1988), 392.
38. Harriet A. Jacobs, *Incidents in the Life of a Slave Girl* (Mineola, N.Y.: Dover, 2001), 64.
39. Ibid., 56.
40. Ibid.

41. Gunnar Myrdal, *An American Dilemma*, vol. 1 (New York: McGraw-Hill, 1964 [1944]), 442–443.
42. Jacobs, *Incidents in the Life of a Slave Girl*, 26.
43. Ibid., 66.
44. Ibid., 32.
45. Ibid.
46. Ibid., 66.
47. Ibid., 35–36.
48. Ibid., 62.
49. Ibid., 164.
50. Ibid.
51. Ibid., 135.
52. Gary B. Nash, *Race and Revolution* (Madison, Wisc.: Madison House, 1990), 49.
53. W. E. B. Du Bois, *The Souls of Black Folk* (New York: Bantam Classic Books, 1989 [1903]), 186–187.
54. Walter Johnson, *Soul by Soul: Life Inside the Antebellum Slave Market* (Cambridge, Mass: Harvard University Press.: 1999), 19.
55. See Henry Wiencek, *An Imperfect God: George Washington, His Slaves, and the Creation of America* (New York: Farrar, Strauss, and Giroux, 2003), passim. One oral tradition says that the rape of a black servant was by John Washington's son, Bushrod.
56. I am indebted to Ruth Thompson-Miller for some suggestive comments here.
57. Quoted in *Bartlett's Familiar Quotations*, 15th ed., ed. Emily M. Beck (Boston: Little, Brown, 1980), 556.
58. "Collective Memory," *The Brain from Top to Bottom*, McGill University at http://www.thebrain.mcgill.ca/flash/a/a_07/a_07_s/a_07_s_tra/a_07_s_tra.htm (accessed July 12, 2004).
59. William A. Link, *Roots of Secession: Slavery and Politics in Antebellum Virginia* (Chapel Hill: University of North Carolina Press, 2003), 6.

CHAPTER THREE

1. Quoted in Anthony S. Parent, Jr., *Foul Means: The Formation of a Slave Society in Virginia, 1660–1740* (Chapel Hill: University of North Carolina Press, 2003), 201.
2. Wilbur J. Cash, *The Mind of the South* (New York: Random House, 1941), 51.
3. Andrew Burnstein, "The Inner Jefferson: Portrait of a Grieving Optimist," *Washington Post*, http://www.washingtonpost.com/wp-srv/style/long-term/books/chap1/innerje.htm.
4. These data are from the Monticello website. See http://www.monticello.org/jefferson/dayinlife/wishes/home.html#three (accessed May 9, 2004).
5. Family Guardian Ministry, "Thomas Jefferson on Politics & Government: 32. Racial Policy," http://famguardian.org/Subjects/Politics/ThomasJefferson/jeff1290.htm (ret. May 30, 2004).

6.   At least 187 black people had been held by him, including on his planta-tion, Monticello, which had been in operation twelve years at the time he published *Notes*.

7.   Paul Finkelman, *Slavery and the Founders: Race and Liberty in the Age of Jefferson* (Armonk, N.Y.: M.E. Sharpe, 1996), 127–134.

8.   Garry Wills, *"Negro President": Jefferson and the Slave Power* (Boston: Houghton Mifflin, 2003), 8–9.

9.   Frank Shuffelton quoted at "Jefferson Book is Reissued by Professor," *Currents*, http://www.rochester.edu/pr/Currents/V27/V27N06/story14.html (accessed May 10, 2004).

10. Thomas Jefferson, *Notes on the State of Virginia*, ed. Frank Shuffelton (New York: Penguin Books, 1999 [1785]), 145.

11. Ibid.

12. Ibid.

13. Ibid.

14. Ibid.

15. Benjamin Franklin, "Observations Concerning the Increase of Mankind, Peopling of Countries, Etc." (1751), as quoted in *Benjamin Franklin: A Biography in His Own Words*, ed. Thomas Fleming (New York: Harper and Row, 1972), 105–106. I have changed this excerpt to modern capitalization.

16. Jefferson, *Notes*, 145.

17. John C. Miller, *The Wolf by the Ears: Thomas Jefferson and Slavery* (Charlottesville: University Press of Virginia, 1991), 55.

18. Jefferson, *Notes*, 146.

19. Ibid.

20. Ibid.

21. Myrdal, *An American Dilemma*, 443.

22. Jefferson, *Notes*, 146.

23. Ibid.

24. Ibid.

25. Ibid., 147.

26. Ibid.

27. Ibid.

28. Although Washington had taken a view of Indians who opposed American revolutionaries as "beasts of prey" to be destroyed, he later en-visioned integration of some Indians into the white population. In a 1796 "Address to the Cherokee Nation," Washington laid out a "path I wish all the Indian nations to walk." Washington's path was that Indian Americans give up hunting, operate only as farmers, and assimilate to white culture. See Joseph J. Ellis, *Founding Brothers: The Revolutionary Generation* (New York: Vintage Books, 2000), 159.

29. Quoted in David Stannard, *American Holocaust* (New York: Oxford, 1992), 240.

30. Jefferson, *Notes*, 147.

31. Ibid.

32. Ibid., 147–148.

33. Ibid., 148.

34. Ibid., 149.
35. "Slaves and Freedmen," PBS Special on the Roman Empire, http://www.pbs.org/empires/romans/social/social5.html (accessed June 17, 2004).
36. Jefferson, *Notes*, 149.
37. Ibid., 150.
38. Ibid., 150–151.
39. Ibid., 151. Italics added.
40. Ibid.
41. Ibid., 168.
42. Quoted in Jordan, *White over Black*, 430–431.
43. Quoted in Miller, *The Wolf by the Ears*, 57.
44. Ibid.
45. Thomas Jefferson to Henri Gregoire, February 25, 1809, Library of Congress, http://www.loc.gov/exhibits/jefferson/images/vc80.jpg (ret. June 21, 2004).
46. Thomas Jefferson to Joel Barlow, October 8, 1809, as quoted in Finkelman, *Slavery and the Founders*, 163.
47. Letter to Edward Coles Monticello, August 25, 1814, "The Letters of Thomas Jefferson: 1743–1826; Emancipation and the Younger Generation," "From Revolution to Reconstruction," *Project of Department of Humanities Computing*, University of Gronigen, at http://odur.let.rug.nl/~usa/P/tj3/writings/brf/jefl232.htm (accessed May 10, 2004).
48. George Frederickson, *The Black Image in the White Mind* (Hanover: Wesleyan University Press, 1971), 54–57; Eugene G. Genovese, *Roll, Jordan, Roll* (New York: Random House, 1974), 4.
49. George Fitzhugh, *Sociology for the South; or, The Failure of Free Society* (Richmond: A. Morris, 1854), 82–108.
50. Letter to Edward Coles Monticello, August 25, 1814 "The Letters of Thomas Jefferson."
51. Ibid.
52. A. Leon Higginbotham, Jr., and Barbara K. Kopytoff, "Racial Purity and Interracial Sex in the Law of Colonial and Antebellum Virginia," *Georgetown Law Journal* 77 (August, 1989): 1671.
53. Letter to Edward Coles, Monticello, August 25, 1814, "The Letters of Thomas Jefferson."
54. Ibid.
55. Jordan, *White over Black*, 546–547.
56. Ibid., 546, 558–565.
57. Miller, *The Wolf by the Ears*, 241.
58. "Autobiography," in *The Writings of Thomas Jefferson*, ed. Andrew A. Lipscomb, vol. 1 (Washington, D.C.: Thomas Jefferson Memorial Association, 1903), 72.
59. Jordan, *White over Black*, 429.
60. Ibid., 494.
61. Ellis, *Founding Brothers*, 99–101.
62. Paul Finkelman, quoted on PBS.Org, at http://www.pbs.org/jefferson/archives/interviews/Finkelman.htm (accessed May 10, 2004).

63. Miller, *The Wolf by the Ears*, 58.

64. Quoted in Michael P. Rogin, *Fathers and Children: Andrew Jackson and the Subjugation of the American Indian* (New York: Knopf, 1975), 319.

65. Max Farrand, ed., *Records of the Federal Convention of 1787*, vol. 1 (New Haven: Yale, 1911), 486.

66. Donald E. Lively, *The Constitution and Race* (New York: Praeger, 1992), 4–5. Lively draws on the work of William Wiecek.

67. Herbert Aptheker, *Early Years of the Republic: From the End of the Revolution to the First Administration of Washington (1783–1793)* (New York: International Publishers, 1976), 93.

68. James Madison, *Federalist Papers*, no. 54, from the *New York Packet*, February 12, 1788, at http://www.foundingfathers.info/federalistpapers/fed54.htm (ret. June 21, 2004).

69. Quoted in Ellis, *Founding Brothers*, 118.

70. Letter from James Madison to Dr. Morse, March 28, 1823, James Madison University, James Madison Center, at http://www.jmu.edu/madison/center/main_pages/madison_archives/era/african/elite/q-a-slavery.htm (accessed May 25, 2004).

71. Ronald Takaki, *Iron Cages: Race and Culture in 19th Century America* (New York: Oxford University Press, 1990), 12–14.

72. Ibid., 12.

73. Ibid., 15.

74. Letter from James Madison to Dr. Morse, March 28, 1823.

75. Ibid.

76. Ibid.

77. Letter from James Madison to Robert J. Evans, June 15, 1819, "The Founders' Constitution," Volume 1, Chapter 15, Document 65, at http://press-pubs.uchicago.edu/founders/documents/v1ch15s65.html (accessed May 24, 2004).

78. Ibid.

79. Ibid.

80. Ibid.

81. Letter from James Madison, Jr., to James Madison, Sr., September 8, 1783, Montpelier National Trust Historic Site, at http://www.montpelier.org/hi-enslaved.htm (ret. May 25, 2004).

82. F. Nwabueze Okoye, "Chattel Slavery as the Nightmare of the American Revolutionaries," *William and Mary Quarterly* 37 (January 1980): 13.

83. Quoted in "A Rhetoric of Rights: The Arguments Used in the 'American Conversation' in the Era of the Revolution," E. Pluribus Unum Project, Assumption College, at http://assumption.edu/ahc/1770s/coreargs.html (accessed November 1, 2004).

84. Okoye, "Chattel Slavery as the Nightmare of the American Revolutionaries," 13. From New England to the southern colonies, readers of newspapers were bombarded with advertisements offering to sell enslaved African Americans and to recover runaways.

85. Fritz Hirschfeld, *George Washington and Slavery: A Documentary Portrayal* (Columbia: University of Missouri Press, 1997), 49. See also pp. 16, 37.

86. Ibid., 236.

87. Quoted in Peter R. Henriques, "The Only Unavoidable Subject of Regret: George Washington and Slavery," at http://chnm.gmu.edu/courses/henriques/hist615/gwslav.htm (ret. May 20, 2004).

88. Quoted in Hirschfeld, *George Washington and Slavery*, 65.

89. Ibid, 34.

90. Ibid.

91. Quoted in Peter R. Henriques, "The Only Unavoidable Subject of Regret: George Washington and Slavery."

92. Hirschfeld, *George Washington and Slavery*, 34.

93. Wiencek, *An Imperfect God*, 84–85, 284–285.

94. Ibid., 301–305 and passim.

95. Ibid., 179–180.

96. Hirschfeld, *George Washington and Slavery*, 58.

97. Ibid., 68–69.

98. Ibid., 114–115.

99. Wills, "Negro President," 210.

100. Ibid., 206–212.

101. Quoted in ibid., 127.

102. Quoted in Wiencek, *An Imperfect God*, 352.

103. Jordan, *White over Black*, 465.

104. Miller, *The Wolf by the Ears*, 176.

105. Walter Johnson, *Soul by Soul: Life Inside the Antebellum Slave Market* (Cambridge, Mass.: Harvard University Press, 2000), 113.

106. Jordan, *White over Black*, 431.

107. Ibid., 481.

108. Wiencek, *An Imperfect God*, 356.

109. Ibid., 112.

110. Ibid., 7.

111. Quoted in Jordan, *White over Black*, 273. Modern capitalization.

112. Ibid., 273–274.

113. Ibid., 275.

114. Ibid., 276.

115. "1000 Commemorate One Va. Man's Freeing of Slaves 72 Years Early," *Marietta Times*, 29 July 1991, A1.

116. Wiencek, *An Imperfect God*, 356–357.

117. See the discussion in C. Vann Woodward, ed., *Mary Chesnut's Civil War* (New York: Book-of-the-Month-Club, 1994), xlix.

118. See Elizabeth Fox-Genovese, *Within the Plantation Household: Black and White Women of the Old South* (Chapel Hill: University of North Carolina Press, 1988), 334–360.

119. Keziah G. H. Brevard, *A Plantation Mistress on the Eve of the Civil War: The Diary of Keziah Goodwyn Hopkins Brevard, 1860–1861*, ed. John H. Moore (Columbia: University of South Carolina Press, 1993), 42.

120. Ibid., 95.
121. Ibid., 110.
122. Ibid., 39, 42, 83, 110.
123. Ibid., 87–89.
124. Ibid., 95.
125. Ibid., 82, 110.
126. Vann Woodward, *Mary Chesnut's Civil War*, 642.
127. Ibid., 245.
128. Ibid, 794.
129. Ibid., li.
130. Ibid., 243.
131. See J. A. Rogers, *Africa's Gift to America* (St. Petersburg, Fla.: H. M. Rogers, 1961), 44.
132. Ibid., 123.
133. Vann Woodward, *Mary Chesnut's Civil War*, 208.
134. Joanne Pope Melish, *Disowning Slavery: Gradual Emancipation and "Race" in New England* (Ithaca, N.Y.: Cornell University Press, 1998), 165–167.
135. Ibid., 185–190.
136. Quoted in Kenneth O'Reilly, *Nixon's Piano: Presidents and Racial Politics from Washington to Clinton* (New York: Free Press, 1995), 45.
137. *Jones v. Mayer Co.*, 392 U.S. 409 (1968).

CHAPTER FOUR

1.   Stetson Kennedy, *After Appomattox: How the South Won the War* (Gainesville: University Press of Florida, 1995), 3–20.
2.   W. E. B. Du Bois, *Black Reconstruction in America 1860–1880* (New York: Atheneum, 1992 [1935]), 707.
3.   Melton A. McLaurin, *Separate Pasts: Growing Up White in the Segregated South* (Athens: University of Georgia Press, 1987), 3.
4.   Stetson Kennedy, *Jim Crow Guide: The Way It Was* (Boca Raton: Florida Atlantic University Press, 1990 [1959]), 118.
5.   Ibid., 35–36.
6.   Ana S. Liberato, "Segregation Study" (research study, University of Florida, 2005). Used by permission.
7.   Kennedy, *Jim Crow Guide*, 87.
8.   Ibid., 58, 76–77.
9.   Ibid., 47.
10. Quoted in ibid., 135.
11. P. S. Foner and Y. Taylor, eds, *Frederick Douglass: Selected Speeches and Writings* (Chicago: Lawrence Hill Books, 1999), 715.
12. Du Bois, *Souls of Black Folk*, 119.
13. Minnesota Public Radio and NPR News, American RadioWorks special report, "Remembering Jim Crow," February 27, 2002, transcript in appendix (CD-Rom) to William H. Chafe, Raymond Gavins, and Robert Korstad, *Remembering Jim Crow* (New York: The New Press, 2001).

14. John L. Gwaltney, *Drylongso: A Self-Portrait of Black America* (New York: Vintage Books, 1981), 143–144.
15. Ruth Thompson-Miller, "The Reality and Legacy of Fear: The Consequences of White Oppression under Segregation" research paper, University of Florida, 2004.
16. Gwaltney, *Drylongso*, 236.
17. Audrey O. Faulkner, Marsel A. Heisel, Wendell Holbrook, and Shirley Geismar, *When I Was Comin' Up: An Oral History of Aged Blacks* (Hamden, Conn.: Archon Books, 1982), 158.
18. James Baldwin, *The Fire Next Time* (New York: Dell, 1962–1963), 18.
19. W. E. B. Du Bois, *The Philadelphia Negro: A Social Study* (Millwood, N.Y.: Kraus-Thomson, 1973 [1899]), 394.
20. Quoted in Jacqueline Jones, *Labor of Love, Labor of Sorrow: Black Women, Work, and the Family, from Slavery to the Present* (New York: Random House/Vintage Books, 1985), 23.
21. Theodore Hershberg et al., "A Tale of Three Cities: Blacks, Immigrants, and Opportunity in Philadelphia: 1850–1880, 1930, 1970," in *Philadelphia*, ed. Theodore Hershberg (New York: Oxford University Press, 1981), 462–464.
22. Faulkner et al., *When I Was Comin' Up*, 107.
23. Thompson-Miller, "The Reality and Legacy of Fear."
24. Kennedy, *Jim Crow Guide*, 209.
25. Gwaltney, *Drylongso*, 41.
26. When I did a systematic search on the web using the Google search engine, which looked at millions of websites, for the phrase "white sexual predators," I found only one reference to that concept.
27. Joe R. Feagin and Clairece B. Feagin, *Racial and Ethnic Relations*, 4th ed. (Englewood Cliffs, N.J.: Prentice-Hall, 1993), 224–225; Trudier Harris, *Exorcising Blackness* (Bloomington: Indiana University Press, 1984).
28. Thompson-Miller, "The Reality and Legacy of Fear."
29. Kenneth B. Nunn, "Rosewood," in *When Sorry Isn't Enough: The Controversy over Apologies and Reparations for Human Injustice*, ed. R. L. Brooks (New York: New York University Press, 1999), 435–437.
30. Faulkner et al., *When I Was Comin' Up*, 22.
31. Kristen M. Lavelle, "Facing Off in a Southern Town: Black and White Perspectives on Race and Racism" (master's thesis, University of Florida, 2004). I am indebted to Lavelle for permission to quote from her interviews.
32. Gwaltney, *Drylongso*, 6.
33. See Joe R. Feagin and Harlan Hahn, *Ghetto Revolts* (New York: Macmillan, 1973).
34. Thomas J. Sugrue, *The Origins of the Urban Crisis: Race and Inequality in Postwar Detroit* (Princeton: Princeton University Press, 1996).
35. Ibid., 13.
36. Coretta Scott King, ed., *The Words of Martin Luther King, Jr.* (New York: Newmarket Press, 1983), 31.
37. Thompson-Miller, "The Reality and Legacy of Fear."
38. Ibid.

39. W. E. B. Du Bois, *Dusk of Dawn: An Essay toward an Autobiography of a Race Concept* (New Brunswick, N.J.: Transaction Books, 1984 [1940]), 131.
40. Gwaltney, *Drylongso*, 53.
41. Minnesota Public Radio and NPR news, American RadioWorks special report, "Remembering Jim Crow," February 27, 2002, appendix (CD-Rom) to Chafe, Gavins, and Korstad, *Remembering Jim Crow*.
42. Thompson-Miller, "The Reality and Legacy of Fear."
43. Liberato, "Segregation Study."
44. Ibid.
45. King, *The Words of Martin Luther King, Jr.*, 29.
46. Minnesota Public Radio and NPR news, "Remembering Jim Crow."
47. Thompson-Miller, "The Reality and Legacy of Fear."
48. Baldwin, *The Fire Next Time*, 19.
49. King, *The Words of Martin Luther King, Jr.*, 29–30.
50. Du Bois, *Souls of Black Folk*, 3.
51. Baldwin, *The Fire Next Time*, 134.
52. Gwaltney, *Drylongso*, 101.
53. David L. Chappell, *A Stone of Hope: Prophetic Religion and the Death of Jim Crow* (Chapel Hill: University of North Carolina Press, 2004), 102.
54. W. E. B. Du Bois, *Darkwater* (Amherst, New York: Humanity Books, 2003), 72–73.
55. Martin Luther King, Jr., "Letter from a Birmingham Jail," April 16, 1963, Historical Text Archive, at http://historicaltextarchive.com/sections.php?op=viewarticle&artid=40 (accessed February 10, 2005). I have slightly edited the quote.

CHAPTER FIVE

1. See Garrett Epps, "The Antebellum Political Background of the Fourteenth Amendment," *Law & Contemporary Problems* 175 (Summer 2004): 185.
2. Ibid.
3. Congressional Record, 84th Cong., 2d sess., 1956, 102, pt. 4: 4459–4460.
4. James J. Kilpatrick, *The Southern Case for School Segregation* (New York: Crowell-Collier, 1962), 20–21.
5. Ibid.
6. Lester G. Maddox, *Speaking Out: The Autobiography of Lester Garfield Maddox* (Garden City, N.Y.: Doubleday, 1975), 54. His italics.
7. Quoted in Dan T. Carter, *The Politics of Rage: George Wallace, the Origins of the New Conservatism, and the Transformation of American Politics*, 2nd ed. (Baton Rouge: Louisiana State University Press, 2000), 11.
8. Ibid., 238.
9. Ibid., 237, 417.
10. Albion W. Tourgee, *An Appeal to Caesar* (New York: Fords, Howard & Hulbert, 1884), 127. Italics added.
11. Quoted in O'Reilly, *Nixon's Piano*, 65.
12. Quoted in ibid.

13. Ibid., 84.
14. Ibid., 149.
15. Ibid., 165–166.
16. Quoted in Theodore Cross, *Black Power Imperative: Racial Inequality and the Politics of Nonviolence* (New York: Faulkner, 1984), 157–158.
17. Quoted in Robert Caro, *The Years of Lyndon Johnson: Master of the Senate* (New York: Random House/Vintage Books, 2002), 778.
18. Melton A. McLaurin, *Separate Pasts: Growing Up White in the Segregated South* (Athens: University of Georgia Press, 1987), 98.
19. Stetson Kennedy, *Jim Crow Guide*, 182.
20. Ibid., 216–217. I have deleted the numbering of items.
21. Ibid., 185, 217.
22. Allison Davis, Burleigh Gardner, and Mary Gardner, *Deep South: An Anthropological Study of Caste and Class* (Chicago: University of Chicago Press, 1941), 45.
23. Ibid., 48.
24. Trudier Harris, *Exorcising Blackness: Historical and Literary Lynching and Burning Rituals* (Bloomington: Indiana University Press, 1984), 7.
25. Nedra Tyre, "You All are a Bunch of Nigger Lovers," in *Red Wine First* (New York: Simon and Schuster, 1947), 120–122, as quoted in Harris, *Exorcising Blackness*, 10.
26. Alachua County Historic Trust: Matheson Museum, Inc., Oral History Collection. Interview with Katherine Kincaid Feiber (Gainesville: University of Florida Library, 1994).
27. Ralph Ginzburg, *100 Years of Lynchings* (Baltimore, Md.: Black Classic Press, 1962), 106.
28. Congressional Record, 84th Cong., 2d sess., 1956, 102, pt. 4: 4459–4460.
29. McLaurin, *Separate Pasts*, 134.
30. Lavelle, "Facing Off in a Southern Town."
31. Quoted in Ray Stannard Baker, *Following the Color Line* (New York: Harper Torchbooks, 1964 [1908]), 104.
32. Lavelle, "Facing Off in a Southern Town."
33. Ibid.
34. Minnesota Public Radio and NPR news, "Remembering Jim Crow."
35. Joe R. Feagin, Hernán Vera, and Pinar Batur, *White Racism: The Basics*, rev. ed. (New York: Routledge, 2001), 214.
36. "Eyewitness to Jim Crow," History of Jim Crow Educator's Website, http://www.jimcrowhistory.org/resources/narratives/Edith_Farris.htm (ret. June 6, 2004).
37. "Eyewitness to Jim Crow," History of Jim Crow Educator's Website, http://www.jimcrowhistory.org/resources/narratives/Susan_Huetteman.htm (ret. June 6, 2004).
38. Lavelle, "Facing Off in a Southern Town."
39. Ibid.
40. Ibid.
41. Ibid.
42. Lillian Smith, *Killers of the Dream* (New York: W.W. Norton, 1949), 29.

43. Ibid., 35–37.
44. Ibid., 37.
45. Ibid., 39.
46. Baker, *Following the Color Line*, 218.
47. Quoted in Takaki, *Iron Cages*, 50.
48. Smith, *Killers of the Dream*, 78.
49. Stetson Kennedy, *Jim Crow Guide*, 31.
50. Carter, *The Politics of Rage*, 238.
51. McLaurin, *Separate Pasts*, 67.
52. Martha Hodes, *White Women, Black Men: Illicit Sex in the Nineteenth-Century South* (New Haven, Conn.: Yale University Press, 1997), 1–2.
53. McLaurin, *Separate Pasts*, 70.
54. Kennedy, *Jim Crow Guide*, 237.
55. See Joel Kovel, *White Racism: A Psychohistory* (New York: Columbia University Press, 1984).
56. Takaki, *Iron Cages*, 12–14.
57. Carter, *The Politics of Rage*, 237.
58. McLaurin, *Separate Pasts*, 30.
59. Carter, *The Politics of Rage*, 237.
60. Quoted in Smith, *Killers of the Dream*, 78.
61. Davis et al., *Deep South*, 17.
62. Kilpatrick, *The Southern Case for School Segregation*, 26.
63. Ibid., 43.
64. Ibid., 96–97.
65. Ibid., 192.
66. See Davis et al., *Deep South*, 18ff.
67. George Frederickson, *The Black Image in the White Mind* (Hanover: Wesleyan University Press, 1971), 209, 287–289.
68. Davis et al., *Deep South*, 19.
69. Ibid.
70. Minnesota Public Radio and NPR News, "Remembering Jim Crow."
71. Wilbur J. Cash, *The Mind of the South* (New York: Random House, 1941), 51.
72. Gunnar Myrdal, *An American Dilemma*, vol. 2 (New York: McGraw-Hill, 1964 [1944]), 959.
73. McLaurin, *Separate Pasts*, 37.
74. Baker, *Following the Color Line*, 44.
75. Ibid., 61.
76. Ibid., 215.
77. Carter, *The Politics of Rage*, 237.
78. William Brink and Louis Harris, *The Negro Revolution in America* (New York: Simon and Schuster, 1964), 140–143.
79. Kovel, *White Racism*, 184.
80. Du Bois, *Black Reconstruction*, 707.
81. Ibid., 30.

CHAPTER SIX

1. W. E. B. Du Bois, "What is the Meaning of 'All Deliberate Speed,?'" in *W. E. B. Du Bois: A Reader*, ed. David L. Lewis (New York: Henry Holt, 1995), 422.

2. W. E. B. Du Bois, *The Autobiography of W. E. B. Du Bois* (New York: International Publishers, 1968), 333.

3. Quoted in Philip A. Klinkner and Rogers M. Smith, *The Unsteady March: The Rise and Decline of Racial Equality in America* (Chicago: University of Chicago Press, 1999), 235.

4. Ibid., 3–4.

5. This brief quote is drawn from an interview study of 209 middle-class African Americans across the United States that was conducted by Joe Feagin. I will cite this as Joe R. Feagin, "Black Middle Class Research Study," University of Florida, 1994. For added discussion of some of the quoted interviews and more quotes from these interviews, see Joe R. Feagin and Melvin Sikes, *Living with Racism: The Black Middle Class Experience* (Boston: Beacon, 1994).

6. James Baldwin, *Notes of a Native Son* (Boston: Beacon Press, 1955), 119.

7. Dedrick Muhammad, Attieno Davis, Meizhu Lui, and Betsy Leondar-Wright, *The State of the Dream, 2004: Enduring Disparities in Black and White* (Boston: United for a Fair Economy, 2004), 6–11; and Joe R. Feagin and Clairece B. Feagin, *Social Problems: A Power-Conflict Perspective*, 5th ed. (Upper Saddle River, N.J.: Prentice-Hall, 1997), 119–121.

8. "The National Urban League Equality Index," in *The State of Black America*—2004, ed. Lee A. Daniels (New York: The Urban League, 2004), 15–31.

9. New Jersey Citizen Action, "New Report Highlights Impact of Hidden Practice of Auto Finance Markup on New Jersey Consumers," Press Release, February 23, 2005, at www.njcitizenaction.org/craautofinancpress.html.

10. David R. Williams, "Health and Quality of Life among African Americans," in *The State of Black America*—2004, 115–119.

11. Martin Luther King, Jr., *Where Do We Go from Here?: Chaos or Community* (New York: Bantam Books, 1967), 7.

12. Ibid., 9.

13. Cited in Tim Wise, "Commentary," http://academic.udayton.edu/race/01race/white10.htm (accessed November 24, 2004).

14. Ibid.

15. Feagin, "Black Middle Class Research Study."

16. Ibid. See also Feagin and Sikes, *Living with Racism*, 191–192.

17. Ibid.

18. Ibid.

19. See the summaries in David Wessel, "Racial Discrimination: Still at Work in the U.S." *The Wall Street Journal Online*, at www.careerjournal.com/myc/diversity/20030916-wessel.html (ret. May 26, 2005).

20. "Suit against Microsoft for Its Plantation Mentality," Invisible America, January 5, 2001, http://www.invisibleamerica.com/microseg.html.

21. Yanick St. Jean and Joe R. Feagin, *Double Burden: Black Women and Everyday Racism* (New York: M. E. Sharpe, 1998), 61.

22. Ibid., 56.
23. Kenneth Bolton, Jr., and Joe R. Feagin, *Black in Blue: African American Police Officers and Racism* (New York: Routledge, 2004), 106.
24. I am indebted here to a suggestion of Ruth Thompson-Miller.
25. St. Jean and Feagin, *Double Burden*, 129.
26. Feagin, "Black Middle Class Research Study." For more discussion, see Feagin and Sikes, *Living with Racism*, 145.
27. Bolton and Feagin, *Black in Blue*, 142.
28. Feagin, "Black Middle Class Research Study."
29. Ibid. For more discussion of the longer interview, see Feagin and Sikes, *Living with Racism*, 175.
30. Joe R. Feagin and Karyn D. McKinney, *The Many Costs of Racism* (Lanham, Md.: Rowman & Littlefield, 2003), 46–47.
31. Bolton and Feagin, *Black in Blue*, 174.
32. Ibid., 117.
33. Feagin, "Black Middle Class Research Study." See also Feagin and Sikes, *Living with Racism*, 235–236.
34. See Feagin, *Racist America*, 155–156.
35. Jerome Rabinow, *Students Speak about Racism* (Dubuque, Iowa: Kendall/Hunt Publishing Company, 2002), 109.
36. Feagin and McKinney, *The Many Costs of Racism*, 149.
37. See David Crockett, Sonya A. Grier, and Jacqueline A. Williams, "Coping with Marketplace Discrimination: An Exploration of the Experiences of Black Men," *Academy of Marketing Science Review* 2003 (2003): 1–18.
38. Joe R. Feagin, Hernán Vera, and Nikitah Imani, *The Agony of Education: Black Students in White Colleges and Universities* (New York: Routledge, 1996), 56.
39. Feagin, "Black Middle Class Research Study."
40. See, for example, Rush, *Loving across the Color Line*.
41. Debra Van Ausdale and Joe R. Feagin, *The First R: How Children Learn Race and Racism* (Lanham, Md.: Rowman & Littlefield, 2000), 60–61.
42. See ibid., passim.
43. Leslie Houts and Joe R. Feagin, *Two-Faced Racism*, Routledge, forthcoming.
44. See Benjamin Franklin, "Observations Concerning the Increase of Mankind, Peopling of Countries, Etc." (1751), as quoted in *Benjamin Franklin: A Biography in His Own Words*, ed. Thomas Fleming (New York: Harper and Row, 1972), 105–106.
45. St. Jean and Feagin, *Double Burden*, 83–84.
46. The study by David Figlio is summarized in "University Of Florida Economist Finds that Black Children's Names Hinder Their Educational Development," *The Journal of Blacks in Higher Education* Weekly Bulletin, at file:///C:/Documents%20and%20Settings/User/Local%20Settings/Temporary%20Internet%20Files/Content.IE5/85CF0Z0V/noname.htm#story5 (accessed May 26, 2005).
47. Feagin, *Racist America*, 28–29.

48. Feagin et al., *The Agony of Education*, 88.
49. Ibid., 100.
50. St. Jean and Feagin, *Double Burden*, 205.
51. Muhammad et al., *The State of the Dream*, 8–18.
52. Rebecca Gordon, Libero Della Piana, and Terry Keleher "Facing the Consequences: An Examination of Racial Discrimination in U. S. Public Schools" (Oakland, Calif.: ERASE Initiative, Applied Research Center), 1–3.
53. Ibid., 1. Italics omitted.
54. King, *Where Do We Go from Here?*, 122.
55. Feagin and McKinney, *The Many Costs of Racism*, 78.
56. Eric L. Krakauer, Christopher Crenner, and Ken Fox, "Barriers to Optimum End-of-life Care for Minority Patients," *Journal of the American Geriatric Society* 50 (2002): 182–190.
57. Bebe Moore Campbell, "To Be Black, Gifted, and Alone," *Savvy* 5 (December 1984): 69.
58. Feagin and McKinney, *The Many Costs of Racism*, 115.
59. Feagin, "Black Middle Class Research Study."
60. Bolton and Feagin, *Black in Blue*, 193–194.
61. St. Jean and Feagin, *Double Burden*, 158.
62. Ibid., 165–166.
63. See Robert B. Hill, *The Strengths of Black Families: Twenty-Five Years Later* (New York: University Press of America, 1999).
64. bell hooks, *Killing Rage: Ending Racism* (New York: Henry Holt, 1995), 9–10.

CHAPTER SEVEN

1. National Advisory Commission on Civil Disorders, *Report of the National Advisory Commission on Civil Disorders* (Washington, D.C.: U.S. Government Printing Office, 1968), 1.
2. Ibid., 5.
3. "Black and White in America," *Newsweek*, March 7, 1988, 19.
4. Rush, *Loving across the Color Line*, 128.
5. Toni Morrison, *Playing in the Dark: Whiteness and the Literary Imagination* (New York: Vintage Books, 1992), 11–12.
6. Robert M. Entman and Andrew Rojecki, *The Black Image in the White Mind: Media and Race in America* (Chicago: University of Chicago Press, 2000), 51.
7. Lawrence Bobo, "Inequalities that Endure?: Racial Ideology, American Politics, and the Peculiar Role of the Social Sciences" (paper presented at conference on "The Changing Terrain of Race and Ethnicity," University of Illinois, Chicago, Illinois, October 26, 2001).
8. Joe R. Feagin and Eileen O'Brien, *White Men on Race: Power, Privilege and the Shaping of Cultural Consciousness* (Boston: Beacon, 2003), 101.
9. Joe R. Feagin, Hernán Vera, and Pinar Batur, *White Racism: The Basics*, 2nd ed. (New York: Routledge, 2001), 215.

10. See Leslie Carr, *"Color-Blind" Racism* (Thousand Oaks: Sage, 1997); and Eduardo Bonilla-Silva, *White Supremacy and Racism in the Post–Civil Rights Era* (Boulder, Colo.: Lynne Rienner, 2001).
11. On work efforts, see chaps. 2 and 4 of this book, and Feagin, *Racist America*, 37–174.
12. Feagin et al., *White Racism*, 204.
13. Feagin and O'Brien, *White Men on Race*, 110.
14. Feagin et al., *White Racism*, 205.
15. Leslie Houts and Joe R. Feagin, *Two-Faced Racism*, Routledge, forthcoming.
16. Katheryn Russell, *The Color of Crime: Racial Hoaxes, White Fear, Black Protectionism, Police Harassment, and Other Macroaggressions* (New York: New York University Press, 1998), 69–93 and passim.
17. Feagin and O'Brien, *White Men on Race*, 116.
18. Kim Lersch and Joe R. Feagin, "Violent Police-Citizen Encounters: An Analysis of Major Newspaper Accounts," *Critical Sociology* 22 (1996): 29–49.
19. Ruth Frankenberg, *White Women, Race Matters: The Social Construction of Whiteness* (Minneapolis, Minn.: University of Minnesota Press, 1993), 83.
20. Feagin and O'Brien, *White Men on Race*, 132.
21. Feagin, Vera, and Batur, *White Racism*, 203.
22. Franklin, "Observations Concerning the Increase of Mankind, Peopling of Countries, Etc." (1751), as quoted in *Benjamin Franklin: A Biography in His Own Words*, 105–106. I have changed this to modern capitalization.
23. Quoted in Clarence Page, "U.S. Media Should Stop Abetting Intolerance," *Toronto Star*, December 27, 1991, A27. I also draw here on *Racist America*, chap. 3.
24. Quoted in John Dillin, "Immigration Joins List of '92 Issues," *Christian Science Monitor*, December 17, 1991, 6.
25. Peter Brimelow, *Alien Nation: Common Sense about America's Immigration Disaster* (New York: Random House, 1995), 10, 59.
26. Samuel P. Huntington, "The Erosion of American National Interests," *Foreign Affairs* (September 1997/October 1997): 28ff.
27. Ibid.
28. Personal communication from Victor Romano, May 2004.
29. Van Ausdale and Feagin, *The First R*, 103–105.
30. Feagin et al., *White Racism*, 213.
31. Van Ausdale and Feagin, *The First R*, 1.
32. Charles R. Lawrence, "The Id, the Ego, and Equal Protection," *Stanford Law Review* 39 (January 1987): 323–324; see also Feagin and O'Brien, *White Men on Race*, chap. 1.
33. Maurice Halbwachs, *On Collective Memory*, ed. and trans. Lewis Coser (Chicago: University of Chicago Press, 1992), 38, 52.
34. They kept the journals for several weeks on the average, and in some cases up to 4 months. Houts and Feagin, *Two-Faced Racism*, forthcoming. See Leslie Houts, "Backstage, Frontstage Interactions: Everyday Racial Events and White College Students" (doctoral dissertation, University of

Florida, 2004). I also draw here from Joe R. Feagin, "Legacies of Brown: Success and Failure in Social Science Research on Racism," forthcoming.

35. Houts and Feagin, *Two-Faced Racism*, forthcoming.

36. Feagin, "Legacies of Brown," forthcoming.

37. Feagin et al., *White Racism*, 195.

38. Houts and Feagin, *Two-Faced Racism*, forthcoming.

39. Douglas S. Massey and Nancy A. Denton, *American Apartheid: Segregation and the Making of the Underclass* (Cambridge: Harvard University Press, 1993), 221–223; John R. Logan, Brian J. Stults, and Reynolds Farley, "Segregation of Minorities in the Metropolis: Two Decades of Change" (research report, Center for Social and Demographic Analysis, University at Albany, 2002).

40. Feagin et al., *White Racism*, 192.

41. Isabel Wilkerson, "The Tallest Fence: Feelings on Race in a White Neighborhood," *New York Times*, June 21, 1992, sec. 1, p. 18.

42. Entman and Rojecki, *The Black Image in the White Mind*, 49.

43. Ibid., 51–53.

44. Ibid., 8–9.

45. Ibid., 49.

46. King, *Where Do We Go from Here?*, 5.

47. Philip Moss and Chris Tilly, *Stories Employers Tell: Race, Skill, and Hiring in America* (New York: Russell Sage, 2001).

48. In one 1977 survey of mostly white male local and national leaders in business, farming, unions, the media, and academia, most were overwhelmingly opposed to affirmative-action "quotas" for black Americans. Sidney Verba and Gary R. Orren, *Equality in America: The View from the Top* (Cambridge, Mass.: Harvard University Press, 1985), 63.

49. Feagin and O'Brien, *White Men on Race*, 197.

50. See Joe R. Feagin, "Mythes et realites de l'"Affirmative Action" aux Etats-Unis," *Hommes & Migrations*, No. 1245 (September–October 2003): 29–41.

51. Feagin et al., *White Racism*, 208.

52. Sut Jhally and Justin Lewis, *Enlightened Racism* (Boulder: Westview Press, 1992), 95. See also 96–110.

53. Richard Morin, "Misperceptions Cloud Whites' View of Blacks," *Washington Post*, July 11, 2001, A01.

54. See Feagin, *Racist America*, chap. 6.

55. Feagin et al., *White Racism*, 199.

56. Carter, *The Politics of Rage*, 12.

57. Kevin Sack, "South's Embrace of G.O.P. Is Near a Turning Point," *The New York Times*, March 16, 1998, A1.

58. I am indebted here to an email conversation with Chandler Davidson.

59. Abraham Lincoln himself had the first southern strategy for Republicans. Had he lived, he was planning to develop the Republican party in the South by appealing to the working-class whites (not former slaveholders or the freed blacks). See O'Reilly, *Nixon's Piano*, 49.

60. Kevin P. Phillips, *The Emerging Republican Majority* (New Rochelle, N.Y.: Arlington House, 1969).
61. O'Reilly, *Nixon's Piano*, 292–330. The comment is on p. 327 and was made to John Ehrlichman.
62. Joe R. Feagin and Clairece B. Feagin, *Racial and Ethnic Relations*, 7th ed. (Englewood Cliffs, N.J.: Prentice-Hall, 2003), 175; O'Reilly, *Nixon's Piano*, 375.
63. O'Reilly, *Nixon's Piano*, 378.
64. Feagin et al., *White Racism*, 152–160.
65. O'Reilly, *Nixon's Piano*, 378–400.
66. Office of Civil Rights Evaluation, U.S. Commission on Civil Rights, Redefining Rights in America, "The Civil Rights Record of the George W. Bush Administration, 2001–2004," http://www.thememoryhole.org/pol/usccr_redefining_rights.pdf (accessed April 12, 2005).
67. David A. Bositis, "Blacks and the 2004 Republican National Convention" (Washington, D.C.: Joint Center for Political and Economic Studies, 2004), 1–10.
68. Ibid., 10.
69. Ibid.
70. "The Racist Incident," *Local 207 Organizer*, Issue 41, 17 April 2003, at http://www.afscme207.com/organizers/organizer41_2k3.htm (accessed November 28, 2004).

CHAPTER EIGHT

1. W. E. B. Du Bois, "The Negro's Fatherland," in *W. E. B. Du Bois: A Reader*, 653.
2. W. E. B. Du Bois, *The World and Africa: An Inquiry into the Part that Africa Played in World History* (New York: International Publishers, 1965), 22.
3. Ibid., 45.
4. Ibid., 58.
5. Peter Linebaugh and Marcus Rediker, *The Many-Headed Hydra: Sailors, Slaves, Commoners, and the Hidden History of the Revolutionary Atlantic* (Boston: Beacon Press, 2000), 141.
6. William Brink and Louis Harris, *Black and White* (New York: Simon and Schuster, 1967), 220–222, 278.
7. Ibid., 128–134.
8. Quoted in C. Vann Woodward, *The Origins of the New South, 1877–1913* (Baton Rouge: Louisiana State University Press, 1971), 221–222.
9. Du Bois, *Black Reconstruction*, 30.
10. See Feagin, *Racist America*, especially chaps. 4–6.
11. Ibid., 145–149.
12. See Ani, *Yurugu*.
13. Wahneema Lubiano, "Introduction," in *The House that Race Built: Black Americans, U.S. Terrain* (New York: Pantheon Books, 1997), vii.
14. Ibid.

15. I used many variations of these words: racism, racial oppression, foundation of the nation, foundation of the country, foundation of United States, and founded on racial oppression. There are passing references to the United States as "founded in racism," but none go into depth.
16. William A. Link, *Roots of Secession: Slavery and Politics in Antebellum Virginia* (Chapel Hill: University of North Carolina Press, 2003), 6.
17. Edmund S. Morgan, *American Slavery, American Freedom: The Ordeal of Colonial Virginia* (New York: Norton, 1975), 5.
18. Ibid., 6.
19. Garry Wills, *"Negro President": Jefferson and the Slave Power* (Boston: Houghton Mifflin Company, 2003), 210.
20. Ibid., 5.
21. Ibid., 5–7.
22. Ibid., 8.
23. James Madison, as quoted in Robert A. Caro, *The Years of Lyndon Johnson: Master of The Senate* (New York: Knopf, 2002), 9.
24. Ibid., 9–11.
25. Ibid., 78, 90–94.
26. Robert A. Dahl, *How Democratic is the American Constitution?* (New Haven: Yale University Press, 2003), 52–53.
27. Ibid., 90–94.
28. Du Bois, *Black Reconstruction*, 706.
29. See *Negro President*, 10–11.
30. Mary Frances Berry, *Black Resistance, White Law: A History of Constitutional Racism in America*, rev. ed. (New York: Penguin Press, 1994), 1.
31. Don E. Fehrenbacher, *The Dred Scott Case: Its Significance in American Law and Politics* (New York: Oxford University Press, 1978), 581.
32. Berry, *Black Resistance, White Law*, xii.
33. Du Bois, *Black Reconstruction*, 706–707.
34. Ibid., 707.
35. Douglas Egerton, "On the Haitian Revolution, Toussaint L'Ouverture, and Jefferson," PBS.ORG, at http://www.pbs.org/wgbh/aia/part3/3i3130.html (accessed January 14, 2005).
36. Anders Stephanson, *Manifest Destiny: American Expansionism and the Empire of Right* (New York: Hill and Wang, 1995), xii and xiii.
37. Charles Cochran, as quoted in Stephanson, *Manifest Destiny*, 89.
38. Paul G. Lauren, *Power and Prejudice* (Boulder, Colo.: Westview Press, 1988), 41.
39. Ibid., 262–273.
40. Amy Chua, *World On Fire: How Exporting Free Market Democracy Breeds Ethnic Hatred and Global Instability* (New York: Anchor Books, 2003), 7.
41. Quoted in Nikhil Aziz, "Rac[e]ing Abroad: Exploring Racism in/and U.S. Foreign Policy," *The Public Eye* (Spring 2003): 3.
42. Lewis R. Gordon, *Her Majesty's Other Children: Sketches of Racism from a Neocolonial Age* (Lanham, Md.: Rowman & Littlefield, 1997), 4–5. Some analysts miss this point about how the *white* mind has constantly created

the dominant paradigm and the oppressive continuum running from white to black. An example can be seen in the following comment: "That paradigm, the black-white binary, effectively dictates that nonblack minority groups must compare their treatment to that of African Americans to gain redress." Richard Delgado and Jean Stefancic, *Critical Race Theory: An Introduction* (New York: New York University Press, 2001), p. 67. I am indebted to Roy Brooks for help on this point.

43. Quoted in J. A. Rogers, *Africa's Gift to America* (St. Petersburg, Fla.: H. M. Rogers, 1961), 91.

44. James J. Scheurich and Michelle D. Young, "Coloring Epistemologies: Are Our Research Epistemologies Racially Biased?" *Educational Researcher* 26 (May 1997): 7. For an extended discussion, see Feagin, *Racist America*, 72–73.

45. Quoted in George Frederickson, *The Black Image in the White Mind* (Hanover, N.H. Wesleyan University Press, 1971), 136.

46. Ilan Stavans, *The Hispanic Condition: Reflections on Culture and Identity in America* (New York: HarperCollins, 1995), 32. I draw here on Joe R. Feagin, "White Supremacy and Mexican Americans: Rethinking the 'Black-White Paradigm,'" *Rutgers Law Review* 54 (Summer 2002): 959–987.

47. See Feagin, "White Supremacy and Mexican Americans."

48. See Mia Tuan, *Forever Foreigners or Honorary Whites? The Asian Ethnic Experience Today* (New Brunswick, N.J.: Rutgers University Press, 1998).

49. See Feagin, *Racist America*, 72–73.

50. Leslie Houts and Joe R. Feagin, *Two-Faced Racism*, Routledge, forthcoming.

51. See Feagin and O'Brien, *White Men on Race*.

52. Claire Jean Kim, "The Racial Triangulation of Asian Americans," *Politics and Society* 27 (March 1999): 105–138.

53. See Tuan, *Forever Foreigners or Honorary Whites?*

54. I draw here on Joe R. Feagin and Danielle Dirks, "Who is White?": College Students' Assessments of Key US Racial and Ethnic Groups" (unpublished manuscript, Texas A&M University, 2004).

55. Otto Santa Ana, *Brown Tide Rising: Metaphors of Latinos in Contemporary American Public Discourse* (Austin: University of Texas Press, 2002), 289.

56. Douglass, "The Meaning of July Fourth for the Negro," in *Frederick Douglass: Selected Speeches and Writings*, 196–197.

CHAPTER NINE

1. Frederick Douglass, "The Nation's Problem," in *Frederick Douglass: Selected Speeches and Writings*, 729.

2. Du Bois, Black Reconstruction, 30; and *Jones v. Mayer Co.*, 392 U.S. 409 (1968). See also Andrew Levy, *The Forgotten Story of Robert Carter, The Founding Father Who Freed his Slaves* (New York: Random House, 2005), pp. 194.

3. James O. Horton and Lois E. Horton, *Slavery and the Making of America* (Oxford: Oxford University Press, 2004), 231.

4. I am indebted to Roy Brooks for helping me shape this point.
5. Quoted in Gary B. Nash, *The Unknown American Revolution* (New York: Viking, 2005), p. 224. The essay never found a publisher.
6. David Walker, *Appeal to the Coloured Citizens of the World*, ed. Charles M. Wiltse (New York: Hill and Wang, 1965), 75.
7. W. E. B. Du Bois, *John Brown* (New York: International Publishers, 1962), 263–264.
8. Ibid., 264–265. I use modern spelling here. See also David S. Reynolds, *John Brown, Abolitionist: The Man Who Killed Slavery, Sparked the Civil War, and Seeded Civil Rights* (New York: Knopf, 2005), 262–265.
9. Steve Hahn, *A Nation Under Our Feet: Black Political Struggles in the Rural South from Slavery to the Great Migration* (Cambridge, Mass.: Harvard University Press, 2003), 7; and Philip A. Klinkner and Rogers M. Smith, *The Unsteady March: The Rise and Decline of Racial Equality in America* (Chicago: University of Chicago Press, 1999), 70; and Du Bois, Black Reconstruction, 57–60.
10. W. E. B. Du Bois, *The Gift of Black Folk: Negroes in the Making of America* (Boston: Stratford, 1924), 138.
11. Klinkner and Smith, *The Unsteady March*, 50–51.
12. I echo ideas of Frederick Douglass and Martin Luther King. See King, *Where Do We Go from Here?*, 92. Note too that gender discrimination still barred black and white women from voting.
13. Quoted in *Jones v. Alfred H. Mayer Co.*, 392 U.S. 409, 441 (1968).
14. Juan Perea, Richard Delgado, Angela Harris, Stephanie Wildman, and Jean Stefancic, *Race and Races: Cases and Resources for a Diverse America* (Saint Paul, Minn.: West American Casebook Series, 2000), 140–141.
15. Civil Rights Cases, 109 U.S. 3, 36–37 (1883).
16. *Plessy v. Ferguson*, 163 U.S. 537, 552–553 (1896).
17. James L. Huston, *Calculating the Value of the Union: Slavery, Property Rights, and the Economic Origins of the Civil War* (Chapel Hill: University of North Carolina Press, 2003), 236.
18. See Robert A. Pratt, "*Brown v. Board of Education* Revisited," *Reviews in American History* 30 (2002): 141–144.
19. Nathan Newman, "Remembering the Popular Will for Civil Rights: Robert Caro's Master of the Senate," *Progressive Populist*, June 15, 2002, available at http://nathannewman.org/populist/06.15.02pop.html (accessed Sept. 9, 2003). In this section, I expand arguments from Joe R. Feagin, "Heeding Black Voices: The Court, Brown, and Challenges in Building a Multiracial Democracy," *University of Pittsburgh Law Review*, 66 (Fall 2004): 57–81.
20. *Jones v. Alfred H. Mayer Co.*, 392 U.S. 409, 440-43 (1968). I draw here on Environmental Conservation Organization, "The Constitution of the United States of America: Analysis and Interpretation," http://www.eco.freedom.org/ac92 (accessed February 1, 2005).
21. *Larry Williams, et al., Plaintiffs-Appellants, v. The City Of New Orleans, etc., et al., Defendants-Appellees*, No. 82-3435, United States Court of

Appeals for the Fifth Circuit, 729 F.2d 1554; 34 *Fair Empl. Prac. Cas.* (BNA) 1009; 34 *Empl. Prac. Dec.* (CCH) P34,311.

22. See Feagin, "Heeding Black Voices."
23. Du Bois, *Black Reconstruction*, 706–707.
24. Lakoff and Johnson, *Philosophy in the Flesh*, 556.
25. Paul Thompson, personal communication, April 12, 2004.
26. Howard Zinn, "Changing Minds, One at a Time," *The Progressive*, March 2005, at http://commondreams.org/views05/0210-28.htm (accessed February 18, 2005). I am indebted to Ruth Thompson-Miller and Anthony Orum for suggestions here. Some analysts envision the answer to be expanded social integration of white Americans and Americans of color. Providing common social spaces for whites and people of color, especially African Americans, as neighbors and acquaintances is often helpful in expanding the networking capital of Americans of color and in getting whites to view Americans of color as people like themselves.
27. Levy, *The Forgotten Story of Robert Carter*, p. 194.
28. "Letter to W. H. Thomas," in *Frederick Douglass: Selected Speeches and Writings*, 705–706. In *An American Dilemma*, Gunnar Myrdal noted that his initial focus was on "the Negro problem." Once in the field, he discovered there was only a "white man's problem." See Myrdal, *An American Dilemma*, vol. 1, lxxv–lxxvi.
29. Lillian Smith, *Killers of the Dream*, rev. ed. (New York: W. W. Norton, 1961), 173. Italics added.
30. James Madison, *The Federalist*, no. 51, as reprinted in Alexander Hamilton, James Madison, and John Jay, *The Federalist*, ed. Jacob E. Cooke (Middletown, Conn.: Wesleyan University Press, 1961), 347–353.
31. John Rawls, *A Theory of Justice*, rev. ed. (Cambridge, Mass.: Belknap Press, 1999); I summarize Rawls using some analysis from Avishai Margalit, *The Decent Society*, trans. N. Goldblum (Cambridge: Harvard University Press, 1996), 272–281.
32. Iris M. Young, *Justice and the Politics of Difference* (Princeton: Princeton University Press, 1990), 3.
33. King, *Where Do We Go from Here?*, 4, 9.
34. Young, *Justice and the Politics of Difference*, 173.
35. Quoted in Jordan, *White over Black*, 273. I use modern capitalization.
36. Quoted in ibid., 273–274.
37. Henry David Thoreau, *Civil Disobedience* (Los Angeles: Green Integer, 2002), 25.
38. Lavelle, "Facing Off in a Southern Town." I am indebted to Kristen Lavelle for permission to quote here.
39. Eileen O'Brien, *Whites Confront Racism: Antiracists and Their Paths to Action* (Lanham, Md.: Rowman & Littlefield, 2001), 99.
40. King, *Where Do We Go from Here?*, 154.
41. See Klinkner and Smith, *The Unsteady March*.
42. This is the summary language of the United Nations report. "Summary Record of the 1474th Meeting," Committee on the Elimination of Racial

PUBLISHED BY FIDELI PUBLISHING INC.

MADISON HUNKE

Crossing Blades

To Hannah
Thanks for having my
back when I was new!
Good luck at state and swimming
senior year will be a blast! :-)
— Madison Hunke

Discrimination, United Nations, at http://www.unhchr.
ch/tbs/doc.nsf/898586b1dc7b4043c1256a450044f331/
6d8aee7e356e6498c1256d4e00557f3b/$FILE/G0143983.pdf (accessed
February 18, 2005).

43. Ibid.
44. See Feagin, *Racist America*, 235–271.
45. See Roy Brooks, *Integration or Separation? A Strategy for Racial Equality* (Cambridge: Harvard University Press, 1996), 115.
46. Franklin Roosevelt, "State of the Union," http://www.presidency.ucsb. edu/ws/index.php?pid=16518 (accessed February 28, 2005).
47. Judith Blau and Alberto Moncada, *Human Rights: Beyond the Liberal Vision* (Lanham, Md.: Rowman & Littlefield, 2005), 63.
48. Cass R. Sunstein, *The Second Bill of Rights: FDR'S Unfinished Revolution and Why We Need It More than Ever* (New York: Basic Books, 2004), 124–126.
49. I am indebted to Roy Brooks for this point about the Canadian Constitution. Studies conflict on whether the everyday reality for people of color is better in Canada than the United States. See Jeffrey G. Reitz and Raymond Breton, *The Illusion of Difference* (Toronto, Ontario: C. D. Howe Institute, 1994).
50. Catharine A. MacKinnon, *Women's Lives, Men's Laws* (Cambridge, Mass.: Harvard University Press, 2005), 57.
51. King, *Where Do We Go from Here?*, 209–210.
52. Here I loosely paraphrase Du Bois, *The World and Africa*, 67; see Joe R. Feagin, "Social Justice and Sociology: Agendas for the Twenty-First Century," *American Sociological Review* 66 (February 2001): 1–20.

INDEX

P

Paine, Thomas, 323
Parks, Rosa, 323
Patriarchal family model, *see* Family model, patriarchal
Patriarchism, 29, 85–86, 94, 98, 110
Pennington, James W. C., 64
Phillips, Kevin, *see Emerging Republican Majority, The* (book)
"Plantation mentality," 29, 199–202, 285
Plessy v. Ferguson (1896), 303
Police; *see also* White violence
    brutality, 235, 271
    profiling, *see* Racial profiling
    during segregation, 137, 138–139
    white interest protection, 41
Powell, Adam Clayton, Jr., 162
Predatory ethic, 10
Provisional Constitution of the Oppressed People of the United States, 298
"Psychological wage of whiteness," 268; *see also* Du Bois, W. E. B.
Puritans, 10–11

R

Race
    categories, 13–15, 91, 291
    mainstream approaches, 4–6
    physical markers of blackness, 265
Racial continuum, *see* White-to-black continuum; *see also* Racial hierarchy
Racial formation theory, 6–7, 162
Racial frame, *see* White racial frame; *see also* Social justice frame
Racial hierarchy, xiii, 21–23, 35; *see also* White-to-black continuum
    class, 22
    creation, 8
    definition, 286
    during slavery, 57
    gender, 22
    "honorary white," 290
    immigrant groups, 286–288, 290
    imposing racial-ethnic identity, 291

Native Americans, 284
    physical, 92
Racial profiling, 24
Racism, *see* Systemic racism
Racist America (book), xii
Racist joking, 162, 206–207, 235, 243–244
Racist socialization, 163, 169–171, 240–242, 288
Rape; *see also* White violence
    of female slaves, 15, 59, 74–75, 80–81, 117
    segregation, 19, 134–136
Rawls, John, 310
Reagan, Ronald, 255, 284
Reconstruction, 123
Reed, Ralph, 254
Religion, 64
    colonialism, 10–11
    defense of racial oppression, 10–11, 29, 103, 180, 214
    sexual violence, ix
Reparations, 311
Republican party, 252, 253–258
"Reverse discrimination," 203, 229, 252, 259, 321
Roosevelt, Eleanor, 319
Roosevelt, Franklin D., 318
Roosevelt, Theodore, 161–162
Rushdy, Ashraf, 49

S

Santa Ana, Otto, 292
Segregation, 303; *see also* Jim Crow
    contradictions, 131–132
    desegregation, *see* Desegregation
    economic exploitation, 127–128; *see also* Debt slavery; Unjust impoverishment, segregation
    education, 38–39; *see also* Education, contemporary segregation
    employment, 38–39, 132–133
    informal, 124, 132, 265
    near-slavery, xvi, 33, 129, 150
    northern, 126–127
    police and, 24, 137, 138–139
    as racial apartheid, 124–127
    religious support, 29, 180